NAIROBI AIRPORT

DEPARTMENT OF IMMIGRATION
PERMITTED TO ENTER AUSTRALIA.
24 APR 1996
on
For stay of 12 Month
SYDNEY AIRPORT 34

IMMIGRATION DIVISION BANGKOK THAILAND
A 72 DEPARTED
-6 FEB 1998
SIGNED

IMMIGRATION & ETHNIC AFFAIRS
Person
30 OCT 1999
DEPARTED
AUSTRALIA
SYDNEY 32

TRAVELER'S
KENYA
COMPANION

中华人民共和国
广东省公安厅

上陸許可
ADMITTED
15. FEB. 1996
Status: 4-1-4
Duration: 90 days
NARITA(N)
Immigration Inspector
日本国

ADMITTED
20 OCT. 1998
Status: 4-1-16
Duration: 180 days
Port: HANEDA
Signature

№ 011278
PASSED
THE UNITED STATES
OF AMERICA
NONIMMIGRANT VISA
ISSUED AT
Air Port
U.S. IMMIGRATION
170 HHW 1710
JUL 20 1998

HONG KONG
(1038)
-7 JUN 1997
IMMIGRATION
OFFICER

The 2002–2003 Traveler's Companions
ARGENTINA • AUSTRALIA • BALI • CALIFORNIA • CANADA • CHILE • CHINA • COSTA RICA •
CUBA • EASTERN CANADA • ECUADOR • FLORIDA • HAWAII • HONG KONG • INDIA •
INDONESIA • JAPAN • KENYA • MALAYSIA & SINGAPORE • MEDITERRANEAN FRANCE •
MEXICO • NEPAL • NEW ENGLAND • NEW ZEALAND • PERU • PHILIPPINES • PORTUGAL •
RUSSIA • SOUTH AFRICA • SOUTHERN ENGLAND • SPAIN • THAILAND • TURKEY •
VENEZUELA • VIETNAM, LAOS AND CAMBODIA • WESTERN CANADA

Traveler's KENYA Companion

First published 1998
Second Edition 2002
The Globe Pequot Press
246 Goose Lane, PO Box 480
Guilford, CT 06437 USA
www.globe-pequot.com

© 2002 by The Globe Pequot Press, Guilford CT, USA

ISBN: 0-7627-1009-8

Distributed in the European Union by
World Leisure Marketing Ltd, Unit 11
Newmarket Court, Newmarket Drive,
Derby, DE24 8NW, United Kingdom
www.map-guides.com

Created, edited and produced by
Allan Amsel Publishing, 53, rue Beaudouin
27700 Les Andelys, France.
E-mail: AAmsel@aol.com
Editor in Chief: Allan Amsel
Editor: Anne Trager
Picture editor and book designer: Roberto Rossi
Original design concept: Hon Bing-wah
Based on an original text by Peggy Bond and Michael Bond

Printed by Samwha Printing Co. Ltd., Seoul, South Korea

T R A V E L E R'S
KENYA
C O M P A N I O N

by Jack Barker

photographs by Storm Stanley

Second Edition

The
Globe
Pequot
Press

GUILFORD
CONNECTICUT

Contents

T R A V E L E R ' S
KENYA
C O M P A N I O N

SUDAN

Lokichokio

A1

Kakuma

A1

Lodwar

Lorugumo
Lokiriama

Loiya
Lokitanyala

Lokicha

U G A N D A

Sot
Natic

Sigor

A1

Wagagai

Mount Elgon
National Park

A1 Kitale
C45

Tororo
A104 Webuye

Bungoma A1

Eldoret
A1

Bumala Kakamega
Ebusongo C30 B1 Shikondi
Usengi Akala Maseno

C39 A104
C36
Nabkoi
Sorget

Asembo
Kendu Bay
Homa Bay
Ruma
National
Park

Kisumu
B1
C19 A1
Sondu
Oyugis

B1 Kericho
Ker
En

Karungu
Uriri

Kilkoris

Kisii
Bomet
Gorgor

Lemek

Lake
Victoria

Nyarombo
Nyabikaye
Tarime

Lolgorien

Ntimaru

A1

Kalkoris

C13

Masai
Mara
National
Reserve

C1

Bakit

Serengeti
National Park

T A N Z A N I A

LEGEND

Populations

- ⊙ **NAIROBI** Capital
- ○ Machakos Cities
- ○ Salama Towns

Transportation

- ═66═ Expressway
- ───── Highways
- ━━━━━ Provincial Roads
- ───── Secondary Roads
- ┅┅┅ Railways

Physical Features

- ～～～ National Parks
- ───── Regional Boundaries
- ───── Lakes & Rivers
- ▲ Mountains & Volcanoes
- 800 m
- ✈ Airports

0   40   80   120   160 km

0   20   40   60   80   100 miles

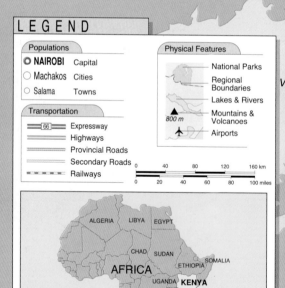

ALGERIA LIBYA EGYPT

CHAD SUDAN

ETHIOPIA

SOMALIA

AFRICA

UGANDA KENYA

ZAIRE

TANZANIA

N

MADAGASCAR

SOUTH
AFRICA

TOP SPOTS

Ride the Lunatic Line

Until the last century Kenya's capital was Mombasa, and Nairobi was just a swamp. What opened up the country's interior was the "Lunatic Line," the railway track laid across the country even before the colonial forces had explored the interior and well before there were any settlers to actually use the railway. In 1896 the first stretches were completed, and for the next three years the track made laborious progress through forest and swamp, across river and mountain. Twenty-eight workers were eaten by lions and countless more died of disease; laborers imported from India were to permanently change the demography of Kenya. By the time the track reached Nairobi, in 1899, sheer exhaustion might have dictated a permanent settlement;

while the railway tracked on to the shores of Lake Victoria and would eventually split off to reach Uganda, the city that is now capital of Kenya took shape.

Nairobi's Railway Museum, on Station Road but best reached by taxi, tells this story, completing the picture with the first trains and carriages to travel the continent.

If the museum experience isn't enough, the railway line itself still provides one of the great train journeys of the world. While road traffic founders in the washed-out surface of the route to the coast, the train runs from Nairobi to Mombasa, every night, in a white-gloved atmosphere of ultimate luxury. For 12 hours — admittedly, sometimes it takes longer — it makes stately progress along the meter-gauge track, passing through Tsavo and down to the steaming flatlands of the coast. Three-course meals prelude nights spent rocked to sleep by the unhurried motion of the ancient train, turned-back linen sheets recreating a golden age of colonial luxury. Dining is on crisp white tablecloths using crockery left over from the colonial era. Sometimes it seems as though the cuisine dates from the same period. Don't expect haute: hope for wholesome.

In first-class compartments just two passengers share a cabin fitted with

OPPOSITE: The Kenya Railway, once nicknamed the Lunatic Express, winds up and down near-vertical Rift Valley escarpments TOP and dashes straight across the flat Tsavo plains BOTTOM. The locomotive used in *Out of Africa* is on display at the Nairobi Railway Museum ABOVE.

borders still with neither electricity nor telephone: the journey takes 24 hours and although the same luxuries are available on board, many travelers find this is just too slow a way of completing a journey that takes eight hours by *matatu*, the packed local minibuses, and one by air. The track east of Nairobi is sometimes washed out and the service doesn't always take passengers.

Reservations are essential for traveling first or second class: reserve the day before, although two or three days in advance is safer, to secure a berth. Without a reservation you'll end up traveling on the benches in third. Reservations can be made in person at Nairobi Station ((02) 221211, one and a half kilometers (one mile) from the city center on Station Road, or at Mombasa Station ((011) 312221, on Haile Selassie Avenue. Reservations are apparently taken by telephone, or perhaps easiest through a travel agent such as Let's Go Travel ((02) 447151 or (02) 441030 FAX (02) 447270 or (02) 441690 E-MAIL info@letsgosafari.com WEB SITE www.letsgosafari.com, Box 60342, Nairobi.

washbowl and served by an attentive drinks waiter: families on the move can link two cabins together. Second-class travel puts four to a cabin but is also perfectly acceptable. Third — crammed wooden seats with chickens in the aisles — might be cheap but is not recommended for overnight journeys. And in Kenya almost all rail trips take place at night. First-class tickets cost Ksh3,000 per person and include all meals. The perfectly adequate second-class fares are Ksh2,100 per person. Third-class travel does not include food, a reserved seat, or even a seat of any kind, but only costs Ksh300.

The journey from Nairobi to Kampala in Uganda is significantly longer and crosses one of the few international

Meet the Past

The prehistory of man is written in the stones of the Rift Valley, and for anyone interested in the birth of mankind, Kenya has archaeological sites and sights galore.

Much of the pioneering excavation that mapped out man's early years was performed by Louis and Mary Leakey. The Rift Valley, which stretches from Ethiopia in the north to Mozambique far to the south, passes down through the length of Kenya, and cradles many of the country's most spectacular lakes. The Leakeys discovered that although the Rift Valley was one of the world's oldest geological structures, comparatively recent volcanic activity had entombed a treasure-house of prehistoric remains and fossils, only now being laid bare by the actions of wind and rain. In many cases, the fossils literally lie on the earth's surface, just waiting to be picked up and identified.

Some of the Leakeys' most important discoveries were made in Olduvai Gorge in northern Tanzania. However there are plenty of important sites in Kenya, often discovered even more recently and still not fully researched even now. One of the world's densest collections of surface fossils is found in the north of the country, at the Koobi Fora fossil site in Sibiloi National Park on the shores of Lake Turkana. Here the combination of lake-floor mud and volcanic eruptions 90,000 years ago has preserved countless animals in pristine fossil form. Just kick away at the ground and every few inches you'll find something.

Recent discoveries of human remains thought to be up to six million years old have thrown the spotlight on the Lake Baringo area and the Tugen Hills. Other sites of interest include Hyrax Hill near Nakuru, a three-hour drive north of Nairobi, home to some of Kenya's earliest inhabitants and still bearing clear traces of their waterside camp and final tomb.

Even closer to Nairobi to the south, within range for a long day-trip or an overnight camping visit, is Olorgasailie,

which is threaded with catwalks, pathways and informative signs, and was inhabited by human beings half a million years ago. Countless hand-axes and animal remains have been uncovered at this site, but so far no human remains have been found. Archaeologists continue their painstaking search.

For the subsequent 500 millennia, pastoral Kenyans trod lightly on the earth and left little trace of their tranquil way of life. Exceptions to this include the coast, where Swahili settlers left stone mosques and villages. Perhaps the best of these are Gedi Ruins at Watamu. This almost complete Swahili village dates back to the fourteenth century, bigger and better than Jumba la Mtwana near Mombasa. Gateway to Kenya's colonial past, Mombasa's most atmospheric sight is Fort Jesus, symbol of the quite justified paranoia of the first years of colonial occupation, and finally stormed by Omani forces from the Middle East.

OPPOSITE: A million-and-a-half-year-old skull TOP of *Homo erectus* is displayed at the archaeological site of Koobi Fora on the shores of Lake Turkana. Fort Jesus, Portugal's toehold BOTTOM on the coast of East Africa. ABOVE: The Chuka dancers of the Meru area.

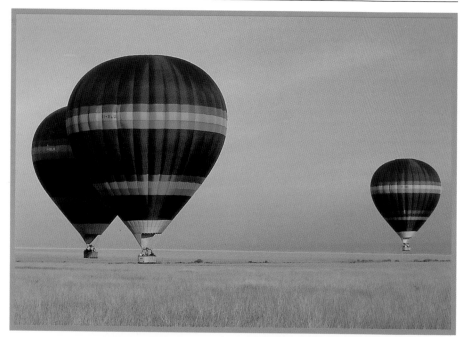

But sometimes it seems the past is still there, an integral part of everyday life. Sail-powered wooden dhows trade up and down the coast, while inland, wandering spear-carrying tribesmen track across vast plains. In Africa the far past is a timeless part of the present.

Take to the Skies

In the cool morning half-light, the roar of the burners heated the air and drove color into the billowing folds of the balloon's spreading canopy. Soon it rose, half-willing and wobbling, into the still air and caught the first rays of the sun on it's upper crescent. Gradually the basket lost weight on the ground and, trembling, strained against the ropes, before smoothly and silently taking to the air.

As the yellow light of dawn lit up the tips of low brush, the balloon glided over the steep banks of the Mara River and out over the open savannah. Peaceful herds of grazing game — wildebeest and zebra, gangling giraffes and purposeful, padding lions — could be seen in the grass far below. A blast on the burner and a family of elephants scattered, suddenly scared,

trumpeting and kicking dust-trails far below. In silence we glided on, over the endless plains of the Masai Mara, sheltered by the distant shades of the mountains of the Rift Valley. Binoculars brought the ground up close as the sun warmed the morning air and bled color into the tranquil scene. Whether dropping low for a closer view or drifting high for Africa's full panorama, the views were magical and the experience serene.

With all ballooning, things start moving quickly when it is time to land. As we dropped towards the ground we were suddenly aware that the gentle breeze, imperceptible at height, was moving us along quite quickly. With a few crisp commands in a broad American accent, our pilot settled us into brace positions on low benches and told us to hold tight to sturdy internal ropes. Striking the ground we turned on our side and dragged for a while as the basket flexed on stones and rocks, until finally we came to a halt. As the balloon collapsed onto the plain we scrambled gratefully clear and in a few minutes we were sipping at the day's first glass of bubbly while a lavish cooked breakfast was being prepared.

Kenya's climate is ideally suited to ballooning, at least in the timeless savannas of the Masai Mara. Unlike Europe, where fickle weather often means flights have to be canceled at short notice, in the Masai Mara mornings are almost invariably calm and cool, perfect for raising these fragile airships. And there is no better way to appreciate the full beauty of the African bush than from the still platform of a viewing basket, suspended high over the heads of some of the world's most exotic animals.

Ballooning in Kenya isn't cheap. It costs about US$380 per person for seats in a 12- or 18-seater basket, although this might be less expensive if reserved in advance through an overseas operator. Three companies offer ballooning in the Masai Mara. Adventures Aloft ((02) 221439 FAX (02) 332170, Box 40683, Nairobi, runs flights from Fig Tree Camp; Balloon Safaris Ltd. ((02) 502850 FAX (02) 501424, Box 43747, Nairobi, takes off from Keekerok Lodge; and Mara Balloon Safaris Ltd. ((02) 331871 FAX (02) 217416, Box 48217, Nairobi, flies from Governors Camp.

Although ballooning has been tried in other areas, it has never been quite as successful. In Samburu, thorns ripped the canopies to pieces and the only place to land the balloon safely turned out to be in the river, which irritated passengers, hippos and crocodiles. For travelers based on the coast, for whom

the Masai Mara would require two flights or several days on the road, the Hilton runs ballooning safaris from Salt Lick Lodge in the Taita Hills, which is much more convenient and even a few dollars cheaper. Their reservations department in Nairobi ((02) 334000 FAX (02) 339462 can take reservations — although they don't always realize this immediately.

Try Out a Treetop Lodge

About midnight, a shape moved slowly in from the forest beyond the lights. At first, it seemed a shadow, but it moved with the authority of the great cats, lethal but extraordinarily beautiful, tan-golden and huge. It was a young lioness, her body glimmering in the lights as she lithely picked her way through grass and brush upwind toward an unsuspecting bushbuck. She reached the last clump of brush that could shield her, the bushbucks only 20 m (60 ft) away, and crouched to wait, only her pointed ears visible above the bush.

Kenya led the way in bringing the night-time game to a wider audience with Treetops Lodge, famous as where Princess Elizabeth was staying when she learned she'd become Queen of England. These days Treetops is nowhere near any trees, as deforestation has taken its toll, but, along with The Ark, still offers overnight game-viewing over their own floodlit waterholes. Although it might seem a bit artificial, the animals are thoroughly habituated, and this can provide some of the most exciting game-viewing experiences in the country.

At The Ark, which is located in the mist forests, you enter along a 100-m-long (330-ft) catwalk and the gate closes behind you, remaining so until your departure the next morning. The order of the day and night? Quiet voices inside and whispers only on the open balconies

OPPOSITE AND FOLLOWING PAGES: A balloon safari provides breathtaking panoramas on a grand scale. ABOVE: Walkways bring the Gura Falls into view in the Aberdares.

and catwalk. Any variety of animals are likely to be grazing, drinking at the pool or eating at the salt lick on your arrival, and sightings are listed in vast ledgers that record the waterhole's status over the years. Buffaloes, giant forest hogs and the resident pair of Egyptian geese greeted us. The hotel's 30 years of statistics show a 50 percent chance of sighting a lion, 88 percent for an elephant, 40 percent for a rhinoceros (probably lower now), 20 percent for a leopard (baited), and two percent for the rare bongo. Buffaloes, baboons, bushbucks, and cute bushbabies are almost guaranteed.

About 6:30 PM, the staff feed the birds along the catwalk. It is a colorful sight — yellows, bright greens, red, orange, and iridescent blue. Thanks to Mike Clifton, our on-duty naturalist, we learned to spot golden-winged and eastern double-collard sunbirds, African rock martins, the pesky speckled mousebirds, and several varieties of weavers, montane warblers, streaky seedeaters, yellow-vented bulbuls, and olive thrush. He identified many more, far too many to remember them all.

Spotted and black genet cats, which are actually in the weasel family, usually chase the birds, and mongooses arrive to pick up the scraps that fall to the ground. At nightfall, cuddly and quite brazen bushbabies arrive to stay until the early morning hours, keeping those who remain awake company. They may try to follow you indoors, tug on your clothes, or sit beside you on a bench. After dark, activity picks up at the salt lick and floodlights are turned on. During the night we were there buffaloes were constantly present. We were also visited by a bull elephant, by forest hogs who were chased away by the buffaloes, by a spotted hyena who just waltzed through, by a white-tipped mongoose and by the 50 or so bushbucks who were continually harassed by the lioness.

Buffaloes drove the bushbucks nearer the lioness. One, a young female, ended up less than 10 m (30 ft) from the feline. Still the lioness waited patiently, knowing the bushbuck's leaping agility and speed. The wind changed, carrying the lion's scent; several bushbuck barked an alarm call, and the herd nervously sidled away, peering toward the darkness.

For the next two hours, the lioness lay motionless as the bushbucks edged nearer and scampered away, hungry for the grass but suspicious. Finally, she made a dash at one and missed, and they all bounded into the forest. Until nearly 4 AM, we could hear their sharp barks as she stalked them down the mountainside.

Experience a Camel Safari

The gentle pace of a strolling camel provides one of the best ways to experience Kenya's wildlife and spectacular landscapes, and no animal could be better suited to a long journey through the bush. First, ships of the desert are very strong, and a single camel can carry a load that will keep the average hiker living in luxury. They don't need to spend most of their days eating and drinking, and can keep going as long — or rather longer — than their human keepers. And finally, they form a comfortable steed — with a refreshingly high viewpoint. Ride sidesaddle for maximum comfort.

A camel's long range can take riders far from roads and civilization, and generally a camel safari will only be slightly more expensive than the equivalent lodge-based trip, with comforts varying according to your exact requirements. Simple safaris get close to nature with fly-camps and meals around the flames of a campfire. Vehicle assistance is needed if you want to arrive each evening to a pre-erected luxury camp with East African walk-in tents and en-suite bucket showers.

Yet another advantage of a camel safari is the real chance to get to know the local people. Most camel handlers are Samburu warriors (*morans*) and know the land. It's always useful to have a *moran*

OPPOSITE: Three zebras TOP watch as camels BOTTOM drink.

along, partly because they don't get lost but also because lions are scared of these braided men in red. *Morans* also act as guides, knowing most of the people along the way, including children too small to acknowledge, busy attending to father's cattle, young warriors striding through the bush looking for something to kill, or elderly women, leaning on sticks, tracing lonely tracks across vast spreading plains.

On my first day out on a camel safari, I met a newly circumcised brave, dressed in black, plastered with ash and with a dead bird tied round his head. At night, after putting up my complex and cumbersome tent, my Samburu *moran*, called Tched, simply rolled up his ochered braid of hair, folded himself flat on his back, pulled his red blanket up over his eyes, and went immediately to sleep, straight as a pole.

There are specialist companies that offer camel safaris, almost invariably in the arid north of the country. Probably the cheapest of the established operators is Yare Safaris Ltd. (/FAX (02) 214099

E-MAIL yare@africaonline.co.ke, Box 63006, Nairobi, based two kilometers (slightly over a mile) south of Maralal on the Nyahururu–Nairobi Road, with prices starting at around US$500 per person for seven days; longer trips are possible. More upmarket operators include Desert Rose Camel Safaris ((02) 228936 FAX (02) 212160, Box 44801, Nairobi, which operates eight-day safaris around the Lake Turkana area from their beautiful lodge in the northern Rift Valley, and Simon Evans, who runs safaris around the Ewaso Ngiro River in Samburu district: make reservations with Let's Go Travel ((02) 447151 or (02) 441030 FAX (02) 447270 or (02) 441690 E-MAIL info@letsgosafari.com WEB SITE www.letsgosafari.com, Box 60342, Nairobi. More casual safari experiences can also be undertaken at any small town in the north: the cheapest safari experience I've ever been offered was a US$10-a-day proposition from an unemployed Turkana graduate trailing three borrowed donkeys around the village of Baragoi, north of Maralal.

Ride the Rapids

One man has done more than any other to open up inland Kenya to the world of whitewater rafting, and that is Mark Savage, who — between taking expeditions scaling the peaks of Kenya's mountains — has run his zodiacs along the lengths of every navigable river in Kenya, and a few that aren't.

Regular clients include the British Army, for whom he trains instructors, but trips are usually tailored to the requirements of his clients, from first-timers to experienced rafters. One-day trips take place on the Tana River, starting from Nairobi. One option starts with three kilometers (two miles) of class II and III whitewater, followed by six kilometers (four miles) of calm scenic river (paddling) before completing the day with an exhilarating six kilometers (four miles) of fast class IV and V rapids.

Alternatively, a quieter day has been tailored to the requirements of ornithologists: a scenic, bird-filled float of three to four hours over eight kilometers (five miles) of river within easy reach of Nairobi. At least 100 species of bird have been regularly spotted by the guides on this stretch of the Tana, who are fully trained to identify fast-flitting rarities. Another one-day trip runs the length of the Muthoya North River for a distance of 22 km (nearly 14 miles) and a drop of over 450 m (1,450 ft). The water is not very big — the river is narrow and low-volume — but technically very difficult; lunch and drinks are carried on board the zodiac inflatables, so everybody prays that it won't capsize, at least until the afternoon.

For whitewater enthusiasts, or anyone wanting a different "take" on Kenya, longer trips are also available. The Athi River is raftable from near Nairobi all the way to the coast — a distance of 450 km (280 miles) that takes 21 days, and can be

OPPOSITE LEFT: Samburu *morans* are great camel handlers. RIGHT: Lions in Samburu National Reserve establish a licking order. BELOW: Brownwater rafting on the Ewaso Ngiro River.

combined with walking and caving in the Chyulu Hills. However it's the first 80-km (50-mile) stretch of the Athi River that is most popular: three days combining medium-grade whitewater with the sights and sounds of a scenic stretch of the river. Much of the time the launches run along the borders of Tsavo East, and wildlife abounds: bushbucks, giraffes, buffaloes and elephants are frequently seen, while crocodiles and prolific bird life are constant companions.

Talk to Mark Savage though and it's clear he has one particular favorite: the three-day trip rafting the Ewaso Ngiro River. This starts west of Barsalinga with a roller-coaster 35 km (22 miles) over almost continuous rapids. Extensions to this trip can continue east for a further 100 km (62 miles), through Samburu National Reserve and up to Chandler's Falls in Shaba National Reserve. All along the way game abounds: even lions have been spotted during rushed glances from the bucking platform of the paddling zodiac. For safety reasons, two boats are the minimum to run this route, with four people on each, but often Mark Savage is able to combine two or more groups to make this experience possible for smaller groups.

The lower age limit for whitewater rafting is 14, with parental consent, but there's no upper limit: it depends on individual health and fitness. Old 40-year-olds have found it hard, while a 72-year-old grandmother new to the sport was a complete convert and booked again. Full safety equipment, including lifejackets and crash helmets, are supplied and must be worn. Camp is on scenic points along the river, with two-person dome tents, airbeds and sleeping bags provided. Perishables are carried in a freezer trailer, along with soft drinks and beer, and while lunch is cold and casual, dinner has five courses, all cooked over a wood fire. May, June, July and November, December, and January are the best months, as rafting is dependent on water levels, but there can be too much water for some routes. In any case, rafting trips run year-round on one river

or another. Rates start at US$95 for a full day's rafting from Nairobi, including meals, beer and transport. Contact Savage Wilderness Safaris Ltd. (/FAX (02) 521590 WEB SITE www.kilimanjaro.com, Thigiri Road, Box 44827, Nairobi.

Game Fishing

Suddenly the twin caterpillar engines cut and the tubby boat wallowed to a halt. In the silence, the racing of the reel, letting line out into the ocean, was loud. One of the rods was taut and trembling. We had a bite. The air filled with shouts and activity. A crewman pushed me towards the rod, the 36-kg (80-lb) line spinning out from the Shimano reel. While I pulled at the rod to strike the fish, two deckhands feverishly reeled in a kilometer of line from the other eight rods, clearing the way for me to play the fish. My rod, friction reel whirring out line, jumped and fought my arms as I was ushered into the "fighting seat," a racked wooden chair built out of rough-cut planks and sturdy metal fitments. It looked rather like an early dentist's homemade treatment chair.

A sailfish, blue and glittering graceful, broke the surface of the ocean 275 m (900 ft) behind our slackening boat with a sun-glinting splash. In a desperate attempt to break free of the one-inch hook, it had flipped into the air to try to

void its stomach. The fish was getting tired. I started to haul in, taking the strain by pumping the rod, reeling in as I dipped the tense, bowed tip.

The sailfish crescented above the surface again, sail flashing lower and tired, and I kept reeling in. In the final moments the silver-sided form could be seen weaving exhausted below the stern of the boat, and then deckhands were pulling at the line, maneuvering the sailfish into position so they could grab its bony bill with thick protective gloves, remove the hook from its mouth and insert a tag. It wasn't a record-breaker —

Lake Victoria's Nile perch can take some landing. It can be useful to have some local help.

about 35 kg (77 lbs) — but it was my first game fish, and a lot taller than me. As my moment of glory faded, the deckhand took over an even more important job: sluicing water through the exhausted fish, waving its bony snout in the warm oxygenated surface layers to get the fish's powerful tail muscles working again. Once revived, it was pushed free and I watched the silvery-blue shape snake off at a tangent to the safety of the deep.

Most of Kenya's better operators have caught up with environmental considerations, and now feature the tag-and-release program, where instead of being killed and weighed the fish are fitted with a small identifying tag and released back into the wild. Game fishing, though, will never be a sport for the softhearted. The trauma of being towed around the ocean on the end of a hook will always prove fatal to some fish. On the day I was fishing, one of the three sailfish caught had been hooked in the gills and had no chance of survival. Meanwhile a 16-kg (35-lb) wahoo was destined for the pot. Swordfish, famous fighters now being caught at night in Kenya by boats trailing diving-light lures, often die of exhaustion in their struggle.

But you don't have to catch a big game fish to experience the thrill of fishing. And the best outing I had was where I caught least. "In America they'd laugh at you for going fishing in a boat like this," Ken Adcock, son of Mombasa fishing legend James Adcock, told me as we set off in a seven-meter (20-ft) canoe built from mango wood in a timeless, narrow, deep design. Rolling on the swell a couple of miles offshore, we powered after horizon specks of flocked feeding birds, slowing to approach as they dive-bombed, speckling the water with white splashes as they hunted bite-sized shoals of fry. Below the water would be the ocean carnivores: tuna and snapper, chased in turn perhaps by sailfish and shark. Stressed by their position halfway up a food chain, any of these fish might be panicked into mistaking our lures for an exotic snack.

Each shoal would drop away as our boat shadowed close. So there was only time for one cast, maybe two, before the fish moved to the deep and birds wheeled off to another bit of ocean. Standing insecure on the rocking canoe we flicked our rods to send crazy-colored rubber squid across the water, winding in, frantic and fast, the hooks skimming and splashing across the choppy waves. A bite: my line went tight and I started to reel in. My red rubber octopus had caught a myopic dorado. Three kilos (seven pounds) only, but this time, I felt, caught with skill. And anyone who seriously considers tagging and releasing a dorado has never really worked up a decent appetite.

Fishermen in Kenya are spoiled for choice. Bad times for offshore fishing are May, June and (in the north) July, when rough sea conditions mean the boats can't clear the fringing reef and many operators close their doors. Even at this time of year there's still fly-fishing in the rivers streaming off Mount Kenya, especially for browns and rainbows in the Burguret and Nanyuki rivers; you can rent fly tackle at the Naro Moru River Lodge. For lake fishing, upmarket lodges at Mfangano and Rusinga islands in Lake Victoria offer full equipment to hunt down Nile Perch. And you can always go native. Local boats might lack sophisticated tackle, but plenty of Kenyans live off the waters of lakes Turkana, Naivasha and Baringo. It's a great way to settle in to the Kenyan pace: just make sure the boat you rent isn't likely to sink.

Brush up Your Birding

Few countries are as rewarding as Kenya for bird watching. And one of the best places to settle down with binoculars is at Lake Baringo. Flat waters, dotted with floating cabbage, are home to countless species, including Humprick's hornbill.

A Goliath heron feeds on a shoreline in Nairobi National Park.

On my last visit, I caught sight of a group of colorful Madagascan bee-eaters. Hyrax clamber round the Baringo Cliffs while kingfishers dip into the waters of the lake. Boats paddle carefully in shallow waters, a constant haunt of hidden hippos, who seem to get annoyed at the beat of engines. Resident ornithologist at Lake Baringo Lodge (reservations through Block Hotels ((02) 535412-4 FAX (02) 545954 WEB SITE www.blockhotels.com), Stephen Heparsa-Laach, told me not to be concerned. "The hippos at Naivasha are far more aggressive."

A pity and a worry. Naivasha might not be as quiet and remote as Baringo, but the bird life is just as prolific, as at all the flamingo-pinked lakes that glow blue along the floor of the Rift Valley. And Kenya has plenty of different habitats, from swamp to desert to coastal wetland regions. The enthusiastic birder will find different species on the hot humid coast, on the open savannas, in the inland forest and swamps and around tall mountain peaks. Whether predator or prey, all Kenya's birds share exceptional beauty and aerial grace.

For the determinedly red-blooded, there's one further sport these birds can provide. In the Galana River area, just outside the borders of Tsavo East National Park, you can make reservations for vacations with Hemingways ((0122) 32624 FAX (0122) 32256 WEB SITE www. hemingways.com, Box 267, Watamu, and go out to their tented camp. In the bright light of dawn, you can walk out from your luxury camp into the bush, admire the thrilling sound of these beautiful birds' morning song, wonder at the flash of their feathers, lift your rented gun, and blast them from the sky.

Specific bird-watching specialist companies include Bataleur Safaris ((02) 227048 FAX (02) 891007, Mezzanine Floor, Hilton Building, Mama Ngina Street, Box 42562, Nairobi, and the rather more expensive East African Ornithological Safaris ((02) 331191 or (02) 222075 FAX (02) 330698 or (02) 216528 E-MAIL eaos @africaonline.co.ke WEB SITE www.savannah camps.com, P.O.Box 48019, Eleventh Floor, Fedha Towers, Standard Street, Nairobi. Birders arriving in Nairobi might want to call Nature (previously the East Africa Natural History Society) ((02) 749957 or (02) 741049, Box 4486, who operate bird walks at 8:45 AM every Wednesday, meeting at the National Museum.

Meet the Animals

It's all very well seeing Kenya's game, but sometimes it's tempting to make contact that much closer. There are a couple of opportunities to get close to Kenya's wildlife. In Nairobi's Giraffe Sanctuary ((02) 891658 endangered Rothschild's giraffes lean over to extend long gray tongues to slurp up afternoon tea: cattle nuts, held out on flat palms. Travel north to Nanyuki and Laikipia, where Sweetwaters camp is home to a tame rhinoceros. Once orphaned by poachers, he now thinks he's a pet, trundling around after guests like a big — very big — dog; he likes having his stomach tickled. Book Sweetwaters through Lonhro ((02) 216940 FAX (02) 216796, Box 58581, Nairobi (US$205 per double, full board): it's just about close enough for an overnight visit. At a more modest outlay of time and money, Nairobi's Maasai Ostrich Farm ((0150) 22505/6 lets you get close to these ungainly birds, and on Sunday afternoons you can

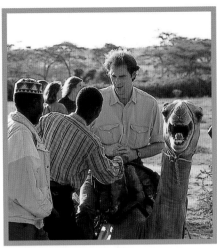

ride them. If the ride gives you an appetite, you can always tuck into an ostrich steak at the Carnivore Restaurant ((02) 602993, around the corner on Langata Road.

Race to Victory

My camel lay like a large desert iceberg, legs concertinaed in the dust. "Hello, Charlie," I said and wondered if I should pat him on the head. Languidly Charlie turned around and gave me a camel's gaze of indifferent contempt, chewing slowly. I wondered if he'd spit. Or maybe bite. Irritated by some small bite he shook his head violently and I jumped back.

Then Tched, the camel handler, pulled on the ropes attaching the loose bundle of sticks and foam rubber laughingly called a saddle. Charlie brayed in irritation, giving me a grandstand view of enough teeth to scalp a hairdresser and an insider's shot of his latest meal. "Don't annoy him," I advised Tched, who smiled shyly. He was an ochered Samburu warrior who hardly spoke Swahili let alone English. He planted his foot against Charlie's flank, pulled harder, and this time I was sure I could

OPPOSITE: An elephant meets an olive baboon at Amboseli National Park. ABOVE: Saddling up for the Camel Derby. FOLLOWING PAGES: Feeding time for orphan rhinos.

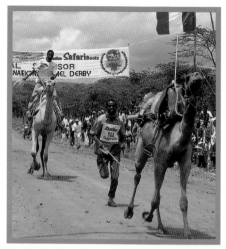

hear some serious irritation in Charlie's anguished bray. Tched stood back, indicating I should climb on. It was time to race.

I had signed up to ride in the Camel Derby at Maralal in northern Kenya, which takes place every year in July. Originally started to educate the locals about the environmental advantages of camels in this harsh land, it is nothing like the competitive Middle Eastern races with professional 11-year-old jockeys and pedigree steeds. In Maralal, the name of the game is endurance and anyone can play. I had entered the 10-km (six-mile) amateur category. The night before, I'd ridden a camel for the first time.

Reluctantly I scrambled aboard and began a slow lurching ascent. Against a background of shouted orders and flicking switches, Charlie unfolded long joints, heaving up at the front, and then high at the back. I was tipped forward in my seat, perched insecurely looking down on an audience of Samburu tribesmen who scattered clear in case I fell off on them. More shouts and a final heave: Charlie straightened his front legs and my seat flattened out, leaving me two and a half meters (eight feet) in the air. It seemed much more and the ground a long way down.

For a minute Charlie appeared to be reconsidering his original decision to stand, until Tched applied a stick and we lurched off. With a certain ungainly grace, Charlie strolled up to the starting line before a thousand spectators: groups of tribesmen looked on from under shady trees while women and children, festooned in beads, hung onto the fences that kept spectators and racers apart.

Fewer than half the racers in the amateur race were foreigners; they included a 10-year-old boy, an American woman in her seventies, an Australian television journalist and a couple of overlanders.

A brief countdown was lost in the background noise and the race was underway. One camel set off in the wrong direction, and a few others, including Charlie, showed no particular urge to go anywhere, but in a minute or two we all thundered down the track between cheering (or were they laughing?) spectators.

We raced along the dirt road from Yare Safari Camp, down and through the town of Maralal, a Wild West scene of clapboard houses and shady verandahs, and back. Charlie was clearly aware he was in for a long haul and shambled off at a gentle trot.

Camel psychology is still a closed book to me. Camels only need food or drink every few days, and Charlie showed none of a horse's enthusiasm for the road home. I muttered endearments, encouragement, and threats, but he didn't seem to speak English. I watched the camel in front, shuffling along on feet the size of dinner plates, running like two tired knock-kneed men jammed into a pantomime suit. It was getting further away. I looked over my shoulder. The competition was falling back too. Psychology was cast to the wind as the race became a battle of wills, my acacia whip flailing against his tough hide, my voice wearing hoarse with continual threats and entreaties which fell on large, indifferent ears. I kept him trotting — barely.

Fifty minutes after I'd started, Charlie lollopped over the finishing line, to rapturous applause from the crowd whose enthusiasm didn't seem to have been diminished by 11 camels before me. Charlie sank to the ground and I tottered about on rubber legs, while occasional bursts of applause indicated the arrival of another racer. The 10-year-old boy had come third and I thought I'd done quite well to finish. Out of 25 starters, 19 made it across the finishing line. Despite the fact no riders wore protective helmets — Kenya, after all, is a land of adventure — there had been no casualties.

The Camel Derby brings together half the country's tourist industry in a convivial, off-duty mood. A tented town makes the camp look rather like a luxury refugee camp, humming with life and a great place to make contacts.

In the aftermath on Monday, the overland trucks threaded off in various directions and the tents were dismantled, packed and dispatched to Nairobi and beyond. Once more birdsong could be heard in the Safari Camp and herds of zebra grazed closer. A small group of travelers set off on a camel trek lasting days or maybe weeks. For another year the Camel Derby was over.

Maralal is 350 km (217 miles) north of Nairobi, the road paved for much of the way. Allow five hours by fast car, or a day by *matatu*, changing at Nyahururu. To get the dates of the next Camel Derby, call Yare Safaris Ltd. ℂ/FAX (2) 214099 E-MAIL travelkenya@iconnect.co.ke, Box 63006, Nairobi.

Track the Migration of the Wildebeest

Every year, by some mass instinct, the Masai Mara sets the scene for one of nature's greatest wonders: the migration of the wildebeest. On some unspoken signal, many millions of these animals, broad-shouldered and slim-hipped, crowned with powerful horns, start off on a long and hazardous trek between Kenya's Masai Mara and Tanzania's adjoining Serengeti Plains. In endless lines they flood through the bush, trailed by lions, following instincts that have driven their movements since time immemorial.

Although at any time of year the Masai Mara is one of the only places in Africa to see the dense herds of game that once covered Africa before the arrival of man, concentrations build up to inconceivable levels when the annual migration happens. The exact timing depends on the weather, but every year, sometime between July and September, over a million wildebeest and hundreds of thousands of zebras arc through the Masai Mara National Reserve in uncountable crowds on their circuit around the plains of the Serengeti, following the rains in search of fresh pastures. Some predators trail, others lie in wait. The wildebeest add up to nine million kilos (20 million pounds) of meat to the park's predators through their long trek. Perhaps the best place to watch the drama of this natural wonder is on the banks of the Mara River, as nervous animals rush in a panicked crossing of the crocodile-filled waters. At this time of year all the Mara's predators are fat and contented, while the wildebeest mow down the lush wet-season growth of long savannah grass.

The Masai Mara is best reached by air from Nairobi, although if traveling on a budget there are plenty of operators who arrange transportation by road. Contact Let's Go Travel ℂ (02) 447151 or (02) 441030

OPPOSITE: The start line LEFT and trouble at the finish RIGHT.

FAX (02) 447270 or (02) 441690 E-MAIL info @letsgosafari.com WEB SITE www.letsgo safari.com, Box 60342, Nairobi, or choose any of the operators listed in TAKING A TOUR, page 76, to arrange your visit. See THE MASAI MARA, page 145, for details on the Mara camps and lodges.

Rave It Up at Lake Turkana

I stared at the sunset. On either side, red, but the center was dyed a brilliant jade. It was the Jade Sea, Lake Turkana, reflected in the sky. I'd never seen anything like it. I'd been dragged from the high-street restaurant where a sign painted on the wall said, "We give you the best service no matter how long it takes" and out on the street. But my new friends had no interest in waiting for service, however good, nor in looking at the sky.

"Come on. We'll miss the film." My companions were impatient. "It's *Demetrius the Greek*." By way of encouragement they recited whole scenes from memory, filled me in on the plot. They pulled me away from the sunset. "How tall are you?"

The Catholic mission has the television. Every Sunday they fire up the generator, plug in the video, and point the screen out through a doorway. A sea of 150 little faces, cross-legged, gazed up into the cathode glare: adolescents, strictly ranked by height, had a more distant view, and I worked out why I'd been asked my height as I squinted at the dated colors of a very old movie. Gasps followed every blow, giggles every kiss. Well, not so much followed. Often a voice from the crowd would beat the actor to their lines, and everyone knew each twist of the simple plot. Heroic Christians wow dissolute Romans. Then Chartlon Heston froze as the video broke down. The audience, chattering excitedly, didn't seem disappointed or surprised. Without hanging around in the hope of any repair they flooded out of the mission compound and split into countless paths that traced the stony ground, home to their clustered *manyattas* — reed or mud dwellings.

Soon the sounds of chanting echoed across the desolate landscape from clusters of round Turkana huts. There wasn't much moon, but the stars gave plenty of light. I followed faint trails, silver threading through the piled boulders of a barren land, and I discovered the locals don't mind spectators. In circles they chanted out traditional songs, while the men danced, pogo-ing across a charmed circle of spectators, in competitive groups or taking huge solo leaps, men singing and bare-breasted women helping the chorus. Shyly the women clapped and assisted, subordinate but interested, especially in the highest jumpers. I asked a spectator to translate the lyrics, expecting tales of romance and love. Far from it. All the songs were about cattle, cows with large humps, bulls with nice horns.

Which was rather sad. In the desolate rocky wasteland that was home to these Turkana, the land isn't rich enough to support many animals. A few goats were the limit of most people's wealth and the constant complaint amongst young men is that the cost of a new bride is far beyond their means. But dancing the night away costs nothing, and until Turkana girls get married they're free to flirt as much as they like. I slipped away at about 10 PM. Early. From all directions the sound of private parties continued well into the night.

This scene was at Loyangalani on the shores of Lake Turkana, a stiff 12-hour drive or charter flight north of Nairobi.

However, through much of rural Kenya every weekend is a celebration. Where there's electricity there are concerts of local music and thumping discos held by overloaded speakers. And beyond the reach of mains power, where a white face is a novelty, the people are invariably pleased to welcome visitors to far more elemental festivities, the very different traditional dances of very traditional societies. One thing that can blunt this natural welcome though is a photographic camera or video. With such cultures it is easy to give offense, and the easiest way to do so is to take a picture.

Crossing time for wildebeest on their annual migration in the Masai Mara.

YOUR CHOICE

The Great Outdoors

For many visitors, Kenya *is* the great outdoors. Sun-baked bush stretches as far as the eye can see, mountains glow blue on the far horizon. Exotic animals graze on thorny bushes, predators wait to pounce … and that's the problem. Hungry wild animals keep many visitors to Kenya confined to their four-wheel drives, nervously watching the drama of the bush through the safe hatch in the roof of their vehicle. Unlike some other African countries, walking is not permitted in most of Kenya's national parks for the simple reason that there's too much game; the outdoor experience will generally be spent peering out of the viewing panel cut into the roofs of most safari vehicles.

Most visitors will spend the better part of their visit in Kenya's national parks. The **Masai Mara** is, without doubt, the best of all in terms of the sheer numbers of animals seen. Joined across the unfenced border with Tanzania's Serengeti National Park, it has unbeatable concentrations of plains game, trailed by plenty of predators. It provides some of the best game viewing at all times of the year (especially during the wildebeest migration see TRACK THE MIGRATION OF THE WILDEBEEST, page 31 in TOP SPOTS) and also has some of the best lodges, maintained by a constant stream of visitors. This park is usually put at the end of any tour of Kenya to makes sure the safari ends on a high note.

Well-served by flights from Nairobi, **Amboseli** is a small park set around a swamp, with the brooding mass of snow-capped Mount Kilimanjaro providing a dramatic backdrop (when clear of cloud). In the dry seasons (from July to September and January to April) huge herds of elephants can be found around the central swamp, and the plains can be atmospheric as they are tracked by whirlwinds kicking up the dust in baby tornados. Since most of the trees have died (either because of salinity in the soil or from being pushed over by ellies) it is sometimes just a little bit desolate.

OPPOSITE: Shaba National Reserve is one of Kenya's least visited. ABOVE: Normally placid, this elephant is starting to get twitchy.

Tsavo was the prime game area before the Masai Mara appeared on the international scene. It is by far Kenya's largest park, and is divided into two parts by the main Nairobi/Mombasa Road. **Tsavo West** is to the south of the road, running up to the slopes of Mount Kilimanjaro across the border in Tanzania. It is one of the most accessible and rewarding of the national parks, with a varied landscape on volcanic soils, and a good amount of wildlife. The animals here are fairly shy but the game-viewing experience is all the more rewarding for it. **Tsavo East** is to the north of the main road, and is even larger: however, much of the park, once closed to visitors while poachers decimated the elephant population, is now restricted to small groups on expensive walking safaris. The southern section, however, has a sprinkling of very worthwhile lodges and some good game-viewing. It is relatively accessible from Mombasa, and so is popular with visitors to the coast.

While these are the major parks, there are a number of smaller parks which can be even more rewarding, and can ideally be combined as part of any safari. Top amongst the "minor" parks is **Samburu**, north of Mount Kenya, where the arid landscape is a dramatic backdrop to game of all kinds, and you know where to find it: the game will be near the water. Traveling to Samburu, visitors will have passed the remote mountainous landscape of the **Aberdare National Park**, where the breeding populations of rhino and elephant can, in the lush growth, be a bit hard to see, and the peaks of **Mount Kenya National Park**, a varied and spectacular landscape, are only really accessible to experienced hikers and mountaineers.

The main road to Nakuru links three more national parks. **Longonot** and **Hell's Gate** national parks protect a dramatic volcanic landscape south of Lake Naivasha, better for hiking than game-viewing, while **Nakuru National**

Looking out over the Leno Valley from the Tot Escarpment.

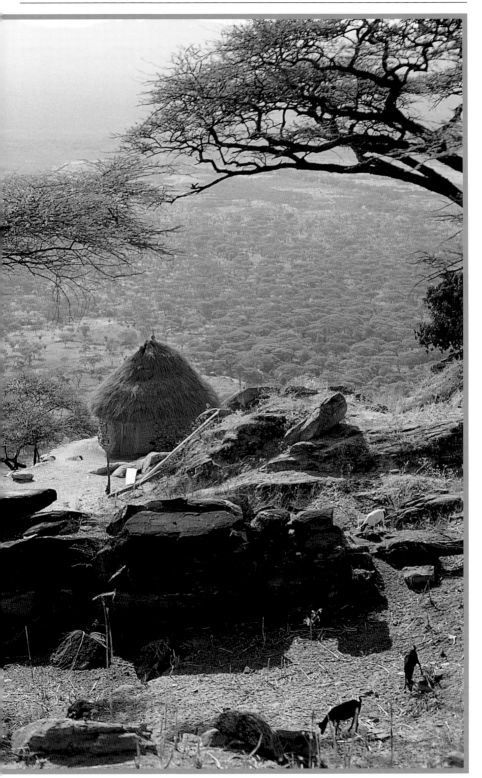

Park surrounds the waters of flamingo-pinked Lake Nakuru in a park-like environment dense with game — you won't want to step out of your car here.

Other national parks well worth a visit include **Meru National Park**, off-limits for many years thanks to bandits and poachers but now reopening to a select few, and, far to the north by the shores of Lake Turkana, the arid fossil-strewn desert of **Sibiloi National Park**. And finally the most accessible of them all: **Nairobi National Park**, where the full range of plains game – and predators – live a wild life in hearing distance of the humming sound of the city's traffic.

From the coast, most visitors in search of wildlife come inland to Tsavo National Park, or to the small but beautiful **Shimba Hills National Reserve**, a fenced stronghold of the sable antelope and a full range of predators. There are marine national parks here too: guarding the coast off **Wasini** to the south, **Watamu** and **Malindi** to the north, and **Kiwayu** near the border with Somalia.

Alongside the national parks, there are a number of natural reserves. Practically, most regulations, entry fees and hours are the same: the difference is that natural reserves are policed and controlled by local councils rather than by the centralized Kenya Wildlife Service. For a private, generally more expensive and less regulated wildlife experience, there are a number of private reserves owned and operated by individuals or groups of farmers; there are also community ranches, owned, but not always run, by local pastoral tribes with ancestral rights over the land. These are listed in the relevant sections of the touring chapters in this book.

Outside the protected areas, Kenya has plenty of fine hiking country, where there might not be too much wildlife, but at least you can escape from your vehicle and explore the countryside.

Some of these are areas where subsistence farmers have long displaced animals. The slopes of Mount Elgon on Kenya's western Ugandan border are threaded with paths and trails where wildlife poses little threat. But where the risk from animals is reduced, humans can be more of a problem: check the security situation by asking around, since border areas are often sensitive. Weeks can be spent on extended treks along the inter-village trails in the Nandi and Cherangani Hills in western Kenya, which is a memorable way to meet Kenya's welcoming people, even if on a tight budget. Camping out in these populous districts is not wise: better to come to an arrangement with a villager to stay with their family or use one of the mountain huts. You won't be short of offers and you will generally get the family bed. This is a brave option too, though, and it would be insensitive and unwise to flaunt your wealth with photographic equipment or even expensive clothes. Bear in mind that medical facilities are few and communications can be poor, so falling off mountains is not advised.

The most popular area for hikers is **Mount Kenya**, where a guide is usually advisable. Mountaineers definitely need a guide: many climbs are technical and demanding. Contact the Mountain Club of Kenya ((02) 501747, Box 45741, Nairobi, or Savage Wilderness Safaris Ltd. (/FAX (02) 521590 WEB SITE www.kilimanjaro.com, Thigiri Road, Box 44827, Nairobi. If in the Mount Kenya region, Joseph Muthui ((02) 242627 FAX (02) 250734, Box 391, Naro Moro, offers friendly and flexible guide services.

Those with just a day to spare can head out of Nairobi to the **Ngong Hills**, but not alone: over the past few years it has been the spectacular setting for plenty of robberies.

Other areas are safe simply because the countryside is too inhospitable to support enough wildlife to be dangerous. Usually the problem is lack of water: most of northern Kenya is classed as desert, a rugged world of exceptional beauty and piled dried boulders where dramatic color-shifts mean even the same view constantly changes. Dotted by the red robes of nomadic hunters, trekking in the drylands takes planning, and preferably a camel. Once more, camping out here is only advisable in groups.

Some areas of Kenya can be explored on foot simply because that's the only way to travel. The forests of **Arabuko-Sokoke** near Watamu Bay on the northern coast (see ARABUKO-SOKOKE FOREST, page 276 of THE COAST) or of **Kakamega** in the west (see KAKAMEGA, page 164 of WESTERN KENYA) are threaded with narrow game trails. No danger of being eaten here: even the lithest predator would find it hard to stalk prey in the thick undergrowth. Buffaloes can make

faster progress than fleeing humans, so if you meet an angry one, climb a tree. In such forests, the greatest risk is getting lost: underneath the jungle canopy it would be easy to lose your bearings. In practice it's not such a problem, as both these forests have friendly and informative guides determined to show you around, and there's little chance of escaping their helpful attentions.

To walk amongst wildlife takes more than nerve — you'll need an armed ranger, a watchful eye and a thorough respect for Nature's killing machines. In general, animals steer well clear; although they're used to cars and safari vehicles, predators and prey alike tend to take flight at the first whiff of a human on foot. Notable exceptions include hippos and buffaloes: easily the most dangerous of all Kenya's wildlife and always to be treated with the greatest respect. If traveling with an experienced guide, the risks are small, and walking safaris are specialties of some of the most inviting private game reserves, often

OPPOSITE: Sheldrick's Falls in Shimba Hills National Park. ABOVE: A diver explores Kenya's fragile coral reef.

bordering national parks, that have set up in Kenya over recent years. Two of the best are **Sweetwaters**, reserved with Lonhro ((02) 216940 FAX (02) 216796, Box 58581, Nairobi (US$205 per double, full board); and **Lewa Downs**, bookable through Bush Homes of East Africa ((02) 350703, (02) 571661 or (02) 571592 FAX (02) 571665 E-MAIL bushhome@africaonline .co.ke WEB SITE www.bush-homes.co.ke, Box 56923, Nairobi (from US$325 per night, full board).

Many visitors, especially those who've been on different types of safaris before, find there's no better way than a walking safari to get a feel for the bush, and it is undeniable that seeing an elephant on foot is a very different experience to spotting one from the high viewpoint of a car. Especially if it's coming your way.

Sporting Spree

For the sports-inclined, Kenya offers a special welcome. On every flat patch of land, goalposts seem to have been put up for soccer matches, and rugby too is very popular. But few travelers arrive in Kenya with a whole team at their disposal, so for most visitors it's the individual activities, such as fishing, golfing, diving, mountaineering and horseback riding, that provide the sporting high points of their stay in the country.

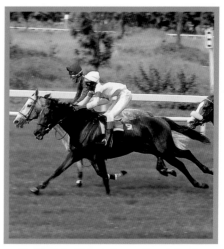

Golfers in Kenya have the pick of some of the world's finest greens, often enlivened by crocodiles and hippos adding their own special frisson to water hazards. Nairobi has a range of golf clubs, most of which offer special guest membership rates to patrons of the city's most famous hotels. There are six high-quality 18-hole golf courses in the Nairobi area: the best is the Windsor Golf and Country Club ((02) 862300 FAX (02) 802322, 13 km (eight miles) from the city center off Garden Estate Road. Another ten 18-hole courses are within easy reach of Nairobi around the Rift Valley and the central highlands. Golfing safaris can be arranged by UTC (trips include tours and nanny services) ((02) 331960 FAX (02) 331422 WEB SITE www.unitedtour.com, Box 42196, Nairobi; or Let's Go Travel ((02) 447151 or (02) 441030 FAX (02) 447270 or (02) 441690 E-MAIL info@letsgosafari.com WEB SITE www.letsgosafari.com, Box 60342, Nairobi.

Malindi, Diani and Mombasa have good courses, while most other major towns have the facilities to play nine holes at least. In Kenya, the clubhouses are often cozy time-warp zones that retain the atmosphere of colonial days; in quiet settings, the rush of the modern world seems to pass them by. A game of golf is a great way to unwind from the excitement of life on safari. For further information, contact the Kenya Golf

Union ((02) 763898 WEB SITE www.kgu
.or.ke, Box 49609, Nairobi.

Horseback riding and **horseracing**
are big in Nairobi. Throughout the year,
the Nairobi Racecourse on Ngong
Road holds events almost every other
weekend. This can be a great day out,
and although it is never quite going to
match the famous races of Europe or
the United States for sheer scale and
pageantry, it makes up for it with a
cheerful and convivial atmosphere in
the stands. A bar, a restaurant and the
chance to place some really small
bets (Ksh20 or about 30 cents is the
minimum) make this an ideal way to
pass a Saturday or a Sunday afternoon.
Everyone says the races are fixed, but
then who cares? Look in the sporting
pages of the *Nation* newspaper to see if
there's a race on or call the East African
Jockey's Club ((02) 561002.

If you want to ride yourself, it's a
great way to experience the country.
Lessons and horse rental are available in
Nairobi from Arifa Riding School ((02)
882937, Marula Lane, Karen, Nairobi,
while the Kitengela Polo Club ((02)
882782 also offers picnic rides and polo
lessons. For long-distance horseback
safaris and up-country operators contact
Let's Go Travel ((02) 447151 or (02)
441030 FAX (02) 447270 or (02) 441690
E-MAIL info@letsgosafari.com WEB SITE
www.letsgosafari.com, Box 60342,
Nairobi. One United Kingdom operator

who specializes in offbeat farmhouse
and horseback safaris is Art of Travel
((0171) 783 2038 FAX (0171) 738 1893,
21 The Bakehouse, Bakery Place,
119 Altenburg Gardens, London
SW11 1JQ.

Mountain biking is relatively new to
Kenya, where ancient bone-shaking
bicycles are the usual transportation
for impoverished farm workers. It can —
for the fit — be a great way to see
the country, perfect for exploring the
footpaths and game tracks of Kenya.
A new operator opening up this field of
African travel is Bike Treks ((02) 446371
FAX (02) 442439, (or reserve with Let's Go
Travel, above), while more expensive
bike tours are now being promoted in
the north by luxury operator Cheli and
Peacock ((02) 604053/4 or (02) 603090/1
FAX (02) 604050 or (02) 603066 E-MAIL
chelipeacock@africaonline.co.ke
WEB SITE www.chelipeacock.com,
Box 39806, Nairobi.

Deep-sea fishing has been popular
since Hemingway's day. All along the
coast of Kenya, operators offer charter
boats for fishing trips, with a new
specialty of night-fishing with diving-
light lures for swordfish. The north is
best known for sailfish, while the south
prides itself on marlin catches.

OPPOSITE TOP: Horseracing at Nairobi Racecourse,
and, BOTTOM, windsurfing on Diani beach. ABOVE
LEFT: Driving in the Masai Mara and, RIGHT, on
track in Samburu.

North to south, every major town is home to at least one reliable operator for tag-and-release fishing; where fish are released live into the wild. In Malindi it is Kingfisher ((0123) 21168 FAX (0123) 30261, E-MAIL kingfisher@swiftmombasa.com, Box 29, Malindi. Ten kilometers (seven miles) to the south, Watamu Bay is home to Hemingways ((0122) 32624 FAX (0122) 32256 WEB SITE www.hemingways.com and Ocean Sports ((0122) 32008 FAX (0122) 32268, Box 100, Watamu. Just to the north of Mombasa, Hallmark Charters Ltd. ((011) 485680 FAX (011) 475217 is at Mtwapa Creek. Head south to Diani Beach, and Grand Slam Charters can be reserved through the Safari Beach Hotel ((0127) 2726 FAX (0127) 2357. Towards Kenya's southern border with Tanzania, Shimoni is base for Sea Adventures Ltd. FAX (011) 227675 and the famous Pemba Channel Fishing Club ((011) 313749 FAX (011) 316875.

Lakeland game fishing is also possible on Lake Victoria, where huge fish are regularly caught. Mfangano Island Camp is booked through Governors Camps ((02) 331871 FAX (02) 726427 WEB SITE www.governorscamp.com, Box 48217, Nairobi (extremely expensive, all-inclusive), or try Rusinga Island Club ((02) 574689 FAX (02) 564945 E-MAIL ras @swiftkenya.com, Box 24397, Nairobi (extremely expensive, all-inclusive).

Scuba diving attracts enthusiasts from all over the world. Diving off the Kenyan coast is notable for pelagic sightings and countless shoals of smaller fish. The Indian Ocean here has twice as many fish species as the Red Sea and rewards snorkelers and divers alike. Reputable operators, from north to south along the coast, start in Malindi, and can be reserved through the Driftwood Beach Club ((0123) 20155 FAX (0123) 30712. A good school in Watamu is Aqua Ventures ((0122) 32008 FAX (0122) 32266. In Mombasa, the top operator is Buccaneer Diving, based at the Whitesands Hotel ((011) 485926 FAX (011) 485652. At Diani, the largest operator is Dive the Crab, which can be booked through Safari Beach Hotel ((0127) 2726 FAX (0127) 2357.

To explore the spectacular waters of the southerly Kisite Marine Park, diving is operated by the Wasini Island Restaurant ((0127) 2331 FAX (0127) 3154 or Pemba Diving Ltd. ((0127) 2331 FAX (0127) 3151.

Whitewater rafting is an increasingly popular way to explore Kenya, although not many of the seven major rivers are suitable. Just one operator exploits Kenya's raftable rivers, which include the Athi, the Tana, the Muthoya, or the Ewaso Ngiro. Day excursions or longer river-based safaris out of Nairobi are offered by Savage Wilderness Safaris Ltd. (/FAX (02) 521590 WEB SITE www .kilimanjaro.com, Thigiri Road, Box 44827, Nairobi (see RIDE THE RAPIDS, page 21 in TOP SPOTS).

The Open Road

Sadly, though Kenya does have roads, few would describe them as "open." At first sight, driving in Kenya would seem to be the action of the terminally insane. I prefer to see it as an adventure. Drivers who are prepared to face the challenges will be rewarded with some of the finest views in the world, the chance to spot exotic game by the side of the road, and the unbeatable sense of satisfaction inherent in independent exploration.

There are a number of truly spectacular drives. The newly surfaced and little-used C51 from Marigat to Eldoret passes through the Tugen Hills in an endless succession of switchbacks and turns, combining ease and beauty; but many of the country's greatest drives match beautiful landscapes with quite demanding conditions. The C71 heading north to the eastern shores of Lake Turkana is an adventurous epic journey that few visitors — or even Kenyans — ever manage. Dropping down to the Masai Mara from the west or north, over the Oloolo or Mau Escarpments, provides vivid memories no amount of time can erase. The coast road breezes through the

The Talek River in the Masai Mara Reserve: a dry-season magnet for game.

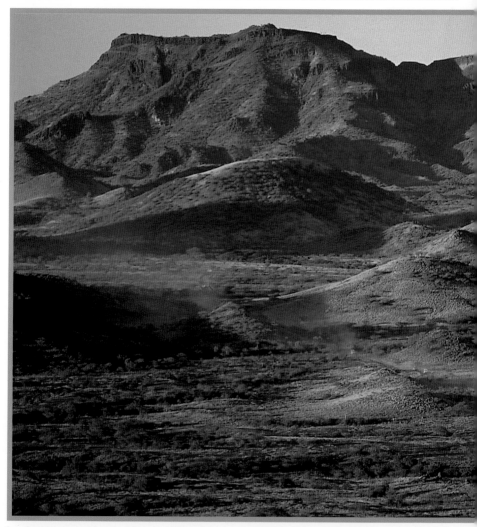

lowland heat with patches of jungle and farmland, strips developed for tourism, and other communities where life goes on at the speed of the seasons. And whenever the sun gets too tempting, the sheltered waters of Kenya's Indian Ocean shore are never more than five minutes away. If you can cope with the slow belching traffic heading north out of Nairobi, the view on cresting the African Rift Valley stretches seemingly forever.

For most motorists the point of arranging their own car is to link specific outlying settlements and a chosen range of national parks. In the 1970s it was quite normal for visitors to rent a car and just explore in a huge loop. As car-rental has become more expensive and security less certain this is a less common, but still rewarding, experience; however be ready to invest considerable time and money in the venture. An ultimate tour of the country could, with 63 days and US$20,000 dollars to spare, be structured as follows:

Days	Destination
1–2	Nairobi: museum, other sites, national park
3–4	Lake Naivasha and Hell's Gate National Park
5–7	Aberdare National Park
8–11	Mount Kenya National Park
12–13	Meru National Park

This would be very much a "dream ticket" ultimate safari, but could easily be divided into less ambitious sections for those with less time or money. To travel in the back country and the wilder game parks a four-wheel drive will be essential, preferably a Mitsubishi Pajero, Landrover or Toyota Landcruiser. Check with the car-rental companies listed on page 289 in TRAVELERS' TIPS.

Before you leave, make sure your vehicle is roadworthy, that it has good tires and a good spare (two spares, and extra tubes and patches if you intend to attempt East Turkana and the Chalbi Desert), a functional jack, and at least one extra jerry-can for gas. Check that your vehicle is in tip-top condition, and doesn't overheat or burn too much oil. Any troubles you may have near Nairobi will be multiplied tenfold in the desert. If your vehicle isn't equipped with a five-gallon jerry-can for radiator water, ask at gas stations — you should be able to pick up a used plastic one cheaply.

Read the sections of this book pertinent to the areas you want to visit (especially the Northern Frontier District) before venturing into them. In the desert of the Northern Frontier District, for example, gasoline is even rarer than water; it's *very important* to call ahead and reserve gas at the few places listed, if they have some.

Wherever you drive in Kenya, the journey is spiced by the beauty of the landscape and the details of everyday life (the roadside shacks and shops, colorful costumes and gentle smiling people), and game glimpsed feeding by the side of the road or racing, flustered, away from your car. Drive on. In the end, perhaps all you need to know is that you drive on the left side of the road.

Conditions are harsh in the Northern Frontier District, but the views superb.

Backpacking

Backpacking in Kenya is easy, cheap and recommended, although travelers should be ready for a completely different experience of the country than their more moneyed counterparts will find in lodges and game-parks.

Whatever the style, on a budget, the travel experience is going to be crowded. Clunky ancient buses, packed minivan *matatus*, or fast station wagon expresses hurtling between cities all have one thing in common: they're always packed to capacity and beyond. Don't carry too much luggage: often it will stay on your lap, and bulky backpacks will be a constant burden. It will be the lucky backpacker who avoids any experience of breaking down on Kenya's poor roads. When and if this happens, it is important to be flexible: if your *matatu* is clearly not about to be fixed by nightfall, flag down any passing vehicle. Whether truck or car, your chances of getting a lift are better as a backpacker than a local Kenyan, not least because you are most likely to be able to pay for the favor.

If the light is failing in a patch of country haunted by buffaloes, lions or bandits, all of whom are immediately interested in a wounded *matatu*, getting to the nearest town should be your first objective: there will be plenty of time

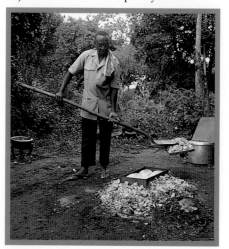

later to fret about your special status and the eventual fate of your fellow passengers. Generally they arrive, tired and dusty, a few hours later.

In normal circumstances hitchhiking is no longer safe between the major cities, but in very rural areas it can be the only way to travel, and is regarded as normal. All passengers are expected to pay for their rides, and you should be ready for it to take some time. I once spent eight days hitching to Lake Turkana, a distance that took me as many hours returning in a fast car. Near urban areas, transportation is so plentiful — and cheap — that few people try to hitch, and in any case it is not safe. Bear in mind that the poorest foreign backpacker will be far wealthier than most Kenyans, and will be assumed to have valuable baggage. The first car to stop might not be a Samaritan.

Accommodation in Kenya can be very cheap, in small B&Ls ("Boarding and Lodgings") that range in comfort from clean-sheeted double beds with en-suite bathrooms and gushing hot water, to small, insect-ridden sheds

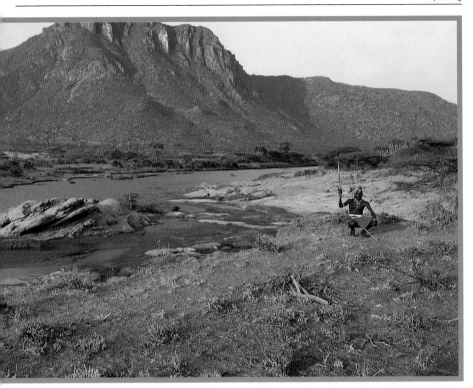

with a long-drop toilet, half a candle for lighting, a rag of a towel and a bucket in case you demand a shower. Rates as low as 50 cents allow travelers on any budget to visit Kenya for extended periods, but conditions won't always be comfortable. Don't get too hopeful when you see a sign saying "Hotel": often this just means restaurant and doesn't necessarily mean they provide accommodation. Small restaurants serving local food are usually cheap and welcoming: there's a sink to wash your hands before and after eating, as cutlery is a luxury. In any case, the local staple, *ugali* (maize), is best eaten with the fingers and mashed into the rest of the meal: eaten with a fork it's completely tasteless.

Seeing Kenya's game is where backpackers might lose out. You have to choose between blowing your hard-kept budget and just giving it a miss. Park entry fees vary down from US$27 a day: enough to keep public transportation well clear. Ostrich, zebra and buffalo glimpsed from a crowded *matatu* is the most that can be expected from public transportation. Unless you strike it lucky and find someone — by hitching or starting up a conversation in a bar or hotel — who has a car and can give you a lift to a national park, the only way of ticking the "Big Five" — elephant, lion, buffalo, rhino and leopard — off your list is to reserve a quick camping safari through a budget operator (see TAKING A TOUR, page 76 of this chapter).

However, backpackers in Kenya can have the best time of all. They are more likely to meet the local people and find out about local culture first hand. Backpacker centers include Lamu Island off the northern coast, where many visitors stay for months, and the distinctly untouristy center of Maralal town to the north of Nyahururu. Don't let a shortage of funds stop your visit, as traveling on a budget will give you even more opportunity to come to know the Kenyan urban culture than tourists

OPPOSITE: Campfire cuisine tastes even better in the bush. ABOVE: Local guides are best in the remote Shaba Reserve.

cosseted in luxury lodges out of the main towns will ever get. If money is really short you can just leave the game viewing until you're older. And richer.

Living It Up

Kenya pioneered mass safaris, but it also saw the birth of the earliest luxury safaris. Now it once more has some of the classiest lodges in Africa and the most extravagant tourist opportunities.

Unfussy and, with all its luxuries, vaguely decadent, the Kenyan high life is not something you usually have to get dressed up for. Only in East Africa are the most exclusive places to stay campsites. The country's most luxurious establishments are generally the simplest, and the idea of total paradise for most Kenyans — and visitors — is to take a **private tented safari**.

They are not campsites as we know them. The tents are made from heavy canvas, are large enough to walk around and usually offer en-suite facilities. Even if the shower consists of a bucket swinging from an overhanging tree, there will be a chain of Kenyans making sure the water, heated over open fires or by solar panels, gushes hot. Dining is often under the stars, with silver service, linen tablecloths and cut glass, lit by the flickering light of hurricane lamps and the dancing shadows of a campfire. Instead of the grand buildings of the great European hotels, in Africa the magnificent landscapes and prolific game take center stage: accommodation is modest and practical, with the luxuries being the view from the wooden deck of your tent or lodge, and the sophistication provided by the company of fellow travelers and the insights of your hosts around a communal dining table.

Even amongst the lodges the trend has been relentlessly upmarket, as smaller, more luxurious properties have been developed for the overseas markets, while established properties that once catered to the very rich have succumbed to the temptations of the mid-market tour

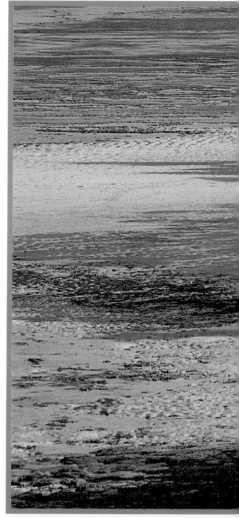

groups. Those who can afford to do so take **private chartered flights** to get well away from the crowds.

Road travel in Kenya will knock most of the luxury out of your itinerary, and well-heeled travelers generally take to the air. There are scheduled services, of course, but there's nothing quite so handy as having your own plane: two charter companies include Boskovic Air Charters Ltd. ((02) 501219 FAX 505964, Box 45646, Nairobi, and Tropicair ((0176) 32890/1 FAX (0176) 32787 E-MAIL tropicair @kenyaonline.com, Box 161, Nanyuki: costs are (approximately) US$1.68 per mile (1.6 km) for a Cessna carrying two passengers, with a minimum of 500 miles.

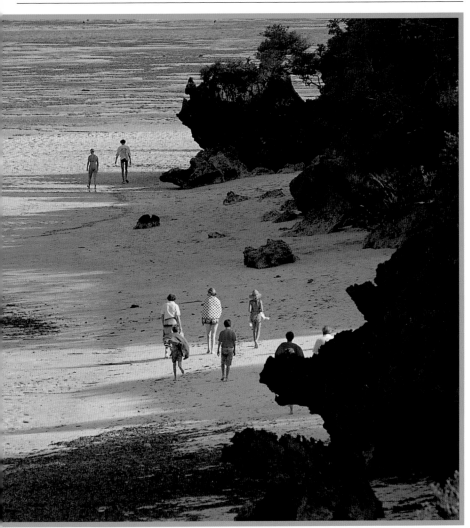

Three Nairobi-based associations, between them, are responsible for marketing most of Kenya's more luxurious lodges and camps. **Mellifera** ((02) 574689, (02) 577018 or (02) 567251 FAX (02) 564945 E-MAIL Mellifera@swift kenya.com, Box 24397, Nairobi, operates central reservations for a number of lodges, including one (Loisaba) that uses a helicopter (with leather seats, eight-stack CD and air conditioning) for luxury tours of the remote northern regions. Mellifera's other partners include Cottars 1920s Camp, offering period luxury near the Masai Mara, Galdessa Camp in the wilds of Tsavo East, and Nderit Estate on the banks of Lake Naivasha.

Members of a number of Kenya's long-established East African dynasties, most of whom have grown up in the bush alongside the country's wildlife, have linked together in creating **Bush Homes of East Africa** ((02) 350703, (02) 571661 or (02) 571592 FAX (02) 571665 E-MAIL bushhome@africaonline.co.ke WEB SITE www.bush-homes.co.ke, Box 56923, Nairobi. This organization provides the opportunity for the more dynamic descendents of the old East African aristocracy to bring remote and

ABOVE: Diani Beach is a favorite with travelers and also popular with European tour operators. OVERLEAF: Buffalo drink at Mountain Lodge's waterhole on the slopes of Mount Kenya.

much-loved parts of Kenya to a wider audience through private parks and reserves, the best known of which is perhaps Lewa Downs. Others include Rekero on the eastern side of the Masai Mara, Lokitela Farm on the slopes of Mount Elgon, Kitich in the northern Mathews Range and Sirita Siruwa between Nairobi and the Tanzanian border. The group also offers the mobile luxury of Patrick's Camp, which follows the dry season from Solio to Tsavo East and Tsao West national parks. Two of their properties bring exclusive luxury to the coast: Tana Delta Camp and Takaungu House, near Kilifi.

Finally, **Cheli and Peacock** ((02) 604053/4 or (02) 603090/1 FAX (02) 604050 or (02) 603066 E-MAIL chelipeacock@africa online.co.ke WEB SITE www.chelipeacock .com, Box 39806, Nairobi, is a long-established agency that coordinates a scattering of specially smooth and sophisticated small lodges around the country, including Elsa's Kopje in Meru National Park, Tortilis near Amboseli and Kiwayu on the remote northern coast.

As the luxury end of East African travel booms, even the mainstream operators have established — or refurbished — their best properties to offer more sophistication to high-spending visitors. Thus **Governors Camps** ((02) 331871 FAX (02) 726427 WEB SITE www.governorscamp.com, Box 48217, Nairobi, has developed Ilmoran in the Masai Mara; the **Heritage Group** ((02) 446651 or (02) 447929 FAX (02) 446533 E-MAIL info@heritagehotels.co.ke WEB SITE www.heritagehotels.co.ke, Box 74888, Nairobi, has opened 10-bedded "Explorers Camps" in the Masai Mara and at Kipungani, on Lamu Island; while the **Conservation Corporation** ((02) 441001/5 FAX (02) 746826 E-MAIL info@conscorp.co.ke WEB SITE www.ccafrica.com, Box 74957, Nairobi, has built Bateleur Camp alongside its already quite luxurious Kichwa Tembo in the Masai Mara. All these properties are described in more detail in the touring chapters below.

Camping in Kenya doesn't always mean roughing it.

Family Fun

The excitement of watching the world's wildlife walk from the pages of books and onto the savanna by your safari vehicle will bring a smile to the face of any child. The sheer size of some of nature's wonders can't fail to impress, and the experience sets the groundwork for a lasting interest in wildlife and conservation in almost every child.

Perhaps strangely, Kenyan **safari operators** have been slow to tailor their arrangements to this emerging market. The first to do so was the Heritage Group ((02) 446651 or (02) 447929 FAX (02) 446533 E-MAIL info@heritagehotels.co.ke WEB SITE www.heritagehotels.co.ke, Box 74888, Nairobi, which runs a portfolio of lodges and hotels around the country, and takes considerable pride in running "Adventurers Clubs" on all their properties. These introduce children ages four to fourteen to the African world with an irresistible combination of wildlife tracking, spear-throwing sessions, bow-and-arrow or beadwork making and lizard-hunts, not to mention plenty of time in the pool. To appeal across the board, the Heritage Group has larger lodges, such as the Voyager Safari Lodge in the Masai Mara and the Voyager Mombasa Beach Resort, which offer cheerful and communal clubs with up to 40 children at a time running around on chaotic treasure hunts. At their medium-sized properties, such as the 27-tented Samburu Intrepids and the Mara Intrepids in the Masai Mara, groups are smaller and the clientele more select.

Parents love it — they often join in — and although other operators are lumbering into position to launch their own imitations, it is the Heritage Group's clubs they are likely to be copying: this is where you should look for the best childcare program for some time to come.

One thing to bear in mind is that children don't, on the whole, enjoy traveling too much or moving too often. It is better to pick a destination and stay

there rather than undertake ambitious mobile safaris, especially with long road journeys. Under the age of five or so, children probably won't appreciate some of the more wonderful sights, and might remember instead long hours spent in vehicles and in the company of strangers, and the break of their routine. Renting a car is one option, as this will give you the freedom to stop where necessary and alter plans to suit changing requirements. Bear in mind that you probably won't find a child-seat in Kenya and should bring your own. Bring too a light collapsible stroller as many hotels have long paths between rooms and public areas.

Children aged six or above are usually transformed by the experience of nature and the excitement of **camping out** and eating around a bonfire. Flat spots can occur driving along dusty roads in the middle of the day: bring plenty of things to entertain them. Excellent children's toys are on sale locally. Handcrafted from wood or wire, these can often provide hours of entertainment for the imaginative child, and hours of entertainment might actually be needed.

Parents will also want to bear in mind that, in the wild, infants of all species are generally prey. Some of the unfenced **game lodges** don't accept children simply because they don't want to see their

OPPOSITE: A swimming pool is an ideal refuge from the midday sun. ABOVE: The Thinker — an olive baboon.

guests eaten, and their minimum accepted ages can vary: some lodges aren't prepared to take children under seven, while for others, 12 is their lower limit. Check ahead with your selected lodges to see if they have any special restrictions.

Fenced lodges are generally far more accepting of small children. And for warm, loving childcare, there is no better place than Kenya. With one of the world's highest birthrates, they get plenty of practice: the majority of the population is under 15 years of age. There aren't that many facilities especially for children, though: normally they're just included in adult activities from a very early age, and for most Kenyans this generally means work.

Kenya is an exotic destination at all levels and the average child's fascination with the surroundings can be dangerous. It can take time and a consolidated effort to persuade them not to drink the water. Nairobi's **Snake Farm** might be a good early stop if children are unaware of the dangers of venomous snakes, as they will get the chance to see a selection in relative safety.

Most resort hotels have **babysitting and nanny services** that are staffed by well-trained and practiced professionals, but it is well worth considering hiring a nanny for the duration of your stay, to ensure continuity of attention and consistency of care. Rates are not too expensive. Let's Go Travel ((02) 447151 or (02) 441030 FAX (02) 447270 or (02) 441690 E-MAIL info@letsgosafari.com WEB SITE www.letsgosafari.com, Box 60342, Nairobi, should be able to assist in this.

Health is of course the major problem. To ensure clean toilet facilities, stay in mid-range hotels and lodges. Most good hotels have links with reliable and well-qualified doctors and most mainstream Western drugs are available to those who are able to pay for them, but bear in mind that in case of injury or serious illness good medical facilities are generally limited to the major cities.

For general child maintenance, you can buy all the **basics**, including sterilizer, diapers and baby food in the supermarkets of any major town, but your favorite brands might only be available — if at all — in the boutiques of the better hotels. Disposable diapers, preferred brands of baby food and motion-sickness pills should all be brought along in case they are unavailable: hats, sandals and sunscreen are also wise supplies to carry.

Malaria is a special problem. Even if young children can be persuaded to swallow malaria medicine — not always easy — it's still important to minimize their exposure to mosquitos in the morning and evening. Which means nets: not every child's favorite way to go to sleep. Risks of malaria are much lower in the cool up-country air than in the steamy climate of the coast — a fact that, with young children, might end up dictating much of your travel itinerary.

In rural areas, it's accepted to view the whole country as a playground. This indeed is what the local children do if they haven't been taken out to work the fields. But there are a few establishments set up specifically to cater to children. There are two **waterslide centers** that should be top of the list for parents: in Nairobi, Splash is next door to the Carnivore Restaurant, and in Mombasa there is Pirates on Nyali Beach, where waterslides through the day will keep children entertained, at least until 6 PM when both are turned back over to the adults. In Nairobi there are several opportunities for children to get right up close to animals, but this should not be attempted if they are young or naturally nervous: at Nairobi's **Giraffe Sanctuary** a raised platform allows kids to feed endangered Rothschild's giraffes, but children younger than eight might find the animals just a little big. Although Nairobi's **Maasai Ostrich Farm** gives a unique opportunity to get close to the world's largest birds, it is important to remember that ostriches don't hide their heads in the sand: when scared they let out a disemboweling kick which, designed for predators, can easily fillet a human.

Children love Kenya but constant supervision is essential. There are crocs out there!

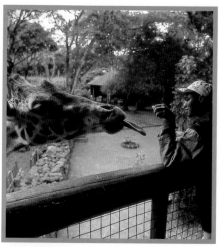

In the coastal resort hotels, most of the **swimming pools** are surveyed by alert lifeguards, but don't leave children unattended, especially on the **beach**. Occasional strong currents can be a danger and the tropical waters contain unexpected hazards from hard-to-spot stonefish to fluffy-looking sea urchins.

And whatever older children may claim, discos in Kenya are rarely suitable for teenagers, or even most adults.

Cultural Kicks

Kenya has a lively theatrical scene, based in Nairobi, and the self-censorship of the 1970s started to fade in the more overtly malcontented 1990s. The best

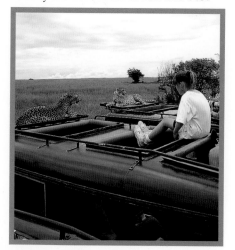

theater is generally thought to be Nairobi's small Professional Center ℂ (02) 225506, in Parliament Road, which puts on modern works from Africa and classics from the West — usually with fast-talking ad-libs reflecting the concerns of the local audience. It's a small theater where the audience feels directly involved, and some of their musicals are well worth catching; contact the center to find out what they're showing. The National Theater ℂ (02) 220536, Moi Avenue, just opposite the Norfolk Hotel, also puts on good performances, with the focus clearly on African drama and Kenyan writers. Sometimes this means that you won't understand a word! Ask what's on and don't forget to ask which language will be used. More live performances are put on at the adjacent French Cultural Center ℂ (02) 336263, Loita Avenue, and the Goethe Institute ℂ (02) 224640, also on Loita Avenue near Uhuru Highway in the city center. Although primarily intended to present the French and German cultures (respectively) to a Kenyan audience, they also showcase Kenyan art and dance. Call for schedules.

Tracking down good art can take rather longer. Most commercial art in the city center tends to be aimed squarely at the tourist market, with an unrelenting focus on wildlife scenes: professionally executed, but too much can wear thin. To see good contemporary **Kenyan art**, check out the upper floor of the National Archives, in the old Bank of India building on Moi Avenue. The National Gallery and, of the private galleries in the town center, Gallery Watatu on Standard Street can usually be relied upon to show some works by new artists of interest, at least until they are sold.

Much of Kenya's cultural heritage is not based in theater or flat, representative paintings, but in vivid and organic **sculptures** in wood or stone. There's a tradition of copying though, and it can be hard at first sight to distinguish real originality and flair from cheaply produced products made on industrial scale. All it takes to get your eye in is to take a look at some quality sculpture. Some can be found, as you'd expect, at Nairobi's National Museum on Museum Road, while still more is jumbled on the floor of the National Archives. African Heritage off Kenyatta Avenue is a combination shop/museum/restaurant where some of the finest handicrafts and sculptures from Kenya and Ethiopia can be found and bought. As an added attraction, live African music is played on Saturday and Sunday afternoons. The Africa Cultural Gallery on Mama Ngina Street in the Jubilee Insurance building displays some high-quality modern sculpture — often at high prices.

More of Kenya's culture is encapsulated in **dance and costume**. Once more, your first stop should be the National Museum. However, displays that are more dramatic are on offer in the capital. The Bomas of Kenya on Forest Edge Road, just past the national park main gate, offers daily displays of traditional dancing every afternoon between 2:30 PM and 4 PM. Somewhat disconcertingly, these are performed by a professional dance troupe who quickly switch among Kenya's tribal cultures, which might

maintain athletic standards of dancing but detracts from the authenticity.

A rather better experience of potted culture awaits visitors to the Bombolulu Center, just south of Nyali Bridge in Mombasa. The center also has tribal *manyattas* (reed or mud) dwellings and costumes. Other ways of experiencing local dance styles are more haphazard: many lodges persuade their local communities to show off the local dances, while travelers will find it quite easy to gatecrash local dances that take the place of television in outlying communities: just follow the noise after nightfall and find fireside hop-alongs where the music is by voice and drum, and the lyrics mainly focused on cattle.

To track down the rich musical traditions of the present day, it helps to have a Kenyan guide: it's quite hard to find live **local music venues** in Nairobi, as most turn to the more moneyed tastes of white and Asian communities. Worthwhile venues that specialize in

OPPOSITE TOP: At Nairobi's Giraffe Sanctuary these magnificent creatures eat from your hand. But in the Masai Mara, BOTTOM, it's safer to stay on the roof. ABOVE: Entertainment by Kamba dancers from the Machakos region.

and children. The warriors will be elsewhere, and cash transactions the only point at which visitors and tribes people interact. The main thing that ruins the experience for all concerned is the omnipresent camera. Taking photos and videos always causes offence and really is best avoided. If you want a good quality picture to take home, buy a postcard, rather than seeing it all through the restricting viewfinder of a cheap camera. Things get much better if you have — or can borrow — some small children for company. Young people of all races can quickly form a common bond, and the sight of a young *mzungu* is the easiest way to get young Maasai girls to break into wreathing smiles.

Shop till You Drop

First-time visitors to Kenya are likely to be overwhelmed by the onslaught of souvenir sellers. Prices start high, especially for visitors with the pallor characteristic of a new arrival, and an American accent is a real drawback in negotiations.

But persist and there are real bargains on offer. Artisanship can be high, although you'll have to expect this to be reflected in the price. It is worth paying more for something that will persist as a thing of value than buying cheaply something you'll be embarrassed to give away on your return. Whatever you're buying, knowing more about what is available and the quality to expect will help you gain the upper hand in the long and convoluted bargaining process.

Bargaining is usually necessary, apart from a few fixed-price shops and hotel boutiques. Even then it's always worth pointing out flaws or trying for a reduction. Some people find it a frustrating waste of time while the vendors invariably regard it as an endlessly interesting duel of wits. Their opening price depends on any

African music include the Ngong Hills Hotel on Ngong Road, the Makuti Park Club in Nairobi South B Shopping Center, and the nearby Peacock Inn. These regularly provide local music, with the big nights being Wednesday, Friday and Saturday. Local bands lured by foreign dollars line the hotel waterfronts along the lively Bamburi Beach to the north of Mombasa Island. In general, authentic local music is easier to find on the weekends in the less cosmopolitan provincial cities. Just ask at your hotel, but specify that it's live African music you're after (mime a guitar) or you'll get directions for the nearest disco if you're lucky, and to a brothel if you're not.

Many visitors are fascinated by the **tribal customs** and traditions of Kenya's pastoralists: the nomadic Maasai and Samburu people, who are most often seen across the countryside outside the national parks and reserves. To meet with these people, and to begin to understand thier way of living, takes care. Most of the lodges will offer visits to Maasai *manyattas*, but following such well-worn tourist trails is almost always a depressing experience of overpriced curios amongst a few shabby huts occupied by women

ABOVE: Mombasa's Jain Temple is a vibrant blast of Hindu culture. RIGHT: The colorful dress of Kenya's rural pastoralists.

number of factors, one of which will be how much money they think you have. The first secret of successful bargaining is to avoid getting bounced into making an offer higher than what you think the product is actually worth. If in doubt keep quiet, and don't let a big opening price persuade you to revise your initial estimate of value upwards. Once you've named a price you will be expected, if not to shift upwards, at least to stick to it. An offer once made cannot be retracted without causing real offence. An occasional and rather dishonorable way of getting the keenest deal can be to bargain on the basis that you're buying five — or ten — of whatever object is being discussed, and then, at the last minute, decide just to buy one.

Woodcarvings can represent exceptional value. Napkin rings, salad servers, elegant hardwood bowls and coasters, if well made, are always useful. Stylized stick sculptures, masks festooned with matted hair, and herds of miniature carved rhinos can travel less well. "Makonde statues," usually of people and with a high ebony gloss, are often just lighter wood dyed with shoe-polish; check the quality by the weight, although it is best, in general, to buy blackened lightwood — there are more souvenir vendors around than surviving ebony trees and it is illegal to carve Kenyan ebony.

Basketry is an art form in Kenya, and prices often very low indeed. Craft shops invariably have a stock of handmade place mats, fruit bowls and laundry baskets, painstakingly crafted and often using natural dyes. For more substantial products like sofas, dog kennels or carports, head out to the Racecourse Road. Sisal handbags are strong and hardwearing, but check how much they cost, imported, back home. This is essential information to the bargaining process, as often, even at their source, you'll end up paying more.

Soapstone sculpture is found in almost every Kenyan souvenir stall, and all originate from mines near the village of Tabaka near Kisii in the west of the country. Often beautifully carved and

painted, it is also very cheap, considering the hours of work that go into carving and polishing. Once more, bowls and plates are most likely to be useful, but bear in mind that soapstone is heavy: think ahead to how far you'll have to carry it.

Tribal beads characterize many goods fashioned by the Maa tribes, which include the Maasai, the Samburu and Turkana. From key rings to necklaces, these are often exceptionally beautiful and easy to carry, and provide a lifesaving income to traditional women working from their home *manyattas*. Price should depend on quality: watch carefully to make sure it does. In the same category, **shields**, **spears and tribal regalia** are more expensive if actually used rather than purpose-made for the tourist industry. These can be cheaper bought in their region of origin but if that isn't possible and you're in Nairobi on any Tuesday, check out the Maasai Market, which takes place on waste ground off Muranga Road one day a week. Quality is often very high and the prices low. Metal **bracelets** and **necklaces** are tempting buys but beware: within a few hours of use they often dye your skin with metal impurities, which lessens their beauty and usefulness considerably.

The single most underrated product available in Kenya is its **cotton fabric** — batiks and weavings produced for the highly critical local market. *Kangas*, designed for women, are sold in pairs, with one half used as a papoose for the inevitable child. In thin cotton and delicate patterns, they also generally have a proverb included in the design. Ask the vendor to translate the message. My favorite reads "Don't sleep with fleas." *Kikois* derive from the coast: generally striped, they have their origins in Islamic Lamu, are made in thicker cotton and are designed to be worn by men. Other fabrics on offer include

TOP: Watch painters at work in Nairobi's art galleries. BOTTOM: Cowrie-shell necklaces are very much part of Kenyan culture.

batiks, often designed to be stretched and hung, with prices totally dependent on the quality of workmanship and the textile used. Pay a lot for a lot.

In general, one of the best places to buy handicrafts is Nairobi, which attracts some of the best produce from all over the country. Shop at the **Central Market**, however, and expect to pay dearly for the privilege. Around a small core of vegetable sellers are poised ranks of sharp salesmen selling products usually of indifferent quality but always at premium prices. Better is the **Kariakor Market** (named after the World War I "Carrier Corps" in which many Kenyans "decided" to help the British war effort), off Racecourse Road east of the city center, where you'll be rubbing shoulders with local shoppers rather than other tourists. Or let your money go to a good cause: some of the best outlets are run by charities or have a proportion of their revenue going to a good cause. Two of these in Nairobi include the **Undugu Shop** in Woodvale Grove, Westlands, with a wide range of handicrafts benefiting several charities around Nairobi, or the **Utamaduni Crafts Center**, Bogani Road, Langata, where 18 specialist shops trade on behalf of the Kenyan Wildlife Service.

Short Breaks

Kenya might seem a long way to go for just a short time, but there are plenty of short breaks that can give a vivid feel of the country in just a few days. On a short break, there is little point in driving yourself as this is not a place to drive jet-lagged and even small distances on the ground will take longer than you expect. Both Kenya Airways ((02) 210771 or (02) 229291 FAX (02) 336252, Box 41010, Nairobi, and their subsidiary Flamingo ((02) 210771 FAX (02) 823612 fly to Kenyan airports, including Eldoret, Kisumu, Lamu and Malindi, on a daily basis from the international airport. Most domestic flights go from Wilson Airport, five kilometers (three miles) south of the city center on Langata Road: passengers

from the international airport therefore do not need to travel in to the city center to transit for their domestic flight. The largest operator here is the main regional airline, Airkenya Navigation ((02) 501421/3 FAX (02) 500845 E-MAIL info@air kenya.com WEB SITE www.airkenya.com, Box 30357, Nairobi, that flies daily to Lamu, Kiwayu, Amboseli, Nanyuki/ Samburu/Lewa Downs, Mombasa and, of course, the Masai Mara, with regular services also to Malindi. For charter flights, the main operator is Boskovic Air Charters Ltd. ((02) 501219 FAX 505964, Box 45646, Nairobi.

Don't cut things too fine on the way back though: internal flights in Kenya are liable to delay and a missed international link can stop a short break being short.

If it's your first visit to Kenya and you have little time, there's really no contest. Kenya's main international attraction lies in its wildlife. As such the **Masai Mara**, the country's most game-filled national park, is the obvious choice. Fly-in safaris can quickly reach most of the main lodges, meaning that within hours of leaving your desk it is possible to be immersed in the famous migration of wildebeest. You won't be the first — or indeed the only — person with more money than time; most of the mainstream travel companies are used to arranging short breaks in the Mara and many have daily departures — by air or road — at prices far lower than you would be able to arrange independently. But be warned that even two nights in the Mara will seem rushed after six to eight hours on a poor road with the same prospect again on the way home. Charter flights and many small, dirt airstrips open up the most remote parts of Kenya as realistic destinations for increasingly busy travelers to pack the African experience into just a few days.

Most of Kenya's more expensive lodges are well used to collecting clients from the local airport and just as capable of arranging short game-spotting breaks,

Africa's giant baobab trees can live for more than 1,500 years.

as well as being valuable parts of longer tours. Choose one that combines several immediate activities such as riding, as well as tame — or at least reliable — game since there's not going to be time to tune in thoroughly to the wild. Although a town with an airport is ideal, most of the more expensive lodges have access to private airstrips.

A short break is probably not the best time to experiment with complicated travel arrangements within Kenya. Internal flights are subject to overbooking and schedules change. Although individual lodges are described in detail later in this book and contact details are given, in the context of a short break it is probably wise to use a major Kenyan operator accustomed to making travel arrangements on the ground such as Let's Go Travel ((02) 447151 or (02) 441030 FAX (02) 447270 or (02) 441690 E-MAIL info@letsgosafari.com WEB SITE www.letsgosafari.com, Box 60342, Nairobi, or UTC ((02) 331960 FAX (02) 331422 WEB SITE www.unitedtour.com, Box 42196, Nairobi.

If restricted to travel by car it is best not to aim too far from Nairobi. The main safari operators are well able to supply vehicles and drivers to explore, or you can rent a car of your own, but ambitious itineraries overland snarl up in heavy traffic and poor roads. Distances feel longer than they look on the map and although you will see a lot of Kenya, you

might not enjoy it. Sensible objectives for short breaks starting in Nairobi generally head north up the spectacular **Rift Valley** and include **Lake Naivasha**. Not only beautiful in itself, it is good for bird watching, spotting hippos and relaxing, and is only a two-hour drive north of Nairobi. There is a good range of accommodation options, but it's popular with city weekenders too: reserve ahead.

Lake Nakuru is a two-hour drive further north from Naivasha and contains an underrated park surrounding a flamingo-filled lake — a good place to spot game of all kinds including black rhinoceros.

Beyond the Rift Valley are the **Aberdare Mountains**, a drive of five hours north from the capital. These cloud-kissed mountains are unspoiled and little visited: partly because the roads are so bad within the park. It's easy to get stuck, which is not an excuse accepted by many airlines for missed flights. So it's safest to stay instead at the Aberdares Country Club, where the greatest danger is a low-flying golf ball; and if time permits reserve a night spotting game at The Ark. See THE ABERDARE MOUNTAINS, page 208 in CENTRAL HIGHLANDS for further details.

An alternative destination, a five-hour drive from Nairobi, is **Sweetwaters**

ABOVE: Three-horned chameleons blend in with the leaves. OPPOSITE TOP: Bird watching on Lake Naivasha. BOTTOM: Zebras in Samburu take no notice of safari vehicles.

Reserve. This private sanctuary is near Nanyuki and is home to a tame rhinoceros called Morani who likes to have his stomach scratched. The reserve also houses Kenya's largest chimp sanctuary. Night drives in search of leopards are a specialty here.

If time is really short, a matter of a few hours between connecting flights, there's the chance to spot almost all the "Big Five" — elephant, lion, buffalo, rhino and leopard — within half an hour of the airport in **Nairobi National Park**. Even a taxi driver can be persuaded to drive through, although you're likely to see a lot more from the higher position of a safari vehicle, and a qualified driver/guide, possibly linked by radio with other vehicles and park rangers, is much more likely to find you good sightings. Within hearing distance of the hum of Nairobi's traffic, the 120-sq-km (46-square-miles) of the national park contains everything from rhinoceros to cheetah: only elephants are banned as they knock over too many trees. The best way to see it is on a half-day tour: minivans and drivers are available at reasonable rates through Let's Go Travel, or with other operators such as UTC.

Fly into Mombasa's international airport and a whole range of different opportunities opens up along the coast. If time permits, it's best to make the three-hour drive to **Watamu**, for a quick dive, game fishing, or conventional water sports. Not a bad way to fill the decompressing hours, as 24 hours are needed after scuba diving before any flight. If time is really short, though, there are plenty of worthwhile dives and beaches even nearer Mombasa: **Bamburi Beach** is barely 20 minutes by car from the airport. To the south, the Likoni Ferry puts you on a good road to **Diani Beach**, an hour and a half away, which offers a waterfront array of package hotels with a good, if faintly sanitized, atmosphere.

Your beach hotel will, in any case, be surrounded by exotic plants and animals: look closely and however luxurious the facilities, there'll never be any doubt you're deep in Africa. Watamu is backed by the **Arabuko-Sokoke Forest**, in Mombasa itself, the resident hippopotamuses are just part of the attraction of the **Bamburi Quarry** Nature Trail, and at Diani Beach the beachfront hotels share their surroundings with colobus monkeys. For a short-break safari experience from a coastal base, ideal for overnight stays, head back inland from Mombasa to the **Shimba Hills Forest Lodge** or **Kwale Elephant Sanctuary**, both within two hours of Mombasa and with transportation readily arranged from Mombasa's hotels or through UTC.

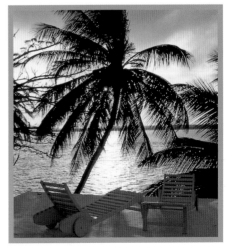

OPPOSITE: Five out of Kenya's seven rivers start from the Aberdares Mountains. ABOVE: Hippos yawn through the day. RIGHT: Lamu Island is perfect for a beach break.

Festive Flings

As most of their lives are devoted to surviving through years of continuing recession, most Kenyans need quite a lot of encouragement to come out and party. The many religions of the country provide the vital spark.

For the majority **Christian** population, the biggest public celebration is Easter, with Christmas, as in the West, being a quieter, more low-key display. And it is the Christian calendar that dictates Kenya's national holidays. However, **Muslims** make up 30 percent — and rising — of the population, so their big festivals are also observed, especially on the coast. The beginning and end of Ramadan and the Muslim New Year are the cause for major celebrations, but exact dates will vary from year to year — the biggest parties happen at Eid. Maulidi, the Prophet's birthday, is celebrated most in Lamu, with processions and parties; it too shifts date every year.

Meanwhile a significant minority of **Hindus** celebrate the colorful festivals of their own religion, especially inland. Once more, the exact dates vary and predicting them even a year ahead is a matter for an astrologer familiar with the lunar calendar. Further festivals particular to specific tribal groups are also observed but rarely advertised. Ask around.

Some of the biggest festivities are entirely secular, grouped around government-run agricultural shows. These tour the provincial cities and can provide an insight into Kenya's rural way of life.

For most "Kenyan Cowboys," the endangered, hard-drinking white Africans, the last weekend in May is party time. To attend you'll need initiative and probably some camping equipment, as the precise location of festivities moves about. From the coast, they converge on Diani for an anything-goes sporting extravaganza called

"**Diani Rules**," the secret being that there are no rules. To track down this year's Diani Rules, a good starting point is the Safari Beach Hotel ((0127) 2726 FAX (0127) 2357, Box 90690, Mombasa. On the same weekend the Nairobi population decamp in their green Range-Rovers and baggy shorts to a secret location in the heart of the bush for an unique rally called the **Rhino Charge**. The aim is to cover 10 checkpoints over the course of a day while clocking up the minimum mileage: many cars don't make it, but the weekend in the bush has become a Kenyan tradition. One operator who can help you find this event, and can even arrange for you to enter if you give plenty of notice, is Rafiki Africa Ltd. ((02) 884238 FAX 710310 E-MAIL safarico @arcc.or.ke WEB SITE kilimanjaro.com/ safaris/rafiki, Box 76400, Nairobi.

Most of the small towns around Kenya tend to be quiet and low-key most nights of the week. If you are planning a night out, however, Fridays and Saturdays are often the time for serious drinking and dancing, with music continuing, a little more calmly, through Sunday.

Galloping Gourmets

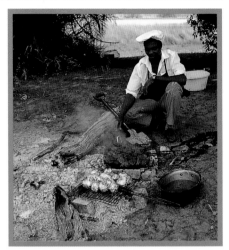

East Africa is not known as a gastronomic paradise. So Kenya comes as a pleasant surprise. The best chefs are the subject of hot competition amongst Kenya's top restaurants and lodges, and standards are often extremely high. They are helped by one great factor: Kenya's range of climates that run from the snow-capped peaks of Kilimanjaro through the temperate highlands and down to the steamy tropics of the coastal belts. Great cooks can pick and choose from the finest ingredients, be they lobster, Aberdeen Angus grazing manicured fields, or humped, zebu cattle bought from pastoral herders. Meanwhile, a thriving agricultural sector produces almost every type of fruit: strawberries and apples rival the finest of Europe, while mangos and papayas are just some of the tropical specialties. Everything is locally grown, glistening fresh and tasting of rich Kenyan soil. As a result, the best restaurants and hotels are free to specialize in every type of world cuisine, working with the best ingredients.

These advantages do not apply so readily to the local cooks at traditional restaurants, whose aim is generally to provide cheap, filling dishes at minimal cost. Often the cooking equipment is limited to a saucepan and a small clay oven filled with firewood. However the local Kenyan cuisine should be a feature of every visitor's experience of the country, and can often be delicious, especially at better restaurants. The cheaper versions are likely to be a central feature for travelers on a budget.

In the mornings, the standard diet at local establishments is *mandazi*, home-cooked doughnuts washed down with a mug — or two — of hot, sweet tea. Local restaurants are often open only at lunchtime, and serve a limited menu that comprises maize (*ugali*) with beans and a tough stew made from whatever meat was available that morning, often goat, and perhaps a plate called spinach but usually kale. *Matoke* is something of a luxury: this Ugandan specialty is made from mashed green plantains. *Githeri* is a vegetable stew with everything put in, sometimes meat. Thanks to the Asian influence, a common side-dish is chopped chapatis.

Generally Kenyan food is eaten with the hands, partly because knives and forks are a comparatively recent sophistication, but also because many of the dishes, especially *ugali*, need to be kneaded with the fingers to become at all palatable.

Almost every hotel will advertise "*Nyama Choma*," the classic Kenyan dish of roast meat, usually goat. Perhaps surprisingly in view of the primitive conditions in which they are prepared, meals are often absolutely delicious. Even the meanest shack can sometimes surprise. However most good hotels will put on Kenyan dishes, prepared to the highest standards, for their guests to experience local styles of cooking.

On the coast, the long maritime tradition has made coconut milk and the spices of Asia integral ingredients in meals that reflect the cosmopolitan influence of many cultures. The basis is invariably fish from the ocean.

LEFT: Kenya's Muslims celebrate the holy days of Islam according to the lunar calendar. ABOVE: Cooks in Kenya lack sophisticated kitchens, but the cuisine can be superb.

Meanwhile the pastoral tribes, such as the Maasai and Samburu, live entirely on blood, "milked" from the necks of their cattle, and milk — this does not, to my knowledge, figure on any international hotel's menu.

Only in the cities, Mombasa and Nairobi, will visitors to Kenya have the chance to experience a true variety of cuisines. Kenya's widespread Asian influence means that there is a wide range of — often excellent — Indian restaurants. Urban Kenya has some world-class restaurants specializing in French, Japanese, and Chinese cuisine. Tourist lodges and hotels offer a range of classic recipes and small establishments specialize in Ethiopian or West African traditional menus. If just seeing Kenya's wildlife isn't enough, restaurants such as Nairobi's Carnivore Restaurant on Langata Road, or the restaurant at the Safari Park Hotel, 14 km (nine miles) north of the city center, offer special all-you-can-eat selections where the animals of your choice are grilled and carved onto your plate. Zebra steaks hover between the flavors of cow and horse; giraffe has a gamey edge; while crocodile, despite tasting rather of lobster, invariably manages to turn my stomach with its reptilian texture.

For drink, the choice reflects an enthusiasm that leads many visitors to assume that this is Kenya's elusive national sport. Although there is a full range of soft drinks available, my favorite is Stoney, the local ginger beer. As for real beer, countless versions are produced, all tasting much the same, sold in half-liter bottles and all of about the same strength — four to five percent alcohol. Kenyans take their choice of brands very seriously, and will often refuse a drink if the label's wrong. Tusker is the market leader, White Cap favored by more mature drinkers, Export for the upwardly mobile (if you believe the advertising, which most Kenyans do), and Malt (sold in smaller bottles) for epicures. Cans of Castle Beer, from South Africa, are a relatively new

arrival, and tourist lodges and hotels will sell a range of imported beers. Sometimes, to justify high prices, they only serve imported beers. Beer in tourist lodges will be sold chilled, but most of the drinks handed through security cages in local bars will be warm. Specify "*baridi*" if you'd like your drink chilled, and hope they have a working refrigerator.

For wine, some drinkable brews are produced in the Naivasha area, but nothing that would have serious tasters reaching for their wallets. Papaya wine is an interesting experience — worth one try at least — but most good wines in Kenya have been imported from South Africa.

Most rural Kenyans have never tasted wine, and can't afford beer. They rely on *changa'a*, distilled from maize in huts and *manyattas* all over the country. Fiery and potent, newspaper stories often report drinking binges that end in sickness, blindness and death, but Kenyans sipping and stirring their homemade spirits in the privacy of their own huts insist this is an evil rumor put about the government to boost tax-paid sales. It's better though to stick to the local spirits; vodka, whiskey or rum, sold in bottles or 30-ml (one-fl-oz) sachets (called mini-packs) by small bars and shops throughout the country. Tear the mini-pack open with your teeth and mix the contents with anything that will mask the taste.

Special Interests

Kenya has a wide range of special interest tour operators. They are often focused on specific sports, in which case they are listed in SPORTING SPREE, page 40. But not everything in Kenya has to do with sport. More appropriate, perhaps, are directed at Kenya's spectacular wildlife. The following specialists cater to focused travelers.

TOP: The wildlife's on your plate at Nairobi's Carnivore Restaurant. BOTTOM: Kenya's farms provide a steady supply of fresh fruit.

BIRDWATCHERS

Kenya is a paradise for birdwatchers. A range of habitats is available: the arid north, the Rift Valley lakes, forests at Kakamega in the west and at Arabuko–Sokoke on the hothouse lowlands, swamps at Saiwa, and the different habitats of the famous national parks mean that every species of East African and European migrant bird is represented. See BRUSH UP YOUR BIRDING, page 24 in TOP SPOTS.

ELEPHANT WATCHERS

If spotting birds is just too fiddly, elephants might better fill the viewfinder of your field glasses. The professional elephant-watcher is Cynthia Moss, who has spent years in Amboseli studying these great pachyderms. As a famous elephantologist, however, she's likely to be wary of video-toting tourists.

There is someone who can help. Iain Douglass-Hamilton, one of the prime activists who persuaded CITES (Convention on the International Trade of Endangered Species) to ban the trade of ivory and thus save Kenya's elephants from extinction in the 1980s, operates Elephant Watch Safaris ((02) 242572 FAX (02) 243976 E-MAIL oria@iconnect.co .ke or olerai_town@net2000ke.com, which orchestrates close encounters with one of Africa's most fascinating animals, with prices from US$300 per person, per night, in the northern Samburu district.

LITERARY TOURS

Kenya's great literary traditions are reflected in a number of special attractions. Remember *Out of Africa*? **Isak Dinesen's** house in Nairobi has been lovingly preserved as a recreation of the pioneer years where Happy Valley was a larger-than-life world at the frontier of civilization. The modest grace of her plantation house puts the experience in perspective, and even the shortest visit will bring her novels to vivid life. Much of the film was shot in the grounds, although interior shots were taken in a studio. But the ghosts of the past are so stained in the wood that after visiting the house one question remains: how much was fiction?

Kuki Gallmann shot to fame with the best-selling *I dreamed of Africa* (now a feature film starring Kim Bassinger) and is still resident in Kenya. She used her income from the book to establish a private reserve in the Laikipia region and, at it's heart, a stunning lodge northeast of Lake Baringo called Mukutan Retreat. Three chalets in the style of African rondavels are built into the rock of Mukutan Gorge, they are run as an exclusive home-stay where Africa takes center stage. The main person doing the retreating, however, is Kuki herself, and guests she hasn't met socially are positively discouraged. It's a wonderful, but very expensive, place, and you shouldn't expect to get Kuki along with the (hugely expensive) overnight rate. Her long-awaiting follow-up book, *African Nights*, was a depressing account in which all the central characters steadily die. But hopefully your own company will be more cheerful, over dinner, as you look out over Mukutan's stunning view.

Even more important was **Joy Adamson**, whose books about Elsa the Lioness introduced Africa's wildlife to a world audience. Until then lions had been seen as little more than targets. Her writing, often filmed, changed forever the relationship between Western cultures and nature. Joy Adamson's famous house, Elasmere, set on the Naivasha Lake shore towards Kongoni Game Valley, is a pleasant and very quiet place to stay and soak up the atmosphere of a private ranch. This was where her life with lions brought Africa to millions and thrust conservation issues onto the world stage. Less a hotel experience and more like staying in a private house, the friendly staff are happiest when they find guests are familiar with Joy Adamson's life and work, and committed to conservation. Reservations can be made directly from Elasmere ((0311)

Water is the lifeline in the arid north of Kenya.

21055 FAX (0311) 21074, Box 1497, Naivasha (expensive). Much of her research, if that's the right word, with lions took place in Meru National Park, where Elsa's Kjope, run by the upmarket operator Cheli and Peacock Ltd. ((02) 604053/4 or (02) 603090/1 FAX (02) 604050 or (02) 603066 E-MAIL chelipeacock@africa online.co.ke WEB SITE www.chelipeacock .com, Box 39806, Nairobi, is set up in honor of her memory. Her last years were spent in Shaba Game Reserve, where she met her end in a dispute with a 14-year-old boy — with a knife — she had peremptorily dismissed without pay. There's a memorial here, where she was stabbed, but her original camp was taken down: only the site remains. It's an interesting place to visit because it picks out one incident seen very differently by black and white Kenyans. From one side, it was an example of savage murder. From the other it exemplified the high-handed way (usually white, usually female) conservationists sometimes treated Africa's wild animals with greater consideration than they did the people. Either way, if you want to find out more, the only lodge in Shaba is the Sarova Shaba Lodge ((02) 713333 FAX (02) 718700 E-MAIL reservations@sarova.co.ke WEB SITE www.sarova.com, Box 72493, Nairobi. For access, there are scheduled flights with Airkenya ((02) 501421/3 FAX (02) 500845 E-MAIL info@airkenya.com WEB SITE www.airkenya.com, Box 30357, Nairobi, to nearby Samburu.

Taking a Tour

Although many travelers prefer the freedom and flexibility of making their own travel arrangements, in Kenya this will rarely, if ever, save money. Kenya's tour operators are able to negotiate special rates and discounts at lodges and hotels around the countryside that cannot even be dreamed of by the individual traveler. At lodges in the

The cliffs around Lake Baringo teem with life, a paradise for birdwatchers.

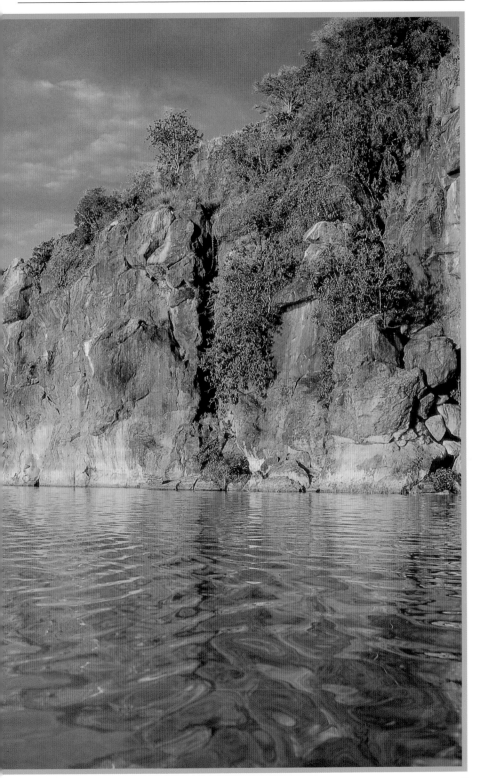

Masai Mara, for instance, a tour operator will be paying just US$30 for a bed that would cost an individual six times as much. Whether for a safari or a beach break, reserving with a tour operator often works out cheaper than going it alone.

Tours of Kenya are generally structured round visits to the national parks, listed under THE GREAT OUTDOORS, page 35, and more fully described under their relevant sections in the touring chapters. Itineraries vary, though even the shortest, these days, include the Masai Mara. Because the Mara is rather out on a limb in the southwest of the country, this means there is certain to be a fair amount of traveling involved: quickly by air or laboriously overland. Overwhelming with its wildlife in the migration season (July to October) the Mara is much less impressive when it has rained and all the wildlife has dispersed. At these times it is worth looking to other, dryer regions.

Other parks can be linked sequentially: for example, Nakuru, Aberdare, Samburu and Meru; or alternatively Amboseli, Tsavo West, Tsavo East. It is worth trying to reduce your travel time when choosing your safari, as long overland journeys are expensive and tiring.

When **choosing a tour operator**, the first decision is whether to make your bookings before your arrive or when you arrive in Nairobi. There are advantages on both sides. Overseas operators will offer all the consumer protection available in your home country, and the better operators will also ensure that the itinerary you finally purchase will meet your requirements. Tour operators based in Nairobi, however, can sometimes offer more up-to-date knowledge about more adventurous itineraries and plan your trip more closely around the prevailing weather conditions. Here we list first some of the most respected operators in Kenya, some of whom also have overseas representation, before going on to mention the better of the overseas operators.

The ultimate way to travel is on an elegant **private safari**, some of which claim to recreate *Out of Africa*, while others are camping trips that are more

realistically like African safaris at the turn of the last century. The most common are minibus tours that race you, at six to nine persons per vehicle, along the rattling, potholed dirt tracks from one park or reserve to the next. Tours catering to visitors with specific interests such as ornithology or photography are also available.

On a private safari, which is the most expensive of the options, you can tailor destination, itinerary, and schedule. However, once these details are established, it can be difficult to change them, particularly during the December to February high season, as the safari operator has to reserve hotels, guides and campsites and sort out other logistics. Many private safari operators have their own tented camps and gourmet cooks, and some have access to private game refuges.

Organizing a private safari requires a good rapport between the traveler and operator. And not a little money: expect to spend anything from US$300 to US$1,000 per head, per day. If you take this alternative, try to contact the operator *directly*, to minimize misunderstandings and to get a sense of his or her viewpoint and methods of operation. Discuss your wishes and the particulars involved. Since you'll be investing a sizable amount of money in your trip, take time to ensure it will meet your expectations. Allow several months for correspondence, and don't hesitate to use the telephone, although the Internet provides an increasingly useful source of up-to-date information and fast, cheap communications. Before you start, read up on the various sections in this book to decide what areas of Kenya interest you the most.

SAFARI OPERATORS IN KENYA
Among top safari operators are **Cheli and Peacock Ltd. (** (02) 604053/4 or (02) 603090/1 FAX (02) 604050 or (02) 603066 E-MAIL chelipeacock@africaonline.co.ke

In rural Kenya, life is still lived according to ancient traditions and ceremonies.

WEB SITE www.chelipeacock.com, Box 39806, Nairobi, and **Abercrombie and Kent** ((02) 334955 FAX (02) 228700, Box 59749, Nairobi, both of whom offer extreme luxury but at prices that can be a bit frightening. If packaged travel just isn't your bag and you want to try a private tented safari without breaking the bank, there are a number of local operators who offer this service. Vehicles and standards vary, however. One known and trusted local operator (well, actually it's run by an expat New Zealander, but he knows the country well) is **Chameleon Tours** (/FAX (02) 860541 or (02) 891375 E-MAIL chamtour @africaonline.co.ke WEB SITE www.chamel eonafrica.com, Box 15243, Nairobi, who can offer tented expeditions from as little as US$200 per person per day. This will get you comfort rather than luxury, but personally, I think this is more appropriate for a bush environment.

For specialist wildlife expeditions in search of gorillas in Zaire and longer private tented safaris way off the beaten track, one Kenyan operator which has received particular praise from film companies and private parties for personal service at reasonable cost is **Rafiki Africa Ltd**. ((02) 884238 FAX (02) 710310 E-MAIL safarico@arcc.or.ke WEB SITE www.kilimanjaro.com/safaris/rafiki, Box 76400, Nairobi.

These companies will provide private safaris in comfort, with knowledgeable guides for groups of any number of people, according to their own special requirements. For more generic tours, though, the bulk of Kenya's tour operators undercut these operators substantially, using minibuses with viewing hatches cut into the roofs (though they may use four-wheel drives on occasion). They usually leave Nairobi on regular schedules and offer neither flexibility nor personalized service but can provide excellent value. The better operators will guarantee that every client at least has a window-seat, though few provide enough space for everyone, simultaneously, to peer together through the rooftop hatch. Of this category,

the most reliable are: **Abercrombie & Kent** who offer both private safaris and organized tours; **United Touring Company (UTC)** ((02) 331960 FAX (02) 331422 WEB SITE www.unitedtour.com, Box 42196, Nairobi, and **SOMAK** with offices in Nairobi ((02) 535500/2/3 FAX (02) 535175, Eighth Floor, Corner House, Mama Ngina Street, Box 48495, and Mombasa ((011) 313871/2 FAX (011) 315514, Somak House, Mikindani Road, Box 90738, Mombasa. All of these also sell their safaris to international tour operators, but as these add on their markup before selling it on to you it's usually best to book directly.

Among younger, more adventurous and more impecunious travelers, camping safaris are justifiably the most popular. Safari companies spring up like desert roses after the rain, some departing the scene with equal rapidity, using trucks decked out with bench seating to up passenger numbers to achieve economically viable group size. For about US$80 per person per day, depending on the size of group and destination, these operators provide transportation, meals, tents, camp beds, and game drives or walking tours. Usually you are expected to bring your own sleeping bag, although even that can be provided at an extra cost, and usually there'll be someone to do the cooking.

Because these groups often take you into inhospitable wilderness, it's wise to rely on someone with experience and reputation. Consistently praised by their clientele are **Gametrackers Ltd**. ((02) 338927 FAX (02) 330903 E-MAIL Game @africaonline.co.ke, Box 62042, Nairobi, and **Safari Camp Services** ((02) 228936 FAX (02) 212160 WEB SITE www.kenyaweb .com/safari-camp, Box 44801, Nairobi (operators of the famed Turkana Bus). Even cheaper companies direct-sell on the streets of Nairobi. Three that have been around for long enough to acquire a veneer of respectability include **Savuka** ((02) 225108; **Kenia** ((02) 223699 FAX (02) 217671 or (02) 444572 WEB SITE www.gorp .com/kenia/; and **Come to Africa Safaris** ((02) 213186. However, these are just the most established of a rather risky end of the industry. Providing the safari experience for as little as US$50 a day, they don't venture far from the standard trail or offer much in the way of backup, service or information, but for many young travelers they offer the only affordable way to meet Africa's wildlife. Industry insiders suspect that they can only maintain their prices by cheating the national parks out of much-needed revenue on entry fees.

One example of what can go wrong on these cheap safaris happened to me in the city of Nakuru. Our driver/guide interrupted our dinner to tell us the morning game-drive would have to be delayed. Our vehicle had broken down. He suggested that we spend the morning in town while he got the car fixed. The infamous mechanics of Nakuru had struck again. In this case our safari vehicle had been sabotaged in the hope of stopping our morning visit to the national park. Each client had prepaid park entry fees of US$27, but two of us also had night flights to catch in Nairobi.

A few hours detained by a back-street garage would mean racing direct to the airport, releasing the park entry tickets for sale on the black market. I looked at the engine. Exhaust fluid was leaking from the joint between manifold and muffler. Could be simple to fix: but with a couple of stripped threads and a few inventive mechanics it was easy to see how the job could be stretched. It was a bit difficult. I wanted him to go and fix the problem immediately while we finished our meal. But for him to do this would have gone too far to admitting the con. I insisted that we take the game drive, at least, the next morning. Even though it wasn't ideal to put up with a noisy car, it removed the motive to draw out the repair.

This wasn't the only problem I found on a recent trip investigating cheap safaris. Others included breaking down in the Masai Mara — not so funny next to five angry lions — and being abandoned by the side of the road for half a day. This

The hyena plays an essential role as scavenger of the savanna, but will kill his prey when he can.

meant that instead of providing the evening game drive, our vehicle could slip into the national park on a minor track under the cover of dusk.

In most cases, making reservations locally doesn't even save money. Kenya's cheapest safaris rely on subcontracted minivans with no history of maintenance and drivers who don't speak English and would never be featured by international tour operators. Savings evaporate as bulk reservations cut out the benefits of tracking down safaris privately. Move up a notch to the middle of the market and service improves dramatically. Even backpackers are better advised to keep off the absolute baseline: beyond a certain point economies can only be made at your expense.

When safaris go wrong, there's more than convenience at risk: in isolated national parks, untrained guides or mechanical problems with subcontracted vehicles both spell danger. International tour operators choose reputable ground operators, and if difficulties arise they are an easy target for complaints or legal action. Make reservations in Nairobi and any dispute will be resolved in a place where Africa's wildlife can really charge: a Kenyan courtroom.

To make sense of the bewildering choice available, it is often a good idea to use a local travel agent. **Let's Go Travel** ((02) 447151 or (02) 441030 FAX (02) 447270 or (02) 441690 E-MAIL info@letsgo safari.com WEB SITE www.letsgosafari .com, Box 60342, Nairobi, has been consistently recommended by travelers over the years for being knowledgeable, efficient, and helpful without being pushy. They specialize in coming up with travel plans for independent travelers and are based above the Continental Supermarket in ABC Place, Waiyaki Way, Westlands, with offices also in Karen ((02) 882505, above Karen Provision Stores, and in the City Centre ((02) 340331 FAX (02) 214713, Caxton House, Standard Street. Another reputable operator is **Express Travel** ((02) 334722 FAX (02) 334825 E-MAIL expressk@africaonline.co.ke, Standard Street, Box 40433, Nairobi.

BOOKING FROM ABROAD

Internationally, **Abercrombie & Kent** is a leading operator at the top end of the market with 30 years of experience arranging travel in Africa. A&K has offices in the United States ((708) 954-2944 US TOLL-FREE (800) 323-7308, 1520 Kensington Road, Oak Brook, Illinois 60521; in Australia ((03) 9699 9766, 90 Bridgeport Street, Albert Park, Melbourne, Victoria 3206; in the United Kingdom ((0171) 730 9600 FAX (0171) 730 9376, Sloane Square House, Holbein Place, London SW1 8NS; and in Nairobi ((02) 334995 FAX (02) 228700, Bruce House, Standard Street, Box 59749. **SOMAK Travel** has offices in the United Kingdom ((0181) 423 3000 FAX (0181) 423 7700, Harrovian Village, Bessborough Road, Harrow on the Hill, Middlesex HA1 3EX.

From the United States, leading operators include the **African Adventure Company** ((954) 781-3933 US TOLL-FREE (800) 882-WILD, 1600 Federal Highway, Pompano Beach, Florida 33062, which offers a range of African programs and safari choices. **Mountain Travel Sobek** ((510) 527-8100 US TOLL-FREE (800) 227-2384, 6420 Fairmount Avenue, El Cerrito, California 94530, specializes in hiking, rafting and adventure travel for travelers based in the United States.

Africa Travel Centers are specialist safari outlets, and have offices in the United States, Australia and New Zealand, all sister companies to the London-based Africa Travel Shop. Contact details are: in the United Kingdom ((0171) 387 1211 FAX (0171) 383 7512, 4 Medway Court, Leigh Street, London WC1H 9QX; in the United States ((908) 870-0223 FAX (908) 870-0278, 197 Wall Street, West Long Branch, New Jersey 07764; in Australia ((02) 9267 3048, Level 12, 456 Kent Street, Sydney NSW 2000; in New Zealand ((09) 520 2000, 21 Remuera Road, Box 9365, Newmarket, Auckland.

The sun sets over Lake Turkana, the Jade Sea.

Welcome
to Kenya

Open savanna dotted with lions, cheetahs, antelopes, elephants and giraffes; skies the color of coal and blood as the sun sets; warriors leaning on their spears in the dry desert air as they watch their herds; grass-roof huts clustered behind thornscrub fences, the miraculous stars of clear African nights — all these images haunt ancestral memories and childhood reveries. Modern, exciting, cosmopolitan Kenya, "the pride of Africa," has incomparable parks and reserves that resurrect this vanished world. Here, with excellent accommodations at more than

to a community ranch or lesser-visited areas, where you'll share the experience with a local guide whose time-honored way of life is so very different to that of the West. The arid, thinly populated north of the country best protects, by its sheer harsh remoteness, this timeless lifestyle.

For others it is the beach that beckons: miles of sandy shoreline, protected by its offshore reef, where diving and deep-sea fishing are just some of the alternatives on offer.

And finally, there are the people. The populated centers of Nairobi, Nakuru and

reasonable prices, you can still see the earth in its pristine beauty. And because the Kenyan people have an ethic, a tribal philosophy if you will, of welcoming strangers and sharing with them, it is a uniquely warm and friendly place to travel.

There are myriad ways to explore the diversity of this country. For most visitors the main draw is the wildlife, coexisting spectacularly with ochre-painted pastoralists and their herds of cattle. To get really close to wildlife, choose a popular national park, where, although you will share the views with other minibus game vehicles, the animals themselves, no longer scared of tourists, will ignore their human audience and follow their natural pace of life. Or head off

Kisumu, sweltering on the banks of Lake Victoria, are open and friendly communities where, with a bit of caution, visitors find a warm and ready welcome.

No other destination will repay you with such lasting memories of the most diverse experiences and adventures. Whether you are traveling on public transportation and staying in basic local hotels, flying into luxury lodges in the heart of the bush, or renting your own four-wheel drive and traveling off on your own, you're assured, in Kenya, of an unforgettable travel experience.

OPPOSITE: A Samburu warrior. ABOVE: Ground transportation is the best way to get to know the wildlife.

The Country and Its People

Twenty million years ago, Kenya extended from the Congo to the Indian Ocean as a vast equatorial plain on the island continent of Africa. A carpet of thick tropical forest and woodland covered the flat and rolling plains. Animals of all stripes and colors inhabited the ground, branches and treetops, among them a variety of forest-dwelling, slender, muscular, and apelike primates we now call dryopithecines.

But Africa collided with Eurasia in the next few million years, creating the Mediterranean. This imperceptible but implacable grinding of the continents gave rise, literally, to Kenya as it is now. Over the land bridges from Africa to Eurasia crossed numerous species; the climate underwent drastic changes, and the drying habitat of the dryopithecines was invaded by the ramapithecines, whose teeth were more adapted to the harsh diet found in the woodlands and open country.

The collision of the continents, though spanning millions of years, was catastrophic in its impact: Africa was split centrally north to south by a vast, sheer fracture. The molten lava underlying the continental plates escaped from volcanoes and poured across the land, over millennia, pushing up the earth's crust more than 1,093 m (3,586 ft), even as the shifting tectonic plates pulled it apart. In 15 million or so years, it deepened what we members of the subspecies *Homo sapiens* now call the Rift Valley, and created the great volcanoes of Mount Kenya, Mount Elgon and Mount Kilimanjaro.

In the north, the Rift extended into what is now Ethiopia, creating the enormous and landlocked Lake Turkana, former source of the Nile, and often called the Jade Sea because of its marvelous green color. As the southern extension of the Rift Valley deepened, it cut off segments of earlier tropical rainforest. Its varied altitudes and climates preserved or gave rise to a diversity of ecosystems, including semiarid desert areas, grasslands, woodlands, and alpine meadows, habitats that offered new biological niches for the emerging ramapithecines. As the lava flowed and the volcanoes spread, they pushed the earth's crust down, widened the Rift Valley floor, and filled extinct craters with lakes, until the valley walls soared a vertiginous 914.4 m (3,000 ft).

FROM JUNGLE TO SAVANNA

As the valley walls rose, they cut into the clouds that, for millions of years, had carried the continent's wind drift from West to East Africa. Over long stretches of time, they blocked the rain's passage to the east, over what is now the majority of Kenya.

The lands changed in response: instead of unending tropical forest, the drier climate produced woodlands and savanna (treeless plain or a tropical grassland of seasonal rains and scattered trees). Like regiments cut off from retreat, patches of lingering tropical forest endured, preserving vegetation and animal species like those still found in West Africa, and antedating Kenya's rise from the equatorial plain. Such vestigial tropical areas, with their unusual vegetation, birds, and insects, include the Arabuko-Sokoke coastal forest south of Malindi, the Kakamega Forest north of Lake Victoria, and smaller areas along the lower reaches of the Tana River.

As the climate and vegetation altered on the East African plains, so did the animals that lived there. The drier climate, the seasonal rains, and the sparser forest gave rise to great herds of ungulates protected by the open spaces. Like many of today's apes, *ramapithecus* were omnivorous, eating leaves, stalks, berries, fruits, insects, eggs and meat. At some point, perhaps because its prey moved out to the expanding savanna, *ramapithecus* left the jungle and the woodland.

Such excursions favored upright locomotion, which, although it requires more energy per distance traveled, has many other benefits. It broadened the range of vision and freed the hands.

TELLING THE FIRST STORIES

Perhaps the thinner forest shelter in the woodland and savanna encouraged *ramapithecus* and its peers to band together; at some point they learned to feed not only themselves and their offspring but also others. Communal sharing of food developed, as did language.

The circumcision ceremony is a complicated ritual: this Samburu adolescent is preparing for the operation that will turn him into a warrior.

About three million years ago, *ramapithecus* began to walk habitually upright. "Hunter-gatherers," Kenya's world-renowned paleontologist Richard Leakey (the son of Louis and Mary Leakey) was to call them. These hunter-gatherers dug for roots and berries; they harvested nuts, seeds, shoots, edible leaves, bird and reptile eggs, insects and fruits; they learned to hunt live animals and feasted on dead ones when the opportunity arose.

As the *ramapithecus* lifestyles bacame more communal, the need developed for a broader language — to convey such matters as the location of foodstuffs, or to argue the division of spoils or the tactics used to achieve them. These issues all became part of the story that enlarged the hunter-gatherers' experience — the same way we humans still have of sharing and building on each other's experience.

Fossil remains of *ramapithecus* have been found in various locations in Africa, southern Europe, and Asia. These fossils constitute three distinct hominid types (including our direct ancestor, *Homo habilis* — able man — and two separate australopithecines), and have been variously estimated to be between two and five million years old. It's possible that man's ancestors existed in Asia and Europe during this time, but their remains have not been found, or that for climatic or other reasons, they ceased to exist except in Africa.

HOMELAND OF OUR ANCESTORS

Through extensive archeological digs on the shores of Kenya's Lake Turkana, in Tanzania's Olduvai Gorge and at the juncture of southern Ethiopia's Omo River with Turkana's northern shore, the Leakeys and other scientists have discovered tools and fossilized bones of several different hominids. These include the complete skull of a human ancestor who lived by Lake Turkana a little over two million years ago, and younger skulls of up to a million and a half years old.

Traces of hominids and the two australopithecines from a million to a million and a

Tribal dwellings as sketched by a mid-eighteenth-century traveler to Kenya.

The Country and Its People

half years old have been found outside Africa, but after that point, none have appeared in Africa or anywhere else except man's direct ancestor, *Homo habilis*. But, once again on the shores of Lake Turkana (at Koobi Fora) a team of paleontologists, led by Richard Leakey, later found remains of a more recent human ancestor, *Homo erectus* (standing man). Leakey's Homo erectus was a million and a half years old, predating others of its species that lived in many parts of Asia (Peking man) and Europe up to a half million years ago.

Africa, Eurasia, Asia and Europe. Their descendants painted cave interiors, fashioned sculpture, and celebrated the burial of their dead.

They improved the arts of habitation and war, literature and music, and learned to herd the ungulates they formerly stalked, farm the land, and set up property. These advances led to even greater warfare and dissension, but also to the building of cities, roads, universities, industry, and now the rockets that take them into space, far from the ancient plains of Kenya.

From *Homo erectus* evolved *Homo sapiens* (thinking man), and 50,000 years ago came modern human beings, anatomically unrecognizable from ourselves. But it was the find of *Homo erectus* skulls at Lake Turkana that proved for the first time that man's ancestor evolved in Africa.

About the time of *Homo erectus*, the shape and precision of stone tools became finer than was necessary for their immediate purpose. Anthropologists think this resulted from their growing language skills.

Through changing climates, the advance and retreat of northern glaciers, new shifts in continental drift, and the narrowing and widening of the Mediterranean Sea, *Homo erectus* and his peers went on to populate

NATURE UNPOSSESSED

"… they walked about their country without appearing to possess it … they had not aspired to recreate or change or tame the country and to bring it under their control … had accepted what God, or nature, had given them without apparently wishing to improve upon it in any significant way. If water flowed down a valley they fetched what they wanted in a large hollow gourd; they did not push it into pipes or flumes, or harass it with pumps. Consequently when they left a piece of land and abandoned their huts, the bush and vegetation grew up again and obliterated every trace of them, just as the sea at each high tide wipes out footprints and children's sand-castles, and leaves the beach once more smooth and glistening." (Elspeth Huxley, *The Flame Trees of Thika*.)

Because the ancient residents of inland Kenya built no castles, roads, or cities, few clues exist as to their recent history. Through archaeology, we know that approximately eight to nine thousand years ago, Kenya became the home of primitive hunters, probably related to the others of southern Africa. About 2000 BC, pastoral Cushitic tribes from Ethiopia moved into western Kenya in search of new grazing land. Some two thousand years ago, other pastoral and agricultural migrants settled the Rift Valley, and by AD 100, there may have been 1,400 pastoral communities living among what are now agricultural populations on both sides of the western Rift Valley.

These tribes migrated along the valley, interacting with other tribes from what are now Uganda, Ethiopia, Sudan and Tanzania. They exchanged and developed cultures that are identifiable in present-day tribes, such as the Kambas in central Kenya, the Kikuyu on the slopes of Mount Kenya, the Luo along the shores of Lake Victoria, and the Kalenjins on the high slopes of the western highlands.

When trade routes were established in the seventeenth century, the Europeans found four basic population groups: the Hamitic, Nilotic, Nilo-Hamitic and Bantu. The National Museum in Nairobi has superb ethnological displays of numerous tribes within these groups. Today, many still keep their social structure and traditions, though their lifestyles and dress have not completely escaped the influence of the West. It is not uncommon to see tribal members exchange their traditional clothes for Western garb.

The Hamitic tribes (Galla, Somali, and Rendille) came originally from the north, settling in the Tana Valley and northern Kenya between 1300 and 1500. The Nilotic people (Luo) migrated from Sudan along the Nile River to settle along the shores of Lake Victoria. According to Luo tradition, they were led to Kenya by two brothers, Adhola and Owiny. Near Mount Elgon, they quarreled and the tribe split. Adhola and his followers stayed around Mount Elgon; Owiny with his supporters settled the area south of Kisumu.

The Nilo-Hamitic tribes, which originated in Sudan, inhabit most regions of Kenya: the Turkana are found near Lake Turkana in the north, the Suk south of the lake, the Kalenjin tribes (Nandi, Kipsigis, Marakwet, Tugen, etc.) in west-central Kenya, and the Maasai in the south.

The fourth group consists of Bantu-speaking peoples who are spread throughout southern Africa. In Kenya, the Bantu tribes (Kikuyu, Meru, Embu, Chuka, Tharaka, Kamba, and other smaller tribes) live around and to the south of Mount Kenya. The Luhya

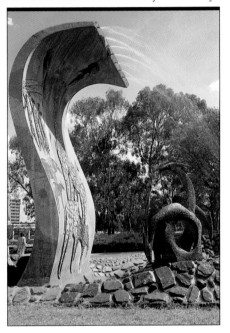

to the northwest of Lake Victoria, and the Nyika along the coast are also Bantu.

The ancestors of the coastal Bantu came to the Tana and Juba river valleys from the Taita Hills before the Galla; some Bantu tribes were probably assimilated into the Arabic coastal empire. The Bantu tribes in central Kenya did not arrive until much later. The Kikuyu, now Kenya's major tribe, may not have reached its present location until about 1800. The whites and Asians, Kenya's two newest "tribes," began to move to the interior at the end of the nineteenth century.

Remains OPPOSITE of *Homo erectus* are displayed at the archaeological site of Koobi Fora on the shores of Lake Turkana. Nairobi University, with starkly modern architecture and art ABOVE, has students from every corner of Kenya and the world.

The Country and Its People

THE COAST — A DIFFERENT HISTORY

The Kenyan coast, on the other hand, has been visited throughout history by personages familiar to students of Western and Eastern civilizations. Alexander the Great certainly sailed the Indian Ocean, but whether he reached Kenya is not known. During the first century, a Greek merchant named Diogenes (though not he who went looking for an honest man) undoubtedly spent a portion of his life here. His log, *The Periplus of the Erythraean Sea*, is one of Western civilization's earliest documented records of East Africa. It describes Kenya's coastal inhabitants as "men of the greatest stature, who are pirates ... and at each place have set up chiefs."

These coastal chiefs were probably Arab traders who had settled and intermarried among the Bantu tribes. Their communities were actively involved in trade with Arab, Indian and Indonesian merchants. They sold foodstuffs (wheat, rice, sesame oil and sugar), cloth, hardware, porcelain and glassware in exchange for ivory, rhinoceros horns, tortoise shell, palm oil and, in some areas, slaves and gold. Here, native and foreign influences merged into a new culture and a new language, Swahili, today one of Kenya's official languages (English is the other).

A century later, the Greek-Egyptian geographer and mathematician Ptolemy included Kenya, which he called Parum Litus, in his *Geography*. Despite its many errors, this work remained the authority on Africa until the sixteenth century. There is no record that Ptolemy ever visited inland Kenya, yet he documented lakes and mountains with relative accuracy.

Trade followed the rhythm of the monsoons. Numerous dhows, pushed by the northeast winds, or *kaskazi*, arrived in Kenya between November and April, departing between May and October when the *kusi*, or southeast winds, began. Coastal communities, each with its own autonomy, developed, but trade remained under Arab control until the fourteenth century.

Local builders make skillful use of natural papyrus to fashion their dwellings.

The Country and Its People

From the time of Ptolemy (second century) until the eighth century, no major changes took place in the coast except for the advent of religion. Schisms within Islam over the selection of Mohammed's successor drove religious refugees to Kenya in search of a new homeland.

These new Arab immigrants, who were neither merchants nor sailors, helped turn the Kenyan coastal settlements into sophisticated cities built from blocks of coral that were carved from the barrier reef: crisp, white architecture with narrow streets, ramparts,

numerous mosques, sultans' palaces, and urban housing with elaborate courtyards for the well-to-do. Remnants of these cities still exist at Manda, Malindi, Mombasa, Pate, Lamu and Kilifi, and are most visible today at Gedi, where the extensive ruins of an ancient city still stand.

Kenya's coastal treasures were traded in the richest kingdoms of the ancient world. India, China, Indonesia, Malaysia, Ceylon, Persia, Arabia, and the countries of the eastern Mediterranean were favored destinations for ivory, rhinoceros horns and palm oil. El Idrissi, a thirteenth-century Andalusian historian of the court of the Norman king of Sicily (a distant cousin of Richard the Lion-Hearted), claimed that iron ore exported from

Malindi was the reason for the high quality of Toledo's swords and knives.

Similarities in style, culture and language among Kenyan coastal peoples gave early voyagers the impression of a unified empire. In fact, except for brief periods, they existed independently and in relative peace, until the arrival of the Portuguese in 1498. This marked the end of the most prosperous period for coastal Kenya.

PORTUGUESE DOMINATION

During the late fifteenth century, under the reign of King John II and his son, Henry the Navigator, Portugal began a period of extensive ocean exploration aimed at breaking the Arab monopoly of the spice trade from India.

After Dias rounded the Cape of Good Hope in 1488, the Portuguese decided they had found the route to India, and began planning an extended expedition up the East African coast. With four vessels under his command, Vasco da Gama left Portugal on July 8, 1487. In November, he passed the Cape and began traveling the East African coast, whose residents soon discovered the Portuguese preached "vulgar" Christianity, and responded with reserve and hostility.

News of the Portuguese predated their ships' arrival in Mombasa on April 7, 1498; they were attacked and quickly retreated to Malindi. Da Gama's log reports that Malindi's sultan received them warmly: "For nine days we had fetes, sham fights and musical performances." Having replenished the ships' stores and acquired a navigator, they set sail with a favorable *kusi* and reached Calcutta on May 23. Three months later, Da Gama began his return voyage, making another call at Malindi.

On subsequent expeditions, the Portuguese were welcomed at Malindi but met continued open hostility in Mombasa. Cabral, who on a voyage to Kenya in 1500 accidentally sailed far enough west to claim Brazil for Portugal, sacked Mombasa before returning home.

In 1505, Portugal decided to install itself permanently in its new territory, and sent Francisco de Almeida as Viceroy of India. For reasons more strategic than commercial, it decided to capture the Arab positions along the East African coast. Mombasa was again sacked during d'Almeria's four-year struggle for control. Once victorious, the Portuguese imposed strict and often brutal rule, reserving for themselves a better part of the local resources and wealth; only friendly cities, such as Malindi, were spared. The Kenyan coast, for the first time in its history, was unified into a single empire.

It was, however, an empire that no longer enjoyed commercial supremacy, but strained from the antipathies between conqueror and conquered. The Portuguese were never able to revive the once prosperous trading cities, perhaps because they failed to provide traditionally traded commodities, or perhaps because the Kenyans ignored their European goods and culture. As a result, the coastal people shifted from a mercantile to an agricultural way of life.

The Portuguese stayed for almost three centuries. At Mombasa, they ultimately felt compelled to build Fort Jesus in 1592 to maintain control, but even this imposing Italian-designed fortress did not put an end to local hostilities.

In 1595 or 1596, the Swahili governor of Pemba was poisoned for becoming a Christian; at the beginning of the 1600s, Sultan Ahmad of Mombasa, generally considered an ally, repeatedly complained of insulting treatment by the Portuguese. His son and successor, Hassan, quarreled openly with Portuguese officials in 1614 and fled inland. Hassan's brother was then allowed to rule for four years before the Portuguese replaced him with a young nephew, Yusuf Chinguliya, whom they promptly sent off to an Augustinian priory at Goa, India, for 13 years of "education."

Upon his return to Mombasa, Yusuf renounced Christianity for his native Islam, and massacred all the Portuguese at Fort Jesus. After defeating a punitive force of 800 Portuguese sent from Goa in 1632, he demolished the fort and left Kenya for Oman. He continued naval raids on the Kenyan coast, but by 1635, the Portuguese had regained control of Mombasa and rebuilt Fort Jesus.

The Portuguese never recovered from their defeat at Fort Jesus; for the next half-century, they battled raids from Omani merchants exercising Yusuf's claim to sovereignty and anxious to regain control of the East African waters. A three-year siege of Fort Jesus brought an end to the Portuguese presence in Kenya in 1698, except for two years (1728–1730) when they briefly held Mombasa.

"You have concealed and preserved
Dreadful secrets
Unrevealed.
Nothing remains
But deathless fascination."
— Amin Kassam, *Fort Jesus*

The Portuguese departure, however, did not bring independence to the Kenyan coastal cities. The Iman of Oman appointed governors who too often quarreled among themselves; commerce continued to wane. In 1741, Mombasa's Mazrui family claimed sovereign control of the island. Opposed to any foreign domination even though it be Muslim, it began the task of unifying the political and economic structures of the coastal cities.

Some coastal cities soon tired of Mazrui domination. In 1817, Pate requested the aid

Johann Rebmann OPPOSITE, one of several proselytizing eighteenth-century missionaries who also explored the hinterland, notably Mount Kilimanjaro. ABOVE: Children at a present-day missionary school.

of the Sultan of Oman, one Seyyid Said; a resolute and aggressive young ruler who at age 15 had assassinated his regent for supposedly not acting in his best interests. Pate's request opened the way for Said to reestablish the Omani empire in East Africa. He easily gained control of Pate and the northern Kenyan cities, but failed to take Mombasa when the Mazrui allied themselves with English forces in the Indian Ocean, who were at the time trying to stop French slave traders.

With the British flag flying over Fort Jesus, Said admitted the futility of attacking

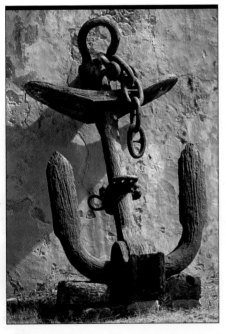

and began negotiations. In 1822 he signed an anti-slave-trafficking agreement; the English removed their protectorate from Mombasa, giving Said control over the entire Kenyan coast.

Finding East Africa more to his taste than the Omani countryside, Said moved his capital to Zanzibar in 1832, where he began an intensive, highly successful commercial development program. He transformed Zanzibar into a gigantic clove plantation and directed the planting of sesame crops on the mainland. The British remained in East Africa with their headquarters in Zanzibar, ostensibly to enforce and strengthen antislavery agreements, but actually to obtain a foothold in the prosperous new land.

On Said's death in 1856, Zanzibar and East Africa were split from Oman. His successor, Seyyid Majed, with support from the English, maintained control of the African portion of the empire, and continued both Said's policies and his close association with England. His brother, Seyyid Bharghash, took over in 1870. Under severe pressure from the English, Bharghash forbade all slave trading in East Africa, by sea or land, and prohibited the entrance of slave vessels into his territorial waters. His reign saw the beginning of the partition of East Africa and the fusion of the two separate histories of Kenya.

THE INTERIOR EXPLORED

The antislavery movement drew European attention to the great expanse of Kenyan land waiting to be claimed, and the legions of "heathen" that could be converted to Christianity. During the second half of the nineteenth century, a handful of missionaries and explorers were lured to Kenya by these challenges, and provided the first more-or-less complete geographic picture of the interior. In previous centuries, coastal Arab traders had established trade routes to Lake Victoria; these, however, did not cross Kenya, but went south of Mount Kilimanjaro through Tanzania, then up the western side of the Rift Valley. This was the general route taken by Burton, Speke, Stanley and Livingstone on various expeditions seeking the source of the Nile.

In 1846, German missionaries representing the English Lutheran Church Missionary Society settled in Rabai, about 20 km (12 miles) northwest of Mombasa. Although not truly the hinterland, Rabai was beyond the coastal belt of Muslim influence. The missionaries, Johann Krapf, Johann Rebmann and Jakob Erhardt, made several proselytizing expeditions to the interior, but did not find the residents much more interested in Christianity than had the Portuguese. From Krapf came Europe's first geographical information about Mount Kenya; Rebmann provided data on Mount Kilimanjaro. Krapf also transcribed Swahili into Roman letters, and published a Swahili dictionary, grammar, and translation of the New Testament.

In 1872, a well-armed German exploratory expedition led by Dr. Gustav Fischer came to investigate the possibility of colonizing the interior. His forces reached the Lake Naivasha region but were ambushed in Hell's Gate Gorge by *moran*, or Maasai warriors. Defeated, Fischer retreated to the coast; German colonial activities shifted south to Tanzania.

The English Royal Geographical Society funded the next major European expedition. Its president, Lord Aberdare, intrigued by the descriptions from Krapf and Rebmann, sent a young Scot, Joseph Thomson, with a small expeditionary force to find a direct route for European traders from the Kenyan coast to Lake Victoria.

Thomson left Mombasa in March 1883 with 143 men, and was soon met by Maasai warriors who arrived in the guise of a peace party. But "as the day wore on," Thomson later wrote, "matters became ominous. The warriors grew boisterous and rude. One of them tried to stab me because I pushed him away and we had to remain under arms from morn till night. On the morning of the third day, our worst fears were realized. We had been deluded and entrapped and we knew they were about to take their revenge on our small party for their failure to annihilate Fischer."

Thomson retreated hastily to Mombasa, regrouped, and began again. Choosing a more northerly route, he crossed the slopes of Mount Kenya, named the mountains to the west after his patron, Lord Aberdare, located Nyahururu Falls (for many years called Thomson's Falls), and arrived on the shores of Lake Victoria near the present-day Kenya–Uganda border. On his return, he detoured north to map Mount Elgon.

Thomson's adventures were filled with encounters with hostile Maasai, countless animals, sundry illness and injuries, witchcraft, stunning panoramas and intriguing discoveries, all of which he recorded and published on his return to England. His tales captured the imagination of Europeans looking for adventure. And the safari business was born.

Kenya's most isolated region, the north, was explored by Count Teleki von Szeck in 1887; he named Lake Rudolf (now Lake Turkana) in honor of a Hapsburg prince.

COLONIALISM

And so began what historians have termed the colonial period of Africa, when individuals at negotiating tables in Europe decided, with the stroke of a pen, the fate of the African peoples and the boundaries of present-day African countries. In 1879, it was estimated that more than 90 percent of the African continent was self-governed. By 1900, all but a tiny percentage was governed by European powers.

In 1886, England's Prime Minister, Lord Salisbury, and Germany's Chancellor, Otto von Bismarck set the present-day boundaries of Kenya and Uganda; an international commission ruled that Sultan Bharghash's holdings on the coast extended only 16 km (10 miles) inland. England then negotiated a £17,000/year lease of the Kenyan coast that remained in effect until the nation's independence, when the Sultan ceded the territory to the new Kenyan government.

The Imperial British East African Company, which was chartered in 1888, became the

OPPOSITE: An anchor outside Fort Jesus in Mombasa, one of the few reminders of Portuguese domination of the Kenyan coast. ABOVE: Some of Kenya's colorfully dressed city dwellers.

administrative and development arm of British colonialism. It purchased valuable goods from Kenya, particularly ivory, in exchange for less-valuable English goods. The enterprise collapsed in July 1895, causing a Victorian financial crash. The British government acquired the floundering company for £200,000, and the territory became officially known as British East Africa. Construction of the Uganda Railway from Mombasa to Lake Victoria began, fulfilling a Kikuyu/Maasai prophecy of an iron snake breathing fire and smoke.

Mombasa retained its position as the major port, with the remaining coastal cities losing all of their previous prosperity. A new nation built around the railroad emerged. As Sir Charles Eliot, Commissioner of British East Africa in 1903, put it, "It is not an uncommon thing for a line to open up a country but this line literally created a country."

The building of the Mombasa–Uganda Railway, so-named because it would connect Uganda with the Indian Ocean, aroused controversy in England, which had made an interest-free loan for its construction. The £5.5 million loan for this "Lunatic Line" was later written off as a gift. The saga of this railroad is well-told in Nairobi's Railway Museum, and in Charles Miller's *The Lunatic Express* and P.H. Patterson's *The Man-eaters of Tsavo*. They tell the heroic story of man's defeat of nature, of thousands of imported Indian laborers who came to build the railroad, of those who stayed permanently and of scores killed and eaten by lions.

Nairobi emerged as the administrative and business center of a country thrust into the twentieth century by the influx of Western (primarily British) settlers, entrepreneurs, developers, explorers and missionaries.

Kenya's colonial history reads very much like that of the Americas, with the appropriation of native lands, with smallpox and measles epidemics, mass slaughter of wild animals, clearing of forests for agriculture, subjugation and confinement of indigenous peoples to reserves, and massive campaigns of "depaganization."

The colonial government chose the temperate plateau between Nairobi and the Rift Valley, the best agricultural land in the country, as Crown Land. In these White Highlands, the government adopted a policy of

not selling to Asians, and an unwritten policy of assuming that no land belonged to the Kenyan tribes. Officially, if the government mistakenly sold or leased lands still occupied by an African, the European purchaser was supposed to advise the government and give up title to the land. In practice, this policy was rarely implemented.

With little or no regard for African rights, white settlers cultivated large expanses of land, using virtually free African labor to plant a variety of crops. The most profitable of these was coffee, which Africans were banned from growing. Big-game hunting and safaris came into vogue, especially after visits by Winston Churchill and Theodore Roosevelt. Although Roosevelt sought fame as a hunter, existing accounts portray him as a terrible shot and a very poor sportsman.

The great variety of African animals, principally lions, leopards, elephants, rhinos, buffaloes and antelope, as well as countless species of birds and reptiles, were slaughtered without quarter. A European community, somewhat loosely organized by the eccentric Lord Delamere, developed with all the trappings of genteel colonial life: antique furniture, European-style homes, formal dinners, polo matches, horse races, and clubs.

The easy lifestyle was briefly interrupted by World War I. Husbands left their wives in charge of plantations, or shipped them home to England, and rode off to fight the Germans in nearby Tanzania. The war in East Africa was not a major British military effort, yet it brought Tanzania under British control via a League of Nations mandate.

In the first years after the war, British veterans were lured to Kenya under the "Soldier Settlement Scheme," whereby land was given away in lotteries and sold on long-term, low-interest credit. The influx of settlers caused a labor crisis; Africans were understandably reluctant to work their own land for someone else at a tiny percentage of the return. The colonial government began to put pressure on the chiefs to direct their subjects into European employment.

Many of the old settlers returned to neglected plantations in need of both labor and money. As Elspeth Huxley describes it in *The Mottled Lizard*:

"So it was a question of starting again, more or less from the beginning, and in the meanwhile everyone had spent his capital. To balance this, the managers of the three main banks in Nairobi were in an expansive, benign and optimistic frame of mind. They conferred large overdrafts upon their customers, rather with the air of monarchs dispensing orders and stars, and details such as rates of interest and terms of repayment were considered by both parties to be almost too insignificant to be brought into the conversation at all. Happily for the banks, who

"Many other farmers were in the same boat. Some went off to hunt elephants, others to work as transport contractors or as road-gang overseers for the Government, one man to collect the skeletons of hippos on the shores of Lake Victoria, pound them up and sell the resultant bonemeal as fertilizer. Another way to turn a modest penny was to recruit labor for the sisal companies, or for some other large employer. One of our neighbors … had taken to this.

"One day he rode over to propose to [Father] that the two of them should go together

in fact charged eight percent, their liberality was rewarded by the stabilization of the rupee, which had been worth 1s. 4d., at the rate of 2s. This meant that one evening [you] went to bed owing £2,000, and woke up next morning owing £3,000; by a stroke of the pen, the banks had gained a bonus of fifty percent at the expense of everyone who had borrowed from them, which meant almost every farmer in the country.

"Because of the state everything had fallen into during the war we could not expect an income from the coffee for three or four years, and … [Father] doubted whether Mr. Playfair and the overdraft would support us, unaided, for as long as that. So he … cast about in all directions for ways of tiding things over…

to a district he knew of, hitherto neglected by other recruiters, in search of stalwart young men willing to put their thumb-marks on a contract binding them to work for six months on some distant plantation… They would get one shilling for each recruit delivered to a prospective employer."

In 1920, there were approximately 9,000 Europeans in British East Africa, most clamoring for London to give them self-rule. London responded by renaming the territory the Kenya Colony and Protectorate, for lofty Mount Kenya, and restating its policy in the Devonshire White Paper of 1923: "Primarily Kenya is an African territory, and His

Many photography shops take photos of their customers: selling film is often only a sideline.

Majesty's Government thinks it necessary definitely to record their considered opinion that the interests of the African natives must be paramount, and that if and when those interests and the interests of the immigrant races should conflict, the former should prevail ... In the administration of Kenya His Majesty's Government regard themselves as exercising a trust on behalf of the African population."

Until after World War II, to which Kenya sent many native regiments, a succession of colonial governors administered Kenya with

TOWARD INDEPENDENCE

It was from the educational system, a random assemblage of missionary establishments, that Kenya's national spirit, for the most part a story of Kikuyu dissatisfaction and resistance, sprang. The Kikuyu population was growing, yet was hemmed in by the White Highlands and the forest around Mount Kenya. Many members of the tribe went to work on European plantations; others left the land for Nairobi.

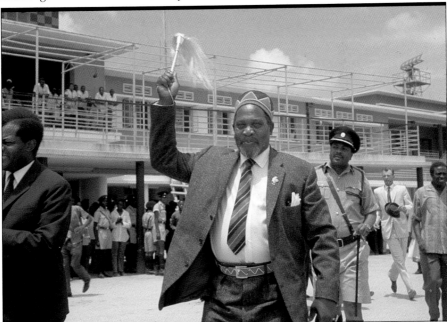

little regard to the Devonshire Paper. Julian Huxley, after a 1929 tour to evaluate education in Kenya, summed up the prevailing situation: "On top of all this variety of nature and man there impinge Western civilization and Western industrialism. Will their impact level down the variety, insisting on large-scale production to suit the needs of Europe and Big Business, reducing the proud diversity of native tribes and races to a muddy mixture, their various cultures to a single inferior copy of our own? Or shall we be able to preserve the savor of difference to fuse our culture and theirs into an autochthonous civilization, to use local differences as the basis for a natural diversity of development?"

After World War II, Harry Thuku, a Kikuyu government clerk, began organizing Kenya's first nationalist group, the Young Kikuyu Organization — for which he lost his job and was arrested and eventually banished to Kismaiya, a small town on the northern Kenyan coast. This fractured the movement, but only briefly. In 1924, the Kikuyu Central Organization (KCA) was formed, with Jomo Kenyatta as secretary.

The Africans were particularly incensed about colonial interference in tribal customs, such as female circumcision, as well as the

OPPOSITE: Musicians TOP and a gourd craftsman BOTTOM are part of a more variegated coastal lifestyle. ABOVE: Mzee Jomo Kenyatta, first president of Kenya.

misappropriation of native lands for European settlement. These and other grievances were carried to London in 1929 by Jomo Kenyatta, who remained abroad in London and Moscow for 15 years, organizing the African rights movement, studying anthropology at the London School of Economics, and publishing a study of Kikuyu life and customs, *Looking on Mount Kenya.*

London responded to Kenyatta's pleas with a series of studies and reviews. One conducted by the 1934 Kenya Land Commission found that 47.5 percent of the

regulation," to justify its actions, claiming that a copy of *Mein Kampf* had been found at KCA headquarters and that its leadership had been suspected of consorting with the Italian Consulate in Nairobi.

The ban did not stop the nationalist movement. It gave rise instead to the Kenyan African Study Union, a multi-tribal organization that became the Kenya Africa Union (KAU) six years later. On Kenyatta's return from England in 1946, he assumed leadership of this party that was to form the government of independent Kenya.

4.4 million hectares (17,000 sq miles) of the highlands reserved for European settlement were not being cultivated. Twenty-five percent lay fallow and another 20 percent was occupied by African squatters, who were allowed to stay so long as they worked part-time for the European farmer, on his terms. At that time, the coffee ban, in which the government prohibited Africans from planting coffee by requiring a license that was virtually impossible to secure, was also still in effect.

These conditions catalyzed the nationalist movement, primarily under the KCA. In 1940, the leaders of all African organizations were arrested, detained, and their groups banned. The government invoked a "defense

After World War II, there were four Kenyan communities — African, European, Asian (primarily Indian) and Arab — all demanding independent and equal representation. Even though the KAU was multi-tribal, it was primarily Kikuyu, and the Africans were divided by tribal affiliations, the Asians by religious beliefs, and the British by the differing attitudes of farmers, businessmen, educators and missionaries. Only the Arabs had a common front, but they were too few to be a major political force. Everyone, however, found fault with colonial rule; some made their viewpoints known in unorthodox ways:

"After the Legislative Council passed an ordinance requiring men of all races to carry an identity card with fingerprints, many whites erupted in fury. Until that time, only Africans had been required to carry identity cards, a measure which they intensely resented. Across the White Highlands, angry meetings were held at which the more zealous whites advocated open defiance of the new law ... At one stormy meeting in Nakuru, a member of the Legislative Council who supported the ordinance was faced with an opponent who strode up and down the gangway of the hall with two large pistols hanging from his belt, fixing a threatening eye on anyone voting against him. In the end, the administration retreated. A compromise was reached by which those who could complete a form in English and provide two photographs were not required to be fingerprinted." (Martin Meredith, *The First Dance of Freedom*.)

Others used traditional avenues in opposing unfair laws. The Kikuyu chief, Mbiyu Koinage, asked the Land Commission for the return of his lands, which had been appropriated for a European coffee farm. He was awarded about one-tenth of the acreage he claimed and ordered to comply with the coffee ban by removing the coffee bushes growing there. Koinage took the case to court and lost.

But the KAU grew stronger. Government policies were challenged by strikes that were often ruthlessly suppressed. In his 1948 annual report, the District Commissioner of Nakuru in the Rift Valley noted that there was thought to be a clandestine movement among the Kikuyu called "Mau Mau." What had caught his attention were oath-taking ceremonies that took place among the inhabitants of the Mau Escarpment. These bound individuals to political objectives such as land reform. Oath-taking ceremonies were outlawed in 1950, during a rash of ritual murders in the Rift Valley, whose victims were primarily Christian Kikuyus who had refused to take the oath.

The killings increased in 1952 and began to include outlying English farmers. Chief Koinage's son organized the Kenya Christian Association advocating peaceful change. The KAU organized a meeting, attended by more than 25,000, where leaders including Jomo Kenyatta denounced the Mau Mau movement. But the Mau Mau now had too much momentum. On October 20, 1952, England proclaimed a state of emergency. Jomo Kenyatta and 82 other nationalists were arrested. Rather than crippling the Mau Mau, this seemed to incite them.

"On March 27, 1953, they pulled the worst of their raids, the Lari Massacre, in the course of which more than 200 Africans of all ages and sexes, living in a compound whose chief was a friend of the British, were murdered and mutilated hideously. And with this horror the Mau Mau war entered a grim phase ... And as counterbalance, the whites began to direct their determination and their superior weaponry into complementary savagery: torture, subversion, and bribery of captured Kikuyu; morbid floggings at the prison camps, where African soldiers were instructed to use Mau Mau methods on suspected inmates, often supervised in these outrages by English officers; the berserker mania that seized the minds of so many 'civilized' Europeans ..." (Peter Ritner, *The Death of Africa*).

Meanwhile, Kenyatta was brought to trial, convicted of organizing the Mau Mau, and sentenced to seven years in jail in Lodwar and Lokichar. The trial was a farce — the chief witness was bribed with two years' study in an English university with all expenses paid and guaranteed government employment on his return. The magistrate received £20,000 to leave Kenya immediately after announcing his verdict.

Even though the KAU leader was no longer Kikuyu, but a Luo, Walter Odede, the government banned the organization and all native groups. It also created fenced "protected villages" where Africans were required to live, and brought in British troops to "enforce" the peace.

During this time, a new constitution, which promoted multiracial participation, was adopted. African politicians complained that democracy was impossible while hundreds of people remained jailed and political organizations banned. In 1955, the colonial government announced that regional political parties could be formed "to encourage a simple and orderly development of African political life."

The Tana River, red with erosion, seasonally greens the arid eastern plains of Kenya.

Under the new constitution, eight communally elected Africans would represent five million constituents, and 14 Europeans would represent 5,000. The Africans refused the Colonial Office's offer of six more seats; in the 1958 elections, all African candidates pledged to refuse office in a move to reject the constitution. Boycotts and protests followed. These maneuvers finally resulted in the all-party, all-race "Lancaster House Conference" in London in 1960.

From the start, the British Government, which had regained political control of the country during the Mau Mau war, made it clear that Kenya was destined to become an African country. A transitional multiracial government, tipped slightly in favor of the African majority, was endorsed, and national political parties were allowed. Two parties emerged: the Kenya African National Union (KANU), which supported a strong central government which would have its seat in Nairobi, and the Kenya African Democratic Union (KADU), which advocated a federal, decentralized government.

UHURU

When the British released Kenyatta from detention in 1961, he gained the leadership of KANU and a seat on the Legislative Council. Two and a half years of disputes between the two parties resulted in a compromise constitution which provided for considerable regional autonomy and a date for the end of colonial rule:

"Kenya regained her *Uhuru* (Freedom) from the British on December 12, 1963. A minute before midnight, lights were put out at the Nairobi stadium so that people from all over the country and the world who had gathered there for the midnight ceremony were swallowed by the darkness. In the dark, the Union Jack was quickly lowered. When next the lights came on the new Kenya flag was flying and fluttering and waving in the air. The Police band played the new National Anthem and the crowd cheered continuously when they saw the flag was black and red and green. The cheering sounded like one intense cracking of many trees, falling on the thick mud in the stadium." (Ngugi wa Thiong'o, *A Grain of Wheat*.)

Four days later Kenya was admitted to the United Nations. With a Kikuyu, Jomo Kenyatta, as president and a Luo, Oginga Odinga, as vice president, independent Kenya adopted policies to encourage foreign investment and participation in the economy while internally restructuring the government to overcome tribalism.

Since agriculture was the basis of the economy, the new government gave priority to the problems of land distribution and ownership. Within five years of independence, through a land resettlement program mainly financed by Britain, one-fifth of the Highlands reverted to African hands. During the 15 years of Kenyatta's rule, Kenya's economy flourished and social services reached a greater number of people. On the political front, the KADU merged with the KANU in 1964, making Kenya a single-party state. The KANU was challenged only briefly, when Vice-president Odinga formed the Kenya People's Union (KPU) in 1966, after he was forced to resign from the government because of his "leftist" views. Three years later, the Minister for Economic Affairs, a Luo named Tom MBoya, was assassinated by the Kikuyu and violence broke out in Kisumu, the Luo heartland: Odinga and his KPU were blamed. Using tactics learned from the colonial government, Kenyatta detained Odinga and other KPU leaders and banned the KPU.

Kenyatta remained in office until his death on August 22, 1978. He was succeeded by David Arap Moi, a Kalenjin who had become vice president when Odinga resigned in 1966.

Moi continued the basic policies of Kenyatta and remained in power after elections in 1983 and 1988, but amid growing controversy that included an amendment to the constitution that changed voting from secret ballots to voting by lining up, widely and correctly seen as a step backwards for democracy. Councilors from the country's majority Kikuyu tribe were removed from many positions of power and further constitutional changes dissolved the separation between judicial and executive areas of government. Despite this divided opposition,

OPPOSITE: Coastal Kenyans TOP have turned their mangrove swamps to a profit — poles for construction. BOTTOM: The narrow, dusty streets of old town Malindi remain the domain of hand-pulled carts and pedestrians.

intertribal violence in key areas enabled Moi to win further elections in December 1992, but many international agencies were dissatisfied with the results: aid programs were suspended and the economy suffered. For the 1997 elections, Moi changed the constitution to allow himself a further term of office, and in an atmosphere of increasing tribal unrest — especially in the Rift Valley and around Mombasa — scraped in for what is widely considered to be his final term of office. Over the last 10 years, freedom of speech has increased greatly in Kenya and be to be significant threats to Kenya's democratic tradition.

Central to Kenya's economic survival is the creation of jobs and industries to generate foreign exchange. Tea surpassed the traditional "big money" export, coffee, in 1988, while tourism led both in foreign revenues. However, tourism is a fragile industry. Kenya's main international draw is its national parks and most visitors come to see the animals. A rash of poaching in late 1988 caused such a dramatic fall in animal numbers and such security problems in the

the voices that are heard are expressing widespread dissatisfaction with a political regime riven with corruption and cronyism. Nearly 40 years after independence, Kenya remains the most stable country in East Africa and perhaps in all of Africa. Nonetheless, it faces problems of overpopulation, unemployment and insufficient foreign exchange to buy needed imports.

To the casual traveler, tribalism is not readily apparent, except perhaps in the obvious difference in dress. But tribal problems exist and can be fanned for political ends: many political analysts feel that therein lies the greatest threat to Kenya's stability. Moi's amendments to the constitution, the basis of Kenya's independence, might also prove to national parks that tourism suffered. Increased pressure on the government by the East African Wildlife Society and tour operators brought about more stringent antipoaching measures. No sooner were the most pressing environmental problems brought under control than human factors started to threaten. Tribal conflict surrounding the 1997 elections and the occasional, internationally reported, incidents of violent crime brought personal security to the top of the agenda: the tourist industry all but collapsed, bringing the economy grinding to a halt and starving the Kenya Wildlife Service of funds.

Things are currently starting to turn around. The powerful political figure of Nicholas Biwott — a man who strikes fear into many Kenyans — has been put in charge of tourism, and a newly pragmatic approach to Kenya's chief foreign exchange revenue source can be detected. Entry to the national parks, once bled dry by forgery, has been computerized and is newly secure. The country still offers a warm and sincere welcome to foreign visitors, and crime, in Nairobi at least, has been brought under control. This is just as well. Without tourism Kenya's wildlife has little chance of survival.

LAY OF THE LAND

Slightly smaller than the state of Texas, but larger than France, Kenya lies on the equator and is bordered by the Indian Ocean, Somalia, Ethiopia, Sudan, Uganda and Tanzania. In a stretch of 800 km (500 miles) from east to west, the land rises from the reef-fringed sandy beaches of the Indian Ocean to the mile-high plateau of Nairobi, higher still to the lofty snow-capped summit of Mount Kenya (Africa's second-tallest mountain), then drops across the Great Rift Valley to Lake Victoria — 1,157 m (3,795 ft) above sea level. From south to north along another 800-km (500-mile) axis, the Kenyan countryside contrasts jagged, forested mountains, and lush red-soil agricultural lands with Lake Turkana and the timeless, sandy-colored dusty desert that covers more than one half of the country.

Before the formation of the Rift Valley, Kenya's climate and vegetation were probably uniformly tropical. The gigantic eruption that created the Rift also triggered dramatic climatic changes. After millions of years of evolution, Kenya's climates are now dramatically varied — semiarid, tropical, temperate, alpine and arctic. Only the visitor who wishes to climb to the peaks of Mount Kenya, Mount Elgon or Tanzania's Mount Kilimanjaro, however, need prepare for temperatures below freezing. Some day, nowhere in Kenya will warm clothing be necessary, according to United Nations Environment Program (UNEP) scientists in Nairobi. The country's overall climate is warming and its desert growing, due to the greenhouse effect.

Kenya's varied climates and vegetation are home to an endless parade of animals, ranging from miniature antelope only 25 cm (10 inches) tall to six-ton elephants. To enjoy this animal carnival to the fullest, patience is needed. Kenya has approximately 90 species of ungulates or grazing animals, along with innumerable predators and scavengers, 1,500 different birds, hundreds of aquatic and reptilian species, and countless types of insects and arachnids. With 10 percent of Kenya's land and a portion of its coastal waters devoted to the preservation and protection of flora and fauna, you are never more than a few hours from one of 48 national parks and game preserves where animals still reign supreme, and where man is only a spectator.

THE COAST

Kenya's 480 km (300 miles) of coast along the Indian Ocean is world-famous for its sand beaches lined with palm trees and backed by rocky inlets and mangrove swamps teeming with miniature aquatic life. The beaches are protected from harsh ocean waves by extensive, multicolored coral fringe and barrier reefs. These shelter hundreds of aquatic species, such as the graceful black-and-white striped Moorish idol, electric-blue striped blinny, lacy basket starfish, prickly sea urchins and spongy sea cucumbers, which are protected in the Kisite, Watamu, and Malindi Marine National Parks.

The reefs have for centuries also provided building material for coastal cities, and served as a deterrent to sharks visiting waters near bathing beaches. But there are exceptions! Those who swim on the eastern side of the reef should *always* be alert for sharks.

Inland of the beaches runs a narrow coastal plain three to twenty kilometers (two to twelve miles) wide in the south and 150 km (90 miles) wide along the Somalia border in the north. The wider northern plain was formed by Kenya's largest river, the Tana, which meanders from its source on the slopes of Mount Kenya for 1,120 km (700 miles) to empty into Ungwana (Formosa) Bay between Lamu and Malindi. Some areas of the plain are suitable for agriculture,

Cooling themselves lazily in the Mara River, hippopotamuses look more tranquil than they actually are. They kill more people than lions!

but most are dry scrub. A few stretches of thick coastal forest are protected as natural reserves.

An ever-present wind off the Indian Ocean brings relief from the average daytime temperature of 30°C (87°F). Even in the cooler summer season, night temperatures rarely fall below 20°C (68°F).

Along the coast, rainfall is frequent but of short duration, except during the April to June monsoon season. A tropical cloudburst may slow the unsuspecting visitor, but Kenyans casually proceed along their routes,

CENTRAL PLATEAU AND HIGHLANDS

The plateau beyond the coastal plain ascends gradually to the central highlands in the south, and across the Ethiopian border in the north. With only a few low valleys and monotonous but unique vegetation — flaming thorn trees, monstrous upside-down baobabs, and scrub — the plateau conveys a sense of endlessness, a place described by Elspeth Huxley as a horizonless void where "you could walk straight across to the rim of the

knowing it will soon be followed by sun and drying wind. Annual rainfall along the coast and coastal plain is 1,000 to 1,250 mm (40 to 50 inches); but even in May, the peak of the monsoon season, seven hours of sunshine is normal per day (situated on the equator, Kenya has 12 hours of daylight year-round). Tourism to the coast is affected, however, by the trade winds that turn on the shore from May to November. Hitting the northern coast in particular, these coat the beach in seaweed and prevent boats from crossing the sheltering reef. In the north, many hotels close completely over this period, and even in less affected regions, such as Mombasa and Diani in the south, few visitors will be found in these months.

world." Here in Tsavo East and Tsavo West national parks roam elephants, buffaloes, Grevy's zebra, giraffes, lions, aardvarks, impalas and antelope, including the miniature five- to six-kilogram (10- to 12-lb) dik dik, and gerenuks which stand on hind legs to feed. Guinea fowl, francolins, blackheaded orioles and red-billed hornbills are only some of the birds you can expect to find.

In the northwest, the Rift Valley and Lake Turkana cross the plateau, changing the landscape. The vegetation is much the same but sparser: Kenya's growing desert. Sibiloi National Park, along the shores of Lake Turkana, protects several hundred square kilometers of Pleistocene era fossil beds and the "cradle of mankind."

The plateau is dry and hot, with average daytime temperatures of 34°C (93°F). Rainfall is minimal, between 250 to 500 mm (10 to 12.5 inches) per year; the area suffers from periodic drought. Yet the meager vegetation sustains a large variety of wildlife, including elephants, giraffes, zebra and antelope which have been pushed by human and livestock expansion from the more temperate lands.

South-central Kenya, termed the Highlands during colonial days, is split by the Great Rift Valley. High tablelands with forested volcanic mountains, savannas and a temperate climate, the Highlands have, in modern times, become a highly populated region.

Here, the savannas are interrupted by deep green valleys, narrow canyons with cascading waterfalls, and steep, rugged mountains. Although not as high as 5,895-m (19,650-ft) Mount Kilimanjaro in Tanzania, at 5,199 m or 17,085 ft, Mount Kenya is taller than Europe's highest peak, Mont Blanc. The days are pleasantly warm and the nights cool. In Mount Kenya and Aberdare national parks live many of the same animals that inhabit Tsavo, but they are joined by other animals not adapted to the arid plateau.

Mount Kenya, on the eastern side of the Rift Valley, and the Aberdare Mountains on the west capture up to 3,000 mm (120 inches) of rain per year, while the lower rich agricultural lands receive between 750 and 1,000 mm (30 to 40 inches): primarily from March to May, the "long rains," and from October to December, the "short rains." As on the coast, although a lot of rain can fall, it generally does so quickly, and in the worst season, April and May, Nairobi and the highlands still average five hours of sun per day. Climate change has made these seasons less dependable, however, and these once reliable dates have, over recent years, varied drastically.

In Nairobi and other low-lying plateau areas, temperatures are comfortable year-round at 10° to 14°C (50° to 58°F) at night and 22° to 26°C (72° to 79°F) during the day. When traveling to high altitudes the visitor will generally experience an average drop of 0.6°C (1°F) per 100 m (328 ft), descending to below freezing on Mount Kenya and the Aberdare Mountains. Evenings in the low mountains are usually brisk, with temperatures around 7°C (45°F) not unusual.

TROPICAL JUNGLE

The western slope of the Rift Valley descends to an elevation of 1,157 m (3,795 ft), where the world's second-largest freshwater lake, Victoria, covers 69,490 sq km (26,830 sq miles). With such a large surface area, Lake Victoria — its islands, papyrus beds, creeks, bays, and beaches — has created a tropical microclimate. Hippos and crocodiles inhabit the shores, as do Egyptian geese, flamingos, cormorants, blue herons, pelicans, Marabou storks and other flying species. The enter-

taining hammerkops and jacan or lily trotters go about transported on the backs of hippos.

Only here, on the surrounding hills and valleys near Kakamega, will one still find in Kenya the tropical forest of African jungle movies, with its monkeys, baboons, bush duikers, forest hogs, buffaloes, waterbucks, bongos and eagle owls. Rainfall here reaches 1,000 to 1,300 mm (40 to 50 inches) per year, and day and night temperatures are more distinct — 14° to 18°C (58° to 64°F) at night and 30° to 34°C (86° to 93°F) during the day.

OPPOSITE: The hardy acacia tortilis survives in soil scorched by drought. ABOVE: Kenya's jungles are paradises of birds, dense vegetation and waterfalls.

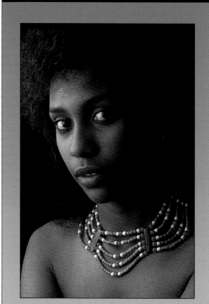

Nairobi
and
About

THE CAPITAL

Unless you are flying into Mombasa for a beach break, your trip to Kenya is most likely to begin in Nairobi, a bustling city whose ultramodern skyline loses some of its glitter as the buildings get increasingly shabby near street level. In fact, they tower over a sometimes daunting but always exhilarating street-life that does take some getting used to. As Nairobi is over a mile above sea level, its climate is temperate and not too drastic an adjustment for travelers arriving from colder northern climates, but it's not a city where many visitors to Kenya spend much time.

On most travel itineraries Nairobi only figures as a first-night jet-lag dispersal point, before travelers head out to the national parks. After the safari experience, they are flown back early (in case of flight delays) and frightened by tales of crime and lawlessness into hiding in hotel day-rooms until their overnight outbound flights depart. This is a real shame, because there is far more to Kenya than the wildlife experience, and Nairobi is one of the best places to explore the culture and society of East Africa's most accessible societies. Over the last few years crime levels have been brought down significantly, and those who have come to know and love Kenya will find Nairobi a civilized and inviting focus of the social, cultural and financial aspirations of most urban Kenyans.

Nairobi is today one of the most important commercial centers in East Africa, and the largest city after Johannesburg and Cairo. Its official population is currently estimated at four and a half million, and growing at three percent a year.

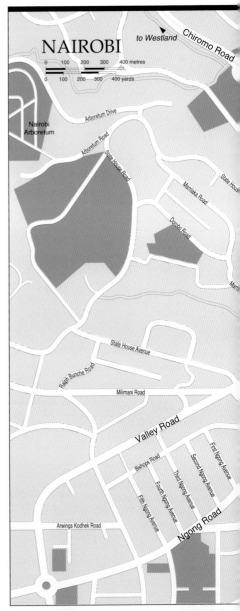

NAIROBI   to Westland

BACKGROUND

Nairobi, "the place of cold water" in the Maa language spoken by the Maasai, was not inhabited until George Whitehouse, chief engineer for the Mombasa–Uganda railroad, decided in 1899 to make this papyrus bog his construction headquarters and the railway's principal nerve center. Almost overnight, a boom town sprang up on the "black cotton" soil that expands to a sticky, impass-able mud when wet and contracts to a solid crust when dry.

"With its irregular lines of weather-beaten tents and faceless, barrack-like corrugated iron bungalows, Nairobi at the turn of the [twentieth] century bore a not altogether inexact resemblance to a miniature Dachau without walls. There was a main thoroughfare called Victoria Street which became a canal of thigh-deep mud whenever rain fell. A proliferation of the cramped, fetid shops known as *dukas* pockmarked the town, and at the western end of Victoria Street sprawled [an Indian] bazaar … Other points of interest were a post office, a soda water factory and a shaky timber structure known as Wood's Hotel which doubled as a general store and which burned down several times before being abandoned as a poor insurance risk. Social life centered on a singularly uncongenial heap of wood and corrugated iron which railway officials and other British

residents were pleased to call their club." Thus did Charles Miller, author of *The Lunatic Express*, a chronicle of the Mombasa–Uganda railway, describe Kenya's future capital.

The railway was finished on December 19, 1901. The British East African Company soon realized that it could not entice the Kenyans to produce enough export crops to keep the £5 million investment paying for itself. Thus began a publicity campaign to attract European settlers with offers of cheap land in return for crops that would provide freight for the new line.

The scheme was only a minor success. It brought settlers by the thousands, many of whom were more interested in getting rich quickly than working the land. Although the land was fertile, it was difficult to clear and maintain. European crops were often attacked by tropical blights and parasites.

Nonetheless, many European settlers fell in love with Kenya and stayed. Nairobi, not their homesteads, became the center of commerce and society.

And although Nairobi has evolved into an international center with a character all its own it has still retained a strong feel of a frontier city, on the edge of a wild and rugged country. The Norfolk Hotel, from which Elspeth Huxley began her journey to Thika, has been restored and enlarged, and is now an international class hotel. Another popular European watering hole in the early days, the Stanley Hotel, has been replaced by a modern structure housing the five-star New Stanley Hotel. The city is cosmopolitan, with its mosques, temples, churches and a

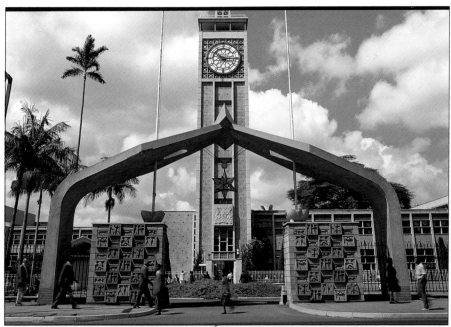

In 1906, the colonial offices were moved from Mombasa to this new city that now had the air of a Wild West town. Men carried guns; brawls were not infrequent. Parties were wild and uninhibited, lasting for several days until the participants staggered out of town back to their farms and ranches. Indian merchants dominated businesses, Europeans controlled the banks and administrative services, and Africans were relegated to a subservient role, a formula that has remained much unchanged to the present day. As the naturalist I.N. Dracopoli described Nairobi in 1914, it was "neither African nor European but seems to combine in one city the discomforts of two civilizations without the advantages of either."

synagogue; its international organizations such as the United Nations Environment Program, Food and Agriculture Organization and World Health Organization; its multinational businesses and foreign embassies. For most of the correspondents covering the neighboring countries of Somalia, Uganda and beyond, Nairobi is the city they call home.

Yet it has retained some of its original flavor. The Indian *dukas* have grown up into a great variety of shops throughout the city. The dust and mud still exist, and the population is still exploding faster than jobs can be created and houses constructed.

The inhabitants are warm and helpful. The city offers every modern comfort but on Kenyan terms. It is good to remember that

Nairobi is Africa and the tropics. Little happens immediately, but it happens. A phone call to Europe or the United States during business hours can go through instantly or take up to an hour. Faxes usually go through instantly, especially outside office hours in the United States or Europe, and Internet access is just starting to open up international communications. Meanwhile domestic communications remain in the dark ages. Trying to make internal telephone calls is one of Kenya's great frustrations: lines often drop out of service, ring endlessly or just don't

impression, and a disproportionate number of robberies happen in a visitor's first 24 hours. There are ways to make your transition easier. If a visa is required (regulations do change, though currently a tourist visa costs US$54 or £35), either obtain it in advance or, if at the airport, make sure you have the correct change, in dollars or sterling. Leg it quickly from the plane to get a good place in the line and to clear passport control. In the arrivals hall, collect your luggage and check it is intact (make a fuss here if it isn't, before clearing customs) and then stow any valuables

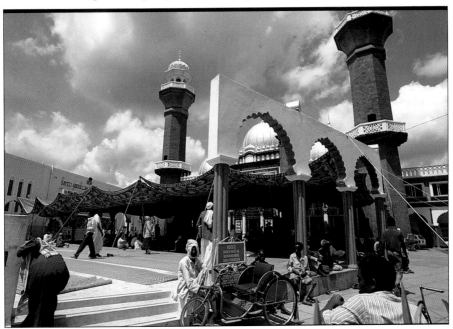

work, and the whole process becomes quite expensive without making any usable connection. Industry and commerce carry on their business in a quiet vacuum untroubled by effective or efficient communication, and to avoid ulcers it is easiest to regard this as a liberating experience. Satellite communications and cell-phones have started to improve the situation in Nairobi and the major cities and it is hoped that expanded coverage will bring effective and affordable communication to the hinterland over the coming years.

— cameras, jewelry, etc. — in relative peace and privacy. There are banks and ATM machines both before and after customs: it's best, if possible, to change money first and stow your money and papers securely. Then, and only then, are you ready to pass through into the inevitable sea of taxi touts.

To get into town, there is an office of Kenatco taxis as well as a line of taxis offering rides into the city for a fixed price, currently Ksh1,000 to most hotels. Lower prices can be negotiated with other, unmetered cabs if you're feeling up to the hassle.

AIRPORT ARRIVALS

First-time visitors to Nairobi International Airport rarely emerge with a favorable

OPPOSITE: The Parliament Building on City Square is a landmark of Kenya's *Uhuru* (Independence). ABOVE: Friday prayers outside Jamia Mosque in downtown Nairobi.

Between 6:15 AM and 8:30 PM the no. 34 bus runs into the central bus station, with tickets costing just Ksh30, but you'll probably be sharing the bus with a few professional thieves who might need discouraging by your generally alert disposition and steely resolve. Personally, and especially after an overnight flight, I find a taxi less stressful.

Once you're established at your hotel, Nairobi is all yours.

GENERAL INFORMATION

There is no official tourist information office in Nairobi — a foretaste of the help you can expect in more remote parts of the country. So you'll be relying on the, necessarily biased, advice given by commercial organizations. Fortunately, the Kenyan tradition of upright civility means the advice most travelers get is better than they deserve. A good place to start would be **Let's Go Travel** ((02) 447151 or (02) 441030 FAX (02) 447270 or (02) 441690 E-MAIL info@letsgosafari.com WEB SITE www.letsgosafari.com, Box 60342, Nairobi.

To get about, extremely battered **taxis** can be found outside most hotels and tourist attractions, but if you need to call one the leading companies are Kenatco ((02) 225123, (02) 338611 or (02) 230771 and, for a gray London-type taxi, Kenya Taxi Cabs Association ((02) 215352. Otherwise there are always plenty of taxis in most of the places you'll need them, many barely roadworthy. Arrange the fare before you set off and don't be scared to bargain: the usual rates are generally much lower than you end up paying.

A medical emergency (dial (999 from any phone) would have to be an emergency indeed before checking into the under-funded public hospital, the **Kenyatta National Hospital** ((02) 726300, Arwings Kodhek Road. Better, here, to go private: two hospitals with good reputations include the **Consolata Sisters' Nazareth Hospital** ((02) 335684, Riara Ridge Road, Limuru (25 km or 18 miles outside Nairobi), or the more central **Aga Khan Hospital** ((02) 740000, Third Parklands Avenue. If you need to get to these hospitals from the bush, the **Flying Doctors Service** (Amref) ((02) 501280 or (02) 602492 FAX (02) 336886 and **AAR Health Services** ((02) 717375/6 are the heroes who might save your life.

Nairobi is the best place in Kenya to pick up your e-mail, with plenty of Internet cafés, generally good connection speeds and competitive rates. One chain (of three) with good connection speeds is **e-world** with branches on Halie Selassie Avenue, Moi Avenue (junction with Kimathi Street), and Barclay Plaza on Loita Street. Alternatively, try **Browse Internet Access** ((02) 251947 WEB SITE www.browseinternet.co.ke, Norwich Union House, Fourth Floor, Mama Ngina Street, opposite the Hilton and open from 7 AM to 9 PM daily.

ORIENTATION

The city center lies on both sides of Kenyatta Avenue, bounded by Uhuru Highway to the west, University Way to the north, Moi Avenue to the east, and Haile Selassie Avenue to the south. The grid of reasonably well-marked streets below the high-rise buildings is compact and enjoyable to walk around during daylight hours, but stay alert and don't carry any obvious valuables. At night taxis are preferable. The same is true all day long if you venture too far across Moi Avenue to the east. After a block or so you'll be in the densely-populated Latema/River Road area, where you'll find the city's cheapest accommodation, most upcountry bus offices and a selection of cheap, local bars. It's an area to be cautious in.

Follow Uhuru Highway northwest (its name changes to Chiromo Road) and after two miles (three kilometers) you'll reach the Westlands district. This suburb is, increasingly, the area of choice for the better bars, businesses and restaurants escaping from the seething action of the inner city. It's quite normal to spend plenty of time shuttling between the city center and Westlands by taxi, at Ksh300 or so a time.

As a newly arrived tourist, don't be surprised if you are approached frequently by young men offering their services as guides to help you find a hotel, safari operator or car rental. They can be helpful but more often are just annoying. Once you get a tan and have found your way around town, you probably won't be bothered as much.

Mosques built by Kenya's Muslim minority are among Nairobi's most graceful buildings.

If you do decide to deal with one of these young men, never follow him down alleys or to businesses that do not have offices. Even some of the Nairobi offices are nothing more than a front for services that are not readily available. There is an abundance of legitimate tour operators, car rental businesses and travel agencies, so there's no need to risk swimming with sharks.

WHAT TO SEE AND DO

The city center is mainly a place to shop, eat, meet and drink. There are some attractions in the central area but not many. It is also possible to visit **Parliament** and the **Kenyatta Conference Center**. Both are situated around City Square, set around the statue of Mzee Jomo Kenyatta and his mausoleum with an eternal flame. Parliament is open to the public, but during a session you must obtain a permit from the gatehouse on the corner of Parliament Road and Harambee Avenue to visit the public or speakers' gallery. If Parliament is not in session, the guards can usually arrange a tour of the building. When a conference is taking place or there are visiting dignitaries in town, City Square is brightly decorated with flags and drapes, but despite the bougainvilleas and manicured lawns the area is just too clean, too free of traders, to give much of a feel of Nairobi. The main reason to visit used to be to go, for a fee, to the top of the conference center for a panoramic bird's-eye view of the city but it's no longer the highest, or even the best, vantage point these days. The gleaming highrise **ICEA Building**, on Kenyatta Avenue, with its glass-walled lift, is currently the most popular place, with a tip to the security guards in order, or less trodden are the stairs of **View Park Towers** on Loita Street, where you can even go up at night to watch the parade of mismatched headlights thread through the potholes of the city's main roads.

The **National Archives** ((02) 228959, Moi Avenue opposite the Hilton, Monday to Friday 8 AM to 4 PM, Saturday to 12:30 PM, free, are worth a visit, being the nearest the city center gets to a non-commercial art gallery / museum. Downstairs there are a great number of ethnological artifacts, refreshingly — or frustratingly — free of any organized

presentation, and on the upper gallery there is an interesting collection of historic photographs. Tourists are also steered towards the **Jamia Mosque**, near the City Market, though quite why, considering non-Muslims are not allowed in, I fail to see. At any rate, it's in all the guidebooks.

Broaden your horizons beyond the central city grid, however, and there are plenty more attractions within a short taxi range.

First visit should be the **National Museum** ((02) 742131-4 WEB SITE www.museums.org.ke, open 9:30 AM to 6 PM daily, Ksh200, located

just over two kilometers (less than a mile and a half) from the city center on Museum Hill. It provides an informative orientation to Kenya's paleontology, geology, ornithology, ethnology, history and wildlife. It also has a small gift shop whose prices may be slightly higher than some of the downtown shops, but the proceeds go to the museum, a worthy cause. Guides, who are in theory free but generally expect a tip, should be available on request. Adjacent to the museum is the **Snake Farm**, which houses an extensive collection of poisonous and nonpoisonous African snakes, crocodiles, tortoises and fish. Admission is Ksh200. It is safer to see these creatures here than in the wild.

Near the railway station, at the end of the potholed Ngaira Avenue south of Haile Selassie Avenue, is the **Railway Museum**, Station Road, 8:30 AM to 5 PM daily, Ksh200. Even though it's quite close to the station I'd take a taxi here as the access road looks unsafe to me. A lot of the exhibits, a collection of period trains and carriages, are rusting gracefully in the open air. Coach No. 12, from which Superintendent C. H. Ryall was dragged and eaten by one of the man-eaters of Tsavo, is also here: look in the main museum for the picture of the lion dragging the body clear. The locomotive that was used in the filming of *Out of Africa* is also well preserved, along with a fascinating photographic display of the building of the "Lunatic Express," and a collection of memorabilia from the railway and Lake Victoria steamers.

Nairobi has several parks and green spaces. Although **Uhuru Park**, across Uhuru Highway from the city center, is not generally safe even during the day, the **Nairobi Arboretum**, five kilometers (three miles) northwest of the city center on Arboretum Road, has been restored to its former glory, and **City Park**, three and a half kilometers (just over two miles) northeast of the city center on City Park Road, is the third largest. Here, you can enjoy the tropical vegetation and bird life on foot, but even in daylight, strolls here can be insecure.

Better then to take to a car and make a first safari to **Nairobi National Park** ((02) 500627 FAX (02) 505866, Box 42076, on the outskirts of the city limits. Turn off the residential street into the any of the park gates, pay the entrance fee (steep at US$20 for adults, US$5 for children, Ksh200 for the car, although this is less than many other parks in Kenya), and suddenly you're transported to the vast open plains of Africa, fenced, but full of all the native animals. A troop of olive baboons are residents of the main gate area, but you can expect to see plenty more than these. There are ostrich, zebras, impalas, gazelles, jackals, giraffes and warthogs amongst the 80 species of large mammals present. You'll perhaps spot rhinos, cheetahs, lions, hippos and crocodiles. Within its 117 sq km (44 sq miles) it contains all the "Big Five" except the rather unmanageable

elephant. If you don't have a guide, ask the rangers at the gate, who generally have a good idea where to find the rarer animals. It is hard to describe the sudden thrill of being surrounded by such a variety of wildlife with the noise of Nairobi traffic faint in the distance. The park fills in the area between the (domestic) Wilson Airport and the main (international) Jomo Kenyatta Airport, and can be incorporated in a slow, circuitous, expensive but highly rewarding route between the two, much favored by tour operators with VIP clients.

For those with a serious interest in conservation, within the park it is possible to make an appointment to see the **David Sheldrick Wildlife Trust Elephant and Rhino Orphanage** ((02) 891996 FAX (02) 890053, 11 AM to noon, entry by donation. Here visitors come a distant second to the priorities of the animals, but this is an unusually accessible chance for the seriously interested to watch some groundbreaking conservation work. There are manned entrance gates all around the park but the main gate, off Langata Road near the Carnivore Restaurant, has a further couple of attractions. There is a café, a brand-new walking trail, and a Mini Animal Orphanage (open 8 AM to 5:30 PM daily, entrance costs US$5) where animals are looked after before being returned to the wild.

It is perfectly possible to travel round the park in a rented car, though you'll see more

OPPOSITE: The Uhuru Monument celebrates Kenya's struggle for independance. ABOVE: Modern buildings, interspersed with jacaranda, bougainvillea and palm trees, are features of urban Nairobi.

from the higher perspective of a minibus: most of the safari companies will run tours of the park for about US$50 but generally not at the optimum dawn and dusk periods. Check with **Let's Go Travel** ℂ (02) 447151 or (02) 441030 FAX (02) 447270 or (02) 441690 E-MAIL info@letsgosafari.com WEB SITE www .letsgosafari.com, Box 60342, Nairobi, or **UTC** ℂ (02) 331960 FAX (02) 331422 WEB SITE www .unitedtour.com, Box 42196, Nairobi, for further details.

One kilometer (half a mile) past the park's main gate are the **Bomas of Kenya** ℂ (02)

891801 FAX (02) 891401, Forest Edge Road, with a collection of huts built in the traditional styles of the different ethnic groups. Energetic but uninspiring examples of tribal dancing are laid on for tour groups, with performances at 2:30 PM and 4 PM Monday to Friday, 3:30 PM and 5:15 PM Saturdays, Sundays and holidays, Ksh300. On weekends there's a disco after the main show.

For Isak Dinesen fans, her house in the smart suburb of **Karen**, 15 km (nine miles) south of Nairobi, has been restored and turned into the **Karen Blixen Museum** ℂ (02) 882779, Box 40658, Nairobi, Karen Road, 9:30 AM to 6:30 PM daily, Ksh200, with a museum featuring an exhibition of her life and work amongst the original furnishings and decor. The setting for the image-forming *Out of Africa* experience is far smaller and more human than you'd expect; the grounds contain early farm machines and are well maintained. Many tour operators offer half-day tours that take in the Karen Blixen Museum and the nearby **Giraffe Sanctuary** ℂ (02) 891658 FAX (02) 890973,

Box 15124, Koitobos Road, three kilometers (one and a half miles) off Langata Road, open 10 AM to 5:30 PM, entrance Ksh250, where each afternoon visitors can feed cattle nuts to endangered Rothschild's giraffes. It's not just their necks that are long: their tongues have nervous tourists squealing in excitement, but the sanctuary actually does sterling work in preserving this exceptionally rare and vulnerable giraffe species. There's a tea-house and, if you're feeling flush, an extremely expensive but small and exclusive hotel here.

The **Denys Finch-Hatton Memorial** in the Ngong Hills used to be one way to recapture the romantic isolation of colonial times: now the private owner charges entrance fees and the atmosphere has gone. It's better to stroll off alone, relax under the trees and let Kenya seep into your soul as it did into the young author's.

From the top of the Ngong Hills is a magnificent view, but it is not safe to go alone. In the past few years there have been several muggings and robberies here. In spite of an ever-present security force, it is suggested that you park your car at the police station at the foot of the hills and take a police escort. Single women, or even two women alone, should definitely not make the hike alone: even Kenyans don't.

A carry-over from colonial times are the races at **Nairobi Racecourse**, 10 km (six miles) northwest of town on Ngong Road, which take place one weekend out of two. Check the sports pages of the *Nation* newspaper to see if there's racing scheduled during your visit. The races are usually a lively gathering where everyone knows both horses and riders and the even the bookies seem to know the winner in advance. Admission is Ksh200 and the first race is at 2 PM. Racecourse Road, outside the grounds, is lined with traders and a is good place to hunt for folding chairs, wicker furniture and large-sized earthenware pots.

SHOPPING

In a city where there are few government-run galleries and museums, the commercial organizations step in to fill the breach. Even if you're not going to buy, some of Nairobi's shops contain the best selection of cultural arts and crafts you're likely to find in the country, although prices are often steep.

Curio and craft shops and stores are found everywhere in the city center. You can bargain in most but generally only with cash. Expect to pay near full price if you use a credit card. Before buying, shop around, because prices and quality vary greatly. To get some idea of the best quality available check out **African Heritage**, on Banda Street, a combination café/museum/shop and, on weekends, live music venue. Prices reflect quality. For possibly the worst quality and value head to the **Central Market**, where a central core of vegetables is ringed by balconies of sharp salesmen. Many visitors prefer to head out of town and buy where they know excess profits are going to a good cause: the **Undugu Shop** in Woodvale Grove, Westlands, has a wide range of handicrafts and Ethiopian antiques sold to benefit a number of charitable projects around Nairobi. An even wider range of products is available at the **Utamaduni Crafts Center** in Langata, where 18 specialist shops trade in a center opened by the Kenyan Wildlife Service. For safari clothes, try **Colpro** in Kimathi Street: it outfitted Michael Palin on the BBC *Pole to Pole* television show. Behind banked and junky tee-shirts they run a specialist outfitting department with a full range of gear that can be tailored to fit.

The **East African Wildlife Society** runs a shop on the mezzanine floor of the Hilton Building, on Mama Ngina Street and City Hall Way; proceeds help support their wildlife projects. Several artists sell their work only here. Some unusual items are produced with the American or European buyer in mind, such as hand-painted animals on handkerchiefs and scarves. The Society sell its own "impala" tie and a safari board game which makes a great present for children and adults alike. From it you can learn Kenyan geography and the names of animals in Swahili. The Society also has a selection of books on Kenya.

Books in Kenya are not expensive, and the selection is excellent. It is a good idea to bring a book or two on safari because, once in the game parks, you will generally have a couple of hours in the mid-afternoon when

reading on the verandah of your room or tent or around the swimming pool will be as energetic as you feel. There is a wealth of good literature available. There are also many coffee-table books on Kenya and its animals that you may want to take home. For children, the East African Publishing House has two beautifully illustrated legends, *The Hot Hippo* and *The Greedy Zebra*, for Ksh230. They are good for the read-aloud-ages and are written at a third-grade reading level.

For the best selection of books in Nairobi, go to the bookstore in the New Stanley Hotel,

the **Select Bookshop** on Kimathi Street, or the **Text Book Center** located in the Sarit Center, Westlands.

Near the bus station, the **open market** on Mfangano Street and Hakati Road serves the nearly 50 percent of Nairobi's population who inhabit the area bounded by Moi Avenue and the Nairobi River. The market is similar to those of country villages, and a great variety of dried beans, *ugali* (white maize meal), rice, potatoes, cabbages and the other essentials of everyday Kenyan life are sold.

Your first day in Nairobi is probably not the best for bargaining: traders here take a special pride in judging how long tourists have been in the country, and newcomers are easy prey for these astute business people. Their aim is to get you to place a value on their offerings: say a price and you're hooked,

OPPOSITE: Cotton and silk fabrics in Nairobi shops are as colorful as the butterflies and birds of the national parks and reserves. ABOVE: The temperate climate means every sort of fruit and vegetable can be found in Nairobi's markets.

so just stay quiet. After a safari or two, schedule a day in Nairobi for shopping; you'll feel much more in control and be able to enjoy the frantic excitement of the market. Then you'll be ready for the **Maasai Market**, which takes place 9 AM to 3 PM Tuesdays by the traffic circle between Muranga Road and Kijabe Road, near the Meridian Court Hotel, where you can bring down prices by trading unwanted cosmetics or tee-shirts of your own. For woven sisal and wooden furniture (for example, wooden directors chairs for about US$10 each), the best market is **Kariakor Market** (a corruption of "Carrier Corps"), between Racecourse Road and Ring Road. If traveling with children it might be worth checking out some of the soulless but stress-free shopping malls. The best are the Sarit Center, Westlands, and the Yaya Center, Arwings Kodhek Road, Hurlingham, but although the Kenyans are very proud of their malls they won't impress visitors from the West.

WHERE TO STAY

The good news is that there is no shortage of hotel rooms in Nairobi, and it is rare to have trouble finding a bed. The bad news is that it is quite easy to understand why none are in special demand. International-standard hotels generally price themselves for room only, and this is perhaps just as well: facilities in the haven of your own private space are good, including satellite television, air conditioning and mini-bar, while few offer especially exciting menus or food. Mid-range hotels seem to be feeling the effects of Nairobi's long recession, and usually give off the distinct air of investor neglect, while the cheapest hotels sometimes double as brothels. The choice here gives you some idea of what to expect.

Extremely Expensive

Of all the places in Nairobi to stay, the most expensive — and unusual — is **Giraffe Manor** ((02) 891078 FAX (02) 890949, Koitobos Road, which is part of the AFEW Giraffe Sanctuary off Langata Road. There are just a few rooms and you might find an endangered Rothschild's giraffe poking its head through your window in search of a snack.

Very Expensive

At the high end of the spectrum are the international-class hotels; rates here are for room only. The two best-known are the veteran landmarks: the **Norfolk Hotel** ((02) 216940 FAX (02) 216769 WEB SITE www.kenyaweb.com/lonrho-hotels/norfolk/norfolk.html, Harry Thuku Road, Box 5851, where the rooms are okay but the food ordinary, and the equally famous **New Stanley Hotel** ((02) 333233 FAX (02) 229388 E-MAIL reservations@sarova.com, Kenyatta Avenue and Kimathi Street, Box 30680,

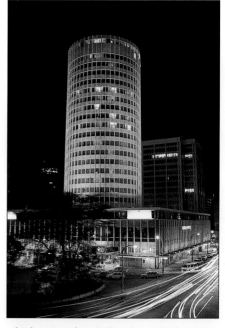

which costs a few dollars less. The latter has a good restaurant (closed Sunday nights) upstairs but the food at the ground floor café, where the landmark "thorn tree" that used to carry travelers' notices has been replaced with an unimpressive sapling, is ordinary. It's hard to avoid the feeling that you're paying for the history at both these places, though if I had to choose I'd go for the Stanley, as you can walk out of the front door and straight to the city center. From the Norfolk you have to pass a bit of a mugger's gauntlet, past the university, to get into town.

The **Hotel Inter-Continental** ((02) 335550 FAX (02) 210675, City Hall Way and Uhuru Highway, Box 30353, could do with a facelift.

The **Holiday Inn Mayfair Court Hotel** ((02) 740920 FAX (02) 748823, Parklands Road, Box 74957, is simply overpriced. The best of the luxury range though is currently the **Serena Hotel** ((02) 711077 FAX (02) 718012 E-MAIL cro@serena.co.ke, Nyere Road, Box 46302, which is a member of the Leading Hotels of the World and priced appropriately at US$200 for a double. These prices do not include meals.

Expensive to Mid-range

Mid-market the choices open up further. The **Hilton International** ((02) 334000 FAX (02) 339462, Watalii Street off Mama Ngina Street, Box 30624, is central and although the rooms haven't any great character they're acceptable for the price (expensive). Less expensive and just as central is the moderately priced **680 Hotel** ((02) 332680 FAX (02) 332908, Box 43436, Muindi Mbingu Street, or on the edge of the city center, the **Hotel Ambassadeur** ((02) 336803 FAX 211472, Moi Avenue, Box 30399 (mid-range).

For a bit more character head just above the center to Nairobi Hill for the graceful and welcoming **Fairview Hotel** ((02) 723211 FAX (02) 721320, Bishops Road, Box 40842 (mid-range), while nearby is the huge and rather run-down **Panafric** ((02) 713333 FAX (02) 715566 E-MAIL reservations@sarova .co.ke WEB SITE www.sarovahotels.com, Box 72493, Kenyatta Avenue (mid-range). Near the National Museum is the **Hotel Boulevard** ((02) 227567 FAX (02) 334071, Harry Thuku Road near Museum Hill, Box 42831 (mid-range), whose main advantage is the location. In the up-and-coming suburb of Westlands there are two middle-range hotels orientated towards the package market, but although tour operators get cheap rates they are definitely expensive for the individual traveler: the **Landmark** ((02) 535412-4 FAX (02) 545954, Chiromo Road, Box 40075 (expensive) is the better of the two, and is within walking distance of two of the city's best bar/restaurants.

Inexpensive

There are a few town center hotels in the Ksh1,000 to Ksh2,000 range, filled mainly — but not exclusively — with a Kenyan clientele: the friendly **Terminal Hotel** ((02) 228817,

Moktar Daddah Street, Box 66814, has now been ruined by the opening of a sedate — but surprisingly loud — bar downstairs. Sleep is impossible until the early hours. The idiosyncratic **Parkside Hotel** ((02) 333348 FAX 334681, Box 53104 (inexpensive), overlooking the Jevanjee Gardens (not safe at night), provides good value and its small "Wiseman's Bar" is quietly contained in the heart of the building.

The **Iqbal Hotel**, Latema Road, is most guidebooks' favorite amongst the "cheap" downtown Nairobi hotels in the rather dodgy River Road area (very inexpensive for a bed in dormitory, double, or triple rooms), but I can't for the life of me think why. You cannot make reservations and may even have to put your name on a waiting list for dingy rooms that are not even en-suite. It does have a useful notice board, and is handy for the infamous Green Bar, but otherwise seems to have little to recommend it. There are several other dirt-cheap lodgings in the surrounding River Road area, but it's not a good place to be looking for accommodation after dark.

Long-term visitors on a budget, such as aid workers or fledgling businesspeople, can't do much better than the **Heron Court** ((02) 720740 FAX (02) 721698 E-MAIL herco @iconnect.co.ke WEB SITE www.heronhotel .com, Milimani Road, with cheap rooms and excellent-value apartments. The downstairs bar is lively but kept well separate from the accommodation.

For the cheapest rooms, with nothing like the Green Bar or its equivalent for your neighbor, try the **Nairobi Youth Hostel** ((02) 721765, Ralph Bunche Road, Box 48661 (very inexpensive). It is an International Youth Hostel Association member.

In the suburb of Parklands, reached by the No. 107 bus, is **Mrs. Roche's Guest House**, Parklands Avenue, where you can take a bed in one of her cabins (inexpensive) or camp in the garden (very inexpensive). Mrs. Roche has been renting beds for more than 25 years and can provide you with interesting and sometimes helpful information. It is popular with overlanders on their way to or from the Cape.

The lights of the Hilton International Hotel sparkle in Nairobi's clear night air.

WHERE TO EAT

Nairobi offers a superb variety of restaurants in every price range. According to the Tourism authorities, there are over 200 different cafés, restaurants and snack bars offering a choice of more than 20 different cuisines, but there are probably twice as many as their estimate. Nairobi is one of the few places in Kenya where you'll be able to pick and choose your meals; Mombasa, on the coast, is the other.

In Nairobi, nearly every nationality is well represented, although there are few American fast-food chains. There is, however, Kenyan fast-food — fish and chips (the fish is fresh Nile perch, but the chips usually greasy), curries, sausages, kebabs and stews. These "stand-up and eat" shops are found everywhere in Nairobi; often the food is good at Ksh50 to Ksh150 per serving. Before selecting an establishment, look discreetly at what others are eating. If it looks appealing and the surroundings relatively clean, try it. Avoid salads and cold meals. Your best bet in a tropical environment is hot food, because cooking keeps bacteria to a minimum.

Be sure while you're in Nairobi to try some of its internationally renowned restaurants. A gastronomical treat is the **Carnivore** ((02) 602775, Langata Road, Nairobi. The Carnivore serves spit-roasted wild and domestic meats on an "all-you-can-eat" basis, accompanied by soup, salad, relishes, baked potato, dessert and coffee or tea for Ksh1,000. For meats, there are the standards — spare ribs, lamb, beef, chicken, and pork — and countless varieties of game — eland, hartebeest, crocodile, zebra, giraffe, Cape buffalo, warthog, ostrich or wildebeest — depending on availability. The wild meat comes from game farms in Kenya. For example, the crocodile comes from a farm on the coast that grows crocodiles for their skins. The skins are exported to Italy and Carnivore buys the meat. If you have a non-carnivore in your party, there is a good vegetarian menu or fried trout, fresh from the Carnivore's trout farm on the slopes of Mount Kenya. They also serve the best Irish coffee to be found outside San Francisco.

The Carnivore is very popular, and reservations are advisable. Lunch, from noon to 3 PM, and dinner, from 7 PM to 10:30 PM, are served daily except New Year's Day, when they close to recover from a lavish New Year's Eve bash in the adjacent Simba Saloon (see NIGHTLIFE, page 131). If you make reservations early enough, you can request a table inside around the open hearth where the meat is roasted, or outside on the terrace which is airy and cool. It is a good idea to bring a jacket or sweater in case you are seated outside. The Carnivore is a 10-minute drive from the city center. You can take a *matatu* or bus, but there's a kilometer (half-mile) walk; at night a taxi is always recommended, which shouldn't cost more than Ksh600.

Nairobi has numerous, generally excellent, Indian restaurants. Best is currently the **Minar** ((02) 330168, with three outlets, the original is on Banda Street; they serve some of the best Indian Mughlai cuisine outside India. Their closest rival is the **Haandi** ((02) 448294, Westlands' Shopping Mall. Prices reflect the quality; you can expect to pay between Ksh600 and Ksh1,000 per person for dinner. The menu is extensive and at Haandi's they are happy to prepare special orders off the menu. If you have difficulty deciding, the waiters can explain what each dish is.

A fine Japanese restaurant is the **Restaurant Akasaka Ltd.** ((02) 220299, 680 Hotel, Kenyatta Avenue, Box 47153, formal and traditional in decor and service, especially in the evenings, their lunch boxes make a perfect meal while shopping downtown. The sashimi is fresh (as is most fish in Kenya).

The **Delamere Coffee Shop** ((02) 216940 in the Norfolk Hotel on Moi Avenue has been and still is a favorite tourist hangout. Its atmosphere is relaxing, a good place to sit and watch the passersby while adjusting to the pace of Africa, but the food is pricey and disappointing.

Another popular tourist stop for coffee, tea, or buffet meal is the **Thorn Tree Café** ((02) 333233 of the New Stanley Hotel. The four-story tall thorn tree, once covered with thumb-tacked messages left by travelers, has

---

At Nairobi's Carnivore restaurant, wild and domestic meats are roasted in the open hearth.

been cut down, but the location, in the heart of the city, is some compensation.

There are several good Continental restaurants. Best for French food is the expensive (by Kenyan standards: Ksh1,000 to Ksh1,500 — US$15 to US$20 — for dinner) **Allan Bobbe's Bistro** ((02) 336952, Cianda House, Koinange Street, where reservations are essential and where the food is either homegrown at their private ranch or flown in fresh from the ocean off Somalia.

Drinkable wine has also started to become available in Kenya, mainly imported from

South Africa though some is produced domestically. The local vineyard, Naivasha Winery, produces an excellent white wine, but the reds and rosés are more variable.

For Kenyan food, just look through any number of steamed-up windows: special offerings include *ugali* (maize meal), roast meats, *mboga* (vegetable stew with some meat) and *pilau* (rice with meat) at very reasonable prices (Ksh100 to Ksh200). The **Chic Joint**, on Uhuru Avenue, is one good place for local food and they often have good live African music on weekends. In the city center, the **Harvest House**, Kenyatta Avenue, Nairobi, half a block from the Kipande House branch of Kenya Commercial Bank, offers an African Platter (Ksh300) with a

variety of local dishes. Alternatively, nearby **Simmers** ("the answer on a plate") ((02) 217659 FAX (02) 217632, Kenyatta Avenue, cooks local and regional specialties priced separately. In concept, both these are like a Mexican combination plate, but not in taste. If you like cornmeal or polenta and baked or refried beans, you'll enjoy Kenyan food. It is subtly spiced and hearty. Perhaps Nairobi's best Kenyan food is served at the **Utalii Hotel**, eight kilometers (five miles) out of the city center on the Thika Road. Owned and run as the practical part of the university's tourism department, it is where student chefs and waiters hone their craft with enthusiasm and skill. Tuesday lunchtime is a special Kenyan buffet, but the restaurant offers great value every day and is a favorite with Nairobi residents.

There are also moderately priced Chinese, Korean, and Ethiopian restaurants in Nairobi. All are worth a try.

NIGHTLIFE

Nairobi's nightlife does not, in general, start out lively but, unchecked, can become so. In general, it is best not to walk around at night, nor to hang about waiting for a bus. The sight of a lone *mzungu* (white person) glowing gently in the dark is an open invitation to thieves who then melt away into the shadows. Even for short distances it's wise to use one of the many taxis available. Their minimum fee is Ksh200 so bar-hopping can become expensive.

Popular bars with expatriate workers in the town center start with the **Delamere Terrace** at the Norfolk Hotel and the bistro at the New Stanley. Most of the hotels have their own bars with their particular characters: in the Hilton, for example, the **Jockey's Bar** gives an evening's free beer to anyone successfully downing a yard of ale. Unless you know the trick of twisting the yard to avoid a sudden flood of beer halfway through don't try this — you'll end up with a soaked shirt, a laughing audience and paying for the yard along with the rest of your night's drinking.

Travelers who don't mind being the only white face in a Kenyan crowd are always surprised by the welcome they receive in local bars, for security reasons often located on the first floors of city center office blocks. Try **Tanager Bar** in Rehema House, Kaunda Street, to mix with senior civil servants or **Invitation Bar**, opposite the New Stanley, for a younger crowd of office workers. The infamous **Green Bar** in the River Road area is featured in so many guidebooks it is constantly packed with hustlers and petty criminals geared up to fleece the tourist market — go prepared if at all. For a young, professional atmosphere and the chance to play several games of pool, try the **Klub House** ((02) 742149, Ojijo Road, Parklands, where there is mellow indigenous music every Wednesday and Sunday.

Later at night, when most of the local dives will be infested with at least one too many drunks, the smart money and the *mzungus* (white people) will have moved out of the city center and on to the suburbs: either to the mock-Tudor **Horseman** in Karen, or to Westlands where two bars close together form a focus. **Gypsies'** serves seafood *tapas* and drinkers spill out onto the street, while **Papa Loca** is a Tex-Mex joint with a courtyard. Depending on the crowd, both these bars are quite capable of serving through until 4 AM, but after about midnight serious party animals head on out to the **Simba Disco**, a part of the Carnivore Restaurant, which offers disco at least and usually has a DJ or live music from Wednesday to Sundays. Wednesday is rock, Thursday jazz, Friday groove, Saturday disco and the only noticeably African night is Sunday. The cover charge (after 9 PM) is Ksh150. This is a fairly standard charge for Nairobi discos. As the disco scene changes relatively quickly, it's best to ask at your hotel for other recommendations. The **Cantina Club**, on Wilson Airport Road, features African music, dancers and acrobats. Meanwhile, every night is crowded at both the **Florida nightclubs** in the city center, where you can be sure of the opportunity to meet more prostitutes than you ever knew existed. The current favorite, however, is the **Pavement** on Waiyaki Way in Westlands, where there's a pleasant café area and a nightclub where proceedings are kept relatively respectable by refusing entry to unaccompanied Kenyan women. This is where you'll find customers who at least have a serious interest in dancing.

For a more restrained but potentially even more expensive finale to the evening, Nairobi has a choice of casinos. The largest is the original **International Casino** on Chiromo Road, but this area is unsafe at night, even in a taxi: better to go the extra mile to the rather more civilized casino attached to the **Mayfair Court Hotel** in Westlands.

HOW TO GET THERE

The easiest, if not the cheapest, way to travel around Kenya is by air, and this is more true than ever of Nairobi. International flights, and internal flights with Kenya Airways, use **Jomo Kenyatta International Airport** ((02) 822111 or (02) 822206, 15 km (nine miles) southeast of the center. Reconfirm all tickets and check ahead to make sure your flight is leaving when scheduled. Eight flights a day reach Mombasa and there are also flights to Malindi and Kisumu. Internal flights, Airkenya services to Somalia, Kilimanjaro, Zaire and Ethiopia, and charters use the small and friendly **Wilson Airport** ((02) 501941 FAX (02) 501944, off the Langata Road to the south of the city center. Flights from here ferret into both regional airports and obscure landing-strips in the bush. Departure tax is Ksh100.

Nairobi's **Bus Station**, wryly referred to by the locals as "Machakos Airport," is one and a half kilometers (a mile) east of the town center, though tickets are best reserved first at the company offices in the River Road area. It is a fascinating hub of human activity at the end of a working day. Drivers stand, bidding for passengers to overfill their already crowded buses. Vendors hawk food, toys, and other items to passengers through the open windows — often having to run alongside to collect money or give change as the bus pulls out. Buses are loaded with every type of cargo imaginable, all strapped helter-skelter atop, to proceed slowly and cheaply to destinations all around the country. Unfortunately there are pickpockets and thieves aplenty, and there have been numerous incidents of drugging travelers — it's not for the unwary. Of the many bus companies, **Akamba Bus** ((02) 556062, (02)340430 and

For more conventional meals, Nairobi has an abundance of good seafood and European-style restaurants.

(02) 221779, Lagos Road, is one of the largest and most reputable lines, especially useful for the grueling Mombasa route. Their vehicles leave either from their offices in the River Road area or from "Machakos Airport" — check which.

Matatus are quicker, marginally more expensive and, despite a poor record for safety, are a better way of covering long distances. They do not leave from a single central base: rather, they congregate informally in certain areas for each particular route. Just to confuse matters, they change rendezvous from time to time. Taxi drivers usually know where you need to be to catch a *matatu*, and will show you where to board. It is always best to start early as services to less popular destinations thin out through the day. Dawn is the best time to start such a journey.

Due, perhaps, to the shocking nature of the road to the coast there are no direct *matatus* to Mombasa. The best overland way of getting to and from the coast is by overnight train, with sleepers bookable in advance. The **Railway Station** ((02) 221211 extension 2700, at the southern end of Moi Avenue has trains leaving for Mombasa at 7 PM, and at 6 PM to Kisumu. Rail services to Moshi via Voi and Kampala are currently suspended but might resume at any time.

TO THE SOUTH

OLORGASAILIE

The prehistoric site of Olorgasailie and the pink-tinged waters of Lake Magadi in the Rift Valley (see below) can be visited as a long day-excursion or relaxing overnight trip from Nairobi (if you're willing to rough it).

In 1890, geologist John Walter Gregory discovered stone tools and other evidence of prehistoric habitation of this Rift Valley crater that probably contained a lake some 400,000 to 500,000 years ago. It was not until the 1940s, however, that the site was systematically excavated by Louis and Mary Leakey. The Leakeys concluded that the lakeshore had been inhabited by *Homo erectus* of the Acheulean culture, early men who had the same culture as those who had lived in Saint-Acheul, France, during the lower Paleolithic. A variety of tools for skinning animals, crushing bones and hunting, as well as hand axes for which this culture is best known, were unearthed and are displayed *in situ*. Despite the large concentration of tools, no human remains have been discovered. The Leakeys also found a gigantic fossilized leg of an extinct species of elephant. Your Ksh200 entrance fee includes a guided tour by a usually well-informed ranger.

Where to Stay

The only accommodations at Olorgasailie are self-service *bandas* or bunkhouses (Ksh500 per person) and a campsite (Ksh100 per person) run by the National Museum ((02) 742131, Box 40658, Olorgasailie, but you'll need bedding and cooking equipment. Without this it's perhaps best treated as a day trip.

How to Get There

Leave Nairobi, head south past Wilson Airport and the national park and turn left onto the C58. After 40 km (25 miles), just after the village of Oltepesi, follow the signpost to Olorgasailie and turn left to drive one and a half kilometers (one mile) to the site. Alternatively buses do occasionally leave from Nairobi bus station, usually early in the morning. It's not a busy route and it is more convenient to rent your own car or reserve a vehicle and driver from an operator such as **Let's Go Travel** ((02) 447151 or (02) 441030 FAX (02) 447270 or (02) 441690 E-MAIL info @letsgosafari.com WEB SITE www.letsgosafari .com, Box 60342, Nairobi, or **UTC** ((02) 331960 FAX (02) 331422 WEB SITE www.unitedtour .com, Box 42196, Nairobi.

LAKE MAGADI

At 600 m (2,000 ft) above sea level, Lake Magadi is one of the hottest spots in Kenya and the world's second-largest trona deposit (first is California's Salton Sea). This alkaline lake acts as a gigantic evaporating pan in which trona (a solution of sodium salts) deposits are 30 m (100 ft) deep, giving the lake its unlikely pink or green color, depending on the season. The lake is leased by the Magadi Soda Company Limited: signs by the road warn visitors to report their visit to the police station, but permission is freely given.

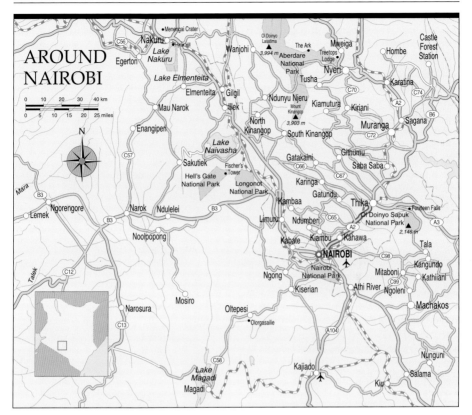

Lake Magadi once received international attention when the flamingos left their normal breeding grounds in lakes Nakuru and Baringo and laid their eggs here. The hatchlings were unable to free themselves from the sticky sodium deposits. A massive rescue operation ensued that took thousands of the stranded birds to safety. The bird life at the southern end of the lake and in the small freshwater swamps is varied enough to make the trip worthwhile for the dedicated bird watcher. This is the only place in Kenya where you are likely to see the chestnut-banded sand plover.

Geologically, the site is unique. Each year, Magadi receives less than 500 mm (20 inches) of rainfall and has an average temperature of 20°C (68°F), varying between 15°C and 41°C (59°F and 106°F). Its evaporation rate is 3,500 mm (120 inches) annually. Thus, theoretically, the lake should be dry. But it is not, and the trona deposits are growing more rapidly than they are mined.

Obviously, local rainfall is not keeping the lake alive, but rainfall from the neighboring areas of the Rift Valley drains into the lake underground. In addition, this underground seepage is being geothermally heated, which accelerates the rate at which the water can leach soda salts from the subsurface rocks. Once the hot water, already rich in soda, reaches Lake Magadi, evaporation takes place quickly, leaving solid trona crystals on the surface of the lake. Some deposits are so solid that cars can drive across them. In spite of the heat, it's fascinating to walk over these Technicolor fields on the factory causeway. The two factories operated by the Magadi Soda Company produce approximately 166,000 tons of soda ash and 40,000 tons of table salt annually.

Where to Stay

The town has, thanks to the factory, a public pool that is free to all comers. You might want to cool off here before beginning the journey back to Nairobi. Camping is possible here if you ask permission, although you're more likely to be invited to stay by a company employee. Alternatively, check in to the **Lower Guesthouse** ((0303) 33000 or (0303) 33278 (very inexpensive).

How to Get There

Leave Nairobi heading south past Wilson Airport and the national park and turn left onto the C58. After 83 km (51.5 miles) you will reach the end of the road and Lake Magadi. Alternatively, most days a bus does leave from Nairobi's bus station early in the morning. It is easier to rent your own car or reserve a vehicle and driver from an operator such as **Let's Go Travel** ((02) 447151 or (02) 441030 FAX (02) 447270 or (02) 441690 E-MAIL info@letsgosafari.com WEB SITE www .letsgosafari.com, Box 60342, Nairobi, or **UTC** ((02) 331960 FAX (02) 331422 WEB SITE www .unitedtour.com, Box 42196, Nairobi.

NORTHWEST OF NAIROBI

Because Longonot Crater, Lake Naivasha and Hell's Gate National Park are so close to Nairobi (within a two-hour drive), it is easy to speed by them in haste to get to more distant safari destinations. Each can be visited on a day trip from Nairobi, but Naivasha is a rewarding overnight stay before continuing west or returning to Nairobi.

LONGONOT NATIONAL PARK

The attractions of Longonot National Park are hiking and picnicking in the ragged volcanic crater, which takes its name from the Maasai "Oloonong'ot" meaning mountain of many spurs or steep ridges. A trail starting at the Longonot police station takes you to the rim. Like the Ngong Hills, security here has been a problem in recent years, so don't hike alone. You will be accompanied by a Kenya Wildlife Service ranger in any case. Admission to the park is US$15, with vehicles charges at Ksh500.

On reaching the rim, your response might be similar to that of Major Joseph Thomson, the first European to describe his visit here, in 1884. "The scene was of such an astounding character that I was completely fascinated, and felt under an almost irresistible impulse madly to plunge into the fearful chasm. So overpowering was this feeling that I had to withdraw myself from the side of the pit."

You can descend into the crater but the walk around the rim offers better views. It

takes over two hours to make the circuit, as the path is narrow and often crumbly. You will need a sturdy pair of shoes. For those not interested in the climb, there are superb views of the crater and nearby **Suswa Crater** from the Nairobi–Naivasha road, where there are scenic overlooks (although the souvenir vendors will make it hard to enjoy in peace). Don't leave your car unlocked anywhere in Kenya, especially here.

How to Get There

To reach Longonot from Nairobi take the Naivasha Road northwest towards Limuru. After 28 km (17.5 miles) the road splits: the new Uplands Road heads on to Limuru and Lake Naivasha, while the B3 forks left.

After a further 22 km (14 miles) turn right onto the C88 signposted for Longonot. Park at the Police Station after 16 km (10 miles).

LAKE NAIVASHA

Lake Naivasha is one of the most beautiful of Kenya's Rift Valley lakes, surrounded by feathery papyrus, marshy lagoons, and grassy shores. It was the setting for M.M. Kaye's mystery, *Death in Kenya*. The story isn't great, but it describes the Naivasha area accurately.

Over the centuries, the size of the lake has fluctuated greatly. In the 1920s a Swedish geologist, Eric Nilsson, found a buffalo skeleton in sediments of a former, larger Lake Naivasha. This buffalo had a horn span of over two meters (six feet) and its teeth indicated that it fed on soft juicy foliage rather than the tougher, drier vegetation that sustains buffaloes of today. Nilsson suggested that this buffalo lived in an environment more moist than prevails at present in the Naivasha basin. Other research supports Nilsson's hypothesis; it is now generally agreed that the Rift Valley as a whole had a colder, wetter environment 10,000 to 20,000 years ago.

Early explorers such as Thomson and Fischer in the 1880s described it as a smaller

Lake Magadi has the hottest climate in Kenya and an unusual resident population of aquatic birds, including the chestnut-banded sand plover.

lake. Records from the 1890s show that during that decade it rose 15 m (50 ft) and was much larger than it is now.

Today the lake water irrigates the surrounding countryside, where much of the fresh vegetables for Nairobi's markets are grown. On the south shore is Kenya's only vineyard, and a plantation that employs approximately 4,000 people to grow flowers that are exported throughout the world. Many of the flowers in the world-famous Amsterdam market are flown there daily from Kenya, though there are mounting concerns about the amount of pesticides demanded to keep these introduced plants perfectly blooming.

From all waterfront hotels you can take a boat to **Crescent Island** (Ksh500 per person and Ksh200 entrance), a private game sanctuary, where you can walk around the island and view, at close range, zebras, waterbucks, giraffes and several species of antelope. Hippos are almost always seen and heard during the boat ride. Bird life around the lake is also abundant.

Where to Stay and Eat

Around the lake are several places to stay. In town is the excellent and fun **La Belle Inn** ((0311) 21007 FAX (0311) 21119, Moi Avenue (inexpensive, B&B). On weekends, this small hotel is often full with Kenyans up from Nairobi, and it can even be difficult to find a seat for coffee or tea. White rabbits nibble the courtyard grass and a caged python provides a touch of local color. In addition to the French fare it offers American-style milkshakes, pizza and superb panini, all served in an atmosphere 40 years adrift in time.

Most tourists, however, will opt to stay on the shores of the lake itself. Here you'll find the **Lake Naivasha Country Club** ((02) 535412-4 FAX (02) 545954, Block Hotels, Box 40075, Nairobi (expensive, full board), which is still the best place to stay, with bird walks, boat rides, and countless butterflies in the garden. On a budget, travelers might choose the famously friendly and very inexpensive **YMCA** ((0311) 30396, Box 1006, which is Spartan but a good base for hiking.

Naivasha's earlier position at the heart of the colonial plantation culture, however, means that it has a number of atmospheric home-stays that are, perhaps, the best way to recapture its timeless appeal. Sometimes these are seriously expensive. **Olerai House** (extremely expensive, all-inclusive, book through Bush Homes of East Africa ((02) 350703, (02) 571661 or (02) 571592 FAX (02) 571665 E-MAIL bushhome@africaonline.co.ke WEB SITE www.bush-homes.co.ke, Box 56923, Nairobi) is the home of Iain and Oria Douglas-Hamilton, activists involved in elephant conservation, and a maximum of 12 guests are treated to an informative and entertaining stay. **Kiangazi** ((0311) 21052 FAX (0311) 21059, Box 719, is another home-stay offering game-drives and excellent cuisine (very expensive, all-inclusive). **Loldia** ((0311) 30024, Box 199, North Moi Lake Road was originally built by Italian prisoners in World War II and still is one of the grandest buildings in the area, with horseback riding a specialty (extremely expensive, all-inclusive). For a really exclusive experience, **Mundui Estate** (extremely expensive, all-inclusive, book through Bush Homes of East Africa) is a two-bedroom cottage offering a full range of activities as well as a swimming pool, croquet and badminton court.

If you are interested in conservation, consider a stay at Joy Adamson's famous house, **Elasmere** ((0311) 21055 FAX (0311) 21074, Box 1497, Naivasha, set on the lakeshore towards Kongoni Game Valley (expensive, full board), which offers a private, home-like experience. This was where Adamson's life was spent working with lions, as immortalized in her writing, which put conservation issues onto the world stage. It prefers guests to have an interest, if not in Joy Adamson's life and work, at least in conservation.

Travelers on any sort of budget here will have to be prepared to look after themselves: bring all your own food and bedding to stay at self-catering **Eburru Guest Cottage** or **Melili Cottage** next door, both bookable through Let's Go Travel ((02) 447151 or (02) 441030 FAX (02) 447270 or (02) 441690 E-MAIL info@letsgosafari.com WEB SITE www.letsgo safari.com, Box 60342, Nairobi (inexpensive).

How to Get There

It's a two-hour drive to Naivasha although the frequent buses and *matatus* that leave

Longonot Crater towers over the Rift Valley.

Nairobi from the lower end of River Road will take rather longer. Drive northwest on Uhuru Highway, which turns into the Chiromo Road, and climb out of Nairobi on one of the country's few stretches of dual lane road — shared, unfortunately, with a lot of heavy traffic — to climb the shoulder of the Rift Valley. It's a spectacular drive.

HELL'S GATE NATIONAL PARK

Nearby is one of Kenya's unsung but most accessible national parks, Hell's Gate (entry

control the herbivore population), it is possible to hike throughout the park. During and after the rains, the road to the gorge is impassable and you will probably have to walk most of the way from the gate if you wish to see the 180-m (600-ft) cliffs, formed by Lake Naivasha's prehistoric outlet.

It is a full-day's hike, 25 km (16 miles) round trip from the park gate to the south end of **Hell's Gate Gorge**. If you don't want to hike the full distance you can usually drive at least to the head of the gorge, six kilometers (four miles) inside the gate.

US$15, children US$5, vehicle Ksh500), shaped by violent volcanic forces millions of years ago. It was here that the German explorer, Dr. Gustav Fischer, was attacked by the Maasai during his 1882 expedition. Fischer's Tower, a volcanic plug near the north entrance, identifies the approximate site of the ambush.

The park has an abundance of herbivores (zebras, impalas, gazelles, klipspringers and buffaloes), an outstanding bird population, a small Maasai population centered in several *manyattas*, and a spectacular red-cliffed gorge with a resident pair of lammergeyers (bearded vultures).

Because there are few or no predators (although lions may soon be introduced to

While hiking you will need to carry water and food; a hat and sunscreen are highly recommended.

The descent into this miniature Grand Canyon is steep at first, but becomes very pleasant as you reach the bottom of the gorge. At the south end you will see, but hear first, the steam of the **Olkaria geothermal station** that now produces much of Nairobi's electricity. Here underground water temperatures exceed 304°C (579°F), one of the world's hottest geothermal sites. Olkaria is expected to eventually supply half of Kenya's energy requirements.

Hiking in the park gives one a sense of the freedom, open space and wildlife that abounded a century ago in Kenya. It is a pleasure to travel on foot with wildlife grazing along the route. The terrain is rolling, and you need not make the trek to the gorge. Even a two-hour walk around the plains looking out on Longonot Cráter is an experience not to be forgotten. During the week there are few visitors and one can explore undisturbed. Fischer's Tower and Hell's Gate Gorge offer every level of rock-climbing difficulty. We watched several climbers scaling the east face of Fischer's Tower, while dozens of rock hyraxes sunned themselves unconcernedly below.

There are several primitive campsites in the park (US$8 per person), but you must bring your own water and food. Ask the rangers at the gate for the best locations.

How to Get There

Access to Hell's Gate National Park is usually from Naivasha: drive south around the lake on South Lake Road where two left turns lead to Elsa Gate and Olkaria Gate respectively. Alternatively, in the dry season (July to September, January to March), Hell's Gate can be reached along a rough track from the B3 Narok–Limuru Road.

FURTHER EXCURSIONS

There are other excursions northwest of Nairobi that can be done as day trips, most notably, starting early and returning late, Nakuru. But while these can be done as day trips, these are also good destinations in their own right, and are detailed in THE NORTHERN RIFT VALLEY, page 181.

EAST OF NAIROBI

The mountainous plateau to the north of Nairobi contains some of the country's wildest landscapes, finest game parks and most inviting communities. Thanks to the altitude the climate is perfect, with plenty of rain, warm days and cool nights, and it is not for nothing that the early colonists established most of their farms here, on land formerly inhabited by the Kikuyu people. Thika is the gateway town to the mist-shrouded forests of the Aberdares and the varied landscapes of snow-capped Mount Kenya, fully described in THE CENTRAL HIGHLANDS, page 203.

To the east the plateau extends to the town of Machakos, before the main road bumps off southwards Mombasa and the wonderful national parks of Amboseli and Tsavo East and West, covered in the EASTERN PLAINS, page 237.

THIKA

The journey to Thika, which took Elspeth Huxley three days to complete in an ox-drawn wagon at the turn of the century, now takes less than an hour on a four-lane freeway. The red dust is still there (though you won't be covered with it), but the papyrus and tall grasses have been replaced by government buildings, apartment complexes, a sports stadium, Kenyatta University, cattle ranches and sisal, pineapple and coffee plantations.

Thika is now a Nairobi bedroom community and manufacturing center that sprawls haphazardly on both sides of the freeway.

Where to Stay and Eat

Still in operation, the **Blue Posts Inn (** (0151) 22241, Box 43, Thika, which offers inexpensive B&B, was the first permanent business site in Thika and a gathering point for the early European settlers. Situated at the junction of the Thika and Chania river, it has attractive gardens that overlook two spectacular waterfalls and is an ideal spot to stop for lunch, coffee or tea. The restaurant is good and reasonably priced (Ksh200 to Ksh300 for a dish), and the rooms have recently been refurbished. The original structure, built in 1907 by a British captain affectionately nicknamed Major Breeches, got its name from its blue hitching post. Most of today's Blue Posts buildings were added in the 1930s and renovated in 1988.

An inexpensive alternative is the **December Hotel (** (0151) 22140, Commercial Street, but be sure to ask for a self-contained room.

How to Get There

Thika is 42 km (26 miles) from Nairobi along the busy Muranga Road. From Thika or Nairobi you can make an interesting side trip to Ol Doinyo Sapuk National Park and Fourteen Falls on the Athi River.

The dramatic landscapes of Hell's Gate National Park.

OL DOINYO SAPUK NATIONAL PARK

Ol Doinyo Sapuk ("big mountain," in Maa) or Kilima Mbogo ("buffalo mountain," in Kikuyu) rises to 2,146 m (7,043 ft) and is the major attraction of this park. It is here that the colonial owners, William Northrup McMillan and his wife Lucie, are buried.

McMillan, a Canadian, and Lucie, an American, came to Kenya in 1905. He apparently won Ol Doinyo Sapuk in a poker game at the Norfolk Hotel. The couple also owned land at Juja, Saba Saba and Ondiri; their 16,000 ha (40,000 acres) at Juja were a private game sanctuary as well as a farm. McMillan spent much of his time studying animals as well as hunting them. Lucie was an avid photographer.

After World War I, McMillan was knighted for his services in the 25th Fusiliers. He and Lucie spent most weekends at their cottage known as "Lucie's Folly" on the slopes of Ol Doinyo Sapuk. McMillan died in 1925 and was buried on the slopes of the mountain. In 1958, a year after her death, Lucie's executors began the long and tortuous proceedings to carry out her last wishes that Ol Doinyo Sapuk be given to the government as a park. There was much interference from relatives. For a long time nothing appeared to happen, though the colonial government gratefully accepted the gift of land and, with it, the stipulation that the area should be known as the McMillan Memorial Park, and that the graves should be cared for.

By 1964, illegal *shambas* or farms dotted the hillsides, and it would have been easy for the new Kenyan government to assert that the squatters needed the land. But it honored the stipulations of the will and today Ol Doinyo Sapuk is a national park.

The view, on a clear day, is superb — Nairobi and the Athi River to the south, and Mount Kenya to the north. The dirt track to the top is rough and steep, thus a four-wheel drive is advisable, particularly after heavy rains. During the period of long rains, from April to June, the road may be closed: it's best to ask in Thika or Nairobi before making the trip.

Even though walking is not permitted during periods of road closures, a climb can

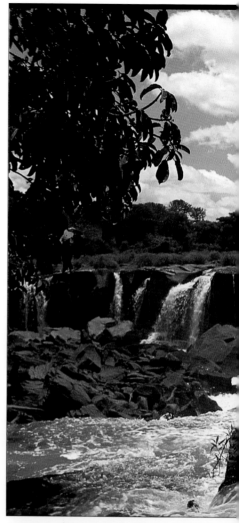

sometimes be arranged with rangers at the gate for a nominal fee. Under no circumstances will a single individual be allowed to hike or climb anywhere within Ol Doinyo Sapuk National Park, due to hostile buffaloes, the predominant inhabitants of the park. If you are lucky, you can also see Sykes' monkeys or black-faced vervets. Unsubstantiated rumor has it that there are still leopards in the forest. During both the long and short rains (April to June and October to December), butterflies are abundant, as is a multitude of wildflowers. Year-round, the ravines are alive with hundreds of species of forest birds. The entrance fee, as for all this grade of national park, is US$15 per person. The park is open from 6 AM to 6 PM.

Fourteen Falls

It's a short drive from Ol Doinyo Sapuk National Park to Fourteen Falls on the Athi River. After a heavy rain, the numerous small cascades merge into a spectacular rush of water. Unfortunately, upstream overgrazing and farming have caused erosion that turns the water a murky red. The avid waterfall lover can descend to the base of the falls along a rocky and often slippery trail. The falls are surrounded by dense tropical vegetation and were used years ago as the setting for one of the many Tarzan movies. Just which one, no one seems to know. Entrance costs Ksh100 per person, with a further Ksh120 for your vehicle.

How to Get There

In your own car, is the short answer, though *matatus* do occasionally leave from the Koinange Street near the New Florida nightclub in Nairobi.

Just a 40-minute drive from Nairobi, Thika is little more than a satellite of the city, and there is little reason to stay overnight here. Few tours head out this way, and it is more popular as a weekend destination for Nairobi residents with their own cars.

Fourteen Falls on the Athi River, a 40-minute drive from Nairobi.

The Masai Mara and the Southwest

At dawn, a vast plain of dusty brown extends before you. The red sun inches above a jagged, distant ridge. In the stillness of breaking light, the morning breeze carries the songs of a hundred different birds and, from afar, the loud roar of a waking lion.

Suddenly, the entire brown plain before you stirs. It begins to move with the surprising quickness of an earthquake, with the thudding of many thousand hooves. In the quick-rising dust, you see that the entire plain was but one herd of wildebeest, aroused now by that lion's roar.

With the earth rumbling and roaring, the wildebeest pour past. It seems they will never end. The air grows thick with their dust and loud with their strange cries. Zebras are passing too — fat, striped, whinnying horses, thousands of them, kicking up their heels. Finally, the herds diminish. Here and there, a loner gallops nervously to catch up, glancing back over its shoulder. And you think, "Ah, the lion's coming."

But no, the ground begins to shake again. More wildebeest are thundering towards you, dashing madly about, bleating, tossing their glossy horns. Still more come, then more, until finally they thin out. Exhausted with waiting, you say, "There, that's over!" only to find you've misconstrued. This entire vast dawn shadow moving toward you across the valley is not bush, as you thought, but wildebeest — hundreds of thousands of them.

No words nor photographs can convey the Masai Mara. It and Tanzania's adjoining and even more vast Serengeti National Park are perhaps the only places left in Africa that retain a sense of the vastness of plains and its game before the coming of the white man.

The standard rule among Kenya outfitters is to save the Masai Mara for last, lest everything that would follow it seem anticlimactic. But as time gets more valuable, many visitors to Kenya see only the Masai Mara, on quick fly-in safaris. It is, without doubt, most amazing at the time of the annual migration (July to October), but even after rain the sheer density of the game here means there is always something to see. But the experience will depend, to a significant extent, on where you go within the national reserve, which covers 1,812 sq km (700 sq

miles), or whether you stay in one of the private game ranches bordering the reserve itself, which can offer an even more private experience free of Kenya Wildlife Service regulations and sometimes (but not always) escaping the lumbering herds of predatory minivans determined to share your every sighting.

To the west the reserve is bounded by the sheer cliffs of the Oloolo Escarpment, then the little-visited highland towns of Kisii and Kericho, and finally the huge mass of Lake Victoria, most commonly reached by small plane from one of the Mara airstrips.

THE MASAI MARA

The Masai Mara is the northern extension of Tanzania's Serengeti National Park. It is far smaller than the Serengeti, with the gazetted reserve area comprising a mere four percent of the Serengeti ecosystem, and of course it is also one of the most visited parks in Africa. Paradoxically this actually makes for better game viewing. There are more tracks and the game is more habituated to the sight of vehicles. Generally, in the Masai Mara, the animals have seen so many minivans and four-wheel drives they carry on playing their role in the drama of the wild world without taking any notice of their eager audience. In the migration season (July to October) the reserve is packed with game of all kinds, but at any time of year it has the highest density of wildlife in Africa. It is possible to count off more species than you have fingers from a single viewpoint here. For sheer numbers of animals and range of species it is, by a comfortable margin, the best park in Kenya.

Until relatively recently, this land was shared among pastoralist Maasai, their cattle, and the wildlife, with occasional incursions by armed hunters. It was only gazetted in 1974, when conservationists and governments decided the needs of Africa's endangered wildlife outweighed the burgeoning Maasai people's need — or even their own — for increased grazing and land. All around the reserve you will see the red robes of warriors and the beaded figures of Maasai

Many Maasai still practice polygamy; many may have 20 or more children.

women. Inside the reserve this all changes: here it's a world of lift-top safari vehicles, pointed cameras and hosts of animals.

By road from Nairobi, the east of the park is several hours closer than the west, and for this reason is always slightly more crowded with safari vehicles, though to be honest they get everywhere. There are other reasons to make the effort to visit the west. By common consent the countryside there is more beautiful, cut through by the important — and large — Mara River, with the dramatic backdrop of the Oloolo Escarpment.

and lions, and the high, steep country in the southeast of the reserve, beautiful and more thickly forested, is an excellent habitat for lions, leopards, giraffes and most other herbivores. And the endless variety here extends to the skies. Some 53 different species of predatory birds have been identified in the Masai Mara, and 430 other bird species. It's not surprising that it is the most popular game area in Africa. Entry fees are US$27 per adult per day, US$10 per child, Ksh500 per vehicle; under a new and probably worthwhile development you'll also be

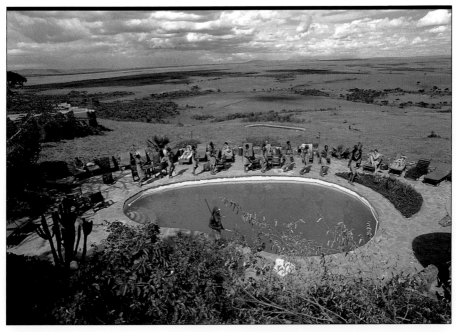

This area, known as the "Maasai Triangle," is where you'll find the largest herds of wildebeest (in Boer Dutch, literally a "wild beast," also known as gnu) and common zebras, and consequently the greatest numbers of predators. Also excellent for game watching is Musiara Swamp and the downstream area outside the Musiara gate, where cheetahs and lions are frequently sighted. The entire course of the Mara and Talek river in the reserve is a good area for elephants, giraffes, hippos, antelope, crocodiles, buffaloes, spotted hyenas, warthogs, black-backed jackals and even the solitary leopard. This isn't to say the western area of the park has all the action, however. The Mosee Plains to the east are good for all the herbivores

charged this to visit the group ranches, owned by displaced Maasai communities or private concessionaires, that border the park. The same tickets cover both ranches and the reserve itself.

In general, the activities in the Masai Mara focus on the wildlife. There are two unusual specialties here, however, to tempt those with a well-stacked wallet. Ballooning is a local specialty (see TAKE TO THE SKIES, page 14 in TOP SPOTS) and costs US$385 per person, or there are also fishing trips — with travel by light aircraft — at Rusinga and Mfangano Island on Lake Victoria. This can be done as a daytrip (allow US$385 per person) or as a very pleasurable overnight (see page 156 for details).

WHEN TO VISIT

Although there is always something to see in the Mara, the best time to visit is during the migration. This is generally from July through October. Low season here is April and May, where rain cuts off many roads and brings high grass: it's hard to see the game, which in any case will have widely dispersed. Low season rates apply through June, however, and this can be a good time to take a gamble as in recent years the seasons have become increasingly erratic.

WHERE TO STAY

Within the park itself there are surprisingly few lodges, all controlled by a small number of major safari companies. If traveling independently they are relatively expensive; tour operators will be paying less than you, so a tour is by far the cheaper option. For this reason, if no other, many independent travelers opt to camp. There are campsites outside most of the gates. Furthest east is Sand River, which is pleasantly located but is also where Julie Ward, a British tourist was murdered in 1998, so it's hard to avoid feeling spooked. Talek Gate has a selection of camp sites, and Musiara Gate's campsite, justifiably popular, is often shared with passing lions. Oloolo Gate's campsites overlook the escarpment and, sometimes, hippos playing below.

It is important to be careful, of course. There are wild animals all around, so don't leave your tent in the middle of the night however many beers you drank before retiring. Security can be a problem, surrounded as you are by hardened communities where poverty is relentless: check with the local situation the park rangers. The reliability of camping changes from season to season in the national parks and it's always possible to become a first, unwelcome statistic. If you wish advance information and think it will help, write to the Warden, Masai Mara National Reserve, Box 60, Narok.

A wiser choice in the Mara is a tented camp or lodge, fenced or unfenced, especially if you can get package rates through a Nairobi, or international, operator. The advantage of an unfenced tented camp is that it's more open, often cooler, and the sounds of the natural world filter closely through the thin canvas of the tent wall. This is, however, a matter of taste: for some people it's an adrenalin rush, while others get no sleep at all as they darkly imagine just what might be bumping against their guy ropes and nuzzling up to their door and would infinitely prefer a fenced, stone-built lodge — an especially good idea if you're traveling with children young enough to wake up curious when a lion grunts outside. One factor that might influence your choice is whether game-drives are included or not. If you're traveling independently with your own vehicle it's better to choose a full-board lodge. Those listed as all-inclusive include game drives in their rates, which will suit those who fly in. Whether tented camps or built lodges, your options within the reserve, once again from east to west, are as follows.

Sarova Mara Camp ((0305) 2386 or (02) 713333 (reservations) FAX (02) 715566 E-MAIL reservations@sarova.co.ke, WEB SITE www .sarovahotels.com, is an expensive, full-board camp that is large but well-landscaped with comfortable, well-furnished tents. It is has the advantage of being the closest camp in the reserve to Nairobi by road. To the south is **Keekerok Lodge** ((0305) 2525 (expensive, full-board), book through Block Hotels ((02) 535412-4 FAX (02) 545954 WEB SITE block hotels.com, a rather touristy but undeniably comfortable lodge that is especially good value in some mass-market packages. There's a pleasant hippo pool with a lone hippo, overlooked by a raised bar on wooden decking.

Cross over to the east of the Talek River to the **Mara Intrepids** ((0305) 2168, reservations through Heritage ((02) 446651 or (02) 447929 FAX (02) 446533 E-MAIL info@heritage hotels.co.ke WEB SITE www.heritagehotels .co.ke, which overlooks the river, where they bait leopard daily (extremely expensive, all-inclusive). They offer especially good programs for introducing children to the wonders of the bush (leaving adults free to go on long, patient game drives). Pricey but recommended. The **Mara Serena Lodge** ((0305) 2252

From the Masai Mara's Limutu Hill, the plains seem to stretch "beyond the rim of the world." OVERLEAF: Wildebeest congregate on the banks of the Mara River.

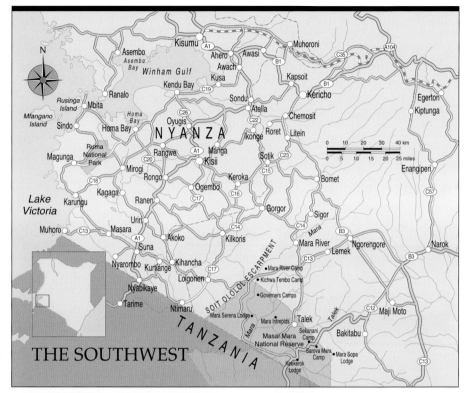

THE SOUTHWEST

or (02) 711077 (reservations) FAX (02) 718012
E-MAIL cro@serena.co.ke, Nyere Road, Box 46302,
Nairobi, is a large but unobtrusive lodge
set high on a ridge which has spectacular
views (very expensive, full board). Most easterly of all are the Governors Camps, with three
options, all extremely expensive and all-
inclusive. The camps overlook a steep gorge
of the Mara River. **Governors** ((0305) 2273 is
the largest, **Little Governors** ((0305) 2040
somewhat smaller, while the most luxurious
of all is **Il Moran**, where 10 lavishly huge tents,
decorated with polished olive-wood furniture,
contain every luxury including (unusually for
the Mara, where water is short) huge, free-
standing claw-footed baths. If, at US$740 all-
inclusive, this isn't enough, a private tented
camp can be rented for parties. For reservations contact **Governors Camps** ((02) 331871
FAX (02) 726427 WEB SITE www.governors
camp.com, Box 48217, Nairobi. These are especially well-situated for Musiara Swamp, but
as road-access is difficult most guests fly in.

Outside the unfenced reserve boundaries
but in the dispersal areas of all the Mara's animals a whole new range of activities opens
up, including cultural visits, game walks and
night drives, free of reserve regulations. A
wider choice of lodges also beckons. From
east to west again, the first option is the **Mara
Sopa Lodge** ((0305) 2196 or (02) 336088
(reservations) FAX (02) 223843 E-MAIL enquiries
@sopalodges.com, Box 72360, Nairobi, whose
pleasant *bandas* make good bases for a safari
(expensive, full-board). To the north, convenient to the main Nairobi Road, is **Siana
Springs Camp** ((0305) 2553, reservations
through Conservation Corporation ((02)
441001/5 FAX (02) 746826 E-MAIL info@conscorp
.co.ke WEB SITE www.ccafrica.com, Box 74957,
Nairobi, a small and select luxury tented establishment, beautifully shaded by mature
trees and with leopard and bird hides, and the
very highest standards of cuisine (very expensive, full board). Further north again and
Cottars 1920's Safari Camp ((02) 884508
FAX (02) 882234 E-MAIL Cottars@form-net.com,
Box 44191, Nairobi, recreates a mythical world
of grace and comfort that might have existed
in the 1920s if they'd had portable fridges, solar
power, and posturepedic mattresses (extremely expensive, all-inclusive).

Back on the boundaries of the Masai Mara is **Sekanani Camp** ((0305) 2454, reservations through Southern Cross Safaris ((011) 471960 FAX (011) 471257, Box 90653, Nyali, Mombasa, which consists of 15 stilted tents and is exceptionally comfortable (very expensive, full board). West and the **Mara River Camp** ((0305) 2186, reservations through Savannah Camps ((02) 331684 or (02) 335935 FAX (02) 216528 or (02) 330698 E-MAIL eaos@africa online.co.ke WEB SITE www.savannahcamps .com, 11th Floor, Fedha Towers, Standard Street, Box 48019, Nairobi, is rather less sophisticated than the other camps in this price bracket, which is not in itself such a bad thing; it is well-thought-of by serious naturalists (very expensive, all-inclusive). **Kichwa Tembo Camp** ((0305) 2465, reservations through Conservation Corporation ((02) 441001/5 FAX (02) 746826 E-MAIL info@conscorp.co.ke WEB SITE www.ccafrica.com, Box 74957, Nairobi, is another very smart establishment (very expensive, full-board) with an even smarter offshoot, **Bateleur Camp** (extremely expensive, all-inclusive), a short walk away through the woods, with period furniture, all comforts, and food and drink included. A short 15-minute drive from here is **Olonana**, run by Abercrombie & Kent ((02) 334955 FAX (02) 228700, Box 59749, Nairobi, a curiously dated but eco-friendly, well-run and integrated establishment that knows how to introduce the wildlife and cultural aspects of the area (extremely expensive, all-inclusive).

There are some more, but these are, in my opinion, the best. And if there doesn't seem to be much for travelers on a budget, I'm sorry, they'll just have to camp — or save by pre-booking a tour. Overland safaris with a couple of nights at the Keekerok or Serena should only cost US$300 or so, including park fees, game drives and meals.

HOW TO GET THERE

While the Masai Mara is impressive, the road from Nairobi is less so. Those who can afford to do so, fly. **Airkenya** ((02) 501421/3 FAX (02) 500845 E-MAIL info@airkenya.com WEB SITE www.airkenya.com, Box 30357, Nairobi, flies twice daily from Wilson Airport, taking just one and a half hours to the airstrip in the east of the reserve for US$188

round trip. The morning departure, at 10 AM, is especially useful for those flying in on an overnight flight.

The conventional route is from Nairobi. Leave the city heading towards Naivasha, but once you've dropped down the side of the Great Rift Valley turn left on the B3 for Narok, where the pavement ends. This small town has seen rather too many tourists to keep the friendly atmosphere of less visited parts of Kenya. It is, however, the last gasoline stop you'll see for a while. Continue on the B3 for 17 km (10 miles) to the Ewaso Ngiro River. At this point it is possible to turn right on the B3 and drive west towards Lemek and the west of the park, but the road can be rough, especially after rain. Only attempt this if you have a good high-clearance four-wheel drive and plenty of confidence. Otherwise keep straight on: the road is reclassified as the C12 and dirt rules for the next 60 km (37 miles) to the park gate. Newly surfaced roads mean five hours driving can get you into the heart of the Mara.

All the major tour operators run daily safaris on this route, but the road is poor and not getting better. Alternatively, it can be approached, with your own transportation, from Kisumu and Kisii, after wandering through the Kericho tea district, Ruma National Park and the coast of Lake Victoria. This allows you to drop down over the Oloolo Escarpment, with the Mara spread out before you in all its vastness — or so it seems. This route is likely to be impassable in wet weather. Take plenty of local advice. Equally, this route can be used to climb up from the Masai Mara to Kisii, Kericho and Kisumu.

KISII

Pretty, full of energy and developing rapidly, with good architecture and dynamic people, the town of Kisii is situated at an altitude of 1,700 m (5,580 ft) and is a welcome relief from the sultry humidity and ubiquitous mosquitoes of Lake Victoria. It is one of the most vital, fastest-growing commercial centers in western Kenya.

Center of the one-and-a-half-million-strong Gusii tribe, Kisii was an area of strife early in this century, when nearly a thousand tribesmen were massacred by the British. Next came massive engagements between the British and Germans during World War I, with the Gusii forced into service as British troops. Now it seems the most peaceful place in Kenya, and its people among the most hospitable.

Sixteen kilometers (10 miles) south of Kisii is the village of **Tabaka**, where most of the world's soapstone comes from. This is the source of racked soapstone candlesticks, animals, vases and bowls that fill countless shelves in all of Kenya's souvenir stalls.

agencies. One is the **Kisco Co-op**, where profits are shared with the artists — see more at their shop on the route between the quarries to the north and the village.

Almost every house in town is devoted to polishing and sanding soapstone carvings, washing the sculptures in water to soften the stone and finally waxing the finished product to give it a characteristic luster. Specialists focus on animal shapes, candlesticks or stylized sculptures, while others polish fruitbowls, either sent for immediate export or delegated for etching and painting. Once

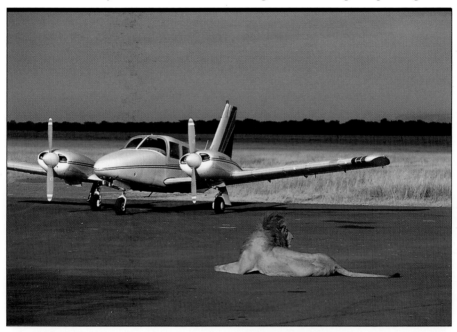

It's hard to believe. The village is friendly and small. The mines are to the east of the village, mountainsides laid bare to the sun and crowds of workers chipping out rocks. Different areas produce soapstone of various colors. The road is filled with workers carrying sacks and bags of stone or staggering under the weight of heavy chunks. Back at the village small, family-run factories carve and polish the rocks on piecework to precise formulae. Artisans — mainly women — chisel, polish and paint, establishing a national art form for the entire country. You won't go short of shopping opportunities. It seems more ethical to sidestep capitalism and shop instead at one of the cooperatives, often set up with the help of foreign aid

racked in Nairobi shops or at Rift Valley viewpoint stalls, there are so many soapstone sculptures they start to look mundane, but at the source the level of skill, craftsmanship and sheer effort is suddenly clear. Prices are low, making this a great place to buy some lasting memories.

From Kisii you can hike up to the **Manga Ridge** (ask directions at the Kisii Hotel), or trek among the green, terraced slopes reminiscent of the Himalayan foothills. You can also drive south to **Tarime** in Tanzania or take the macadam road to **Kilkoris**; from Kilkoris, you can cross the savanna on a dirt road to **Lolgorien**, at the foot of the Ooloolo Escarpment, and suddenly you're back in the land of the Maasai.

The Masai Mara and the Southwest

WHERE TO STAY

Kisii is the best base to explore the area, and there is another advantage: you can stay in the **Kisii Hotel (** (0381) 30134, Box 26, Kisii, a quaint hangover from colonial days, with spreading gardens overlooking the fields just below the hilly and potholed center of town (very inexpensive, B&B). It's a comfortable and friendly place with good food and a bar full of gregarious people most evenings.

HOW TO GET THERE

Those with their own transportation choose between the demanding route up the Oloolo Escarpment from the Masai Mara and two routes to Kisii from Kisumu: fastest is to stick to the A1 heading south towards Tanzania. However, it is well worth the detour to take the tarmac C19 that runs along the coast of Lake Victoria, and then link back with the A1 by taking the 20 km (14 miles) dirt road to Oyugis. It's a spectacular drive and doesn't take much longer. From Homa Bay, it's 45 km (28 miles) of poor but passable tarmac to Kisii.

By public transportation, frequent *matatus* make the three-hour journey from Kisumu. Two bus companies link Kisii with Nairobi three times a day; reserve tickets a day in advance. The trip takes nine hours.

KERICHO

If you were asked the color of tea, you'd probably say brown or black. Once you've seen Kericho, tea will always mean green. For as far as you can see around the town of Kericho, tea plantations carpet the rolling hills. From a distance, the chest-high bushes look soft and cushy. Up close, they are brittle and sharp. Pickers wear oilskin aprons and protective sheaths on their picking fingers.

On any given day, you can usually see a crew (mostly women with male supervisors) working the fields. They move methodically across bright green rows to pick the thumbnail-sized leaves, returning every two weeks to each row. On a good day, a worker can pick up to 70 kg (150 lb) at Ksh3 per kilogram (Ksh1.34 per pound). The baskets can hold

between seven and twelve kilograms of tea and it takes about an hour and a half to fill it. A Luo woman who picked tea for nine years told us that some days were better than others. "After several hours of picking, your fingers always get sore and eventually they are covered with calluses. It is hard work, but a relatively secure job with a wage that is determined by how hard you work." The almost daily rainfall in Kericho has made it the tea capital of Kenya. Over the past years, tea has steadily grown as an industry, surpassing earnings from coffee.

Because most of the inhabitants of the area live and work on the tea plantations, the town of Kericho is mainly a shopping, and not a trading, center. Stores in town cater to the needs of the estate owners and managers as most plantation workers rarely come to town. Nonetheless, the town is one of the tidiest in Kenya and has a beautifully maintained central square.

The area also offers good trout fishing, particularly during the drier months (November to March). The **Itare** and **Kipteget rivers**, each about an hour's drive from town,

OPPOSITE: Lions in the Masai Mara National Reserve have come to accept man and his vehicles as part of everyday life. ABOVE: Tea has replaced coffee as Kenya's largest export crop.

have the best fishing and scenery. They run through the dense rainforest on the western edge of the Mau Escarpment, which has numerous butterflies, birds and wild orchids. Closer to town is the **Mara River** and a short walk from the Tea Hotel is the **Kimugu River**. The Upper and Lower Saosa Dams also offer good fishing, particularly in the evenings. Arrangements for fishing can be made through the Kericho Tea Hotel.

If you don't have time to visit Kericho, but still want to see a tea plantation, there are several near Nairobi. **Mitchell's Kiambethu Tea Farm (** (0154) 50756 gives guided tours on prior arrangement, at a cost of Ksh1,100. They prefer groups to individuals. If you would like some help arranging it, **Let's Go Travel (** (02) 447151 or (02) 441030 FAX (02) 447270 or (02) 441690 E-MAIL info @letsgosafari.com WEB SITE www.letsgosafari .com, Box 60342, Nairobi, are the best people to find a group you can join.

WHERE TO STAY AND EAT

Before or after visiting the fields, you can stop for a cup of tea or a meal at the **Kericho Tea Hotel (** (0361) 30004 FAX (02) 20576, Box 75, Kericho (mid-range, B&B). The pink, Spanish-style hotel was built in 1952 by the then-owner of the surrounding tea plantations, Brooke Bond. It now belongs to African Tours and Hotels. The hotel has an excellent restaurant and well-maintained rooms.

Less expensive and in a rather better (riverside) setting is the **Kericho Lodge and Fish Resort (** (0381) 20035, Box 25, Kericho (inexpensive, B&B). The **TAS Lodge** (no phone) on the Moi Highway in Kericho is the backpacker option and allows camping in its gardens.

HOW TO GET THERE

Kericho is an hour and a half by road and 83 km (52 miles) from Kisumu: travel east along the B1, which continues to Nakuru, Naivasha and Nairobi. From Kisii take the C23, which skirts the Mau Escarpment for a spectacular 115 km (72 miles). By public transportation, frequent *matatus* link Kericho with Kisumu and Nakuru, with plentiful connections on to Nairobi. Overland access from the Masai Mara is possible with a good four-wheel drive if the weather is dry; a beautiful route through the rolling, terraced hills of the Nyanza district.

RUMA NATIONAL PARK

Formerly known as Lambwe Valley Game Reserve, Ruma has 194 sq km (75 sq miles) of rolling savanna mixed with trees and brush. It is set between the lakeside **Gwasi Hills** and the sheer **Kaniamua Escarpment**. Hot, humid and boggy during the rains, it is nonetheless one of the best places in Kenya to see several rare species such as the magnificent, scimitar-horned roan antelope; the huge, curve-horned Jackson's hartebeest; and the diminutive, graceful oribi. You may also see Rothschild's giraffes and the occasional leopard and cheetah.

The park's bird life is spectacular and includes species not likely to be seen elsewhere, such as the barefaced go-away bird, the blue-cheeked bee-eater, the Hartlaub's marsh widow-bird, the yellow-fronted tinkerbird and the African mustached warbler. Despite the battering roads, Ruma is not to be missed.

WHERE TO STAY

The nearest town to Ruma National Park is Homa Bay. Although it suffers from humidity and insects, it offers a good place to stay in the **Homa Bay Hotel (** (02) 229751 or (02) 330820 FAX (02) 227815, Box 42013, Nairobi (US$75 for a double, B&B), which is the best point from which to start exploration of the relatively unknown Ruma National Park.

HOW TO GET THERE

Part of the reason for Ruma's unspoiled status is that it is almost impossible to reach without your own transportation. With a vehicle, the easiest access is from Kisumu, from where the road takes you 104 km (65 miles) southward through the low hills behind the lake, past Mount Homa, which rises over 600 m (nearly 2,000 ft) above the shore in prime hiking country (with a guide). Alternatively, Homa Bay is 59 km (37 miles) from Kisii on good (when dry) dirt roads.

LAKE VICTORIA

The source of the White Nile, Lake Victoria covers 69,490 sq km (26,830 sq miles). It is Africa's largest, and the world's second largest, freshwater lake, and its waters travel some 3,700 km (2,300 miles) to the Mediterranean Sea. It is a huge body of water, the size of Ireland. Most of the time it is blue and tranquil, but it must be treated with respect, as it can change mood suddenly, blowing up into sudden, choppy storms. Lake Victoria would be ideal for swimming, and indeed has plenty of beautiful beaches, but bear in mind that, like most slow-moving or stationary fresh water in Kenya, it is a source of bilharzia, a sickness derived from minuscule flukes that live in snails and bore into the skin to multiply. It is not advised to go bathing. The flukes take a few minutes to burrow through the skin, so dry any freshwater splashes promptly. All this blue water is not completely wasted, however. Kenyans make the most of the lake's opportunities for sport fishing.

This isn't just a white man's sport. Lake Victoria also supplies a major portion of Kenya's protein. In fact, over 90 percent of Kenya's fish catch is freshwater; despite the country's long coast, only 10 percent of the catch is from the ocean. Lake Victoria produces much of this freshwater supply, although its resources have lately been reduced by the replacement of the original tilapia species, highly favored by the local Luo peoples, with the less-preferred Nile perch that, it was hoped, would reduce the mosquito population that causes the humid lakefront region to be so unhealthy.

It took four attempts by fishery biologists and the United States Agency for International Development (AID) before the more expensive perch adapted to the lake in the 1950s, but the introduction of Nile perch, like most experiments with nature, has proved a damaging ecological time-bomb. Current reports indicate that the larger perch have started to prey on the smaller perch, raising the intriguing distant possibility that, at some date in the far future, self-predation will go to its logical conclusion and there will

just be one huge Nile perch in the middle of the lake. In fact, the lake is not deep enough, being little more than 100 m (330 ft) at its deepest. The success of this experiment also spelled disaster for the resident cichlid species, and hit the staple lake-fish, tilapia, which was almost wiped out.

In addition to being favored by the local restaurateurs, the tilapia is a fascinating fish, raising its young in its mouth. The male first clears a nest on the sandy lake bottom and attracts a female, who lays her eggs there; he fertilizes them and she then gathers the

eggs into her mouth and incubates them. She is unable to eat during this entire period. After the fry hatch, the mother guards them for the first 10 days or so, gathering them back into her mouth at any sign of danger and then ejecting them by swimming backward and blowing.

Although it is still possible to fish for tilapia — locals use a simple stick with a hook coated with algae to catch a steady stream of fish usually small enough to return to the water — most visitors to the lake attempt to catch the much larger Nile perch, and generally don't do too badly. The fish grow up to 250 kg (550 lbs) and few visitors return disappointed from a fishing venture.

Traditional Luo basket fishing on Lake Victoria.

RUSINGA ISLAND

Rusinga offers a visit to the birthplace and mausoleum of Tom Mboya, the brilliant young civil rights activist and pro-Western Luo politician gunned down, apparently by Jomo Kenyatta's assassins, in Nairobi in 1969. Mboya was so beloved in Kenya that he stood in the way of an arranged transfer of power from Kenyatta to Daniel Arap Moi, and was accordingly eliminated. His life, accomplishments and burial on Rusinga are recounted in Grace Ogot's *The Island of Tears*, required reading for anyone interested in Kenya or women's literature.

"To Kenyans," Ogot says, "Mboya was one of the greatest men who had ever been born by a woman. To the world beyond the seas, he was a symbol of stability, unity and peace. To the Lake Region people he was a warrior and a hero … He appeared to have been blessed by God of the mighty waters, so that he made blades of grass grow where there was nothing before. He had introduced the ferry which could carry people and vehicles … He had given the island adequate schools, good hospitals and roads. He had encouraged the islanders to adopt modern methods of farming. In ordinary conversation, people would say, 'Oh, it is as miraculous as Mboya's ferry,' or 'It is so big, like Mboya's school' …"

Rusinga Island was also the site of a major find in human prehistory, that of a *Proconsul africanus* skull discovered by Dr. Mary Leakey in 1948. An apelike primate estimated to have lived about 25 million years ago, *Proconsul africanus* may have been a direct ancestor of man, and is similar to two other *Proconsuls* considered likely to have led to the development of the chimpanzee and gorilla.

Most people's reasons for visiting Rusinga are far less cerebral. It currently holds the record for the largest Nile perch fished here, and there are also the full range of water sports on what is effectively an inland coastal resort.

Where to Stay

Rusinga Island Club ((02) 574689 FAX (02) 564945 E-MAIL Mellifera@swiftkenya.com, Box 24397, Nairobi, is the smart place to stay (extremely expensive for full board including all excursions); otherwise there are a couple of small, friendly lodges in Mbita costing a hundredth of the price. Try **Patroba Okgeno Lodge** (0385) 22184, Box 315 (inexpensive).

How to Get There

Rusinga is connected to the mainland by a causeway, even though this is not shown on many maps, and can be reached in an hour by car from Homa Bay, itself two hours' drive from Kisumu. There are occasional lake ferries from Kisumu and along the lakeshore, but these take significantly longer if the hyacinth rafts allow them to leave at all. Most visitors here arrive by light airplane from the Masai Mara: book this through **Mellifera (** (02) 574689, (02) 577018 or (02) 567251 FAX (02) 564945 E-MAIL Mellifera@swiftkenya.com, Box 24397, Nairobi.

MFANGANO ISLAND

Rusinga might be linked to it by causeway, but Mfangano is definitely an island. There's no electricity, piped water or motor vehicles, and life proceeds at the slow pace of a drifting fishnet. Few visitors make it here, apart from day-trippers flying in to fish in the lake, which all adds to its appeal. In the hills an hour's hike above the fishing village of Ukula there are ancient, undated sites of rock art, and the atmosphere on the island is relaxed and friendly — perfect for hiking.

There's only one place to stay, at the **Mfangano Island Lodge** (extremely expensive, all-inclusive), book through Governors Camps **(** (02) 331871 FAX (02) 726427 WEB SITE www.governorscamp.com, Box 48217, Nairobi, with atmospheric rondavels decorated in local style. It offers excellent food, as well as the chance to sip sundowners while fishing for tilapia from the lodge's pontoon as the glassy lake-waters are dyed myriad colors by the setting sun … irresistible. Backpackers can stay with locals.

Access is almost always by light aircraft from the Masai Mara, as Mfangano Island Lodge is owned by the same company as Governors Camps or, for backpackers, by motorized floating *matatu* from Mbita on the mainland.

Early settlers brought nineteenth-century technology to Kenya.

Western
Kenya

The hot, wet west of Kenya doesn't see too many visitors. It's a populous, fertile region where just a few, small reserves hang on in face of population pressures and the need for agricultural land. For those whose interests in Kenya extend beyond the wildlife, however, it is a treasure-trove. A world away from the Muslim coast, far removed from the Kikuyu heartlands of the center and remote from the warring rivalries of the arid north, western Kenya is where you'll find the exhilarating mix of tribal cultures forging ahead into a new Africa. Here unspoiled villages

northern California Coast Range, or of coming down to the Caspian from the Caucasus. It is a sense of the infinity of both land and sea.

The land is green and everywhere cultivated; the water is flat, reflecting the sky, and free of man except when a small boat cuts across it. Above Kisumu, a white Coptic church is set against the slope as if transported from the Cyclades.

The sprawling city of Kisumu has, like Mombasa, a maritime atmosphere due to its former eminence as a major port on Lake Victoria. The upper part of the city contains

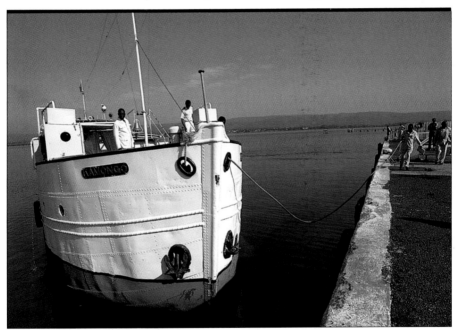

languorously rot in the tropical heat and life proceeds at the pace of growing plants. There are tea plantations and coffee farms, lively markets and the great, sea-like waters of Lake Victoria itself. Take time out to tread the path less trodden in western Kenya.

KISUMU

The capital of Western Kenya is best approached by road. Suddenly, you break through the last of the foothills above Kisumu, and Lake Victoria, resplendent, blue and expansive, lies before you. It feels very much the same as dropping down to the Mediterranean from the French or Italian Alps or the Costa del Sol, of reaching the Pacific from the

many large colonial buildings and residences, set amid more recent shanties and modern structures, on well-shaded wide streets leading down to the port.

At the main traffic circle coming into town you'll find the market and bus station, noisy and teeming with people. Overloaded buses seem to leave every moment for the ends of the earth while black-belching *matatus* are jammed like sardine cans, the squeezed faces of passengers stacked against the dirty windows; other riders hang out the half-shut doors or cling desperately by fingertip to the roof rims and windows, their feet dangling over the speeding pavement.

Kisumu's passenger ferries connect Kenya's major towns and islands on Lake Victoria.

In the days of the East African Community, when Kenya, Tanzania and Uganda were loosely united in a common market and transportation scheme, the port of Kisumu boomed with shipping to and from Kampala in Uganda and Musoma and Mwanza in Tanzania. Since 1977, each nation has become responsible for its own transport networks and the port's business has declined. Yet the town itself is busy, and a walk through its jammed, colorful streets, with their traces of Victorian gingerbread and colonial prosperity, is well worth an hour or two.

It was at Kisumu that the final spike of the "lunatic line to nowhere," the Uganda Railway, was driven on December 19, 1901. It had taken more than five years to build, covered a distance of 920 km (570 miles), cost £5,500,000 and employed a total of 31,983 people, many of whom perished from man-eating lions, accidents, tribal warfare and disease.

Kisumu was called Port Florence in honor of Florence Preston, a woman of great endurance who accompanied her husband, Ronald, the line's railhead engineer, the entire length of the railway from Mombasa to Lake Victoria. It was she who drove the final spike on that last day.

The town was not considered unduly attractive in its early years. One historian, Charles Miller, described it as the least desirable place to be posted in the British Empire, "a pesthouse, conspicuously vulnerable to malaria, dysentery, blackwater fever and a broad range of other tropical scourges. During construction of the railway, an epidemic of sleeping sickness swept the town and took nearly five hundred African lives. For some years, bubonic plague was endemic in Kisumu."

Those days are long gone. Today, Kisumu, though still packed and hot, is an enjoyable stop, especially if one wishes to take a boat across Lake Victoria or continue on southward to Ruma National Park (see page 154). Although Lake Victoria had long served as a transit and shipping zone for Arab slave traders (the lake's indigenous sailboat is rigged with the same lateen sail as the Arab coastal dhow), it was only after the opening of the Uganda Railway that Kisumu acquired commercial status. It soon became the largest Kenyan community on the lake. Despite the failure of the East African Community, Kisumu now has a thriving fish industry, a sugar refinery, marine workshops and flour, textile and cotton mills, threatened only by the rafts of hyacinth that might look pretty but are in imminent danger of stifling all life on the lake.

The **British Council Library** ((035) 45004, at the top of Oginga Odinga, has a selection of books and periodicals. The new **Kisumu Museum** ((035) 40804 E-MAIL kisumuse@arcc .or.ke, on the Nairobi road east of town, is worth a visit, with ethnographic exhibits and more animals than some zoos. The **Kisumu Park**, with orphan leopards and monkeys pacing in cages and an expanse of unspoiled lakefront, is safe-ish for walking as far as the Sunset Hotel, but not, as friendly park wardens are quick to point out, any further.

WHERE TO STAY

Kisumu is an ideal base for exploring western Kenya. The city has two luxury alternatives: the **Imperial Hotel** ((035) 41470 FAX (035) 40345, Box 1866, Kisumu, located on Jomo Kenyatta Highway near Oginga Odinga Road (Ksh3,900 for a double with bed and breakfast), which also offers suites and long-let apartments; and the **Sunset Hotel** ((0345) 41100, Box 215, Kisumu (US$72 for a double with bed and breakfast), located just south of the city center, bookable through ATH ((02) 336858, Box 30471, Nairobi. Get up to the roof for the best view of Lake Victoria and, when the wind's onshore, the vast rafts of hyacinth engulfing the port. Less expensive but still good is the **New Victoria Hotel** ((035) 21067, Box 276, Kisumu, on Gor Mihia Street; doubles with balconies overlooking the city center and lake cost Ksh900 with bed and breakfast. Cheapest is the **Western Lodge** ((035) 42586, Box 276, Kisumu, on Kendu Lane, at Ksh500, bed only.

HOW TO GET THERE

Kenya Airways ((02) 210771 or (02) 229291 FAX (02) 336252 flies once or twice a day between Kisumu and Nairobi. Flight time is one hour, the cost is US$80 one way. Note that in Nairobi, they do not fly from Wilson

Airport but use the International Terminal. Their office in Kisumu ((0345) 44055 FAX (0345) 43339 is on Oginga Odinga Street. Buses and *matatus* leave morning and evening for the six- to eight-hour journey to Nairobi. Trains leave daily for Nairobi at 6 PM, arriving the next morning at 7 AM, although the service can be suspended for long periods, especially during the rainy seasons. Reservations are essential for first- (Ksh2,200) and second- (Ksh1,800) class travel. Kisumu Railway Station is at the lakeside end of New Station Road, and the booking office is open 8 AM to noon and 2 PM to 4 PM.

LAKE VICTORIA TRANSPORTATION

Lake ferries link small towns and islands along the coast to the port, as well as to Mwanza in Tanzania.

Although Kisumu's Port has, over recent years, often been completely clogged with hyacinth, recent breakthroughs using imported weevils to break up the rafts of floating weeds should, if all goes well, open up lake transportation once more. It's not easy, however, to find the passenger port — turn left about midway off Oginga Odinga Road before you get to the Caltex depot and cross to a dilapidated freight yard where you can ask employees for directions to the steamer booking office. There, at a very reasonable price, you should be able to buy a round-trip ticket to any one of several lake communities in Kenya.

Kendu Bay, Kuwur, Asembo Bay and Homa Bay are the main ferry destinations on Lake Victoria, and often there is no way to return to Kisumu until the next day. Similarly, you can leave on Tuesday for Homa Bay, returning Wednesday, or can depart Wednesday and Friday for the port of Mbita (on Rusinga Island) and Mfangano Island, again returning the following day. It's a local boat so fares should vary around the low shilling level. It is possible to get across here to Uganda, although this involves lengthy negotiations with both the immigration department and the skipper of the cargo ferry. The crossing will take 12 hours or more. Be warned that this isn't always a tranquil cruise. The lake can seem placid, then turn rough suddenly.

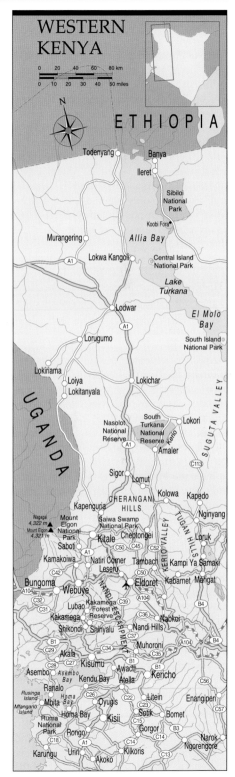

NORTH OF KISUMU

Much of the area between Mount Elgon and Lake Victoria is rolling hills, steep escarpments and narrow valleys. The entire area was once thick tropical rainforest. Kenya's burgeoning population and extensive logging have reduced the original forest to a few scattered remnants, which the government has recently tried to protect by gazetting as forest reserves.

One of the most important of these — well, about the only one that still exists — is the world-famous Kakamega Forest Reserve, located just east of the town of the same name.

KAKAMEGA

Conservationists in Kenya are now attempting to change the status of the Kakamega Forest to a national park, but at present it is just a reserve — and the entry fee is just Ksh100. Unfortunately, this won't pay for any environmental protection measures — well, to be honest not enough visitors make it here anyway — and human encroachment continues apace. The forest, all that remains of the equatorial jungle that once stretched from the Atlantic through the Zaire basin, may not survive for much longer. Kakamega is similar to the equatorial rainforests of West Africa but drier. As a result, much flora and fauna are found in Kakamega Forest that exist nowhere else in Kenya, or probably the world. At least 350 bird species have been identified in the 100 sq km (39 sq miles) that remain of the original forest, including turacos, parrots, trogons, barbets and woodpeckers, honeyguides, greenbuls and crowned hawk eagles.

Whereas the typical North American or European temperate zone forest may contain an average of eight to ten tree species per hectare, equatorial rainforests like Kakamega often have 100 to 150 different tree species per hectare. This amazing diversity of vegetation supports an equal variety of animals; over 40 percent of the mammals in the Kakamega Forest live in the trees, and some amphibians, insects and reptiles never descend to the ground. More than half the mammals inhabiting Kakamega are nocturnal, sleeping during the day in tree hollows or high in the branches.

The proposed Kakamega Forest National Park will provide at least temporary protection to the undamaged part of the forest. This is the portion lying northeast of the town of Kakamega, including nearly half the watershed of the Isiukhu River. However, even if the park is approved, the pressures on the forest are so overwhelming that it will probably not last long as a viable habitat for the rare species still remaining there.

Kakamega's problems are similar to those threatening all the parks, reserves and wildlife of Kenya: logging (both authorized and illegal); firewood collection, which kills young trees; cutting of saplings for household and agricultural use; livestock grazing; and game poaching. The root cause of all these is population growth. Kenya not only has the world's highest birth rate, desertification is expanding and further areas are made unsafe by politically motivated tribal unrest. This means that most of the population settle in areas such as Kakamega and use up its resources.

The flowering plants of Kakamega bloom most colorfully after the long rains, from July to September, when the forest's butterflies are at their peak. From various points in the forest, the hiker can see the grassland, **Nandi Plateau**, escarpments to the east, and the **Kisere Forest** to the north. The major tree species include ebony, podocarp, teak, mukumari (*Cordia africana*) — favored by bees — and seven species of fig including the "strangler fig." The latter is a huge, broad-canopied tree found in most hardwood forests in Kenya, from Lake Victoria to the Matthews Range and the coast. It usually propagates when its fruit is eaten by birds or monkeys, whose droppings may be excreted on the branch of another tree species. The seed then grows, sending down long tendrils to the earth for nutrients and water. Over a period of years, these tendrils multiply, thicken and join, until the fig completely encompasses its host tree, killing it and growing above and around it, to achieve the great height and wide crown often seen in Kakamega.

Specially worth noting in Kakamega Forest are the red-tailed, Sykes' and colobus monkeys, giant forest squirrels up to 65 cm (26 inches) in length and flying squirrels that can glide up to 19 m (60 ft) from tree to tree, the ant-eating tree pangolin, the giant fruit bat, the potto, bushbabies, the rare leopard and more common wild forest hogs, baboons (near the Buyango Hill road), and the occasional duiker that has escaped poaching.

The forest was once home to elephants (exterminated by white hunters before World War I), Cape buffaloes, Uganda kobs (a small,

If bitten, pressure bandages are the only approved method of treatment before medical advice is sought: try to kill the snake for identification. To our knowledge, however, no tourist has expired from snakebite in Kenya for many years.

The Gaboon viper, like its similarly-patterned cousin, the puff adder, which is more common in open country and closer to the coast, is viviparous, bearing its young alive. It may give birth to 80 offspring at a time, all of which, in true snake fashion, are on their own from the moment of birth.

reddish, thickset antelope with ringed horns) and the Defassa waterbuck, all of which are now gone.

Still present, though the tourist is unlikely to see them, are snakes. They include at least five highly poisonous cobras and mambas, and the delightful Gaboon viper, Africa's biggest poisonous snake, which can grow to over two meters (six feet five) and weighs up to 11 kg (25 lbs). Its fangs are over five centimeters (two inches) long. Although its bite is fatal to humans, the Gaboon viper is not usually aggressive unless cornered or annoyed. The tourist who keeps to the trails in Kakamega, and is willing to tread heavily (and carry a big stick), need generally not fear an unscheduled demise by snakebite.

Where to Stay

The **Kakamega Forest Rest House** is famous among ornithologists, naturalists and just plain tourists for self-help rooms in a rotting wooden building set amid a dense grove of trees (US$2 per person); some space is available for camping and if I had a tent I'd use it here. Space is limited, so it's best to make reservations first with the Kakamega Forest Ranger (no phone), Box 88, Kakamega. In any case, accommodation is basic at best. Four kilometers (three miles) to the east is **Rondo Retreat Center** ((0331) 30268 FAX (0331) 20145, $^c/_o$ Trinity Fellowship, Box 2153,

Tranquil Lake Elementeita, another lake where flamingos breed, remains the private domain of the Delamere family.

Kakamega, a restored saw-miller's house where *The Kitchen Toto* was filmed (expensive). Very elegant but no alcohol. For urban comforts you'll need to stay in Kakamega town at the **Golf Hotel** ((02) 229751 or (02) 330820 FAX (02) 227815, Box 42013, Nairobi (mid-range, B&B). It has handsome large rooms overlooking elegant lawns pecked by vultures, a swimming pool and cheerful staff.

How to Get There

Kakamega town is 50 km (31 miles) north of Kisumu on the main A1 road heading north station set among subsistence farms and a recently clear-cut pine forest. If using public transportation, take a *matatu* heading towards Webuye, but you'll have to walk the last stretch from the main road. Going south, you drive 10 km (six miles) toward Shikondi and turn left (east) on to a dirt road at the sign "Forest Rest House" (the sign may be missing, however). Drive the 13 km (eight miles) through the village of Shinyalu, past the reserve boundary and the Isicheno Forest Station and turn left for the last few hundred meters to the Forest

to Lodwar. By public transportation the most frequent *matatus* run from Webuye and Kisumu.

Finding the forest from the town can appear confusing unless you realize that there are two access points into the forest, both, in their way, worth visiting. Thus equally valid directions can send you in opposite directions. With your own vehicle, drive from Kakamega either south toward Kisumu or north toward Webuye. Going north, you pass Lubao and turn right (east) some 16 km (10 miles) from Kakamega, just before the road to Kambiri, at the sign reading "Ministry of Tourism and Wildlife." From there, it's two and a quarter kilometers (nearly one and a half miles) to a forest

Rest House. By public transportation ask for the daily *matatu* traveling between Kakamega town and Eldoret via Shinyalu village and Kapsabet. Ask to be dropped at Isecheno, 10 minutes' walk from the Forest Rest House. At either forest station, it's possible to hire a guide.

South of Kakamega you may see men pushing bicycles laden with large burlap sacks — these are 90-kg (200-lb) bags of maize kernels being transported all the way to Kisumu. Depending where the man began, this may be a distance of 60 km (37 miles) or more, nearly all of it up and down steep hills. For this he receives, if the maize is good, about as much as tourists pay for a quick meal at a lodge.

ELDORET

Above the western edge of the Rift Valley, the countryside levels out on the 2,100-m (7,000-ft) elevation **Uasin Gishu Plateau**. Here are large wheat and cattle spreads intermingled with cedar, fir and pine plantations, reminding one of the American Midwest.

It's hard to imagine this area as the early colonists described it — a veritable paradise filled with animals that had never been hunted. None are to be seen today.

During the Boer War, the area was settled by Afrikaners and in 1912 Eldoret became a town when J.C. Shaw opened a branch of the Standard Bank of South Africa. In *The Mottled Lizard*, Elspeth Huxley describes the event. "[He] had arrived in an oxcart with a too heavy safe which he had pushed out at the back onto a wagon track that traversed the bare, brown plateau. As it was heavy to move, a mud hut had been build round it with two rooms, one for the safe and one for Mr. Shaw. The town then consisted of a few little stores and was called Sixty-four, after the survey number on which it stood. Sixty-four served a sparse community of Afrikaners who had arrived together — men, women, children, babies, predikants and household goods — from Bethel in the Transvaal, and trekked in their semi-covered wagons up roadless, forested escarpment to a promised land."

Today Eldoret is an ideal village. Very much a Moi area, it has had a great deal of investment and, rather to its bemused surprise, has an international airport. So far, however, the only international flights persuaded to land are those on the so-called "slave run" taking workers to Saudi Arabia. It is a center of industry (fabric and leather) and commerce. On the west edge of the shopping district is a small city park, one of the few found outside Nairobi, the state hospital is better than average and there is a private hospital as well, the Uasin Gishu Hospital ((0321) 32720.

Where to Stay and Eat

Whether because it is a commercial center for a large agricultural community or because of its many businessmen trying, over a few cocktails, to find some hometown angle to interest Moi, Eldoret has an abundance of hotels. The best is the **Sirikwa Hotel** ((02) 336858, Box 30741, Nairobi, with a restaurant, bar, and swimming pool (mid-range, B&B). The best of the budget accommodations are the **Kabathaya Hotel and Lodging** ((0321) 22160, Box 832, Eldoret (very inexpensive) and the **New Wagon Wheel** ((0321) 32271 (inexpensive), which does allow camping in the garden.

How to Get There

The international airport ((0321) 61299 is served four time a week by **Kenya Airways** ((02) 210771 or (02) 229291 FAX (02) 336252, Box 41010, Nairobi, flying from Nairobi via Kisumu. Eldoret is on a main freight highway between Kenya and Uganda, with heavy truck traffic and as a result a disintegrating road surface. From Nairobi allow four hours for the journey of 312 km (195 miles). *Matatus* leave from the Nyamakima Bar on Duruma Road in Nairobi, and Akamba buses leave from "Machakos Airport." If heading north the situation is worse: the 70 km (43 miles) between Eldoret and Kitale is dreadful and things don't improve until after Kitale, where most of the trucks turn off for Uganda.

KITALE

Kitale is a pleasant town with a wide tree-lined main street, a large produce market and the **National Museum of Western Kenya**. This small museum has a limited wildlife and ethnology section featuring the Maasai, Turkana, Pokot and Luo tribes. On the grounds are a Turkana village and an agricultural demonstration of "terraced" land to supplement the interior displays on soil conservation; a nature trail leads through a miniature rainforest, a remnant of pre-colonial days. There is also a reasonably priced and usually well-stocked craft shop featuring local wares. Although there's not enough of interest here to plan a lengthy stay, a night here might be inevitable if heading up to Mount Elgon National Park, Saiwa Swamp, or to break the drive to Lodwar and the western shores of Lake Turkana.

The giant groundsel (*Senecio*) grow to 10 m (33 ft) on the highest slopes of Mounts Kenya and Elgon and the Aberdares.

Where to Stay and Eat

There are a number of good mid-range and very inexpensive places to stay in Kitale. The most expensive is the **Kitale Club** ((0325) 20030, Box 30, one kilometer (three-fourths of a mile) on the Eldoret road, an old club that once served as a camp for slaves being marched to export (mid-range). Perhaps this is why the atmosphere isn't that welcoming. Better are the **Lantern** (/FAX 30360, Box 4566, Kenyatta Street, where some rooms have balconies looking out over the town (inexpensive), or the **Alakara Hotel** ((0325) 20395, Box 1984, Kenyatta Street, next to the Post Office (inexpensive). On a real budget the **Mount Loima Lodge** ((0325) 31929, Box 1517, near the market, is adequate (very inexpensive). Those with their own transportation, however, are better off traveling north to take advantage of superb accommodation at Saiwa Swamp (see page 172) or east to Mount Elgon National Park (see page 170).

How to Get There

Kitale is served by several bus companies, of whom the best is Akamba ((0325) 31732. Coming up from Nairobi, book through their River Road office. Seats can be reserved for the return journey, but they only run two buses a day so it is usually a matter of clambering onboard whichever bus looks fullest; Eldoret Express has more departures.

Matatus leave Nairobi for Kitale from the Nyamakima Bar, Duruma Road, every day. Returning, they go every morning to Nairobi (six hours), to Lodwar near Lake Turkana (five hours) and to Kisumu via Kakamega (two hours).

MOUNT ELGON

The massive, cloud-cloaked slopes of Mount Elgon offer a refreshing relief from the hotter parts of Kenya. Mount Elgon, only 877 m (2,877 ft) shorter than Mount Kenya, is far bulkier. In the local language, Maa, the mountain is known as Ol Doinyo Ilgoon, "Breast Mountain," and it massively straddles the Ugandan border. The first European to climb to the top was Frederick Jackson, in 1890.

The highest peak on the rocky crater, Wagagai, at 4,322 m (14,178 ft), is actually in Uganda outside the national park. You may have great trouble getting a guide to take you there, or find yourself on the wrong side of the border without a reentry visa. The Mountain Club of Kenya does not recommend climbing this peak because of the potential border problems and the occasional presence of hostile, armed Ugandan rebels. Recommended instead are short hikes within the park itself, paying the daily fee of US$10 (adult) or US$5 (child), or freely outside the park limits.

Mount Elgon National Park is a hiking and camping paradise that is seldom visited by travellers. Wildlife is plentiful, and there are specified hiking trails to the major caves, along **Elephant Platform**, or to 4,038-m (13,248-ft) **Koitoboss Peak**, the highest of Mount Elgon's peaks in Kenya.

The hiking is especially good because the driving is singularly bad. You will often be denied admission unless you have a four-wheel drive. Indeed, it is doubtful that you could be able to get as far as the gate if you didn't have four-wheel drive. I once met an American family in Kisumu whose rental car could not, even during a dry spell, tackle the steep climb to the Kitum or Elephant Caves, once one of the major attractions in the park.

Along the eastern slope of Mount Elgon is a series of enormous caverns — **Kitum**, **Mkingeny**, and **Chipmyalil Caves**. During colonial times they were inhabited by Maasai and thought to be manmade. Descriptions of them by the explorer Joseph Thomson supposedly inspired the English writer, H. Rider Haggard, to site part of his famed novel *She* in the El Goni caves.

It is now, however, the accepted theory that the caves were dug over the millennia by elephants in search of salt. And there is certainly enough elephant dung on their floors to support this theory. When I visited, I wondered how the elephants could have moved some of the gigantic boulders that littered the floor. This mystery was explained by Mike Clifton, the naturalist at The Ark (see THE ABERDARE MOUNTAINS, page 208). They were deposited there during an earthquake, which coincidentally was filmed.

"A film crew had obtained a permit to set up lights in Kitum Cave to film the elephants at night," Mike said. "On one particular night, while elephants were present and film rolling, the cave ceiling began to fall. The footage was spectacular, with the giant animals fleeing to avoid the shower of rock."

"However, during the next week the director had his film confiscated and his research visa revoked. He was accused of having set off explosives in the cave. Luckily, he was able to prove from seismographic data at the university that there had indeed been an earthquake whose shock waves, not explosives, had caused the rock shower. The footage was recovered and used as part of a television documentary on elephants."

hiking. If they see no problem, the trail starts at the end of the "drivable" track to the northern boundary of the park, and should take from two to three hours. From the peak, a trail leads to the left across glacial moraines down into the crater and the Suam warm springs for a relaxing bath. This walk can be done in a day, but get an early start in order to be out of the park or back to your campsite by the 6:30 PM curfew.

The forests of Mount Elgon are among the most impressive in Kenya, with giant podos (podocarpus), junipers and Elgon

These caves were also the setting for the movie *Quest for Fire*. However, without doubt the caves' biggest claim to international fame was as the suspected epicenter for the Ebola virus — immortalized in the film *The Hot Zone*. Despite several spacesuited research expeditions by American scientific teams, no connection was ever proven. Hard-hit hoteliers blame the international media for yet another scare story. Nonetheless, the caves are eerie, and you'd be wise to bring a flashlight and extra batteries if you wish to explore. Thousands of bats of several species darken the sky as they flock into the dust.

If you want to go to **Koitoboss Peak**, check with the rangers at the entrance of Elgon National Park as to the dangers of

olive trees, the largest variety of olive in East Africa. Some reach heights of 25 m (80 ft). Flowers are abundant in the forest and moorlands at all times of the year, but they are at their peak in June and July, when you can also find several varieties of terrestrial and epiphytic orchids.

The park's animals are extensive but well-hidden. They include the Sykes', brazza and colobus monkeys, olive baboons, civets, genets, the rare golden cat, giant forest hogs, bush pigs, duikers, sunis and bushbucks. Leopards are fairly common but difficult to see, and usually not dangerous. Buffaloes are frequent up to at least 3,000 m (10,000 ft), and

The Mount Elgon Lodge was once a rancher's idyllic estate.

should be treated with extreme caution. Elephants are rare due to poaching, and the black rhino is gone.

Where to Stay

You can either camp in the park or stay at **Mount Elgon Lodge** ((02) 229751 or (02) 330820 FAX (02) 227815, Box 42013, Nairobi (expensive, full board). The lodge is two kilometers (just over a mile) before the Chorlin Gate. Formerly a colonial estate, the lodge has several elegant spacious rooms with large bay windows in the manor house, and double cottages on grounds with sculptured shrubs and formal glades. Alternatively, **Lokitela Farm** (book through Bush Homes of East Africa ((02) 350703, (02) 571661 or (02) 571592 FAX (02) 571665 E-MAIL bushhome @africaonline.co.ke WEB SITE www.bush-homes.co.ke, Box 56923, Nairobi) is a working farm on the slopes of Mount Elgon with a full range of activities and excursions (extremely expensive, all-inclusive).

Days on Mount Elgon are warm, but, like Mount Kenya and the Aberdares, the nights are chilly, near-freezing at the higher campsites. Even when staying in lodges, a sweater and/or jacket will be useful, particularly if there are no logs blazing the dining room's massive two-meter (six-foot) fireplace.

Let's Go Travel ((02) 447151 or (02) 441030 FAX (02) 447270 or (02) 441690 E-MAIL info @letsgosafari.com WEB SITE www.letsgo safari.com, Box 60342, Nairobi, keeps a list of private estates on Mount Elgon which take visitors on an occasional and usually expensive basis; otherwise there are several grassy campsites in the park (US$2 per person), all with running water. **Kapkuru Campground**, 500 m (550 yards) from Chorlin Gate, is at the lowest elevation and would be the best place to stop unless you have plenty of warm clothes and heavy sleeping bags. If you are planning to camp at Mount Elgon, be sure to buy provisions in Kitale. The best way to see Mount Elgon is to camp and hike.

How to Get There

It's not just the security situation nor the limited accommodation that restricts the popularity of Mount Elgon National Park. It's also hard to reach. A four-wheel-drive vehicle is recommended year-round. The best access is through the Chorlin Gate, 27 km (17 miles) from Kitale, via Endebess Road (watch the signs carefully and ask directions if in doubt). It will take the better part of an hour to cover this distance. The road is paved for the first 19 km (12 miles) west from Kitale to the village of Enderbess, which is as far as you'll get by *matatu* — or indeed, saloon car. The rest of the distance to Chorlin Gate is rough — if hitching don't expect more than a couple of vehicles to pass each day.

SAIWA SWAMP NATIONAL PARK

Just north of Kitale is the 26-sq-km (10-sq-mile) Saiwa Swamp National Park, entry US$15 per adult, US$5 per child, created to protect the rare and endangered semi-aquatic sitatunga antelope. First classified by Speke, the sitatunga have highly specialized, splayed and elongated hooves that allow them to spread their weight over a greater area than a normal hoof would permit. They are thus able to move about the swamp, semi-submerged. They swim well and are reputed to submerge, leaving only their nostrils showing, when threatened.

Several tree blinds have been constructed along the western edge of the swamp to provide viewing. As usual, late afternoon and early morning are the best times for watching these normally shy and increasingly rare creatures, but their semi-aquatic lifestyle makes them hard to see. The swamp has also become the home for the white-bearded brazza monkey, and colobus and vervet monkeys, which can be spotted at almost any time of the day. And even if the sitatunga are being shy, there are plenty of bushbucks to keep your interest.

Bird watchers should enjoy the turacos, cuckoos, kingfishers, hornbills and crowned cranes. Following the rains, you will get the extra bonus of innumerable butterflies and mountain orchids. And on very rare occasions, when pushing the dusk curfew, you may find a potto. Perhaps best of all, vehicles can't drive in the swamp so viewing is all on foot.

At any time of the year, the swamp is cool and a wool sweater will be welcome. Also

A rocky outcrop on Mount Elgon.

bring film with a fast ISO (1,000 to 1,600 ISO) rating if you plan to take photos, as there is not much light in the swamp of the sitatunga.

Where to Stay

There is primitive camping (US$2 per person) near the park entrance, with running water, and a *banda* (inexpensive), but this is a bit basic. Better by far to drive six kilometers (just under four miles) to the north to **Sirikwa Safaris Guesthouse and Campsite** ((0325) 20061, Box 332, Kitale, signposted, where the Barnley family offer B&B (expensive to mid-range), camping and *bandas,* as well as guides for hiking and bird watching. This place is one of Kenya's undiscovered secrets and well worth a detour and some time and, most unusually in Kenya, it combines very expensive and comfortable accommodation with more basic accommodation for travelers with less money.

How to Get There

Saiwa Swamp is 18 km (11 miles) north of Kitale off the Lodwar road, while the Barnley's house is six kilometers further on, signposted on the right. There are *matatus* for the determined, leaving from Kitale, but you might well have to pay the fare for the full journey to Lokichar, if not Lodwar. For security reasons, these long-distance *matatus* travel in convoy, leaving at 6 AM and noon.

NORTH FROM KITALE

North of Kitale, banditry and cattle-rustling have caused plenty of security incidents. At time of writing, driving here was only in convoy, but as a result of this there had been no incidents for the last few months. The road has deteriorated too, and only trucks can negotiate the tarmac — cars use the hard shoulder, and even that's slow going. Plenty of time to enjoy the view of the savannas of Trans-Nzoia and along the western and northern slopes of the Cherangani Hills but, in convoy, the only chance to stop is when a vehicle breaks down. After Kapenguria, the last gas before Lodwar, the scenery changes from open rolling hills to steep, forested mountains as you climb Marich Pass. On a clear day to the northwest, you can see jagged, unusually shaped mountains, the

tallest of which is 3,068-m (10,066-ft) Mount Kadam, beyond the Uganda border.

Descending the pass, the road follows the Moran River, clear and fast-running over large granitic boulders. Emerging from the Cherangani Hills, you again look down into the Rift Valley with its extinct volcanoes of varying sizes. To the northwest is 3,325-m (10,910-ft) **Sigogowa** or **Mtelo Mountain,** the Pokot sacred mountain and one of the sources of the Turkwell River. The Pokot bury their dead on the mountain with their heads facing the summit. It used to be possible to hike to the top of Sigogowa, but this is no longer considered safe. Should things change the easiest climb is from the village of **Sigor,** the major Pokot market center, on the north side of Marich Pass.

As you continue north toward the Jade Sea, the scenery becomes less and less varied, more alien. Familiar vegetation begins to disappear as the land becomes more and more arid.

As you go north tall thorn trees dry to sparser, squatter thornscrub to golden grasses and doum palms. And the soils change as well. The traditional African red fades to coral, then pastel pink, and finally to sandy white. The few clouds are like puffballs; dust devils swirl about the barren volcanic hills and across dry river beds where women and children dig for water. There are the familiar livestock — goats, sheep, and cows — but now there are also camels, blending into the sandy scenery. Hares, squirrels, gazelles, sunis and jackals are the major, though scarce, wildlife.

LOKICHAR

The only settlement of any size along the route is Lokichar, where a local mission has organized an excellent Turkana crafts cooperative (which is closed on Sundays). The shop is well stocked with baskets and mats, Turkana bead necklaces and bracelets, wrist and finger knives, carvings, bowls and beaded goat skin aprons. The variety is great, the quality good, the prices fair. There is no middleman taking a cut, so I recommend that you not bargain too ruthlessly here. The proprietor told us that it took a week to make a basket that I purchased for

Ksh40. It is hard to offer less. There's no-where here to stay, however, and no very good reason to tarry.

Lokichar and Lodwar have the unfortunate history of being sites of Kenyatta's detention by the English during the Mau Mau Rebellion. Even today with a paved road they seem remote and it is easy to imagine how alien they must have seemed to Kenyatta, with no electricity or guaranteed source of water after the lushness of Kikuyuland. Certainly the lack of green was a great deprivation to one so unjustly detained.

LODWAR

Lodwar's inauspicious history began in 1933 when a Pakistani trader, Shah Mohammed, arrived with his donkey on the banks of the seasonal Turkwell River. He eventually built a permanent trading center which today is the last stop on the road to Sudan. It now has a 24-hour gas station, and is supported by aid agencies heading north to work in Sudan and smuggled goods coming the other way. Optimistic talk of oil in the region has evaporated and hustlers are especially determined to milk every possible shilling out of the few tourists who brave the drive up from the south. Watch out for these. Most foreigners here are heading for Lake Turkana and there are countless "guides" offering to help. Few of them have been so far, and are totally panicked when they are hired for the trip. Many travelers head for the lake, lured by tales of mythical ferries and dreamtime lodges, only to end up having to sleep in the bush. Sometimes they are then robbed. When they report to the police the reaction is "How could you be so stupid." Hard to say. Perhaps it is the dry, dusty desert that induced some sort of dissociation from reality — and normal caution. For Kenyans it's a hardship posting: teachers, civil servants and soldiers all dread being sent here.

The town blends old and new. On its outskirts are traditional Turkana straw domed-huts. In town, radios blare from concrete buildings. There are a few *hotelis* and restaurants, and large missionary complexes competing for members, one offering "Salvation Music."

Where to Stay and Eat

This is one place where having a fan is recommended. Air conditioning would be better, but at the time of writing, in a hot dusty town that could really do with some, there isn't any. The best place to stay is the politically very correct **Nawoitorong Guest House** ((0393) 21208 FAX (0393) 21572 E-MAIL edfrh @imul.com, Bow 192, Lodwar, run by Turkana women as part of an educational co-operative (very inexpensive). You can spend a bit more at the **Lodwar Club** ((0393) 21252, Box 123, Lodwar, but it's a bit rundown (inexpensive). Both these places are to the east of the town center. In town, the **Turkwel Lodge** ((0393) 21201, Box 14, Lodwar, though it can be noisy, especially at weekends (very inexpensive, B&B). *Matatus* drop their fares at the **Salama Hotel** (no phone), which has basic inexpensive rooms and one of the best restaurants in town, though no alcohol or smoking is permitted.

How to Get There

With difficulty. Lodwar is beyond the reach of bus services, but not far enough for scheduled flights which, depending entirely on aid workers, fly further north. With your own car it is 355 km (222 miles) north of Kitale. It's no closer by *matatu* and it doesn't feel it either, although at least, because they have to travel in armed convoy, at least don't stop too often to pick up fares.

TURKANA'S WESTERN SHORE

Of the two settlements on the western shores of Lake Turkana, Ferguson's Gulf (of which the local village is called Kalokol) and Eliye Springs, neither has many facilities of any sort. Whichever you choose, be ready for an experience of unreality and strangeness. The air is dry, the sun so intense that all color fades. But then there are minute variations in the landscape — bleached sand, golden grasses, sapphire sky and jade lake. Occasionally there is a dash of green, but only in the first week following the rains in October and November or April and May. They dry all too quickly.

The sun rises red to announce each new day as hippopotamuses return to the coolness of the lake. Young Turkana begin their march to the sea to fill sundry containers with the brackish water. Some pause for a quick, playful swim, always aware they share the water with crocodiles. Sacred ibis patrol the shore, cormorants bob for fish and Egyptian geese float silently.

Later the young men arrive with nets which they lay from their raft-like boats to trap Nile perch. Mothers bring their infants to bathe. Children chase and scream along the shore. Some make a game out of washing clothes, stamping on them in their wash buckets as if they were mashing grapes.

For the young, school has been added to this rhythm. Most learn the standard Kenyan curriculum in a thatch hut among the dunes; those whose parents can afford it go to the boarding school in Lokwa Kangoli. What changes education will make in their age-old lifestyle in this dry, fragile environment cannot be foretold.

Their survival is constantly being threatened. The waters of Lake Turkana recede and return, mocking any attempts to build harbors or fish-canning plants funded by overseas aid agencies. Onshore, growing

The shore is a hub of measured activity: graceful human figures gliding on shimmering sand, a herd of sheep and goats browsing the tan, gilded grass, a white, glinting scatter of shorebirds. Northward, the land leaves a blank horizon, where the Jade Sea extends forever carrying your eye off the edge of the globe straight into space in which this earth floats like a tiny speck in a more infinite sea.

As sunset approaches, a glow creeps across the sky like a giant jacaranda dropping its purple snow, and people move gracefully, loads atop their heads, back to their dune dwellings. All is silent except for the snorts of hippos as they leave the water to graze along the shore until the sun rises red again.

African desertification and global climate change are certainly contributing to a long-term change.

Fish have proved the lifeline. In an increasingly competitive market, fish from Lake Turkana are now transported south for sale in the markets around Lake Victoria.

Unlike most national parks and reserves, Turkana's shores can be explored on foot. Although there are plenty of crocodiles, they are generally scared of man and don't appear to be a problem. Trailing gangs of small children are more of a problem, and will make life unbearable for hot, sweaty backpackers traveling on foot. Distances, around the shrinking lake, are huge and the climate unforgiving. Early morning and late afternoon are still the best times because the midday sun is unmercifully hot. Along the shore you can find giant Nile perch skeletons, which I first took to be crocodile bones; and some of the many children who will try to accompany you on your expeditions will offer to sell you croc teeth — the Crocodile Dundees of Africa. They will also pose for a photographic fee, request T-shirts and give you their addresses if you wish to strike up a friendship. If you want to see crocodile bones ask one of the children to show you the way.

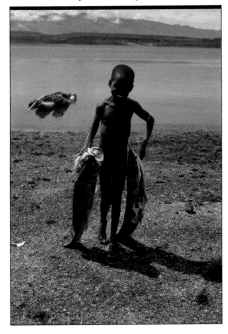

Admittedly there is not a great variety of destinations or sights to see, but the ephemeral quality of the environment weaves its spell.

Where to Stay and Eat

Eliye Springs used to have *bandas* and a lodge, but this is now only a primitive campsite. Water is usually available, but before making the rough 42-km (26-mile) drive, check in Lodwar if anyone knows the latest status of the place. In any event make sure you have enough water for at least one day. The site is usually deserted and tranquil. You will, however, probably be visited by local children once the nearby village becomes aware of your presence. Very few visitors make it here.

Ferguson's Gulf does, in the village of Kalokol, have a few basic huts that will take in visitors. There is also the remains of a luxury lodge: the **Lake Turkana Fishing Lodge** (no phone now) which still serves warm drinks and has rotting *bandas* (inexpensive). The only halfway reasonable place to stay in the area at all is **Lebolo Lodge** (contact through Bush Homes of East Africa ((02) 350703, (02) 571661 or (02) 571592 FAX (02) 571665 E-MAIL bushhome@africaonline.co.ke WEB SITE www.bush-homes.co.ke, Box 56923, Nairobi), which is set in an idyllic lakeside oasis between Eliye Springs and Ferguson's Gulf (very expensive). This is run by long-time Turkana veteran Halewijn Scheuermann and guests here benefit not just from his effective and reliable trucks and boats, but also from his unparalleled local knowledge.

How to Get There

To reach the western shore of Lake Turkana, you continue 24 km (15 miles) north of Lodwar before choosing a lakeside destination — turn right on a dirt road for the 48 km (30 mile) trip to Eliye Springs or stick to the *murram* for the 42 km (26 mile) journey to Ferguson's Gulf. Only Ferguson's Gulf is regularly served by *matatu*: there's one most days, and the trip takes about an hour. Travelers are dropped off at the village of Kalokol and left to walk to the lakeshore past endless Turkana settlements. Harried by local Turkana kids, this can take two hours. Most visitors find their two-litre water bottle lasts them outbound, but there's nowhere to buy another for the long, hot, walk back. Many travelers arrive here looking for a ferry across the lake but there isn't one. Don't sleep out here waiting for onward transportation because this won't eventuate and you will probably get robbed.

CENTRAL ISLAND NATIONAL PARK

One excursion from Ferguson's Gulf is a half-day trip to Central Island National Park. The problem here is finding a boat that will do it, and the park fee of US$15 per adult and US$5 per child will be the least of your prob-

OPPOSITE AND ABOVE: Turkana's El Molo tribe, which subsists principally on fish, is not averse to eating crocodile.

lems. At time of writing, the only person able to organize reliable transportation was the manager of Lebolo Lodge (see above).

Approximately 20 km (12 miles) southeast of Ferguson's Gulf, this island sanctuary is the most concentrated breeding ground for crocodiles in Africa. The five-square-kilometer (two-square-mile) island is three connected volcanic cones, two of which contain fresh water lakes. The island shores are black lava sand and rock, and the vegetation thorny, bleached scrub.

The southern and smallest cone, a five- to ten-minute hike from the shore, is the domain of the crocodiles, a turquoise rimmed lake with an iridescent, almost algal verdancy of brilliant scrub. From the rim above you can see crocodiles cruising like immense sunken logs, only the knobs of their eyes showing. If you are in Kenya during April and May, this crater can be "the" place to be, and not just to get away from the rain. It's hatching season and the crater is alive with squeaks and yelps of the young, who will spend their first year here before heading out to the Jade Sea. Some, however, spend their entire lives in the crater.

A morning trip is usually the best for viewing the reptiles, while the afternoon excursions frequently include a trip to the northern cauldron and its pink flamingos standing one-legged along the shore. As there are supposedly no crocs here, I once climbed down the steep dusty trail to the water's edge. Scorpions leapt from a trailside boulder as I descended. The flamingos rose and circled to the far side of the lake, which is larger than it appears from above. Butterflies rode the updrafts. I walked across the hard, cracked mud where scorpions nest. Further on, flat pinnacles of calcified mud rose above the water, where you can walk as if they were stepping stones. The water's edge is thick with algae and almost too hot to touch. Across the lake the flamingos can appear like a pink ribbon edging the brown pleated crater wall.

Central Island has more than its share of shorebirds, a few hippos and a resident lizard population. I saw several lava-colored reptiles over a meter (a yard) long. As I left,

The barren shorelines of Lake Turkana, the Jade Sea.

four hippos decided they'd had enough of the tourists for the day and blocked the route of the boat. Making light of what could have been a nasty situation, one of our French companions for the trip joked that the hippos only wanted to have their photos taken and to give us their address. And what's more they didn't ask for Ksh20!

If you are on a tight budget, you can sometimes find a local fisherman who'll take you to Central Island for about Ksh500 per boat and hope the park ranger isn't around. If you go this route make sure the boat is seaworthy and has plenty of fuel, and that the crew is experienced. Turkana's weather can change suddenly and winds can quickly whip up meter-tall waves.

For a trip to the island, wear sturdy shoes: sandals just won't make it. Bring a hat, sun screen and water. The island is hot by 10 AM and remains so until dusk.

ACROSS THE LAKE

The third and most exciting of opportunities is a two or three day trip across the lake to **Sibiloi National Park** and a visit to **Koobi Fora** (see page 200). Other than flying to Sibiloi, this is the most comfortable, relaxing way to get there, and crossing Lake Turkana is exhilarating, unless of course you are prone to seasickness. The crossing is not something that can be easily achieved on the spur of the moment: it's not a trip to make in an unreliable boat and in any case you will need to be sure there is a vehicle — with gasoline — at Allia Bay. Plans for the journey must be made in advance: **Let's Go Travel** ((02) 447151 or (02) 441030 FAX (02) 447270 or (02) 441690 E-MAIL info@letsgo safari.com WEB SITE www.letsgosafari.com, Box 60342, Nairobi, can help with charter flights, though for boat transport from Ferguson's Gulf you'll need **Bush Homes of East Africa** ((02) 350703, 571661, 571592 FAX (02) 571665 E-MAIL bushhome@africaon line.co.ke WEB SITE www.bush-homes.co.ke, Box 56923, Nairobi.

From Ferguson's Gulf it takes about three hours to make the crossing to Allia Bay or Koobi Fora. Time of departure depends on the weather; usually the water calms in the afternoon.

At Allia Bay, a guide with a four-wheel drive meets any arrivals and takes them to the *bandas*, prepares any meals (if you've brought food — otherwise you'll starve) and provides transportation to archaeological digs and on game drives. There's no guarantee they'll have gas, however, so bring your own.

For this trip you will have to be self-sufficient. Apart from sturdy shoes, hat, sun screen, wind breaker and a change or two of clothes, don't forget food, fuel and water.

Lake Turkana does exert a spell, and many visitors try to include it into their visit to Kenya. However they often expect to be able to include it into a round-trip journey taking in both western and eastern shores. This rarely works. Few if any boats seem to make grueling crossing between Ferguson's Gulf to Loyangalani where there is, in any case, no reliable transportation south. A speedboat will take at least six hours to do the journey, and if you go with local fishermen you're looking at an adventure that will take a week or so. Those wishing to "close the circle," therefore, will be disappointed. It is worth the trip as there is something captivating about the hot, dusty frontier atmosphere of the northern towns, but you should bear in mind that neither side of the lake is especially secure, and armed cattle-rustlers and bandits travel with far more freedom than motor-bound visitors. Check locally for the current security situation.

The only way back from Ferguson's Gulf is the way you came. There's a certain pleasure in this expedition into the arid north, however. On your return colors are one by one added to the previously monochrome landscape until you are once again into the verdant greens of the Marich Pass. It probably didn't seem quite so green or cool on your northward journey.

An El Molo, fishing from his *ambach* raft, pulls in a crocodile.

The Northern Rift Valley

The East African Rift Valley is supposedly large enough to be seen with the naked eye from the moon, and it runs over 8,000 km (4,960 miles) from Ethiopia on the Red Sea to Mozambique on the southern Indian Ocean. Formed some 20 to 40 million years ago by faulting and warping, continuing still as the tectonic plates floating on the earth's crust pull apart, the Great Rift contains seven lakes in Kenya (Magadi, Naivasha, Elmenteita, Nakuru, Bogoria, Baringo, and Turkana) and is liberally punctured with both recent and ancient volcanic craters. Of these lakes, Magadi and Naivasha are featured in the NAIROBI AND AROUND chapter, on pages 132 and 135 respectively. This chapter will detail the Great Rift lakes of Nakuru, Bogoria and Baringo, the town of Nyahururu, the Laikipia district up to Maralal, as well as the route up to Lake Turkana's eastern shore. The road systems and communications make this a logical way to proceed.

LAKE NAKURU

Lake Nakuru, one of the most beautiful of the Rift Valley lakes, can be visited in a long day trip from Nairobi or an overnight stopover on safari going north or west. The perimeter is protected as a national park, though it is a little manicured and enclosed, and if Menengai Crater and Hyrax Hill Archaeological Site are included then there's enough to keep a visitor busy for two days or more.

Alkaline Lake Nakuru was first mapped by Major Thomson, as was the nearby, smaller **Lake Elmenteita**, which is privately owned by the descendants of Lord Delamere. Lake Nakuru completely evaporated during a dry period from 1939 to 1940, but filled up again during the mid-1940s. By the end of the 1950s it was dry again, and dust devils whipped up and scattered white soda sediments over nearby farm fields. The dust often traveled 64 km (40 miles) away, threatening the productivity of the agricultural lands. The lake refilled in the 1960s and has remained wet ever since.

The lake is world-famous as the feeding ground of both lesser and greater flamingos, which can be distinguished by size and the color of their bill. The lesser flamingo has a deep carmine-red bill, the greater a pink one with black tip. The lesser also has a deeper pink plumage, but unless both species are present, it is difficult to use this as a basis for identification.

Lake Nakuru and a wide strip of shoreline were made a national park in the 1960s and entry is US$27, US$10 for children. It was estimated then that there were, at times, more than a million flamingos on the lake. Ornithologist Roger Tory Peterson described it as "the most fabulous bird spectacle in the world." The concentration of flamingos fluctuates greatly, depending on which of the soda Rift Valley lakes (Magadi, Elmenteita, Bogoria, Turkana or Nakuru) has the best food supply, but even when food is more abundant elsewhere, there are sizable flocks of flamingos on Lake Nakuru.

A species of alkaline-tolerant fish, tilapia, was introduced into the lake in the 1970s, and the number of resident white pelicans has since increased substantially. On the southern and northeastern shores are blinds and viewing platforms from which you can watch the pelicans and flamingos.

Besides the more than 400 species of birds that can be seen in the park there are hippos, reedbucks, waterbucks, bushbucks and, recently introduced, Rothschild's giraffes and black rhinoceros — which are now fenced and under tight security since the poaching of the white rhinoceros in Meru National Park in 1988. Between the lake and the cliffs in the west, large pythons inhabit the dense woodland, and can often be seen crossing the roads or dangling from trees.

MENENGAI CRATER

The 11-km-wide (seven-mile) Menengai Crater is one of the largest in the world. Although you get the best view of it from the Nyahururu–Nakuru road, the easiest access is from Nakuru. When the first European settlers arrived, they found the crater and the surrounding area surprisingly void of inhabitants. Later archaeological finds, however, indicate that the area had been inhabited since prehistoric times.

OPPOSITE AND FOLLOWING PAGES: Once a single tribe, the Samburu and Maasai maintain many original dances and traditions.

Legends about the Menengai volcano, whose name in Maa means "corpse," may account for the lack of nineteenth-century inhabitants. Several tell of scouting and raiding parties venturing into the crater never to be seen again. One story relates how the now-extinct Ilaikipiak tribe celebrated their victory over the neighboring Ilpurko by throwing themselves to death in the Menengai. They supposedly gathered at the edge of the crater, gorged themselves on looted meat, and finally called upon God to witness their mass suicide, as there was nothing left for them to live for since they had defeated everyone worthy of their prowess. Another version claims that the Ilpurko pushed hundreds of Ilaikipiak warriors over the crater rim. Today, there is a satellite tracking station on the rim, although the bush-covered lava floor 500 m (1,600 ft) below is still relatively uninhabited.

The crest of the crater is about eight kilometers (five and a half miles) from Nakuru; follow Menengai Road to Crater Climb. There is a path from the signed, but now defunct, "Campsite and Picnic Area," past the satellite tracking station to a lookout tower. Only on a clear day will you be able to see the opposite wall of the crater. Hiking to the crater is best done with a guide, for reasons of security.

HYRAX HILL

Six kilometers (four miles) east of Nakuru is Hyrax Hill, one of three archaeological sites managed by the National Museum (Koobi

Fora and Olorgasailie are the others). It is open to the public at Ksh200 per person. Here, in 1926, Louis Leakey discovered utensils and bones, some dating from the Neolithic period. Mary Leakey's excavations during 1937 and 1938 uncovered dwellings, a fort, livestock enclosures, a burial mound and a great variety of bones, utensils, obsidian fragments and pottery remnants.

Most of the site has been dated to the late Kenyan Iron Age (the fifteenth and sixteenth centuries AD), but one burial ground is Neolithic. A large stone slab that once sealed it has been removed to display the bones of Stone Age inhabitants. In another site to the north, 19 more Neolithic graves were discovered in an Iron Age burial site. It is interesting to note that in the Neolithic graves, women were buried with their tools, while men were buried alone. This might indicate that even then African women did the bulk of the physical labor — they certainly do today.

There is a small museum housing the finds from the dig and you can walk along the rocks to see the dwellings and burial mounds. An excellent guide, which will help you identify the sites, is on sale in the museum and your entry includes a guided tour by the museum's curator. The site is a bumpy two kilometers (one and a half miles) off the main Nairobi road.

WHERE TO STAY AND EAT

Accommodation is available in the park or in Nakuru town just north of the main gate. Within the park are **Sarova Lion Hill** ((02) 713333 FAX (02) 715566 E-MAIL reservations @sarova.co.ke, Box 72493, Nairobi (expensive, full board); **Lake Nakuru Lodge** ((02) 226778, Box 561, Nairobi (expensive, full board); and camping facilities (US$15 per person), most with running water, but you are warned not to leave anything valuable at your campsite.

The best of the town lodgings is the rather soulless **Midlands Hotel** ((037) 212125, Box 908, Nakuru (inexpensive), or the central **Waterbuck Hotel** ((037) 215672 FAX (037) 214163, Box 3227, Nakuru (inexpensive). As Kenya's fourth largest city, Nakuru also has a great variety of *hotelis* (which can mean anything from the most basic food-hut to a modest hotel), some small restaurants and even a couple of discos, but the town itself has little charm and what character it has is not very prepossessing.

HOW TO GET THERE

Nakuru is three to four hours' drive from Nairobi, an hour and a half beyond Naivasha on the A104 Uplands Road. The lake is 158 km (99 miles) northwest of Nairobi. Motorists should watch out for Nakuru's mechanics: they're famous for staging or faking mechanical breakdowns and then dragging out repairs. A steady stream of buses and *matatus* link Nakuru with Nairobi.

LAKE BOGORIA NATIONAL RESERVE

Some 30 km (19 miles) south of Lake Baringo, as the ruddy duck flies, is Lake Bogoria, a national reserve. This small equatorial lake has geysers and hot springs. There are relatively few good vantage points, but its topaz and green water is strikingly beautiful.

The Maasai know the lake as Mbatibat, the Tugen as Makwaria, and before independence the maps called it Lake Hannington, named for the Bishop of Uganda, who was supposedly the first European to see it. Though history is somewhat vague on the subject, it has been accepted that in 1885 James Hannington, en route to his missionary post in Uganda, sighted the lake from a point, now called **Hannington's Lookout**, northwest of Nyahururu near Chepkererat, and not easily accessible. Hot and thirsty, Hannington's party climbed down the steep wall of the Rift only to discover the water was saline. His luck did not improve: upon arrival in Uganda he was murdered by the Bagandas as he tried to cross the White Nile.

In 1902, the English adventurer/chronicler, Sir Harry Johnston, wrote that a forest of large trees in the center was slowly dying, and speculated that there must have been recent geological activity or an overflow from Lake Baringo. However, nothing supports these theories, and local traditions claim that the lake had always been here, with or without the dying forest.

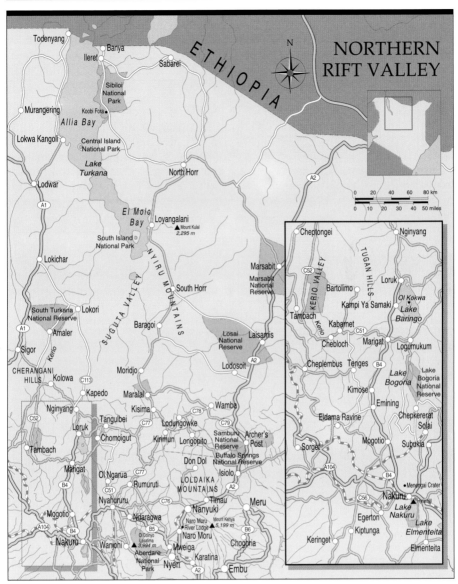

NORTHERN RIFT VALLEY

Sir Harry also noted a large population of flamingos and photographed their nests. Today you can occasionally see some of these giant, pink birds, but they no longer nest in Bogoria's mud.

Along Lake Bogoria's western shore is a bed of hot springs and blowholes that infrequently erupt two and a half to three meters (eight to ten feet) into the air and constantly emit a pungent sulfur smell. These geothermal phenomena are intriguing, but also dangerously hot. Often the surrounding crust cannot support much weight and recently

a visitor fell through the crust and was boiled to death.

Lake Bogoria National Reserve entry fees are US$15 per adult and US$5 for children.

WHERE TO STAY

The **Lake Bogoria Hotel** (/FAX (037) 40748, Box 208, Menengai West, is three kilometers (two miles) north of Loboi Gate, making use of the hot springs for one of its swimming pools, but it is overpriced and strangely dull (expensive). However there are several campsites. The best, and well worth the trip for a relaxing day in the water, is **Fig Tree Campground**, book through the warden ((037) 40746, Box 64, Marigat (US$2 per person, paid at the reserve gate). The campground is on the banks of a crystal clear, drinkable spring which flows into several natural whirlpools.

HOW TO GET THERE

Access to this little-visited reserve leaves much to be desired. No public transportation

400 species of birds. It has an average depth of only eight meters (25 ft) and its three islands (Gibraltar, Teddy Bear and Ol Kokwa) are breeding grounds for the statuesque one-and-a-half-meter (five-foot) Goliath heron, the largest of the heron species.

The area is home to many communities of Njemps, one of three Maa-speaking tribes in Kenya. The others are the Maasai in the south and Samburu in the north. They are unusual in that they have broken the pastoralist's traditional taboo of not eating fish, and live on a mixed diet of fish

reaches it, and you need a four-wheel drive unless the weather has been particularly dry. The road from Nakuru is not recommended. It is easier, and, in the end, quicker, to approach Lake Bogoria from Lake Baringo, 30 km (19 miles) to the north.

LAKE BARINGO

Lake Baringo is a good stopover site to break the long drive across the Rift Valley, or for a two-day trip from Nairobi. Because it is now accessible by paved road from Nairobi, it has become a popular Kenyan weekend destination. This brown saline lake is the most northern of Kenya's six small Rift Valley lakes and is home of hippos, crocodiles and over

and goat meat. Their one-man boats are made from ambach trees, which grow around the lake. Like those used by the Turkana, these raft-like craft float semi-submerged, giving the occupant the appearance of sitting atop the water. Most of the inhabitants of the Lake Baringo area are from one of two Kalenjin tribes, the Pokot and the Tugen. President Moi is Tugen, which may explain the high quality of the roads in this area. They are primarily pastoralists and the land around the lake is severely overgrazed and eroded as a result. If you visit the lake after a rain, the water will have a distinct red tone, while during the dry season (July to September, January to March) it appears browner.

The surrounding countryside is arid, red-soiled and sparsely vegetated with several types of the omnipresent thorn trees and candelabra euphorbias. Termite castles of every size and shape abound. After the rainy seasons, the hillsides are dotted with bright pink but poisonous desert roses.

The shores are a mixture of sand and marsh, which provides some cover and shade for the resident hippos. Many visitors swim and water ski in the lake, which is supposed to be free of bilharzia.

I have seen no crocodiles in Baringo, and a few people swimming round the dock at Ol Kokwa Island. By all local accounts there have been more problems with hippos than crocs. Only the month before I arrived, one boat was attacked and another smashed by angry hippopotamuses. Because the lake is shallow, these aquatic giants can be found anywhere, not just along the shores. Apparently the sound of boat motors particularly annoys them; they are also known to kill people for getting between them and the water, which is their traditional refuge when they feel under threat. If you want to swim, the less-accessible Lake Bogoria (see above) or the swimming pools at Lake Baringo's two lodges might be safer and considerably more relaxing.

WHERE TO STAY

Accommodation options at Lake Baringo are varied. There are a couple of *hotelis* in Kampi Ya Samaki, the only town on the lake, but head out to the waterfront and **Betty Roberts's Campsite** ((0328) 51403 (between 10 AM and noon), Box 1051, Nakuru, with *bandas* for Ksh500 per person or campsites for Ksh400, is one of the nicest campgrounds in Kenya; with running water and showers, and no extra charge for grazing hippos at night.

Next to Betty Roberts's is the luxurious **Lake Baringo Lodge** ((02) 540780 FAX (02) 543810 E-MAIL blockreservations@net2000ke .com, Box 40075, Nairobi, which has very comfortable doubles for US$126 with full board. This is also a good place to eat while staying at Betty's. Because of the influx of weekend travelers, the lodge has a Ksh100 entrance fee for visitors to their bar, gardens, swimming pool and hippo-viewing pier. It

is often waived. As an added attraction, they offer guided bird-watching walks with 400 species to spot.

Just north of town is the dock where boats leave for Ol Kokwa Island. **Island Camp** (make reservations with Let's Go Travel ((02) 447151 or (02) 441030 FAX (02) 447270 or (02) 441690 E-MAIL info@letsgo safari.com WEB SITE www.letsgosafari.com, Box 60342, Nairobi) is a luxurious and peaceful tented camp with double tents for US$200 full board. If you have a day to spend at the lake the island is probably the

most interesting way to spend it; the boat ride costs Ksh600 round trip. You can walk on the island, which is inhabited by thousands of birds, a few waterbuck, and several hundred Njemps and their livestock.

HOW TO GET THERE

The instructions I was given to get to Lake Baringo on my first visit were "Leave Nairobi on the Naivasha Road and at the second roundabout go right," and the directions were spot on. It was more than two hours

OPPOSITE: Remnants of a prehistoric dwelling on the slopes of Hyrax Hill, one of several archaeological sites open to the public. ABOVE: Leafy Lake Baringo Lodge is popular with weekend visitors to the lake.

before I hit the first roundabout (traffic circle) at Naivasha and another hour and a half to the second at Nakuru. Overall, the drive takes about five hours, with the road starting off laden with trucks and buses but improving steadily all the way. By public transportation, frequent buses and *matatus* service Nakuru from Nairobi and other towns, and it is reasonably easy to arrange onward travel to Marigat. From there transportation is likely to become infrequent for the last 21 km (13 miles); carry plenty of water.

NORTH AND WEST FROM LAKE BARINGO

Going north from Lake Baringo is not currently recommended. Although there are two alternative routes that take you through equally beautiful though different terrain, the area is at the heart of some of Kenya's worst tribal conflict. Take advice locally and see if the situation has calmed. Look forward to some difficult driving conditions in any case: the situation does not encourage road maintenance.

There is a choice of routes heading west. The more difficult route heads north from Baringo through Loruk and Nginyang, then crosses the Kerio Valley and River to Tot at the foot of the Elgeyo Escarpment and swings north to Sigor, where it picks up the new section of A1 that goes north to Lake Turkana and Sudan. North of Tot a second dirt track can be taken roughly following the Kerio River through the South Turkana National Reserve and meeting another dirt track from Baringo and Kapedo, then meeting the A1 finally in Lokichar. The latter is a four-wheel-drive adventure through barren hill and desert scrub, crossing the northern end of the magnificent, desolate Suguta Valley, one of the hottest — and the most dangerous — places on earth. During the rains and for several weeks after (or possibly months depending on the scheduling of road crews) these roads are impassable. Even during the dry seasons (July to September, January to March) this route can be dangerous and should only be attempted if you are fully contained (food, water, camping gear, etc.) and have a full tank of gas and at least two full jerrycans.

Timewise it is just as quick to take the longer paved route, a 20-minute drive south from Lake Baringo to Marigat and then west. This is itself a beautiful drive and along some of the best roads in the country, a butter-smooth ribbon of little-used pavement, dotted with local farmers selling wild honey, formerly the route of the East African Rally through President Moi's hometown of Kabarnet to Eldoret. The route begins at Marigat, 19 km (12 miles) south of Lake Baringo. From Marigat, the road climbs steeply into the Tugen or Ilkamasya Hills, offering magnificent vistas of Lake Baringo and, from one upper point, Lake Bogoria, as well as numerous volcanic craters, reminders of the turbulent eruptions that have pockmarked the land over millions of years. The high country, only a little less arid than the lake valley floor, is predictably covered with thorn scrub, but where possible the Tugen have terraced the slopes to grow maize.

Perched atop the Tugen Hills, **Kabarnet** overlooks the lush Kerio Valley. As the administrative center for the Baringo District, the town has complete shopping facilities, a multitude of government buildings and the recently constructed **Kabarnet Hotel** ((02) 336858, Box 109, Kabarnet (inexpensive, B&B).

The **Kerio Valley**, with some of Kenya's richest agricultural land, is a welcome relief after the browns and reds of the lakes. (If you are traveling this section in reverse — Eldoret to Marigat — you probably won't be so impressed with the lush greens or the variety of crops.)

Approaching the western slope of the Kerio Valley, the Tambach or Elgeyo Escarpment, you can't help but wonder how the road will ever get to the top of these sheer, wooded cliffs. But it does in 15 km (nine miles) of twisting, hairpin turns that are a challenge to negotiate in any vehicle. Imagine what these must have been like before they were paved!

About halfway up the escarpment, just past the village of Tambach, you get a full view of **Torok Falls**. If you want to walk to them you will have to do it from Tambach, where you can usually find a guide who will gladly show you the way or accompany you for Ksh30 and provide some local history as well.

NYAHURURU

Leaving Mombasa on March 15, 1883, Joseph Thomson led a ragtag group of 113 "vagabond" porters and other African coastal sailors on what was to be the grandest safari of them all, the first to cross Maasailand and reach the shores of the fabled lake which would be called Victoria, passing by the cascades now called Nyahururu, which in honor of himself he named Thomson's Falls.

Already a famed naturalist and explorer at the age of 24, Thomson was engaged by the Royal Geographical Society to discover if a practicable route existed across Maasailand to Lake Victoria and Uganda. He was soon intercepted by Maasai north of Kilimanjaro, an advance guard of the same *morans* (warriors) who had ambushed Gustav Fischer's party at Hell's Gate the year before. Thomson was forced to retreat to Taveta and then to make a 323-km (200-mile) dash all the way back to Mombasa in just six days.

Rather than give up, he recruited more men and joined an Arab ivory and slave trading caravan as far as Kilimanjaro. From there the Maasai harassed him all the way through the Satima mountains, which he renamed the Aberdares after the president of the Royal Geographical Society. He finally convinced the Maasai he was a wizard by removing, then replacing, a false front tooth and offering to do the same to a warrior's nose, by using a battery to shock them, and by making a magical potion of fizzy Eno fruit salts. After an abortive attempt to reach the top of Mount Kenya, he was forced once more to retreat from the banks of the Ewaso Ngiro by threats of a Maasai attack.

With great relief he passed out of Maasai country, reaching the shores of Lake Victoria on Christmas day, from there traveling north to Mount Elgon, where he visited the Elephant Caves. On the last day of 1883, while hunting for his New Year's dinner, he shot a buffalo which vengefully gored him and tossed him over its shoulder, and which then was killed by one of his men as it prepared to give him the *coup de grace*. Badly injured, Thomson was carried on a litter back to

Meal time for a gerenuk who knows the freshest nibbles are higher up.

Naivasha, where he contracted dysentery and lingered for two months on the edge of death as the Maasai continued to threaten on a daily basis. He finally regained sufficient health to return to Mombasa on May 24, 1884, having traveled 4,839 km (3,000 miles) in 14 months, where he opened a direct route for the first time to Lake Victoria, and completed one of the most difficult and courageous feats of African exploration.

Thomson's Falls, named after this adventurer, are where the Ewaso Narok River pours roiling and brown over a stony ledge into its narrow, forested chasm, perpetual mist rising from the clash of water and rock, rainbows cloaking the green, chilled slopes. An array of souvenir kiosks mars the view of the falls, however, and a quartet of painted "native dancers" may waylay you in an attempt to sell a photo opportunity.

More interestingly, there is a path along the edge of the falls, and a trail you can take to the bottom. However, it is slippery and quite dangerous in places, and it's easy to lose your way; tourists have also been robbed here, thus it's best to check at the hotel desk on trail conditions and safety, and to engage a guide if necessary. At the desk they'll also tell you where to pick up a trail that crosses the river on the bridge above the falls and descends the other side, crossing again lower down and returning to Nyahururu — it's a beautiful walk that takes you into the wall of rainbow and cloud amid the canyon.

WHERE TO STAY

A few minutes walk from the falls, **Thomson's Falls Lodge** ((0365) 22006 FAX (0365) 32170, Box 38, Nyahururu, offers double cottages comfortably overlooking the Thomson's Falls, with grassy campground behind (midrange B&B). Built in the 1930s, the hotel is a relic of colonial times, but has borne the change with considerable grace. The rooms are spacious and very clean with carefully-laid fireplaces, the food ample and good, and the staff friendly. At 2,375 m (7,800 ft) above sea level, Nyahururu can be cold at night, but the hotel bar usually has a roaring fire, and is a cheerful place to strike up a conversation, far more lively than the average sedate game lodge.

The town of Nyahururu itself has a number of small *hotelis*, including the inexpensive **Baron Hotel** ((0365) 32056, Box 423, Nyahuru.

HOW TO GET THERE

Nyahururu is 198 km (124 miles) north of Nairobi, a two- to three-hour drive by *matatu* or your own vehicle. The town itself has little to detain the visitor and Thomson's Falls themselves (and the Thomson's Falls Lodge) are four kilometers (three miles) from the town, which is either a steady and not unpleasant walk or a quick ride by taxi.

EASTERN LAIKIPIA

The Laikipia Plateau covers an ill-defined area the size of Wales, spreading across Kenya to the north of Nyahururu, and west above the Aberdares and Mount Kenya. After World War I, much of the land was handed over to western settlers as ranches or farms, but since then cattle rustling, droughts and occasional tribal conflicts have reduced the population considerably. It is not a national park, but contains within its region some of the best game-viewing available. Protected from the outside world by, among other things, really appalling roads, this is home to four of the world's most important rhino sanctuaries and the "big five" (rhino, elephant, lion, leopard and buffalo) are often seen here. That the experience is also shared with cultural contacts with the resident tribespeople, settlers and ranchers adds a depth to a visit here that is invariably missed, or diluted, in the animal-only national parks.

The scenery varies from the edge of the Great Rift Valley to (when it's clear), the snow-drifted peaks of Mount Kenya, encompassing rivers and waterholes, plains and grasslands. In recent years a new initiative has linked together the descendants of the original, imported and imposed settlers, private ranchers, subsistence farmers and roaming pastoralists to form the Laikipia Wildlife Forum, uniting the community to

The Ewaso Ngiro flows from the slopes of the Aberdare Mountains through arid Samburu country and dries up in the vast Lorian Swamp.

resolve the inevitable conflicts. While it's not the most accessible nor secure area of the country, it is one of the most interesting, and there are a number of characterful establishments that offer very different insights into their particular environments free of any park regulations or entry fees.

WHERE TO STAY

Although charter flights to Laikipia often, for reasons of economy, leave from Nanyuki Airport, for purposes of clarity the lodges

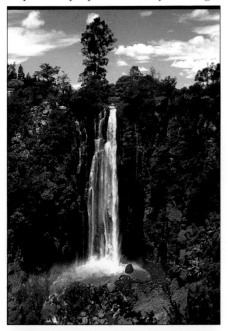

described here are those in the east, best accessed by the C77 as it heads north from Nyahururu. Those in western Laikipia, normally accessed by road via Nanyuki, are covered in the CENTRAL HIGHLANDS, page 212. Budget travelers can skip this section completely: there's nothing below the extremely expensive category here.

The experience depends on where you stay, and even if money is no object, time and the distance between the ranches here will mean you have to choose.

Most easterly is the extremely expensive, all-inclusive **Mukutan Retreat (** (02) 520799 FAX (02) 521220 E-MAIL mukutan@africa online.co.ke WEB SITE www.mukutan.com, Box 45593, Nairobi, owned by Kuki Gallmann,

the Italian-born author of *I Dreamed of Africa*, who lives nearby. Her famous bestseller has now been made into a film starring Kim Basinger. Her second book, which was a long time coming, failed to wow the critics as it is a rather depressing tale in which everyone seems to die. Still, the first book allowed her to set up a huge private reserve in memory of her dead husband and son. At its heart, Mukutan, with just three guest dwellings — generally let to only one party at a time — and sweeping, open views, is certainly stunning and a wonderful place to stay. Allow five hours from Nairobi by car: travel to Nyahururu and continue left on the C77, before turning left on the C51. Most guests here, already paying handsomely for their accommodation, find it more convenient to fly to the nearby airstrip.

Stay on the C77, through Rumuruti and you'll first reach **Mugie Ranch** where there are two accommodation options in a working ranch with plenty of game — lion, Jackson's hartebeest (only found in Laikipia) and all the other dry-country animals of northern Kenya — coexisting with camels, cows and other cattle. There is **Cheli and Peacock's Laikipia Camp (** (02) 604053/4 or (02) 603090/1 FAX (02) 604050 or (02) 603066 E-MAIL chelipeacock@africaonline.co.ke WEB SITE www.chelipeacock.com, Box 39806, Nairobi, a luxury mobile camp that brings guests close to moving predators (extremely expensive, all-inclusive), or the more settled home of **Mutamaiyu House (** (02) 882521 FAX (02) 882728 E-MAIL Bonham.luke@swift kenya.com, Box 24133, Nairobi, a delightful settlers house, atmospherically furnished with antiques (extremely expensive, all-inclusive). The house is run by Anthony and Marie Dodds, who are especially welcoming guides to the area. If you want an introduction to the Pokot, Samburu, Kikuyu and Ndorobo tribesmen, this is a comfortable place to start, and game drives, of course, are included.

Further north and it's more luxury again at **Loisaba (** (02) 574689, (02) 577018 or (02) 567251 FAX (02) 564945 E-MAIL Mellifera@swift kenya.com WEB SITE www.loisaba.com, Box 24397, Nairobi, a very luxurious lodge set on a 150 sq km (58 sq mile) private game reserve (extremely expensive, all-inclusive).

Highlights here include "star beds," in which you sleep under the stars but can wheel the bed back in at the first sign (very rare, up here) of rain. The lodge has a helicopter that flies up the remote Suguta Valley.

North again, Ol Malo (book through Bush Homes of East Africa ((02) 571661 FAX (02) 571665 E-MAIL bushhome@africaonline.co.ke, Box 56923, Nairobi) is run by Kenya legends Colin and Rocky Francombe (extremely expensive, all-inclusive). This is probably the most luxurious of all the lodges in the area, and there's always the chance of seeing an exceptionally rare black leopard, which occasionally has come to drink at the waterhole below the guest buildings.

North again, set on a cliff overlooking the Ewaso Ngiro River, is the **Sabuk Lodge** ((02) 891065 FAX (02) 890266 E-MAIL glen.ewaso @swiftkenya.com, Box 15094, Nairobi, write to Simon Evans, Box 243, Gilgil, Kenya; or make reservations with Let's Go Travel ((02) 447151 or (02) 441030 FAX (02) 447270 or (02) 441690 E-MAIL info@letsgosafari.com WEB SITE www.letsgosafari.com, Box 60342, Nairobi (extremely expensive, all-inclusive). This is also the base for the Ewaso River Camel Hike. Run by Simon Evans, member of a local ranching family, the camel hike allows you to travel on foot and on camel — no experience is required — through the lovely ranchlands and semiarid brush of the upper Ewaso Ngiro; all the way, if you wish, to Samburu National Reserve. Costs for a camel safari are a little higher than a standard full-board park lodge, but include food, camels, mattresses, mosquito nets, laundry and all the bush lore you can ingest. You need to bring your sleeping bag, a good pair of boots and standard safari hiking gear. For more information, see EXPERIENCE A CAMEL SAFARI, page 18 in TOP SPOTS.

MARALAL

Whether traveling independently from Wamba or, more probably, emerging dustily from a *matatu* at the end of its line, Maralal is an atmospheric and relatively secure outpost of civilization, and a good place to relax casually with the local Samburu people. It has two gas stations in a part of the world where one is a lifeline; it also has a range of accommodation and even a small natural reserve to call its own. This mountain town, in its windswept cleft of hills, cedar forest on both slopes imparting a perfumed, resiny flavor to the cool, thin air, is on the edge of civilization. There's electricity, shops, a thriving market, and a throng of souvenir sellers guaranteed to make you wish you were back in the desert. There is a fancy police post with a spanking new flag and new government buildings overlooking an imposing traffic circle, from which sign-less, potholed dirt roads unravel in all directions, one leading by chance to the town itself. The main street, with clapboard verandahs and trees not so much lining the streets as growing in it, has a Wild West feel. Cattle and at least one ostrich wander from shop to shop; Samburu tribesmen are driven in from the bush by tribal conflict, and barefooted gangs of children run around cheerfully. Three bars offer warm (and sometimes cold) beer, and there are a number of surprisingly good restaurants to be found.

If you've missed purchasing Samburu trinkets so far, Maralal's a good place to catch up: trouble in the Rift Valley has brought scores of refugees in from the country and they're having to sell their heirlooms. There are two-piece, wooden-handled, steel-shafted spears made by local blacksmiths for the tourist trade, and the wicked foot-long double-bladed knives known as *simis* or *lalem*, central to every Samburu warrior's health and longevity.

The true *simis*, those the *morans* carry, are cut down from large machetes made in England — look for the brand-name of the machete, such as "Giraffe" or "Birmingham," and the words "Made in England," which are stamped into the steel just above the hilt, and which are carefully conserved when the machete is ground down into a *simi*. The tourist-grade *simis* are made of brighter, lighter Kenyan steel, and will not keep an edge; in either case make sure the goatskin sheath of your *simi* is not split along the edge, or it can give you a nasty cut. The going rate for *simis* is Ksh450 to Ksh600 depending on size and condition; a good spear can cost up to Ksh1,000.

Thomson's Falls.

WHERE TO STAY

Most of the better places to stay here are a serious hike out of town — not something to try after dark in an area where elephants and buffaloes are often found. The **Maralal Safari Lodge** ((02) 211124 FAX (02) 211125, Box 15020, Nairobi, about four kilometers (two and a half miles) south of town, is the best place to stay, even though it is often, rather depressingly, empty (expensive). Their 24 comfortable cedar cabins with fireplaces, a cozy bar and lounge and large dining room all overlook a salt lick and water hole of the Maralal Game Sanctuary, with grazing zebras, buffaloes, impalas, gazelles and elands. Guides from the lodge will take you on a game walk through the surrounding refuge;

early in the mornings both birds and beasts are generally abundant. There used to be a leopard as well but apparently an Italian guest shot it some time ago.

If the Maralal Safari Lodge doesn't fit your budget or lifestyle, **Yare Safaris Ltd.** (/FAX (02) 214099 E-MAIL travelkenya@iconnect.co.ke, Box 63006, Nairobi, three kilometers (two miles) south of town, is a clean and quite classy campground with *bandas* and bunkhouses just to the east of the main road south of town (very inexpensive to inexpensive). There is a range of accommodation to suit all budgets and a campsite used by overland trucks. There's a well-stocked bar, a restaurant, a fake Samburu *manyatta*, and extensive campsites with a beautiful panorama of the surrounding cedar-clad hills. The lodge commonly pulling out at around lunchtime, packed to the gills. The 146 km (91 miles) trip through the Laikipia region and beyond takes three hours if everything goes well, which it often doesn't as most of the route is dirt and punctures are frequent. In your own vehicle it is possible to reach Maralal from Nairobi, a distance of 344 km (215 miles), in a mere five hours.

NORTH TO LAKE TURKANA

For many adventurous travelers, Maralal is the last vestige of comfort on the way north to the eastern shores of Lake Turkana, but bear in mind that the security situation in this part of Kenya is uncertain. Check for up-to-date information on recent bandit attacks and tribal tensions. There's no public transportation — though those with a couple of weeks to spare can hitch — and you'll need your own vehicle, enough gasoline and drinking water, and some stamina. The 210-km (130-mile) trip from Maralal to Loyangalani will take six hours if you're lucky. The small town of Baragoi can usually be relied on for pancakes at least, and there is a simple but comfortable hotel (I've forgotten the name but you can't miss it, very inexpensive), while South Horr will only provide food if you buy some meat and share it with someone who cooks it. Here you can hire a guide to explore the **Nyiru Mountains** and forest all the way to the **Tum Valley**, which offers superb views on Lake Turkana and the desolate expanse of **Suguta Valley**. This area is home to **Desert Rose Camel Safaris** ((02) 228936 FAX (02) 212160, Box 44801, Nairobi, perhaps the best-informed and equipped camel safari operators, who have a new lodge built overlooking the river (see EXPERIENCE A CAMEL SAFARI, page 18 in TOP SPOTS). Otherwise, continue on along the shores of Lake Turkana and to the fishing village of **Loyangalani**.

itself can be rowdy and lively or cavernously empty, depending which safari trucks, if any, are in town, apart from it's annual high-spot, the **Maralal Camel Derby** (see RACE TO VICTORY, page 27 in TOP SPOTS). Yare also organizes camel safaris, accompanied by Samburu *morans*, at unbeatable prices starting at US$500 for a week all-inclusive. This is one of the cheapest places in Kenya to try this reliably. Alternatively, small *hotelis* in town have basic accommodation at very inexpensive prices, starting at a mere US$1 for the **Midpoint Hotel**.

HOW TO GET THERE

Maralal is the end of the line for *matatus*: they leave from Nyahururu, with the last one

LAKE TURKANA

Lake Turkana has a majestic splendor all its own. Like its name, it seems jade, then turquoise gray as clouds mask the sun, silver

Vervet monkeys await nightfall in the forked branches of a doum palm.

at dawn and deep red at dusk; placid as a pond or wild and wind-tossed as the sea, so elementally vast that its far shore seems to fall beyond the horizon, and the curvature of the earth is visible in its limitless north–south expanse.

Four million years ago it appears Turkana, still by far the largest of the Rift Valley lakes, was a huge freshwater lake four times its present size of 7,200 sq km (2,800 sq miles). By two million years ago, sediments deposited from the Omo River and tectonic shifts had diminished the lake to a wide-based

Similar French and Italian dam building on the Turkwell and Kerio Rivers will undoubtedly lessen their peak flows and thus their contribution to the lake.

At the same time, explosive population growth among pastoral tribes, due to improved healthcare without the requisite increase in family planning services, has vastly increased livestock herds and led to catastrophic overgrazing of the parched uplands surrounding the Rift. The consequent denuding of vegetation and soil erosion has altered the climate, reducing or changing rainfall,

system of rivers, channels, and marshes, which may have drained eastward into the Indian Ocean. Since then it has expanded and contracted in the wide low bed of the Rift, has become increasingly saline (average pH is now 9.2), and no longer has an outlet other than evaporation.

The water lost by Turkana to evaporation now generally exceeds inflow from the Omo River and from the meager seasonal rainfall carried by the Turkwell and Kerio Rivers. Today about 435 km (270 miles) long by an average of 30 km (19 miles) wide, the lake is shrinking again, due perhaps to climatic fluctuation, but also to manmade changes. Foreign-aid irrigation projects in southern Ethiopia have decreased the Omo's flow.

and further diminished the lake. All of this strikes home as you look out over Turkana's beaches to its present shores, particularly at Loyangalani.

Bathed by onshore breezes in the palm trees, Loyangalani is a nice place to recover from the rigors of East Turkana. To the east, the imposing ridges of **Mount Kulal**, 2,295 m (7,530 ft), are climbable for those not tired of adventure, and are reputed to offer an inspiring panorama of the lake, the Ethiopian escarpment and out into the **Chalbi Desert**. It's possible to swim in the lake here with only minimal fear of hippos and crocodiles (however, one local told me that a British crocodile researcher was recently devoured here).

As always around Lake Turkana, flocks of children will follow you wherever you go, speaking good English, asking to be photographed for a fee or to sell some trinket. The local population is diverse, comprising remnants of the El Molos, considered the most ancient of Turkana's inhabitants, who live principally on fish, hippo steaks when they can get them and occasionally crocodile meat. They have largely merged into the overpowering Turkana and Samburu peoples, and their language is now considered lost. The remaining 400 or so of

the tribe live on **El Molo Bay**, fifteen minutes' drive north of Loyangalani. For a fee you can visit the village; most visitors find the experience depressingly commercial.

The Turkana and Samburu are more evident, having learned how to fish from the El Molo. Their herds can be seen watering at the lake edge. If the weather is calm, from Loyangalani you can rent a boat for an hour's ride to fascinating **South Island National Park**, a withered volcanic core surprisingly rich with crocodiles and bird life. Birds are not lacking along the entire east shore of Turkana, with flamingos, pelicans, ibis, cormorants and avocets being common.

The waters of Turkana have long been famous for their fish, including a world record

Nile perch (which can exceed 150 kg or 330 lb), tilapia, golden perch and the fierce tiger fish, which can weigh up to eight kilograms (18 lb) and fights like a trout when hooked.

Where to Stay and Eat

Lodging is Loyangalani's only disappointment. The **El Molo Lodge** is now almost derelict, though you might be able to camp there, and the once luxurious **Oasis Lodge**, which you can reserve through Bunson Travel ((02) 221992 FAX (02) 214120, Box 45456, Nairobi (expensive), is really not worth it and no longer has working vehicles or boats of its own — a sure sign, in this part of the world, that it is on its way out. The budget option, at around Ksh500, is cheap but not luxurious: **Mama Shanga's** consists of a few concrete sheds with a padlocked long-drop outside toilet as the only sanitary facilities. Outside the major lodges there are a few basic restaurants — most of which are better than the expensive fare at the Oasis Lodge. My favorite has a sign written on the wall "we give you the best service no matter how long it takes."

How to Get There

There is no public transportation to Loyangalani and even *matatus* stop at Maralal. Those prepared to undergo a participation-camping expedition, with up to 18 young tourists and aid workers traveling together in a truck, can get there on either the Turkana Bus operated by **Safari Camp Services** ((02) 228936 or (02) 330130 FAX (02) 212160 E-MAIL Safaricamp@form-net.com, Box 44801, Nairobi, or its main rival, **Gametrackers** ((02) 338927 or (02) 330903 E-MAIL Game@africaonline .co.ke, Box 62042, Nairobi. With your own transportation, it's a relatively easy three-hour drive from Nairobi to Nyahururu, but soon after this the pavement ends and it takes a rather slower three hours on dirt road to Maralal. From there the road deteriorates markedly and if you complete the last 220 km (137 miles) in less than a further six hours you'll be doing well. Bear in mind that there's no gasoline further north than Maralal unless you call ahead to make sure that there

Crocodiles are found at Turkana and many of Kenya's other lakes and rivers. They are both dangerous and swift.

is some waiting for you at Loyangalani. This might not be possible, so make sure you have some jerrycans. There is an airstrip at Loyangalani if you have the budget for it (allow about US$1,200 for a charter) but then, unless the Oasis Lodge can borrow a vehicle, you'll be stuck.

THE FAR NORTH

If you wish to visit the blazing moonscape of Sibiloi National Park and its fascinating archaeological and paleontological sites, you

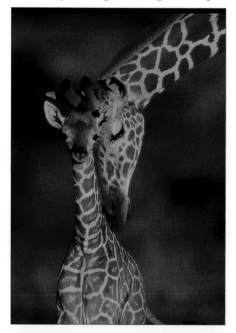

will need your own rugged vehicle, a touching confidence in the local fishing boats and their engines or, better still, access to a small plane. To get there you either cross the lake from Kalakol (see page 179) or drive via North Horr to Allia Bay on Lake Turkana, south of Richard Leakey's digs at Koobi Fora, contained within the Sibiloi National Park. On a slope overlooking the lake a weird assortment of ochre, brown and yellow pillars lie like a broken temple among the gray commiphora brush and tawny grass — petrified vestiges of a once-great tropical forest.

At Allia Bay you can hire a guide (essential if you wish to explore Sibiloi National Park), and drive past the park offices

then two hours north to the peninsula of Koobi Fora, where there's a small museum containing some recent finds. Although it's best to have asked permission in Nairobi (at the National Museum) before visiting Koobi Fora, the resident archaeologists are friendly and if you manifest a reasonable knowledge of and interest in their excavations may offer a quick tour. As well, there are *in situ* fossil elephant, tortoise and crocodile exhibits in the nearby uplands at **Bura Hasuma Hill**.

SIBILOI NATIONAL PARK

Sibiloi National Park is both fascinating and different from any other site in Kenya; considering the terrain and climate, a quite diverse wildlife community exists. It was originally a haven for elephants (the Koobi Fora museum displays a one-and-a-half-million-year-old example), but white hunters shot these out before the World War II. The park's relatively common large animals include the tiang race of topi, common and Grevy's zebras, reticulated giraffes, Grant's gazelles, gerenuks, dik diks, golden jackals, lions, hyenas, a few leopards, a surprising number of cheetahs, many crocodiles and some hippos near the lake.

Many of the fossils that have pushed back the dawn of human history millions of years have been found near Koobi Fora (the name derives from the local Gabbra tribe's word for the commiphora bush common to the area). Building on discoveries made by his parents, Louis and Mary Leakey, at Olduvai Gorge and other locations in Tanzania, Richard Leakey came to the east shore of Lake Turkana because its wind- and water-eroded barrens seemed to offer unusually clear incisions into the sedimentary rocks, which bear, like the piled pages of a manuscript, the decodable history of our human past.

Since 1968, Leakey, his wife Meave, and other scientists have made a series of breathtaking finds at over 200 East Turkana sites including, in 1972, the skull of a *Homo habilis* over two million years old, and now considered to be our direct ancestor. Enough information has been gleaned from the over 6,000 fossil specimens in Sibiloi to form a coherent picture of the development of a gatherer-hunter society as it evolved to language and tool making, as its brains enlarged and, stressed by changing climates and competition, it expanded and diversified until it came to consider itself apart from other animals and favored with dominion over the earth.

In all, the sedimentary deposits of East Turkana have yielded nearly 200 different hominid specimens, including several skulls and other major skeletal sections. Earliest discoveries (three and a half to four million

sive) and something to eat if you bring it. Even in the busy months of July and August, when American archaeologists move in, the *bandas* are generally empty and there's no need to book ahead. However booking is done through the National Musuems of Kenya ((02) 742161 FAX (02) 741424 E-MAIL nmk@africaonline.co.ke, Box 40658, Nairobi, who'll let you pay in advance if you weaken. Without your own transportation, you'll have to rent the resident Landrover (if working and gassed up) at Ksh50,000 per day to get around.

years old) appear to be of *Australopithecus afarensis*, the earliest recognized hominid. More recent specimens comprise three major hominid groups (*Australopithecus robustus, Australopithecus africanus,* and the *Homo* lineage which led to today's humans); all appear to have lived during the same one-million year period, with *Homo erectus* evolving from the earlier *Homo habilis* about one and a half million years ago.

Entry fees to the park are US$27 per person per day.

WHERE TO STAY AND EAT

At Allia Bay there is a small campground, some basic but comfortable *bandas* (inexpen-

HOW TO GET THERE

Overland, the route is via North Horr, then turning to drive the 130 km or 81 miles (three to four hours) to Allia Bay. The best way though, by far, is by air. Contact Fuf Aviation ((02) 505541. The other way to get there is by boat from Ferguson's Gulf, detailed under WESTERN KENYA, page 179.

OPPOSITE: One of nature's stranger creations, giraffes can make loving parents. ABOVE: Flocks of lesser flamingo pink the lakes of the Rift Valley.

The Central Highlands

Kenya's central highlands contain, in many ways, the best of the country. There are some of the finest parks, such as Aberdare, Mount Kenya and Meru, great national reserves such as Samburu, Buffalo Springs and Shaba, and, of course, the snow-capped brooding bulk of Mount Kenya. Interspersed with this are a host of upcountry towns where all the vibrant urban life of Kenya exists in a gentle climate, warm through the daylight hours and fresh at night. It's the foodbasket of the country and the cultural homeland of the most populous, successful and dynamic tribe, the Kikuyu.

KIKUYULAND

The freeway ends abruptly a short distance north of Thika, as you travel toward the dwelling place of the Kikuyu god, Mount Kenya. This is Kikuyuland, home of Kenya's largest tribe and its first president, Mzee Jomo Kenyatta.

The countryside is cloaked with an infinite number of green tones on terraced hillsides where corn, beans, peas, bananas, coffee, and tea are grown. After the rains in October and November, the flame trees dot the hillsides with orange. A month later, the jacarandas bloom, casting an otherworldly purple glow across the fields.

The land is always a hub of female activity. Brightly dressed women, with infants and toddlers in tow, fetch water, weed and harvest crops, gather and carry firewood, wash clothes in the rivers and ponds, and do whatever is necessary to manage their households. The more affluent women, with babies tied on their backs, have the luxury of going about their journeys with an umbrella to shade them and their offspring. Older children tend cattle, goats and sheep that graze in wooded strips between fields or along the roadside.

MURANGA

Muranga is chiefly important as the last major city before you need to decide between three roads heading north. Those that split to go around Mount Kenya do so further north, but at Muranga a turning heads off to Nyeri and the Aberdare Forest. There are,

however, one or two things to see here and it is worth a quick stop. Formerly Fort Hall, Muranga is still the district headquarters, with modern administrative buildings and the **Church of St. James and All Martyrs**. In the church is a mural of the life of Christ as an African, designed by the Tanzanian artist Elimo Njau. It was consecrated in 1955 by the Archbishop of Canterbury as a memorial to the Kikuyu victims of the Mau Mau Rebellion.

At the turn of the century, Muranga was little more than a military outpost administered by officers of the King's African Rifles. Many of the commanders spent their time shooting animals and leading occasional punitive expeditions to settle intertribal disputes or settlers' problems with their Kenyan workers. Justice was frequently expedient rather than fair.

You can find accommodation at Muranga, if necessary, although it will be basic. One of the best central hotels is the **Rwathia Bar** ((0156) 22527, Market Street (very inexpensive). With your own transportation there are better options out of town on the main A2 highway: the **Muranga Mukawa & Lodges** ((0165) 22542, Box 207, Uhuru Highway (inexpensive), and **Muranga Tourist Lodge** ((0156) 22120, Box 52, Uhuru Highway, in the direction of Thika (inexpensive).

To get to Muranga, catch a *matatu* from Accra Road in Nairobi heading to Embu (or Karatina, or Nyeri) as they all stop off here, and ask to be let off. The town is 87 km (55 miles) from Nairobi on the A2.

KARATINA

North of Muranga, turn left for the market town of Karatina, a popular stop for tour vans going to Aberdare and Mount Kenya national parks. There are a few stalls selling tourist items, but inside the concrete-walled open market all is local business — fresh fruits and vegetables, dried beans of every color and size, rice, *ugali*, houseware and soap. It is worth stopping just to see the cabbages as large as basketballs. Woman vendors pass the time weaving baskets and the ever-popular Kenyan bags. If you want to buy cattle,

Vervet monkeys look sweet but watch out: they are skilled at stealing your lunch.

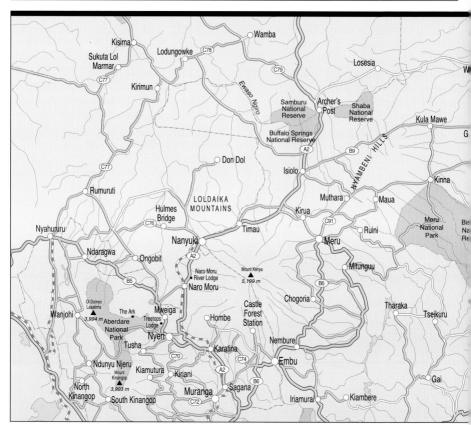

as one does, here you will find the largest selection in the country.

In the market's southeast corner, women treadle sewing machines to repair torn garments or sew new ones to the buyer's specifications. The best market days are Tuesdays, Thursdays and Saturdays. Usually, no one objects to your taking an overall picture of the market, but be sure to ask if you want to photograph a single individual or a small group.

Good and inexpensive accommodation can be found in the **Karatina Tourist Lodge** ((0171) 71522 FAX (0171) 72520, Private Bag, Karatina (inexpensive). The smartest option in the area is 30 km (19 miles) out of town (the turning is signposted off the road towards Nairobi), and this is the **Mountain Lodge** (/FAX (0171) 30785, Box 123, Kiganjo, reservations through Serena Hotel ((02) 711077 FAX (02) 718012 E-MAIL cro@serena .co.ke, Nyere Road, Box 46302, Nairobi, which is one of the best of Kenya's treetop hotels, with great views over a busy floodlit

waterhole (very expensive). At the other end of the scale, the very inexpensive **Three-in-One Hotel** ((0171) 72316, Box 768, will put up travelers on a budget.

Karatina is 41 km (26 miles) from Muranga but otherwise is easiest reached from the town of Nyeri, 27 km (17 miles) distant, within easy taxi or *matatu* distance.

Twenty kilometers (12 miles) north of Karatina, the road splits. The left branch leads west to Nyeri and Aberdare National Park, the other north to Mount Kenya.

NYERI

The main town in the area is Nyeri, formerly a market center for European-expat highlands farmers, now a busy commercial and industrial center and the dropping-off point for Aberdare National Park. Its cemetery attracts visitors to the graves of the famous author and hunter of man-eaters, Jim Corbett, and of the founder of the Boy Scouts, Lord Baden-Powell, who spent the last years of

ENTRAL HIGHLANDS

```
0      20      40      60      80 km
0    10    20    30    40   50 miles
```

B9

C81

Rahole
Kituri
Reserve

C81

Kora
Kituri
Reserve

N

A3

his life in a cottage on the grounds of the nearby Outspan Hotel, and who once said, "Nearer to Nyeri, nearer to heaven."

At the time of independence, the government purchased all lands around Nyeri still in the hands of European farmers, then divided and distributed it by drawing lots among the Kikuyus. These farms are some of the most prosperous in Kenya, harvesting up to four crops of maize per year. However, with the park nearby, farming has not always been easy. Elephants frequently devastate the crops and volunteer fundraisers are still frantically raising funds to build a boundary ditch and electric fence around the park to keep humans and elephants apart, restricting these giant pachyderms to a limited migratory right-of-way. During migration, a herd of elephants will push a younger elephant through the electric fence, and the rangers must then radio farmers along the route to Mount Kenya to have them open their gates so the elephants can pass.

In the town itself, the best hotel, just sliding in below the package market, is the **Greenhills Hotel (** (0171) 4233, Bishop Gatimu Road, Box 313, Nyeri, although it can be noisy on Wednesdays, Fridays and Saturdays because of its packed disco (inexpensive). Backpackers might prefer the pleasures of the **Thingira Guest House (** (0171) 4769, Box 221, located off Kenyatta Road (very inexpensive).

Most accommodation aimed at the overseas market, however, is out of town, and is therefore suitable for people with their own cars or on organized packages. Leading these is the **Aberdare Country Club (** (02) 216940 FAX (02) 216796, Box 58581, Nairobi, 10 km (seven miles) north of Nyeri in Mweiga (very expensive). This is an elegant establishment, but it suffered a considerable knock when a British tourist was killed by robbers within the hotel grounds seven years ago. The rooms, many of them recently built, are large and well furnished and the grounds, looking out on Mount Kenya, are alive with colorful flowers and shrubs, and flocks of peacocks. There is an aviary, a nine-hole golf course, tennis courts and a swimming pool; the trout fishing is reputedly excellent in the section of the river on the grounds. Not only do they operate the nighttime treetop game viewing at The Ark, but the Aberdere is also a good contact point for two of the area's other great attractions: **Solio Ranch (** (02) 763638, Box 2, Naro Moru, or **(** (0171) 420157 FAX (017) 55235, entry fee Ksh1,600, an important rhinocerous breeding center where Kenya's rhino population was saved from extinction, and **Sangare Ranch**, a luxury tented camp (reservations through Savannah Camps and Lodges **(** (02) 331684 or (02) 335935 FAX (02) 216528 or (02) 330698 E-MAIL eaos@africaonline.co.ke WEB SITE www.savannahcamps.com, 11th Floor, Fedha Towers, Standard Street, Box 48019, Nairobi, very expensive). The rival to the Aberdare Country Club is the **Outspan Hotel (** (02) 540780 FAX (02) 543810 E-MAIL blockreservations@net2000ke.com, Box 40075, Nairobi, opposite the CalTec Garage on the Nyeri Road, Nyeri (very expensive). Just as the Aberdare Country Club operates The Ark for nights spent game-viewing, the Outspan operates Treetops.

THE ABERDARE MOUNTAINS

The mountains of the Aberdares, not often visited by travelers, contain some of Kenya's most wonderful forest, interspersed with open moorlands and stretches of savannah. The lowland areas were once settled by Europeans — it is from here the myth of "Happy Valley" was propagated, though there are not many signs now of those halcyon days.

ABERDARE NATIONAL PARK

Established in 1950, the Aberdare National Park (entry US$27, children US$10) covers 590 sq km (230 sq miles), mostly at altitudes greater than 3,000 m (10,000 ft). To the local Kikuyus, these mountains had always been the Nyandaraus, but in 1884, Major Thomson renamed them after Lord Aberdare, president of the Royal Geographical Society that funded his expedition, and the name has stuck.

Because of its high altitude, the park has chilly weather — high rainfall and almost freezing night temperatures — and some of Kenya's most unusual vegetation; bamboo forest and open moorland with tussock grass and giant heath. Year-round, a four-wheel-drive vehicle is recommended; sometimes, even this may not get you through the park's black cotton soil, as the roads wind along the sides of steep, wooded valleys and across the moors. There seems to be little maintenance of any kind and roads are often closed. Even on the open roads it is easy to get stuck — not a very happy situation when, as can happen, you get stuck beside a pride of lions who show no intention of moving.

The road to **Chania Falls** is usually passable, even for two-wheel drives, and the walk down to the base of the falls is like a fairytale with rolling mist, giant lianas, Spanish moss and innumerable flowering plants and trees. Above the falls, the **Chania River** has superb brown trout fishing. Arrangements for trout fishing in the Gura, Karuru, or Chania river should be made through the park rangers.

From the peaks of **Ol Doinyo Lasatima**, 3,994 m (13,125 ft), and **Mount Kinangop**,

Kenyan women caring for their large families.

3,903 m (12,810 ft), are beautiful views of the Rift Valley and Mount Kenya, but these may be shrouded with mist after early morning.

Wildlife is abundant but often difficult to see. Along the roadside are many places where elephants have dug into the soil with their tusks in search of salt. Buffaloes, baboons and impalas are the easiest to find. Lion sightings are becoming more frequent and the Aberdare lions, most of whom have been transported in from ranches, are known to be very aggressive and have attacked tourists. Don't hike to the falls alone.

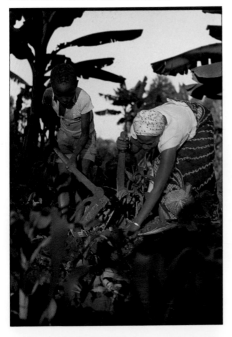

Leopards, including the rare black panther (a melanistic leopard), are found near the Wanderis Gate, but it's a good idea to ask the rangers where they were last sighted. A game driver from the Aberdare Country Club tells the story of a young couple whom he was taking on a private game drive en route to their overnight stay at The Ark. The driver came upon the elusive black panther on the road while the couple were having an argument. Ignoring the panther, they refused to let the driver stop, insisting that they be taken immediately to their rooms. The guide, irate that they did not understand the rare opportunity they had missed, was even more upset that he had not been able to watch the panther himself.

It's worth bearing in mind that the experience at both The Ark and Treetops, involving frequent wake-up calls and activities through the night, can often leave you feeling short of sleep and rather washed out. It's as well to schedule a restful day afterwards, perhaps back at the Aberdare Country Club. For an overnight stay in the Aberdares, you'll want to bring film of 1,000-ISO or higher. Warm clothes can be useful too: year-round night temperatures are near 3°C (40°F). Long pants, wool sweater and windproof jacket are a must, and even then you'll probably feel cold if you stay outside during the night.

Four species of sunbirds and 200 other bird species inhabit the park. Whether you can identify the birds or not, their songs, color and activity are a delight. The best time for viewing Aberdare's wildlife is during first light.

Where to Stay

The only full-service hotel accommodations in the park are **The Ark** ((02) 216940 FAX (02) 216796, Box 58581, Nairobi (very expensive, full board), or at the slightly less pricey **Treetops** ((02) 540780 FAX (02) 543810 E-MAIL blockreservations@net2000ke.com, Box 40075, Nairobi (very expensive, full board). For more on both of these see TRY OUT A TREETOP LODGE, page 15 in TOP SPOTS. Because of the difficulty in negotiating the roads, visitors who come to view animals, not the falls and mountains, stay at one of these two forest night-viewing lodges. Being older, **Treetops** is better known to tourists, but is far less frequented by lions and leopards than The Ark since its surrounding forest has disappeared into firewood and *shamba* construction, some of which can be seen from the lodge in daylight. By all accounts, the Treetops experience is good, but you are paying for the prestige of staying in the place where Queen Elizabeth became queen (her father died while she was viewing the animals), rather than for the accommodations (tiny bedrooms with paper-thin walls and a bathroom down the hall). **The Ark** is generally thought to be better, offering

ABOVE: Kenyan women do most of the heavy household labor, planting crops, carrying firewood and water. RIGHT: The spectacular Gura Falls in Aberdare National Park.

some of the most exciting game watching in Kenya, even if this is under floodlights of animals artificially attracted by salt licks. Neither allows children under seven, though the management has been known to bend the rules with the understanding that your child must be well-behaved and quiet (this rule applies to all guests regardless of age, rank or nationality). Another plus for The Ark is a no-smoking viewing lounge, which is very much appreciated when the outside temperatures drop.

Reservations are a must for The Ark and Treetops; both can provide transportation to and from Nairobi if you don't have your own (at US$75 round-trip) and in any case insist on providing transportation from the Aberdare Country Club or the Outspan Hotel respectively. You may also camp or rent the self-service *bandas* or bunkhouses at the **Aberdare Fishing Lodge** ((0171) 55024, c/o Warden, Aberdare National Park, Mweiga, near the Kiandongoro Gate. The rate is US$15 per person for bunkhouse accommodation, US$10 per person for camping. Bring your own bedding, food, and cooking utensils. Perhaps the best option, if driving yourself or in a party, is to stay at **Tusk Camp**: for Ksh5,000 up to eight people can camp in the wilds of the park. Reserve through Let's Go Travel ((02) 447151 or (02) 441030 FAX (02) 447270 or (02) 441690 E-MAIL info@letsgo safari.com WEB SITE www.letsgosafari.com, Box 60342, Nairobi.

How to Get There

Private vehicles are not allowed to make their own way to either Treetops or The Ark, so most guests arrive on packages from Nairobi. Guests with their own vehicles leave them at the Outspan Hotel or the Aberdare Country Club respectively and are then shuttled into their treetop lodge. It is, of course, possible to drive through the park — with skill, nerve and a four-wheel drive; there are park gates west and north of Nyeri. *Matatus* run from Nairobi to Nyeri but not the two minor roads that turn off for the south of the park. For the central and northern regions the road onwards from Nyeri to Nyahururu, which is served by *matatu*, passes close (within five kilometers or three miles) to the Aberdare Country Club, even closer to Solio

Ranch, and within two kilometers (one and a half miles) of Rhino Gate into the north of the park, but you won't get far into the park on foot before being eaten. You need your own transportion to explore much up here.

NANYUKI

An important air base and training center for, among others, the British Army, Nanyuki is well-positioned as a base to explore the northern flanks of Mount Kenya as well as being a good place to organize charter flights or four-wheel-drive expeditions off into the wilds of eastern Laikipia. Just across the equator, it started life as a basic collection of *dukas* serving the surrounding farms, and did not develop until the railway arrived in the 1920s. Now that the trains no longer run the town has lost some of its optimism, and although there are some charming shops reminiscent of the colonial days — including the "Settlers Store," in operation since 1938, the United Stores, and the Modern Sanitary Stores — there's not a great deal to see here. Worse, the ongoing presence of British soldiers has done little to improve the image of *mzungus* (white people) here. One ray of light, should you need one, is that there is a good private hospital: the Nanyuki Cottage Hospital ((0176) 22684.

WHERE TO STAY AND EAT

Staying in town is only recommended for those who don't have their own transportation, need to be at the airport early, or are interested in exploring the nightlife — of which there is plenty. The best place to stay is the **Sportsman's Arms** ((0176) 32347/8 FAX (0176) 22895, Box 3, Nanyuki, has a certain period charm though this might be hard to identify if they're hosting a loud disco — especially likely at weekends (inexpensive, B&B). The **Nanyuki River Lodge** ((0176) 32523, Box 101, Nanyuki, is best geared up for Mount Kenya climbs and has more facilities, but, once again, can get noisy (mid-range). Quieter is the **Nanyuki Guest House** ((0176) 22822, Box 211, Meru, just along the Nyahururu road (inexpensive).

As is often the case in Kenya, the best accommodation is a way out of town. Eight kilometers (five miles) to the southeast, the **Mount Kenya Safari Club** ((0176) 22960 FAX (0176) 22754, Box 35, Nanyuki, reservations made through Lonrho ((02) 216940 FAX (02) 216796, Box 58581, Nairobi, was founded by actor William Holden and still maintains some traces of Hollywood glamour (very expensive, all-inclusive). The resort offers horseback riding, golf and fishing, and has an animal orphanage in addition to being surrounded by animals in the private Mount Kenya Game Ranch … all good fun.

walks (separately charged). **Ol Pejeta Ranch** ((0176) 23414, Box 763, Nanyuki, book through Lonrho (see above) which is a six-roomed luxury lodge, colonial down to stuffed trophies on the wall and super-rich clients in the leather furniture (extremely expensive, full board).

How to Get There

Nanyuki Airport benefits from its military significance, and has regular flights to and from the Masai Mara with **Airkenya** (US$173)

Northeast of Nanyuki and you are fringing into the west of the **Laikipia** area (see page 193), with its characteristically expensive, but rewarding, private reserves. **Sweetwaters Game Reserve** is where the most famous resident is a tame rhino, called Moran, who trails around guests like a large primeval dog, and a chimpanzee sanctuary for chimps orphaned in their Uganda and Zaire homelands. This reserve contains two establishments once owned by arms dealer Adnan Kashoggi but taken over, in exchange for unpaid debts, by Lonrho. **Sweetwaters Tented Camp** (/FAX (0176) 32409, Box 763 Nanyuki, book through Lonrho (see above) is a well-run tented camp (very expensive, full board), with night drives and game

((02) 501421/3 FAX (02) 500845 E-MAIL info @airkenya.com WEB SITE www.airkenya.com, Box 30357, Nairobi. It is also the base for **Tropicair** ((0176) 32890/1 FAX (0176) 32787 E-MAIL tropicair@kenyaonline.com, Box 161, Nanyuki, a good charter company run by well-respected Kenyan Jamie Roberts, and able to reach most of the luxury lodges in the Laikipia area in less than half an hour. As charter costs are (approximately) US$1.68 per mile (1.6 km) for a Cessna carrying two passengers, this puts Nanyuki firmly on the map for reasonably well-heeled, but not profligate, travelers.

The Aberdare Country Club has magnificent facilities and food.

By road, Nanyuki is 200 km (125 miles) north of Nairobi, 97 km (61 miles) east of Nyahururu, and 90 km (56 miles) west of Meru. All these towns are linked by regular *matatus*, though the C76 to Nyahururu is dirt and bad dirt at that. Be ready for a long slow journey.

MOUNT KENYA

One of the best things you can do in Kenya is to take a trek around or, even better, an ascent of, Africa's second-tallest peak, Mount

Kenya. Named by the various tribes as Ol Doinyo Ebor, Ndur Kegnia, or Kima ja Kegina, it is at 5,199 m (17,057 ft), taller than Mont Blanc, the Matterhorn, the Rockies, the Sierras and most of the peaks of the Himalayas and Caucasus.

Composed of a huge volcanic base and plug whose outer mantle and crater have eroded away, Mount Kenya has three main peaks and a series of subsidiary cones scattered about its crest. The first European, and perhaps even the first person, to reach the mountain's top was the British geographer H. H. Mackinder, on September 13, 1899. He named the taller two peaks **Batian**, 5,199 m (17,052 ft), and **Nelion**, 5,188 m (17,017 ft), in honor of two famed Maasai medicine men.

The third and lower peak, **Lenana**, is 4,985 m (16,361 ft).

During the early era of human history, six to three million years ago, when our ancestors were wandering the shores of Lake Turkana and probably the foothills of Mount Kenya, the mountain was even taller, estimated by geologists to be over 7,000 m (23,000 ft). Since then, the mountain's mass has caused it to sink into the earth's crust, and the combined effects of glaciation, wind and weather erosion have further lowered its peaks.

Both Batian and Nelion are glaciated spires set in a gleaming array of snow-clad cirques and arêtes, like the Matterhorn and many of the Himalayan peaks. They are the province of skilled mountaineers only, with a variety of routes from Grade IV and above, depending on the time of year, and should *never* be attempted without the requisite experience, equipment and guides. Lenana, however, is far more rounded, slightly lower, and beloved by Kenyans because it is accessible to hikers who are fit and reasonably conditioned to altitude.

CLIMBING LENANA

Climbing Lenana is one of the peak experiences of a lifetime — a view of all Kenya awaits you on the top, and if you're lucky enough to reach Lenana at dawn, after a short climb from a hut below, the sunrise across the vast plains and hills of Africa will stay with you all your life.

Mount Kenya is visible from afar, its peaks usually covered with clouds by noon, but often glitteringly free in early morning or just before sunset. Explorer Joseph Thomson was one of the first Europeans to see the mountain, on his epochal safari from Mombasa to Lake Victoria in 1883:

"Suddenly there was a break in the clouds far up in the sky, and the next moment a dazzling white pinnacle caught the last rays of the sun, and shone with a beauty, marvelous, spirit-like, and divine, cut off, as it apparently was, by immeasurable distance from all connection with the gross earth."

Thomson did not reach the mountain itself, having been threatened with extermination by Maasai while encamped on the

Ewaso Ngiro River 24 km (15 miles) away, and forced to flee westward toward Lake Victoria. Today, the locals are more welcoming, and a variety of options are available for those who wish to hike or drive to Mount Kenya's lovely lower slopes or ascend Lenana Peak.

The Naro Moru Route

There are four main routes up Lenana. The most direct and popular, though perhaps less scenic, is the Naro Moru Route. Its advantage is that you can stay a night at the

62211, Box 27, Nyeri, at Ksh400 per night, which is a good place to meet up with other climbers if you want to team up.

First stocked with trout in 1910, the **Naro Moru River** stays clear most of the year, except during and just after the rains. Good fishing for browns and rainbows is also available in the nearby **Burguret** and **Nanyuki** river, although overgrazing, logging, and intensive farming have led to increased turbidity and sedimentation of spawning beds, diminished minimum flows and reduced fish habitat.

marvelous **Naro Moru River Lodge** ((0176) 62212 FAX (0176) 62211, Box 18, Naro Moru (reservations are also available through Alliance ((02) 443357/8, 448000 FAX (02) 448507 E-MAIL alliance@africaonline.co.ke WEB SITE www.alliancehotels.com, Box 49839, Nairobi). Its lovely cedar cabins are spaced among giant podocarp trees, green lawns and gardens along the south bank of the Naro Moru River (inexpensive to expensive). It also offers a bunkhouse and an exposed campsite. It has excellent cuisine, a very friendly staff, more birds on the grounds than you can count, and great fishing for rainbow trout literally at your doorstep. Alternatively there are cheap *hotelis* in Naro Moru village, including a **Youth Hostel** ((0176) 62412 FAX (0176)

You can rent fly tackle at the Naro Moru River Lodge, as well as all the gear you'll need for a hike around the mountain and up to Lenana Peak. The lodge offers everything from hiking boots (it's better, of course, to bring your own) to backpacks and even climbing hardware. It will also arrange porters if you wish, and organize your stays in upper mountain huts depending on your pace and aspirations. Steven Wahome, a member of Kenya's 1989 Mount Everest team, is the manager of the lodge's climbing office, so needless to say you're in very good hands.

OPPOSITE: Lionesses can be tender with their cubs, yet are skillful hunters when they get hungry ABOVE.

To reach Naro Moru, follow the road north through Thika, Muranga, Karatina and Nyeri. If you've come from Aberdare National Park, you can return to Nyeri or take the back road shown on the map to the town of Naro Moru. An intersection just north of the town of Naro Moru leads either two kilometers (one and a quarter miles) west to the Naro Moru River Lodge or 17 km (11 miles) east to the **Mount Kenya National Park (** (0171) 21575, Box 69, Naro Moru (US$15 per day adults, US$5 children, Ksh200 per vehicle) and the start of the Naro Moru route

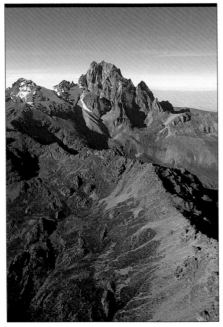

to Lenana Peak. This first 17 km (11 miles) takes you through gradually ascending farmlands and scattered forest over ancient lava flows, then into towering conifer forest with vast clear-cuts where potatoes have been planted between the new seedlings. During the rainy seasons, this section of the road may be impassable due to the huge ruts gouged into it by trucks bringing down harvested potatoes. Usually, you cannot drive beyond the park gate at 2,400 m (7,874 ft); however, if the road's good, you can take your vehicle all the way to the **Meteorological Station** at 3,050 m (10,000 ft).

In any case, it's a beautiful walk from the park gate up to the Meteorological Station, as the conifers give way to hardwoods, then

thick bamboo forest with magnificent vistas over thickly vegetated, mist-shrouded valleys. Once common throughout much of Kenya, the hardwood forests diminished as tectonic movement raised the earth's crust and split the Rift Valley, decreasing rainfall in much of East Africa. They are now found in isolated areas such as lower **Mounts Kenya** and **Elgon**, in the **Aberdares** and the **Mau Escarpment**. This mixture of hardwoods begins at about 1,800 m (5,600 ft) on Mount Kenya, shifts to bamboo and then moorland and heath at 3,200 m (10,500 ft), with the hardwoods more dominant on the south and east slopes due to the prevalence of rain-bearing winds.

Buffaloes are common on the road all the way from the park gate to well beyond the Meteorological Station, and may be dangerous, particularly if they are solitary. If you're hiking, don't get too close: they are very bad-tempered, and old males are especially likely to charge. They're much faster than they look and a lot faster than you. If you encounter them on the trail, try throwing rocks to chase them into the bush; if that doesn't work or if they move toward you, climb a tree as the locals do — and stay up until the coast is completely clear, which can take all day. Similarly, avoid hiking off the main road unless you have a local guide and he's willing to go first; buffaloes have a habit of exploding out of the bamboo thickets and trampling the unwary wanderer.

The Meteorological Station has a campsite and self-help *bandas* with cooking facilities and mattresses but no food. Bushbucks, Sykes' and colobus monkeys, giant forest hogs, eagles and, of course, buffaloes are common near the station, and leopards not infrequent in the boggy meadow below the *bandas*. If you arrive before noon, it's possible to ascend further to **Mackinder's Camp** the same day. But the altitude can suddenly become a problem if you're not acclimated; it's usually better to spend an afternoon hiking up to treeline (3,200 m or 10,500 ft) and enjoying the view. In the afternoons, the weather frequently turns rainy and visibility

---

OPPOSITE: Marabou storks confer in the branches of a thorntree. ABOVE: Mount Kenya, considered the home of God by many Kenyan tribes, is Africa's second-tallest mountain.

drops; the trail to Mackinder's Camp has a section known as the "Vertical Bog" which is best left alone in the rain.

From the station, you break out above treeline in less than an hour, slog up through the bog past the rain gauge and Picnic Rocks in another hour, and soon cross the Northern Naro Moru River, coming upon a marvelous view up and down narrow **Teleki Valley**, the imposing snow-covered peaks glittering above you. Since the station, the vegetation has changed from bamboo and hardwood forest, to stunted trees, to heather

covered glaciers a deep pink and little whips of violet hovering above its icy pinnacles. The black rock-faces, tooth-edged crags, all the weight and massive solidity of those twin towering peaks, Batian and Nelion ... was transmuted into something as light, as airy and ethereal as a phantom ship riding upon a fleecy ocean ...

"The night was cold, our single fly-sheets scarcely broke a chilly wind, damp rose from the ground to penetrate our blankets. So clear was the sky that the Milky Way looked like a plume of spray thrown across it by the

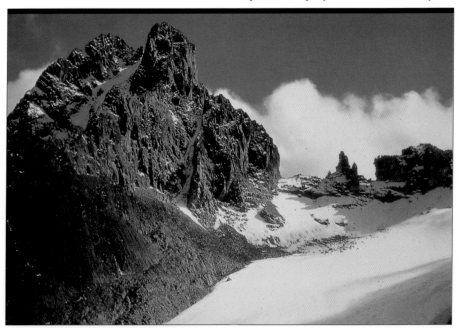

and tussock-grass moorlands, with giant yellow-flowered groundsel (*Senecio*) and giant lobelia standing up to 10 m (33 ft) tall.

While not luxurious, the concrete and rock bunkhouse of Mackinder's Camp will seem more than welcoming. If the clouds have not descended, there is a fine view of the peaks; from the ridge above camp it's possible to climb northward to **Two Hut Tarn** and other small lakes. Sunset on the peaks is beautiful beyond description, but Elspeth Huxley, in 1919, comes closest:

"The land stretched it seemed forever into a setting sun that had inflamed the whole sky with purple, crimson and gold. And then the peak emerged from its sheath of cloud, incredibly sharp and delicate, its snow-

bursting of some colossal breaker and held there in myriad frozen droplets. Above us, the peak loomed silently in darkness. Rocks were black as tarn water, grass a misty gray, mysterious shapes waited on the fringe of our vision, and we seemed to be afloat on some motionless vessel high above all the oceans of the world."

Alternative Routes up Mount Kenya
Three other routes up the mountain deserve special mention. The **Chogoria Route** from the eastern side is the most scenic and strenuous of all the ascents, more popular now the road on the east side of the mountain has been paved to the roadhead at 3,200 m, or 10,500 ft. Above this point, there are some

spectacular views of the incised **Gorges Valley** and **Lake Michaelson**, a "trough lake" dug by glaciation. To reach this route, turn off the Embu–Meru highway north of Chuka at the sign for **Meru Mount Kenya Lodge**. Don't be confused by the grand title: it's less a lodge than a set of huts, self-service *bandas* (inexpensive) but no food or beverages, and a good campsite (very inexpensive); reserve through Let's Go Travel ℂ (02) 447151 or (02) 441030 FAX (02) 447270 or (02) 441690 E-MAIL info@letsgosafari.com WEB SITE www.letsgo safari.com, Box 60342, Nairobi. The lodge is

thick rainforest and fabulous moorlands with long views of the peaks. Noted for its wildlife, Sirimon begins 13 km (eight miles) east of Nanyuki before the bridge crossing the **Sirimon River** and Timau. Leaving the highway, drive 10 km (six miles) through open farmland to the national park gate at 2,440 m (8,000 ft), then another nine kilometers (over five and a half miles) to the roadhead at 3,200 m (10,500 ft), where you'll find a campsite.

From the roadhead, it can take a day to climb the Barrow to **Liki North Hut** at

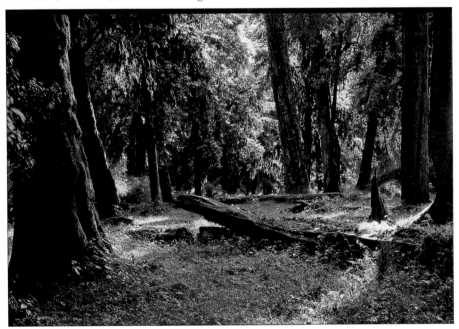

30 km (19 miles) from the highway but it is possible to hike an hour further up to **Urumandi Hut** at 3,060 m (10,050 ft), for a (very inexpensive) bunk bed.

There are magnificent rainforests and bamboo jungle on the way up to Urumandi, and from there it's an exhilarating four- to six-hour hike to **Minto's Hut**, spectacularly set into a bowl of three small tarns. You can stay in the hut or camp, again leaving early (3 AM) if possible. It's a two-and-a-half- to four-hour hike from Minto's to Lenana Peak, with a long scramble over slippery scree, which at this altitude can be more than exhausting.

Alternatively, the **Sirimon Track** is the longest and driest route, much of it through

4,000 m (13,123 ft). If you're in very good condition, you might like to continue on around the wall above Mackinder Valley. This route leads past **Shipton's Caves** at 4,150 m (13,615 ft) — an emergency shelter — and then straight up to **Kami Hut** at 4,425 m (14,518 ft). After Kami, it's possible to circle eastward below Batian across **Simba Col** and pick up the Chogoria route up Lenana. It's also possible to climb Lenana from this side, but this is inadvisable, as the scree makes for significant danger, particularly in the dark if you're trying to reach the peak by sunrise.

OPPOSITE: Mount Kenya's Nelion Peak rewards fit climbers. Much of the route up the mountain passes through montane forest ABOVE.

Finally, a fourth approach is via the **Burguret Trail**, from the **Mountain Rock Hotel** ((0176) 62625 FAX (0176) 62051, Box 333, Nanyuki, eight kilometers (five miles) north of Naro Moru on the Nanyuki road, where there is a very inexpensive campground, mid-range *bandas*, and a restaurant. As at Naro Moru, you can get guides and can drive to 3,000 m (9,840 ft), then follow the **Burguret River** to the Highland Castle Camp at 4,000 m (13,120 ft), and ending at **Two Tarn Hut**, from where a three-hour scramble will take you to the top of Lenana.

Mount Kenya by one route and descend by another, such as Burguret Trail and Sirimon Track, which makes an easy circle. If you can, try to spend a day or two on the high peaks, as the huts are very inexpensive and the views majestically different from each side. Remember that no food or beverages are available, so bring plenty.

If you're thinking of climbing Lenana Peak or just want to hike some of the lower trails of Mount Kenya, it's best to pick up a copy of the excellent *Mount Kenya Map and Guide* by Andrew Wielochowski and Mark

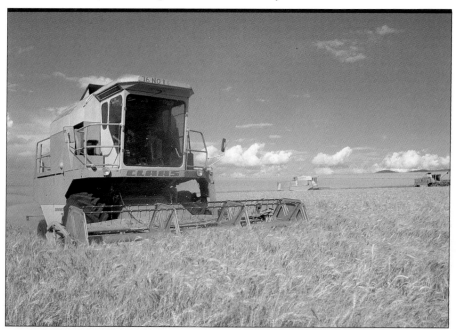

Mountain Practicalities

The scree, or talus, at the top of Lenana, particularly when wet or icy, is difficult for the average hiker. Originally formed by the freeze-thaw weathering of the mountain's glaciated upper slopes, it is loose enough in some areas to take a great deal of high-altitude energy just to get through. Thus if you're not experienced in mountain trekking and scree climbing, consider hiring a guide, who will make your trip a lot more relaxed and see that you don't miss things that are easy to pass by. From about Ksh1,000 per day, it's an inexpensive way to double your pleasure and minimize potential danger.

Another option, if you're not pressed for time and love the mountains, is to ascend

Savage. It is available at most lodges round the mountain and sometimes in Nairobi. The **Mountain Club of Kenya** ((02) 501747, Box 45741, Nairobi, has built and manages many of the huts on the mountain, and has extensive information and guidebooks. Call or find out more at its clubhouse at Wilson Airport, Nairobi, where it holds public meetings every Tuesday at 8 PM.

Guided hikes can be arranged through the following contacts. For the Naro Moru Route, contact **Naro Moru River Lodge** ((0176) 62212, Box 18, Naro Moru. To head up the Sirimon and Burguret Routes get in touch with **Tropical Ice Ltd**. ((02) 740811, Box 57341, Nairobi, who operate from Mountain Rock Hotel. The operators who specialize in the Chogoria Route are **Savage Wilderness Safaris** incorporating **East African Mountain Guides** (/FAX (02) 521590 WEB SITE www.kilimanjaro.com, Thigiri Road, Box 44827, Nairobi. If you want to try technical climbing on the peaks (ice and rock to Grade VI), you have a choice of operators. Call Steven Wahome at Naro Moru River Lodge, Tropical Ice Ltd., or Savage Wilderness Safaris incorporating East African Mountain Guides. For hiking and climbing all routes, try **Joseph Muthui** ((02) 242627 FAX (02) 250734, Box, Naro Moro, a previous member of the mountain rescue team, who is famously patient and good-humored, and charges a very reasonable price.

One final point. If you are hiking independently, the park fees you pay on the way in will estimate how long you plan to stay within the park. Overstay and search parties will be organized. It is especially important, even if you don't overstay, to register with the park authorities when you leave the park, as you are likely to be pursued for expensive search costs.

WHERE TO STAY

Where you decide to stay will partly depend on which route you choose and the lodges and campsites are listed above. If, on the other hand, you want to just have a gentle stroll around the area but haven't the slightest intention of climbing any mountains whatsoever, a good place to stay is the once very smart but now merely comfortable **Mount Kenya Safari Club**, operated by Lonhro ((02) 216940 FAX (02) 216796, Box 58581, Nairobi (very expensive); just before Nanyuki turn right and thread up the mountain for six kilometers (four miles) (see also under NANYUKI, page 213).

HOW TO GET THERE

Most of the routes up Mount Kenya approach it from the western flanks. Leave Nairobi on the Thika road heading north and continue to Karatina, turning right just before Nyeri (signposted Naro Moru River Lodge and Samburu Lodge), and continue on towards Nanyuki. The drive will take about four hours but it can take longer: the road surface is bad, especially in the latter stages. Public transportation will take longer and unless you start very early (leaving by five or six in the morning) will probably involve a change of *matatu* at Karatina and Nyeri. Alternatively, perhaps because it is Kenya's air force center, Nanyuki (see page 213) is well served by air. **Airkenya** ((02) 501421/3 FAX (02) 500845 E-MAIL info@airkenya.com WEB SITE www.airkenya.com, Box 30357, Nairobi, flies every day between Nairobi and Nanyuki, with round-trip tickets costing US$136, and even have a daily service between Nanyuki and the Masai Mara costing US$173 one-way.

For the Chogoria Route, on the mountain's eastern flank, turn right at Sagana or Muranga for Embu and continue towards Meru. At the village of Chogoria turn left for the 16 km (10 miles) of rough track to the self-service Meru Mount Kenya Lodge. Take your own food and bedding. On the eastern slopes of Mount Kenya check locally about the current security situation as this area is at the heart of Kenya's production of *miraa*, the fairly intoxicating drug made of the leaves and stems of a bushy plant common to the Meru area; and drugs and safety rarely go together.

NORTH OF MOUNT KENYA

North of Mount Kenya there are two main wildlife areas that are rated highly by visitors: the popular and groundbreaking private conservancy of Lewa Downs and the very rewarding Samburu National Reserve, with its neighbors, Shaba and Buffalo Springs reserves. North of these and the land dries up and the population density falls away.

The residents in this area are Samburu pastoralists, tall nomads tending their cattle, following a timeless and traditional way of life, and sharing many aspects — including language and appearance — with the Maasai to the south. There are nature reserves further north — most notably Losai and Marsabit — but generally the wildlife coexists with humanity here, in a wild and lawless area where anything can happen. Before traveling on from Samburu National Reserve, carefully check with the authorities

Large farms on the plains surrounding Mount Kenya produce much of the country's wheat.

on the security situation and make sure you are equipped to cope with any mechanical or medical emergency. Up in this part of Kenya public transportation is all but nonexistent and north of Archer's Post the only person who will get you out of trouble is you. The road as far as Isiolo is generally regarded as safe but there have been some problems (bandits attacking tourists) between Isiolo and Samburu National Reserve (though the park itself is safe). North and east of here the security situation is dire, and travel is not recommended.

This is a commercial venture as well: entry to the reserve is US$35 for adults and US$20 for children.

Where to Stay

There are three places to stay here, none of which are very inexpensive. All are bookable through Bush Homes of East Africa ((02) 350703, (02) 571661 or (02) 571592 FAX (02) 571665 E-MAIL bushhome@africaonline.co.ke WEB SITE www.bush-homes.co.ke, Box 56923, Nairobi. The most exclusive is in **Wilderness Trails** (extremely expensive, all-inclusive),

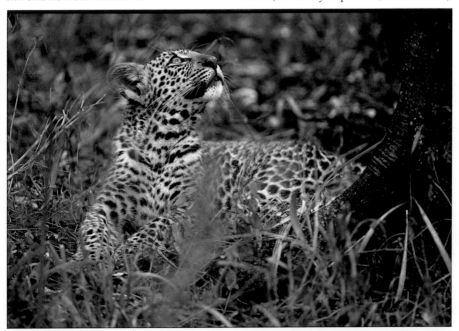

LEWA DOWNS

The Lewa Downs Conservation Center is one of Kenya's most successful blends of conservation, traditional ranching and tourism projects, encompassing an L-shaped patch of land 60 km (37.5 miles) northeast of Nanyuki that was originally set up by Anna Merz, who is well-known for taming orphan rhinos. Well into her eighties, she has since retired to South Africa, but her brand of patriarchal conservationism lives on. There are protected, fenced-in rhinos and there is also a small swamp where a few endangered sitatunga can be found. With daily air links to Nairobi and a fast turnover of visitors, it's a slick and successful wildlife experience.

with three cottages, full luxury cuisine and game-drives included. Step down to **Lewa Tented Camp** (extremely expensive), formerly Lerai Tented Camp, which is sited within the rhino sanctuary itself. The third option here is at Samburu-run **Il Ngwesi Lodge** (very expensive, all-inclusive), which involves the local community directly in its management. Comforts are reduced, with even the shower-water brought up from underground wells by camel, but the lodge remains in the international price range. Good and authentic camel-rides and walking expeditions help, though charging US$20 to visit the local *manyattas* does seem a touch excessive, given how much most guests are already paying into the local community coffers. Following the success of

Il Ngwesi, a new community project has opened to the north, **Tassia** (extremely expensive), book through Let's Go Travel ((02) 447151 or (02) 441030 FAX (02) 447270 or (02) 441690 E-MAIL info@letsgosafari.com WEB SITE www.letsgosafari.com, Box 60342, Nairobi, which is generally self-catering with exclusive use of the whole camp for two to twelve people, but bring your own drinks. There is a standby rate within a week of the booking date, so it might be worth a call at the last minute.

How to Get There

Lewa Downs is normally reached on the daily flights from Wilson Airport with **Airkenya** ((02) 501421/3 FAX (02) 500845 E-MAIL info@airkenya.com WEB SITE www.air kenya.com, Box 30357, Nairobi, priced at US$120 one-way. It can also be reached from the Nanyuki–Isiolo road: the turning is signposted clearly if you're in your own car. Travelers using public transportation will find the game reserve too far from the main road for this option to provide a practicable access, but in any case the overnight fees will scare off any backpacker using *matatus*. Lewa Downs Conservation Center is only 20 km (12.5 miles) south of Isiolo.

NORTH TO ISIOLO AND SAMBURU

On the northern flanks of Mount Kenya, the road from Nanyuki, skirting Mount Kenya to the west, meets that from Meru curving round the eastern flanks, and a turning heads north. On either side are magnificent views: the purple slopes and peaks of the Loldaika Mountains to the west, and the soaring Nyambeni Hills, where most of the country's slightly narcotic *miraa* is grown, to the east. It's not insecure here, at the moment, but it's on the edge: check locally to make sure there aren't too many bandits around before attempting this drive alone. The provincial capital of Isiolo is 30 km (22 miles) to the north of Mount Kenya's ring-road.

ISIOLO

The first thing most visitors to Isiolo remark is its Somali influence. Many veterans were settled here after World War I, and there is also a substantial immigrant population from Kenya's troubled neighbor, making it Kenya's largest Somali city. But there are also plenty of Kenyan tribes represented in this town, which has a strong and irrepressible frontier feel. It's worth spending a little time in Isiolo, for the town is a striking clash of southern and northern desert cultures, with an overflow of the more sultry Meru temperament and a strong Somali influence.

The town itself is reasonably secure, thanks perhaps to three military training colleges and a tank regiment. The general area, however, is not.

If you're heading north, which is not currently recommended, bear in mind that Isiolo is the last sure place to buy gasoline until Moyale, some 525 km (325 miles) to the north, at the Ethiopian border; even on a very grand safari, you may not be traveling that far. Marsabit, a mere 275 km (170 miles) north from Isiolo, may have gasoline at the rundown **Marsabit Lodge** ((02) 229751 or (02) 330820, but don't depend on it unless you've called one of these Nairobi numbers to reserve some.

Isiolo's most famous blacksmith, one Mumin Hassan, who should be well beyond retirement age, known locally as "Ayatollah Khomeini," has almost single-handedly created a thriving industry in daggers, Somali swords, *kols* or curved knives, and other such instruments of mayhem, which he and his flock of sons cheerfully sell to tourists, Samburu warriors and *shiftas* (Somali bandits) alike. Usually, he can be found sitting beneath a spreading euphorbia tree, unfinished dagger in hand.

Isiolo is also a regional center for packing and trading *miraa*, a fairly intoxicating drug. The *miraa* arrives by truckloads early each morning, to be sorted and bound by Isiolo women into bundles of a kilo each (called *kilos*) for resale. Chewed by many northern Kenyans and Somalis, *miraa* is reputed to have a slow, amphetamine-like effect. Although not illegal, it appears to lead to outrageous fantasies and occasionally, when combined with alcohol, to violence, particularly when imbibers have their swords in their belts. Like "uppers" in the

Young leopards are among the most appealing of Kenya's cats.

United States, it is a favorite of long-distance truckers, another reason why the tourist is best advised not to drive in Kenya at night.

Where to Stay

There are several cheap inns for the intrepid traveler. The **Bomen Tourist Class Hotel** ((0165) 2389 FAX (0165) 2225, Box 67, Isiolo, at the end of the alley opposite the new white Barclay's Bank, is the newest and best in town (inexpensive). However the **Mocharo Lodge** ((0165) 2385, Box 106, Isiolo, is much better value and has safe parking (very inexpensive). A luxury alternative 20 km (12.5 miles) south of Isiolo on the Nanyuki Road is **Lewa Downs**, reserve through through Bush Homes of East Africa ((02) 350703, (02) 571661 or (02) 571592 FAX (02) 571665 E-MAIL bushhome@africaonline.co.ke WEB SITE www.bush-homes.co.ke, Box 56923, Nairobi, see above (very expensive).

How to Get There

Isiolo is 285 km (178 miles) north of Nairobi. Traditionally, the preferred route is to the west of Mount Kenya via Nyeri and Nanyuki, though the newly paved road on Mount Kenya's eastern flank makes the route via Meru rather quicker. Early-morning buses and *matatus* link Isiolo with Nairobi, although if you miss the last one (sometimes even 6 AM is too late!) you might face a long hopping journey. Frequent *matatus* link Isiolo with Nanyuki, a center for air travel with occasional *matatu* links west to Nyahururu.

EAST FROM ISIOLO

The fascinating, if barren, area from Isiolo through **Wajir** to the Somali border is only recommended for those with plenty of time who enjoy incinerating desert temperatures and abysmal roads. It is also very insecure and travel here is by convoy only.

If this is the adventure for you, take the **Garba Tula–Mado Gashi** road east from Isiolo, being as usual sure that you have sufficient gas and water reserves, plenty of spare tires and tubes, and food. The countryside is flat, blistering hot and sandy all the way to **Habaswein** at the headwaters of the **Lorian Swamp**, with occasional mirages

or the lone figures of Somali and Borana nomads breaking the isolation of the desert. From Habaswein east, you're in the **North Eastern Province**, Kenya's least populated, and the most remote from central rule in Nairobi.

Again, don't believe any map that shows gasoline at Habaswein (it can be found, occasionally, at Wajir — call ahead to the **Wajir Administrative Center offices** ((0136) 21112, though they may say there is some when there isn't). It's a long 260 km (160 miles) from Isiolo to Habaswein, another 70 km (44 miles) to Wajir, with its single-story white houses, mosque, Foreign Legion-type fortress, cheap hotels (none particularly recommended) and places to eat, and all the camels you can count.

From Wajir, it's another searing 190 km (120 miles) to **El Wak**, with its own fort, camels and *miraa* traders. Beyond it, the road is potholed but paved the remaining 225 km (140 miles) across the **Sardindida Plain** to **Mandera** on the Somali border. Another way to reach this godforsaken patch of the world is on the sandy, flat road from Meru National Park up to Wajir through Garba Tula, via the park's gate beyond Leopard Rock. It's a lawless, frontier land, contested by Somali tribesmen and the older settlers of Borana and Samburu. Cattle thieving is common, with occasional bloody shoot-outs between AK47-toting Somalis and local police if the latter can't get away fast enough. The best advice is to steer clear.

SAMBURU COUNTRY

Although there are plenty of Samburu to the west, around the towns of Maralal and the northern desert regions, Isiolo regards itself as the gateway to Samburu country. These slender, handsome people are known for their quiet friendliness and simple, grave demeanor. They are closely related to the Maasai, from whom they separated in tribal disputes some centuries ago during the migration southward from Sudan and Ethiopia. In the Maa language, which both tribes share, "samburu" means butterfly — the Maasai say because the Samburu fled the tribe, the Samburu say because they flutter around and don't stay put.

Like the Maasai, the Samburu are principally nomadic, wandering their vast, often arid territory in search of grazing for their herds of cattle, sheep and goats. They live on the meat of their sheep and goats, on berries, tubers and wild fruits, and on cow and goat milk, often mixed with blood taken from a vein in the necks of their cattle.

Young Samburu men and women are permitted to have relations, the man providing his lover with necklaces as proof of his affection. The young women are then betrothed to older men, circumcised on the day

Samburu wives and daughters do the majority of the physical work around the *manyatta*, but their word is respected and often outweighs their husbands'.

From the *manyatta*, young Samburu *morans* wander with their herds for days, often months, in search of grazing. They are colorfully dressed in blazing red cloaks, their faces and chests dyed ocher, their *simis* — short, lethal swords made of cut-down machetes — at their waists, their razor-sharp spears always in their grasp. The weapons are not for show. Not infrequently, *morans*

of their marriage, and, thereafter, not supposed to continue relations with the younger men. The young men are circumcised at roughly the same age, but cannot marry until much older, long after they become warriors (*morans*), according to an intricate age-set system that provides multiple brides for older, prosperous men who are or will become the elders (*mzee*) of the tribe.

The Samburu settlement, or *manyatta*, is most often a kraal of several mud, wattle and thatch huts, surrounded by a thorn enclosure in which the herds are kept at night for protection from four- and two-legged predators. Family ties are strong, as are the oral traditions of legends and laws that enliven the fireside. Like most women in Kenya, the

find themselves attacked by *shiftas* (Somali bandits), better-armed and ruthless. No Samburu who sets out to wander the Northern Frontier District with his herds can be assured of returning. When forage in one area is spent, the *manyatta* may be moved also, depending on the season.

The terrain north of Isiolo town contains some of Kenya's finest game parks and most beautiful scenery. Less than 30 km (19 miles) north of Isiolo are the linked areas of Samburu, Buffalo Springs and Shaba National Reserves. They cover a total area of some 430 sq km (170 sq miles). Samburu is the

The common zebra, with stripes across its underbelly, populates the open plains of central and southern Kenya.

most famous, an expanse of semiarid, often volcanic prairies and hills, divided from Buffalo Hills to the south by the serpentine, crocodile-infested Ewaso Ngiro River. It's a good place to spot leopards, for the simple reason that both the Samburu Lodge and the Samburu Serena Lodge bait the most elusive of all the big cats with dangling game.

Although the three reserves can impose their own daily fees even if you are just passing from one to another, or even in transit, this rarely happens. The US$27 per adult and child/student rate of US$5 is averaged across the reserves, with each sharing the revenue of shared tickets. Game-drives commonly traverse from Samburu Reserve into Buffalo Springs, depending on wildlife movements, whereas Shaba is a significant 40-minute drive away by road. There have also been some incidents of robbery both on the road from Isiolo to Samburu and at the public campsites here. Caution is recommended. In the off-season between April and July, most of the luxury lodges here drop their rates by as much as half to fill empty tents and *bandas*.

BUFFALO SPRINGS NATIONAL RESERVE

In many ways, Buffalo Springs, adjacent to Samburu National Reserve, is the most beautiful of the three reserves. Its springs and stream of the same name, with their volcanic pools and black-rock water chutes flanked with tall grass and doum palms, should not be missed. The graceful doum palm often reaches 20 m (66 ft) in height, towering over other riverine trees. It is the only palm species whose trunk and boughs divide into branches, making it instantly recognizable. Baboons and elephants eat its orange-brown fruit, and its leaves are used by people for weaving baskets and mats, so extensively that in many areas the tree no longer exists. Its broad-spreading, V-branched canopies are good places to look for black-faced vervet and Sykes' monkeys.

Both Buffalo Springs and Samburu are excellent areas for reticulated giraffes, the unusual beisa oryx with its lovely straight, long horns and gleaming black-and-white coat, impalas, blue-legged Somali ostriches, waterbucks, Grant's gazelles, dik diks, duikers, warthogs, olive baboons, lions and spotted and striped hyenas. Grevy's zebras, the desert race with large, rounded and fringed ears and narrow stripes that don't meet under the belly, are common in all three reserves. Also frequently seen are gerenuks, the long-necked antelopes that graze like giraffes on the upper branches of thorn trees, and are fittingly named *swara twiga* (antelope giraffe) in Swahili.

Elephants are rare, having been poached by Somalis and, occasionally, Samburu during their annual migrations from the reserves towards Marsabit and the northern plains. But if you're lucky you can see hunting dogs and occasionally cheetahs and leopards along the waterways or in the rocky, inaccessible hills. The cone-like hanging nests of weavers are visible everywhere in the acacias, their gregarious chatter a constant background sound, especially in the mornings.

Where to Stay

The last lodge here, just outside the reserve, is the **Samburu Serena Lodge (** (02) 711077 FAX (02) 718012 E–MAIL cro@serena.co.ke, Nyere Road, Box 46302, Nairobi, which is well-run and comfortable (expensive).

Campsites line the river in the Buffalo Springs Reserve. Now the spate of robberies in the 1980s and 1990s seems to have been stemmed, their use, once more, is generally recommended; at Ksh825 per person on top of the US$27 reserve entry fee. Their sites are even more attractive than those at neighboring Samburu Reserve are. Check at the gate on the current security situation.

The lodge is less than two hours' drive north of Nanyuki, and less than one north of Isiolo along the A2.

SAMBURU NATIONAL RESERVE

From Buffalo Springs, you cross Ewaso Ngiro River on a good bridge, often crowded with baboons, into Samburu. The higher hills at the south end of Samburu Reserve offer lovely views of the Ewaso Ngiro, and the hills and plains of Buffalo Reserve beyond. On the nearer side of the river, the land is dry and thornbush becomes the common vegetation in the barren, sandy soil. The Ewaso Ngiro begins some 300 km (186 miles) to the southwest, on the 4,000-m (13,000-ft) slopes of Ol Doinyo Lasatima in the Aberdares. It has no outlet, disappearing into the vast Lorian Swamp another 300 km (186 miles) downstream of Samburu.

Where to Stay

The most expensive place to stay in Samburu Reserve is the small and exclusive **Larsen's Tented Camp** ((02) 540780 FAX (02) 543810 E-MAIL blockreservations@net2000ke.com, Box 40075, Nairobi (very expensive). Seventeen tents here overlook the river but there are no children's rates, nor indeed children under seven because they're not permitted,

Alternatively, it is possible to camp for just Ksh825 per person downriver from the bridge and the park entrance (accept the offer of an armed guard). Many of the campsites are in superb riverside locations, but are not easy for incomers to find or reserve: most will be taken by established mobile camping operators, for their clients.

SHABA NATIONAL RESERVE

To reach the unvisited and fabulous Shaba National Reserve, you must drive three

and the atmosphere is, perhaps, rather self-consciously superior. The food is good though. The **Samburu Intrepids** ((02) 446651 or 447929 FAX (02) 446533 E-MAIL info@heritagehotels .co.ke WEB SITE www.heritagehotels.co.ke, Box 74888 Nairobi, is noticeably cheaper and, for families, has (like all the Intrepids) an excellent "explorers club" for children (expensive). With 27 luxury tents, it's not too much bigger either and is a very good option.

The nearby **Samburu Lodge** ((02) 540780 FAX (02) 543810 E-MAIL blockreservations @net2000ke.com, Box 40075, Nairobi, where gasoline is available, is the original camp in the area, and still has the best setting, on a bend in the Ewaso Ngiro River, although it is currently rather run-down (expensive).

kilometers (two miles) south from Archer's Post and turn east at the sign for the Sarova Shaba Lodge. From this turnoff, it's about six kilometers (four miles) of rough road to **Natorbe Gate**, the entrance to the reserve. From the gate, a series of roads branch east and south through an arid, volcanic expanse of rugged hills and sharp valleys.

The reserve extends for nearly 30 km (19 miles) along the south bank of the Ewaso Ngiro, with vulture nesting areas visible across the river on the **Bodich Cliffs**, and monkeys frolicking in doum palms along the water.

Back-country tented lodges, such as Larson's in Samburu National Reserve, offer the ultimate in luxury.

In central Shaba, a marsh feeds a seasonal tributary of the Ewaso Ngiro. This is a favorite locale for foraging antelope and their predators, including leopards, cheetahs and lions. It was at Shaba that a resentful ex-employee murdered Joy Adamson in 1980 as she was completing a study of leopards and cheetahs. It is possible to camp where her settlement once stood (sadly, it was never preserved) and there are still plenty of lions about.

Shaba takes its name from a 1,620-m-tall (5,318-ft) volcanic cone just to the south, which has overflowed areas of the reserve with yet-unvegetated black lava. If you feel unusually adventurous, and your four-wheel drive is in good condition, ask the rangers at Natorbe Gate for a guide to accompany you on the narrow track that descends 30 km (19 miles) along the Ewaso Ngiro beyond the reserve, heading eastward to beautiful **Shanriki Falls**. Shanriki Falls are very often referred to as "Penny Falls," after one of Joy Adamson's lions.

Shaba National Reserve is one of Kenya's most beautiful reserves, but visitors are kept at bay by the unforgiving roads of battered lava and the fact that the game, though plentiful, is painfully shy. Photographers here tend to get plenty of pictures of distant, disappearing tails. But for those who like having the bush to yourself, Shaba is an ideal place to visit.

Where to Stay

Excellent camping is available in Shaba, as the *shiftas* (bandits) that put the park off-limits are now kept at bay by a rugged team of well-armed wardens (Ksh825, once more, per person, on top of the US$27 reserve entry fee). To be safe, check with the rangers first at Natorbe Gate. Fortunately there is a lodge here: the **Sarova Shaba Lodge** ((02) 713333 FAX (02) 718700 E-MAIL reservations@sarova .co.ke WEB SITE www.sarova.com, Box 72493, Nairobi, which is a large establishment looking older than its 11 years but offering unpretentious, reasonably-priced accommodation in 85 suites, all with the luxury of full-length baths (expensive, full board). Somewhat isolated, they are also able to offer extras, such as game walks, that are not, strictly speaking, permitted here.

HOW TO GET THERE

Access to Samburu, Buffalo Springs and Shaba are generally by daily scheduled flight from Nairobi by **Airkenya** (US$120 one-way) ((02) 501421/3 FAX (02) 500845 E-MAIL info @airkenya.com WEB SITE www.airkenya.com, Box 30357, Nairobi. It's a seven-hour drive from Nairobi, but public transportation dries up around Isiolo, leaving travelers 31 km (20 miles) short of the three reserves.

NORTHERN FRONTIER DISTRICT

Driving north from Archer's Post you truly enter the Northern Frontier District: lawless, vast, sun-parched and visionary. This area is currently unsafe, however, and is unlikely to become safe in the lifetime of this book, thanks to heavily-armed gangs of *shiftas* (bandits across from Somalia) and warring tribesmen. Before you, dominating the endless stony steppe, is sheer, towering Ol Doinyo Sabachi, a huge table mountain (*inselberg*) which many of the Samburu people consider the home of *Ngai*, God. If you're really determined to travel this road, you will be taken in a convoy of trucks. The only real reasons to do so is to cross over into Ethiopia or, less ambitiously, to visit Marsabit and the Marsabit National Park.

MARSABIT AND ITS NATIONAL PARK

Inselbergs (from the German for "island mountain") are not uncommon in the plains country of Kenya. Like mesas in the American southwest, they are formed of harder or less-jointed rock that withstands erosion better than the surrounding peneplain. Sabachi is certainly one of Africa's most imposing, often cloud-covered, thickly wooded on its lower slopes and atop its broad plateau, whose springs, marshes and grassy meadows are used by the Samburu for grazing in the dry seasons (July to September, January to March). Few travelers appreciate the view too much, as they are concentrating on surviving the endless corrugations on the road. Marsabit's volcanic

Salt deposits among volcanic rock in Shaba are harvested by desert tribes.

mass rises into the fleecy clouds like Shangri-La amid the desert, its coolness paradise after the molten desert. Permanently green thanks to its sudden elevation, it is a colorful place of Rendile and Borana tribesmen, as well as Ethiopian and Somali refugees. There's a bank and a few basic places to stay, the better of which is the run-down **Kenya Lodge and Hotel (** (0183) 2221, Box 176, Marsabit (very inexpensive). Since the lodge in the park closed, this is your best option — there are too many animals in the park to camp there.

A visit to the park, however, is a must. Watered by the mist and clouds of air blown east from Lake Turkana, the volcanic cones of Marsabit contain important remnants of Kenya's upland forest, its often-immense trees cloaked in *usnea* lichens and gray-bearded mosses, its flora and fauna of exceptional beauty and diversity. The country's longest-tusked elephants have traditionally come from Marsabit Mountain, the most famous being Ahmed, who died in 1974 and is now on display, life-sized in fiberglass, at the National Museum in Nairobi (a humorous account of Ahmed's demise and subsequent enthronement is contained in Patrick Marnham's *Fantastic Invasion*).

Although Ahmed enjoyed the protection of President Kenyatta, the president's last wife, Mama Ngina, was more mercenary in her concern for elephants, having by most accounts directed Kenya's largest poaching ring, with the result that nearly all of Ahmed's peers have vanished from Marsabit, their tusks sold via South Africa to the ivory merchants of Japan, China and Taiwan, and the park is seriously encroached. Curiously enough, Mama Ngina's brother followed as Kenya's Minister of Tourism and Wildlife, thus becoming responsible for the safety and well-being of those few pachyderms that escaped his sister's ministrations.

Many other superb animals remain, however, in the 2,100-sq-km (811-sq-miles) Marsabit National Park, including greater and lesser kudus, reticulated giraffes, spotted and striped hyenas, caracals, serval cats, leopards, lions, beisa oryx and the unusual petersi Grant's gazelles, with its near-parallel horns. What's more, the place is an ornithologist's fantasy, its microclimates shifting from cloud forest to blasting desert, the home of 52 different birds of prey. Grebes, herons, spur-wing geese, ducks, teal and pintail can be found around Lake Paradise itself, with the rare lammergeyers (bearded vultures) nesting on the precipitous cliffs of **Gof Bongole**, and many more rare species found in the black lava desert surrounding the park.

Six kilometers (three and three quarter miles) from the town of Marsabit, off the main road from Isiolo, are the **Ulanula** or **Singing Wells**, more looked for than found: ask a local to show you where they are. In the dry season (July to September, January to March) the local Borana herdsmen form human chains to hand up buckets of water from the well's muddy depths, singing when the mood strikes (or for benefit of tourists, when recompense is offered).

How to Get there

There are no *matatus* or other forms of public transportation traveling overland up to Marsabit, and the only way is in your own four-wheel-drive car, traveling in convoy for safety, along a truly awful corrugated track 242 km (150 miles) up from Archer's Post at the northern boundary of Samburu National Reserve. The only sensible way of getting there is by air charter: contact **Fuf Aviation (** (02) 505541 or **Sarman Aviation (** (02) 606416. With either company the cost is likely to be around US$1,200, depending on how long you intend to stay; without your own transportation on arrival, however, you might not want to stay too long.

WEST FROM SAMBURU

If the security situation is suitable, it is possible to drive west to Wamba. Take enough fuel, as the next provisions are in Maralal. There are two remote and atmospheric camps here. **Sarara (** (02) 501853 FAX (02) 608487 E-MAIL acacia@swiftkenya.com WEB SITE www.africatravelreview.com, Acacia Trails, Box 30907, Nairobi, is a community ranch run by the Samburu people and a real chance to get close to the local community and make a (serious) contribution to their finances (extremely expensive). There is also the even more remote luxury of **Kitich Camp**, reserve through Bush Homes of East Africa ((02) 350703, (02) 571661 or (02) 571592 FAX (02) 571665 E-MAIL bushhome@africaonline.co.ke WEB SITE www.bush-homes.co.ke, Box 56923, Nairobi (very expensive). Camp consists of six luxurious en-suite walk-in tents, each for two people, with individual bathrooms and copious bucket showers filled each morning with hot water from the large wood-fed boiler near the kitchen tent.

The spacious dining tent and the guest tents each look out from groves of shady fig trees onto a magnificent small valley with

baggage transported by horses. This is a pleasure for those who've flown in, but even more for those who've drive up: it's a chance to get out of the car. The nearest town is Wamba, which has a good mission hospital — accustomed to snakebites and bullet wounds — which can, in this part of the country, be useful.

How to Get There

Kitich is an eight-hour drive from Nairobi, traveling north on the A2 to Isiolo, through the Buffalo Springs (paying an entry fee) and

the shimmering Ngeng River in its center and the rugged ridges of the Matthews Range rising abruptly on the far side. On the opposite slopes grow 800-year-old cycads, a prehistoric species of palm which is the most primitive extant seed-bearing plant, and some of the largest podocarp and cedar in Kenya. Other plants include six species of hibiscus, crotons, whose bright flowers produce a very sweet honey, and combretum. The valley boasts a population of butterflies unique in the world, with new species still being found, and is a major stopover for European migratory birds.

From Kitich, accompanied hikes through the Matthews Range can last from a day up to eight-day expeditions with food, tents and

forking left for Wamba. Alternatively, travel north to Naivasha, bear left to Nyahururu and complete the second half of the drive on *murram* roads, turning right before, but near Maralal for Wamba. The fact that there are two routes raises the interesting possibility of a short circuit lasting anything from four days to a week. If you don't relish the eight-hour drive from Nairobi, it's possible to fly directly to Wamba and have someone from Kitich pick you up there. There is no regular overland transportation along the C78 that links Isiolo with Maralal so the trip may take many days if hitching. Wamba itself is five kilometers (three miles) off the

As the sun sets on Lake Turkana the sound of drums come alive in the local settlements.

main road and Kitich 40 km (25 miles) further still. This doesn't mean it's impossible, quite, but it will be an adventure. You should be prepared to do some fairly serious walking and to be ready for days on end waiting for a lift.

EAST OF MOUNT KENYA: ELSA'S COUNTRY

Mount Kenya's eastern flanks, traversed by a newly resurfaced road, guide the main road around towards the town of Meru, the Nyambeni Hills and Meru National Park itself, where the film of Joy Adamson's tale of Elsa the lioness awoke the world to the beauty and romance of African wildlife. Traveling north from Nairobi, the first town you'll come to after bearing right at Muranga is the small settlement of Embu. There seems no very good reason to stay here, but if required the **Izaac Walton Inn** ((0161) 20128/9 FAX (0161) 30135, Box 1, on the Meru Road, is a pleasant enough place to settle into a laid-back, vaguely colonial atmosphere (inexpensive to mid-range). Most people, however, put their foot on the throttle to make the most of the new and, if in a *matatu*, frighteningly fast road that heads across the ravine-ridden eastern slopes of Mount Kenya to the town of Meru. Halfway you'll pass **Chogoria**, starting point for one of the best routes to climb Mount Kenya (see CLIMBING LENANA, page 214).

MERU

The town of Meru is a major hub for transportation in all directions, with buses, matatus and even planes rattling off in every direction, traveling to Uganda, Somalia, Ethiopia and beyond. There's a reason for this, and the reason is *miraa*. This green shrub is chewed all over East Africa, stretching time and reducing appetites, and this is where it grows. It's a mild narcotic and something of an acquired taste (I find it quite resistible), but you'll see how much passion it arouses in the Kenyans whenever you board a *matatu* leaving Meru, loaded with bunches of *miraa*. Your rate of progress is slowed to a crawl as it is sold, bunch by bunch, to people standing by the side of the road.

The town itself is pleasantly sited on the northeastern slopes of Mount Kenya, and is the administrative and commercial center of the district of the same name. The town doesn't see many Western visitors but is all the better for that. The Bantu-speaking Meru tribe, related to both the Kikuyu and the Embu people to the south, are thriving and populous, and the **Meru Museum** ((0164) 20482, 9 AM to 6 PM daily, Ksh200, is a good place to find out more. Housed in the oldest building in town, it has ethnographic displays, a collection of medicinal herbs (including *miraa*, of course) and a well-preserved homestead. The market is large, and it's interesting to see the *miraa*-trading area on Moi Avenue.

Where to Stay and Eat

The best place to stay in town, by a comfortable margin, is the **Pig and Whistle** ((0164) 31411, 20574, Box 3160, Meru (inexpensive). It has been in operation since World War I, and various renovations have done little to drag it into the present day. The cabins, either in concrete or wood, are well-equipped (for Meru) and the creaky wooden bar is a delight. Meal prices are reasonable and the food is delicious and ample. More modern is the **Meru County Hotel** ((0164) 20342 FAX (0164) 31264, Box 1386, Meru (inexpensive). There are plenty of restaurants serving African food, probably best at the Meru County Hotel but with plenty of other establishments such as the **Ivory Springs Café**. Just follow your nose.

How to Get There

There is a choice of routes to Meru from Nairobi (290 km or 181 miles), both via Muranga but then passing either side of Mount Kenya. It is faster to come via Embu (since the mountainside road was repaired), but the road through Karatina and Nanyuki can give more pretexts to stop along the way. Allow six hours or so — more in the wet season (April to June, October to early December). Isiolo is 57 km (36 miles) distant. Thanks to its pivotal role in the production of *miraa* Meru is served by plenty of buses and *matatus* (and unscheduled flights), but are often very full when they leave and none are sympathetic to overladen backpackers.

Unless, of course, their backpacks are full of *miraa*, which would be a novelty.

MERU NATIONAL PARK

Meru National Park, 85 km (53 miles) beyond Meru town, is on few itineraries following many years of poor security and the closure of all park accommodation. Now, however, it is gradually opening up again, with the arrival of a new luxury lodge and increased security.

It is one of the most beautiful of all Kenya's parks. Stretching out before you are the golden, rolling plains where Joy Adamson released the lioness Elsa. The park is the locale of the book and later the movie, *Born Free*. The park, 1,812 sq km (700 sq miles), descends in a series of plateaus from the 1,000-m (3,000-ft) Nyambeni foothills southeast across savanna and open woodland to less than 300 m (1,000 ft) on the banks of the Tana and Rojewero river.

Meru contains a variety of ecosystems, from near-desert savanna to tropical marshes and riparian zones, even rainforest (the **Ngaia Forest**). Occasional rugged, reddish-yellow rocky outcrops thrust up from the plateau amid combretum and commiphora scrub, grassland and acacia trees. A series of sizable waterways, including the **Murera**,

Lions often rest during the day on outcrops and termite mounds on the savannah.

Rojewero, **Tana**, **Kiolu** and **Ura** Rivers, flow southeast across the plateau, providing water for wildlife and riparian forest zones of towering fig and tamarind trees, and raphia and doum palms. The northwest section of the park has numerous large marshes packed with wildlife such as **Bwatherongi**, **Mughwango**, and **Mururi Swamp**, all accessible by the park's excellent road system.

Sizable animal populations inhabit the park — lions, elephants, buffaloes, both common and Grevy's zebras (although you'll probably see only the common), reticulated giraffes, Somali ostriches, waterbucks, leopards, impalas, Grant's gazelles, beisa oryx, olive baboons, aardwolves, Sykes' and patas monkeys, cheetahs, caracals, wildcats, serval cats, hippopotamuses and crocodiles, as well as countless birds. Until November 1988, its major attraction was five very tame white rhinos. They were slaughtered by Somali poachers with automatic weapons who opened fire on the rhinos and nearby rangers, who immediately took cover.

The incident created an international outcry; security at the park tightened, but the poachers, of course, were never found. A major result of the ensuing security crackdown was the closure of several remote campsites. This incident has tainted the park's fame, but rhinos or no rhinos, Meru remains one of Kenya's, and the world's, best parks.

Meru offers superb views of Mount Kenya in the early morning and late afternoon, when the clouds usually clear. It has a well-designed road network and the intersections of the park roads are numbered — note them in your head as you pass and it's less likely you'll get turned around. Also, in the rare event that you can procure a map of Meru, these markers are shown.

During and after the rains, when forage and water are easily available, Meru's wildlife is generally more dispersed, but in the dry seasons (July to September, January to

There is a nearly endless series of short and long game drives you can take in Meru, alternating riverine roads with open savanna ones. **Elsa's Camp** on the Ura River is near its junction with the Tana, in the southeast corner of the park. From here, it's less than an hour's drive along the north bank of the Tana to dazzling **Adamson's Falls**, where you will often find hippos and a profusion of birds including the loud Pel's fishing owl. Be sure to check with park rangers as to the status of the road before departing on these itineraries; take a guide if they so advise.

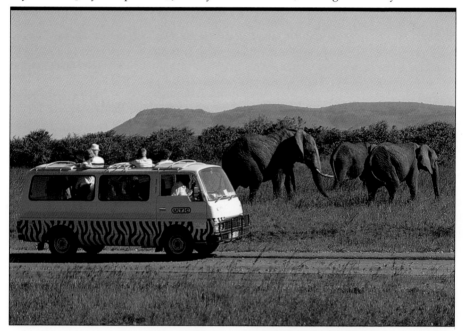

March), it tends to congregate near the rivers, swamps, and ponds, when the marsh in front of the now-closed Meru Mulika Lodge is visited regularly by elephants, buffaloes, impalas, baboons, ostriches and waterbucks.

The northeastern section of the park has the most varied vegetation — magnificent stands of doum palms and whistling thorns. You may not see a lot of game here, but you will often find monkeys and baboons shaking the fruits from the palms. Germination of the doum palm is facilitated by passage through the bowels of an elephant, thus, where you see these palms, it's likely there once were (and may still be) elephants.

Accessible from Meru are the **Bisanadi**, **North Kitui**, **Rahole** and **Kora National Reserves**, all semi-desert except along the banks of the Tana, which they adjoin. The barren, sweeping landscapes and the birds in these areas make the long excursions memorable, but you are also rewarded with excellent undisturbed game viewing.

Before you attempt trips into any of these reserves, however, be *sure* to check with the park rangers on dangers and restrictions. Ever since the rhinos were poached, it has been impossible to make the trip without a ranger/guide. Don't let it disturb you if he climbs into your vehicle armed with an Enfield .303 or a German G-3 automatic rifle. Traveling with tourists offers the rangers a chance to patrol, but he's also there for your security; there are few maps and numerous chances to get lost, and the 6:30 PM curfew is strictly enforced in Meru. Chances are he can point out scores of animals you'd miss alone.

Meru boasts over 300 species of birds. They are everywhere and of all colors of the rainbow. Meter-tall (three-foot) kori bustards often patrol the entrance to the lodge, iridescent superb and Hildebrant's starlings flash about everywhere, and there are four species of honeyguides in residence. Guinea fowl

and francolin are abundant enough to be annoying as they scurry ahead of your vehicle, refusing to give way. They do give way, but not until the very last millisecond, quite unlike the large land tortoise who simply pulled in his head and legs as I approached.

Where to Stay
By far the best place to stay in Meru is **Elsa's Kjope**, run by the upmarket operator Cheli and Peacock Ltd. ((02) 604053/4 or (02) 603090/1 FAX (02) 604050 or (02) 603066 E-MAIL chelipeacock@africaonline.co.ke WEB SITE www.chelipeacock.com, Box 39806, Nairobi, which offers game packages of day and night game-drives, guided walks and fine, Italian-influenced cuisine (very

expensive, all-inclusive). Since the Meru Mulika Lodge closed, the only other accommodation is at designated primitive campsites for US$2 per person, and that *must* be arranged first at the gate or the park headquarters. In consolation, Meru offers some of the best game viewing for travelers allergic to the sight of other vehicles.

How to Get There
To reach the park from Meru, follow the signs in the center of town, taking the macadam highway 30 km (19 miles) northeast (it has marvelous views opening northward on the Nyambeni Hills). Turn right on a dirt road just before the town of Maua (the highway soon turns to dirt also); there is usually no sign to indicate the turn and you may have to ask. This dirt road, which can be difficult during the rainy season, descends 55 km (34 miles) through former forest now jammed with small farms (*shambas*), and lined from time to time with tiny shops (*dukas*).

The parade of women heavily laden with firewood and water containers, of children herding livestock and of men promenading while chewing *miraa*, the local drug, is endless. As recently as 1970, this entire region between Meru National Park and the highway was solid forest, wild and filled with animals. Now, every inch is under cultivation, eroding or being overgrazed — a lesson in the earth's crying need for population control. At the park boundaries such development stops abruptly.

ONWARDS FROM MERU

From Meru, there is an enticing-looking road heading northeast toward Wajir and the Somalia border. Minor routes, on the map, head down toward Garissa. All these roads are lousy: fiendish in the rainy season and blistering when it's hot. Worse, there are just too many bandits and too many guns to make it worth attempting. Think about trying it, fine, but then think again and leave the locals to their local feuds.

OPPOSITE: Once common nearly everywhere in Kenya, elephants have been reduced by ivory poaching to remnant, threatened populations in a few national parks. ABOVE: Most Kenyan tourist hotel rooms are spacious and comfortable, as here in Samburu.

The Eastern Plains

Long before the Masai Mara stole the wild-life show, white hunters in Kenya went to Tsavo on the great Eastern Plains to find, and then shoot, the wildlife. When these early colonists hung up their guns, indigenous hunters took over: in the trackless bush, poachers ran riot, and throughout much of the 1980s, the broad savannahs of Tsavo East National Park were turned into a battleground.

These days things are much improved. Elephant populations, worst hit by the poachers, are recovering, and areas once off-limits to tourists are now open again. Tsavo East National Park, north of the main Nairobi–Mombasa road, now offers many miles of untouched wilderness, and Tsavo West National Park, south of the main road, has areas of spectacular beauty. The volcanic Chyulu Hills, barely crossed by navigable roads, are havens for wildlife dispersing from the national parks through the rainy season, and valuable grazing lands for the cattle of the indigenous Maasai people. Meanwhile, to the west, the small oasis of Amboseli continues to attract huge herds of elephant, all backed by the stunning peak of snow-capped Kilimanjaro.

At the heart of all this is the scattered, unimpressive town of Voi.

VOI

The only settlement of any size on the main Nairobi–Mombasa road is Voi, a simple town that sports several ATM cash machines, a few gas stations and some bars and inexpensive hotels. It is mainly significant as a jumping-off point for the nearby reserves of Tsavo East and Tsavo West.

WHERE TO STAY AND EAT

Although most travelers pass through here on their way to the game lodges in the park, there are places to stay in Voi and it is possible to have quite a good time here. The best place is the **Tsavo Park Hotel** ((0147) 30050 FAX (0147) 30285, Box 244, Voi, with surprising sophistication for such an isolated spot and a good restaurant serving Western staples (inexpensive). On a budget, another good lodging is **Ghana Guest House** ((0147)

2503, Box 492, Voi, quietly run by a woman's co-operative (very inexpensive). Wednesday, Friday and Saturday are disco nights at the Tsavorite Club, in a converted sports hall near the market.

MAN-EATER COUNTRY

" …the lions had a range of some eight miles on either side of Tsavo to work upon; and as their tactics seemed to be to break into a different camp each night, it was most difficult to forestall them. They almost appeared, too, to have an extraordinary and uncanny faculty of finding out our plans beforehand, so that no matter in how likely or how tempting a spot we lay in wait for them, they invariably avoided that particular place and seized their victim for the night from some other camp. Hunting them by day, moreover, in such a dense wilderness as surrounded us, was an exceedingly tiring and really foolhardy undertaking."

So does Colonel J.H. Patterson describe, in his *The Man-eaters of Tsavo*, some of the difficulties he faced when sent by the British Foreign Office in 1898 to direct a section of the Mombasa–Uganda Railway, where the depredations of two ravenous man-eating lions brought work to a standstill. After months of hunting them, during which time they killed numerous workers, Patterson describes being stalked by one lion:

"I again kept as still as I could, though absolutely trembling with excitement; and in a short while I heard the lion begin to creep stealthily towards me. I could barely make out his form as he crouched among the whitish undergrowth … I took careful aim and pulled the trigger. The sound of the shot was at once followed by a most terrific roar, and then I could hear him leaping about in all directions …"

Patterson was finally able to kill another man-eater and capture a brazen third that had entered a railway carriage and killed and carried off one of the line's engineers. Hidden away in Nairobi's Railway Museum there's a photo of the lion doing just that. But man-eating lions have remained part of the lore and mystique of Tsavo.

The distinctive markings of the reticulated giraffes, are specially adapted to blend with its habitat.

THE
EASTERN
PLAINS

Now the biggest park in Kenya, and at 20,807 sq km (8,000 sq miles) one of the largest in the world, Tsavo National Park is an international wildlife and environmental treasure chest. It contains a variety of habitats, geologic/soil types, animals, birds and plants, and offers excellent camping, lodges and other accommodation.

Divided by the Nairobi–Mombasa road and railway into Tsavo West (7,000 sq km or 2,700 sq miles) and Tsavo East (more than 13,000 sq km or 5,000 sq miles), the park is a change from nearby Amboseli. Confusingly, although the two parks are named after their east/west location, in fact they are more defined along a north/south axis: Tsavo East spreads north from the main road, while Tsavo West occupies a C-shaped swathe to the south of the main road.

Tsavo West is hillier, greener and much more vegetated than its northern neighbor, but also has more tourists. For isolation, head instead out into the wilderness areas of Tsavo East. Each has its advantages.

TSAVO EAST

Tsavo East is vast even by African standards. It is the legendary Kenyan wilderness, with limitless vistas across its gray-brown scrub, dotted with baobab trees, to impossibly distant table mountains. Entry fees to the park are US$23 per adult and US$8 per child.

Of its 13,000 sq km (5,000 sq miles), nearly two-thirds (the area north of the Galana River) has spent the last decades off-limits to tourists. This was in part to allow the park to recover from the droughts of the 1970s and the even more devastating poaching wars of the 1980s. Now the area is, once more, opening up to wealthier visitors through walking safaris and mobile tented camps, though movements are still restricted in this area, and you're likely to be assigned, and charged for, a ranger.

South of the Galana River there are no such restrictions and there's more than enough to keep any wanderer occupied for months. The easiest place to start is the main (but not surfaced) C103 road from Manyani Gate, west of Voi, following the south bank of the Galana, with its numerous offshoots up tributary ravines. If you wish, you can take this road all the way to the coast city of Malindi. A highlight of Tsavo East is the imposing **Mudanda Rock**, a flat-topped *inselberg* of Promethean proportions some 13 km (eight miles) south of Manyani Gate. It has a water hole that draws wildlife from miles around, except at the height of the dry seasons (July to September, January to March). Just south of Mudanda Rock, you can turn northeast down the bank of the seasonal Mbololo River, and in 29 km (18 miles) pick up the Galana River road again.

The joining of the Tsavo and the Athi River, which descends all the way from Nairobi, forms the Galana River. It drops from the high plateau country into a narrow canyon at **Lugard's Falls**, named for the adventurer, soldier and antislavery activist Lord Frederick Lugard, who stopped here in 1890 on his way to becoming the proconsul of Uganda. (Surely, the courageous Lord Lugard deserves greater commemoration than this brown, turgid cascade, with its complement of crocodiles basking below.)

From Lugard's Falls, it's an easy half-day drive down the Galana River to Sala Gate. From there, another three hours down the south bank of the Sabaki River brings you to a whole other world in Malindi.

If you've come from Mombasa, Tsavo West or the Taita Hills, the normal place to enter Tsavo East is by the park headquarters at **Voi Gate**. From here, it's a quick drive to several lodges or past the **Kandari Swamp** (which, disastrously, dries out in times of drought) down the north bank of the Voi River. Some 34 km (21 miles) from the Voi Gate is **Aruba Dam**. During the early dry seasons (July to September, January to March), when there's little water to be found in the area, the dam provides a strong draw for wildlife. Here, you have excellent chances of seeing gazelles, impalas, buffaloes, greater kudus, Defassa waterbucks and associated predators.

From the dam, you can follow roads back up to the Galana River or descend further on the Voi, depending on the season. Although Tsavo East is much drier than Tsavo West, its roads can become boggy in the rains and sandblasted ruts in the dry seasons, so proceed with caution.

Foreplay is an intricate part of lion courtship.

Where to Stay

In Tsavo East, there are excellent places to stay, and it's worthwhile spending a day or two wandering this largely unvisited park. Seasonal, between the months of June to November, is **Patrick's Camps**, a mobile tented camp that spends the rest of the year in Solio. Patrick's gets guests closest to the bush through night drives, fly camps and bush breakfasts (extremely expensive, all-inclusive). Reserve through Bush Homes of East Africa ((02) 350703, (02) 571661 or (02) 571592 FAX (02) 571665 E-MAIL bushhome

most expensive, is **Galdessa Camp** E-MAIL www.galdessa.com, reserve through Mellifera ((02) 574689, (02) 577018 or (02) 567251 FAX (02) 564945 E-MAIL Mellifera@swiftkenya.com, Box 24397, Nairobi, on the southern side of the Galana River west of Lugard's Falls (extremely expensive, all-inclusive). Bush breakfasts here are a specialty, followed by walking safaris and fishing on the river. Downstream, and down-market, but much better value, is **Epiya Chapeyu** ((02) 749796 FAX (02) 750990 E-MAIL bigi@formnet.com, Box 14653, Nairobi, which has 20 tents, fairly

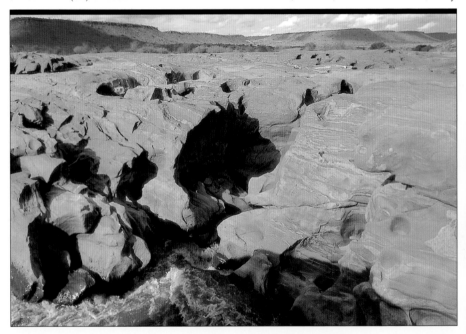

@africaonline.co.ke WEB SITE www.bush-homes.co.ke, Box 56923, Nairobi. Otherwise, the most northerly lodge, accessed through Mtito Andei Gate, nearest to Nairobi, in the restricted area, is **Tsavo Safari Camp** ((02) 227136 FAX (02) 219982 E-MAIL ksc@africa online.co.ke, Box 30139, Nairobi, located 24 km (15 miles) northeast of Mtito Andei Gate on the east bank of the Athi River (expensive, full board). It offers guided tours into the off-limits zone of Tsavo East. It is necessary here to make a reservation, or the guards at the parking lot won't let you cross the river (by boat) to the lodge on the far bank.

Through the western Manyani Gate there are two lodges on the southern banks of the Galana River. Perhaps the best, certainly the

close together, and a relaxed and welcoming, Italian atmosphere (expensive, full board).

Enter the park through Voi Gate, by the park headquarters, and the **Voi Safari Lodge** ((02) 336858 FAX (02) 218109, Box 30471, Nairobi, is nearby (expensive, full board). It is justifiably famous for its endless panorama across the dry savannah and two water holes that entice a multitude of beasts. This is also where Tsavo East's most popular campsite, which also has a few basic *bandas*, is found. Guests here share the place with Daphne Sheldrick's orphaned elephants, now grown up. If you're not careful, you might end up sharing your food as well. These elephants have no fear of man, which is potentially a very dangerous situation: watch out.

Follow the seasonal Voi River and you'll reach Aruba Dam, where there is currently a **campsite** and plans for a lodge. Either way it's worth a visit for its game. Follow the river to **Satao Camp**, reserve through Southern Cross Safaris ((011) 471960 FAX (011) 471257, Box 90653, Nyali, Mombasa, a luxury tented camp built on a (seasonal) island (expensive, full board). It is in the heart of the park and, if coming from Mombasa, is better reached from Buchuma Gate.

Entering the park along the dirt C103 road from Malindi, one of the first places to stay

Airkenya flights into Tsavo are currently suspended, and charter flights (try Boskovic Air Charters Ltd. ((02) 501219 FAX 505964, Box 45646, Nairobi) are now the quickest way. Tsavo East has airstrips at Lugard's Falls, Aruba Dam and Satao Camp. In your own vehicle, the first park gate coming from the capital is at Mtito Andei (literally meaning "the place of the vultures"), 236 km (147 miles) from Nairobi, 249 km (156 miles) from Mombasa, or, further east, at Voi, 334 km (208 miles) from Nairobi and 151 km (94 miles) from Mombasa, where the park

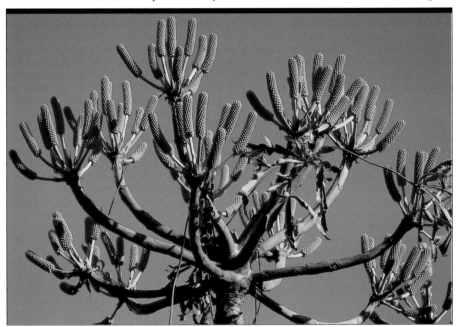

is far downstream, just outside the park boundaries on the coast side by Sala Gate. **Tsavo Buffalo Camp** ((0147) 2547 FAX (0123) 30715 E-MAIL coralkey@africaonline.co.ke, Box 556 Malindi, is the cheapest option without camping and easiest to reach from the coast but you'll need your own vehicle for game drives (mid-range). Nearby is **Kulalu Camp**, reserve through Hemingways ((0122) 32624 FAX (0122) 32256 Box 267, Watamu, or **Ocean Sports** ((0122) 32008 FAX (0122) 32266, Box 100, Watamu, much favored by bird-shooting Kenyans (mid-range).

How to Get There

Access to the lodges in the huge expanses of Tsavo East depends on their specific location.

headquarters are found. Both Voi and Mtito Andei are served by *matatus* but there is no public transportation into the park itself.

TAITA HILLS

Sitting somewhat strangely between Tsavo East and Tsavo West are the Taita Hills. Set against the broad plains, they rise steep and forested, punctuated with crashing creeks and waterfalls. It was from their tallest peak, Vuria, at 2,209 m (7,247 ft), that the missionary Rebmann saw Kilimanjaro's white spire in 1848, the first European to do so.

The wild landscapes OPPOSITE of Tsavo East and are home to exotic plants such as this toothbrush plant ABOVE.

The hills are home to the friendly Taita people, of whom the explorer Thomson spoke fondly. Their settlements are centered on the bustling hill town of Wundanyi and the terraced slopes between Voi and the Tanzania border. To reach the Taita Hills, leave Tsavo West by the Maktau Gate and drive toward Voi. The area between Maktau and the town of Bura was the site in World War I of intensive fighting between the British and German troops. The latter, under the command of Colonel Von Lettow-Vorbeck, were trying to cut the Mombasa–Uganda Railway.

Maktau or west all the way to Lake Jipe. Check with the people in Bungule first as to road conditions, and whether the gate's open. From Bungule, you can also attempt the drive across to **Mackinnon Road** on the Mombasa–Nairobi highway — again, ask first about road conditions.

Where to Stay

The best, but not the cheapest, place to stay here is in a private reserve known as the Taita Hills (but in fact on the less dramatic lowlands) and operated by the Hilton Group.

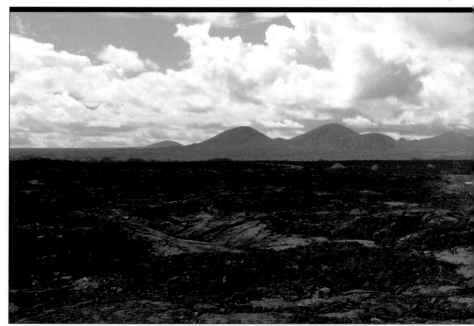

If you're in an adventurous mood, or like military history, there's a rough road (often impassable in the rains) leading southeast from the next town, **Mwatate**, across the arid flatlands, called "durststeppe" (thirst plains) by the German troops. This leads to the sheer escarpments of **Kasigau Mountain**, 1,641 m (5,384 ft), where blistering battles were fought between the Germans and British for control of the region's only water sources.

Providing your vehicle is in good shape and you have plenty of gas, you can turn west at **Bungule**, the town at the foot of Kasigau Mountain, to reenter Tsavo West by the Kasigau Gate. This takes you into some of the finest, and emptiest, terrain in the park, with the possibility of swinging north up to

Entry is US$24 per person, which is included for guests of the **Taita Hills Safari Lodge** (very expensive, full board), just outside the reserve. There are two more places to stay in this price bracket. The **Salt Lick Lodge** (very expensive, full board), in the south of the reserve, is the one that always appears in the photographs — stilted tents on a wide, game-strewn plain — while the **Hilton Safari Camp** (very expensive, full board) is probably the nicest, with no electricity (but no children under seven either). All three can be booked through **Hilton Kenya ℂ** (02) 334000 FAX 339462, Box 30624, Nairobi. This is the only place in Kenya apart from the Masai Mara where it is possible to go ballooning: it's cheaper too, at US$250 per person;

reserve through Hilton. On a budget, and to see the people rather than the animals, there's basic but clean accommodation just outside the small town of Wundanyi at the **Hills View Lodge** ((0148) 2417, Box 1262, Wundanyi (inexpensive); market days are Tuesday and Friday.

How to Get There

The most common way to reach the Taita Hills is from Mombasa. The road is paved all the way, and the drive takes just three hours. Nairobi is just too far — and the road too poor

visitors than its neighbor across the main road. The landscape of Tsavo West is everywhere spectacular, with wide valleys, rivers, ridges and peaks. The most famous of Tsavo West's sites is **Mzima Springs**, where rainfall collected in the porous volcanic rock springs forth at the rate of 225 million liters (50 million gallons) a day, more than 10 million liters (over two and a half million gallons) an hour, into a pool and stream full of crocodiles and hippopotamuses. Here, you can walk along an interpretive trail and even descend to a partially submerged lookout to

— to make this a sensible option from visitors based inland. The turning to Taita Hills is at Voi, 140 km (87.5 miles) from Mombasa and 300 km (187 miles) from Nairobi, where the A23 forks west towards Mwatate and the two Hilton lodges are 55 km (34 miles) on. This road continues on to Moshi and then Arusha. This means it is possible to get here by public transportation: change *matatus* at Voi for one heading to Taveta, Kenya's border town with Tanzania, but then there's no transportation into the game reserve.

Tsavo West

More accessible, and with more accommodation options, Tsavo West receives more

watch the animals swim by. Schools of fat barbel inspect the tourists from the far side of the glass. Unfortunately, some three-quarters of Mzima's flow has been diverted by pipeline to Mombasa, to serve as the city's water supply. This has reduced its downstream flows and aquatic life. Despite this, the springs remain a miracle of nature, a green outpost of tamarind, wild date, raphia palms and wild figs amid Tsavo's dry expanse.

An adventurous itinerary from Mzima is to follow the south bank of the **Tsavo River** east on the dirt track, winding in and out of the many luggas draining from the south. This is *definitely* four-wheel-drive country, and may

The lava fields of Tsavo West stretch to the distant mountains.

be impassable even then. It's best attempted with two vehicles (hopefully one can go for help when the other's incapacitated), and has proved fatal to unprepared tourists in the past. It's well worth the effort, but *not* for the faint of heart, or the inexperienced.

Less dangerous, but also four-wheel drive only, is the track along the river's north bank, 35 km (22 miles) from the Ngulia intersection (number 18) to Tsavo gate. The cardinal rule in any backcountry wandering is: *do not leave your vehicle.* If you do, you can become prey to various carnivores, lions in

of Tsavo's carrying capacity. After they had eaten all the grass and shrubs, the elephants tore down the trees to get at the bark and softer top branches. In the process, they fundamentally altered the vegetation of Tsavo West and turned Tsavo East from a forested savanna into desert and plains.

With vegetation depleted, drought followed. The elephants died by the thousands. As they began to recover, the poachers came to finish off those left. There are few elephants remaining in Tsavo now, but since the Kenyan government enforced proclamations to hunt

particular, alarm or irritate a passing herbivore (buffaloes and hippos kill more people in Kenya than lions do), or what's most likely, succumb to heat and dehydration. Unless you're positive no one will be looking for you, and that there's no way another vehicle will pass (overflights of most parks are common), stay in your car. *Always* let someone know (a park ranger or lodge personnel) before attempting any backcountry driving.

Only 20 years ago, Tsavo was host to the largest herds of elephants still left in Africa — with counts of up to 20,000 at a time. People who have seen them speak of elephants covering the entire surface of the land as far as the eye could see. But such a concentration led rapidly to a degradation

down poachers (including those with government ties), numbers are now recovering.

The outlook for the black rhino is bleaker. Thirty years ago, there were up to 9,000 in Tsavo alone; now there are none in Tsavo and probably fewer than 500 in Kenya. Only by massive international fund-raising efforts are numbers slowly starting to creep upwards.

To the north, Tsavo West extends up to the **Chyulu Hills**: steep volcanic hills that bump parallel to the main road, dividing the dispersion areas of Tsavo and Amboseli. The road from Tsavo West passes over lava beds so new that not a blade of grass has grown. To the north, the most recent cones stand naked and black. One, named Shetani ("devil" in Swahili), is thought to have erupted most recently 200 years ago; a trail of several kilometers winds around the flow but the lava has folded into many caves that shelter leopard, so check with the rangers at Kilaguni Gate before hiking.

Tsavo West's southern extent borders with Tanzania around the shores of Lake Jipe. Lake Jipe appears to have been visited by ancient Greek mariners whose belief that it was a source of the Nile was quoted by Ptolemy. Ptolemy's map of Africa, completed in the second century, was used well into the 1500s. Just north of the lake are the extensive sisal

Where to Stay

A number of excellent lodges in Tsavo West have, over recent years, suffered rather from the long-term consequences of drought and then poaching. The most expensive is **Finch Hattons** ((02) 604321 FAX (02) 604323 E-MAIL finchattons@iconnect.co.ke, Box 2443, Nairobi, with luxurious tents set around a hippo-filled spring (very expensive, full board). Service and cuisine is very smooth here, with crystal glass and silver.

Less formal is the **Voyager Safari Camp** (it used to be called Ziwani Tented Camp)

plantations begun by the eccentric and brilliant Captain Ewart Grogan, an incredibly wealthy timber exporter who in 1898 walked 7,250 km (4,500 miles) from Capetown to Cairo (supposedly for a fiancée he then decided not to marry), and later posted a mining claim on the city of Nairobi. Amid the sisal is **Grogan's Castle**, the huge, rambling, disorganized mansion that he built in the 1930s.

As pretty as Lake Jipe but less commercialized is **Lake Chala**. It straddles the Tanzania border 10 minutes north of **Taveta**. Follow the dirt road east of Taveta northward until you see a small hill: this is a crater, with Lake Chala inside it. Descend with care, there are crocodiles in the lake. Entry fees to the park are US$23 per adult and US$8 per child.

E-MAIL info@heritagehotels.co.ke WEB SITE www.heritagehotels.co.ke, Box 74888, Nairobi, to the west of the reserve (very expensive, full board). With just 20 comfortable tents and under the management of the very professional Heritage group this is a good place to stay, and because it is outside the park boundaries, it can offer walks and other activities. In the heart of the park, and surrounded by all its exuberant small animals, is **Kilaguni Serena Safari Lodge** ((02) 710511 FAX (02) 718103, Box 48690, Nairobi (very expensive, full board). Overlooking two busy waterholes, there's always some-

OPPOSITE: The magnificent views of Tsavo West are easily accessed. ABOVE: Mother lions are gentle with their cubs and ferocious in their defense.

thing to look at here. Even if it's out of your budget it's a good place to stop for lunch. East towards the Ngulia Rhino Sanctuary, **Ngulia Safari Lodge** ((0147) 2698, Box 42, Mtito Andei, is famous among ornithologists for the migrating birds from Russia and western Europe that stream by in autumn (expensive, full board). The lodge also offers self-catering *bandas* (inexpensive). The **Lake Jipe Lodge** ((02) 227623, Box 31097, Nairobi, on the shore of the lake is becoming run down, but does offer dhow trips on the lake (expensive).

Keep a fire going during the night to keep the more aggressive of predators at a distance, and be sure to leave nothing in your tent during the day, lest it fall prey to baboons or other primates.

There are excellent self-help *bandas* at **Ngulia** and **Kitani Safari Camps** (inexpensive, bring your own beverages and food), operated by Let's Go Travel ((02) 447151 or (02) 441030 FAX (02) 447270 or (02) 441690 E-MAIL info@letsgosafari.com WEB SITE www .letsgosafari.com, Box 60342, Nairobi, but these may be full in peak season.

If you've brought a tent, Tsavo is a great place to use it, even if just to store your gear: nothing can beat the millions of sharp, bright stars visible in Tsavo's clear night sky. There are good campsites in the park, as well as very inexpensive self-help *bandas*. One of the best is located just west of the **Chyulu Gate** (US$12 per person, payable at the gate). There are thatched verandahs to place a tent under or next to, along with fireplaces, running water, showers and toilets. You can also camp at the **Mtito Andei** and **Tsavo Gates**, not far from the Nairobi–Mombasa highway; at **Ziwani**, where there are more self-help *bandas*; and at **Lake Jipe** on the Tanzania frontier, with its astounding views of Kilimanjaro and Tanzania's Pare Mountains.

How to Get There

Tsavo West is on the main road between Nairobi and Mombasa, although it is rather nearer Mombasa and the coast. From Nairobi take the A109; how long the journey will take depends on the state of the road. Once the trip used to take six hours, but it has been known to take twice as long. The nearest gate to Nairobi is at Mtito Andei. From here it is 40 km (25 miles) to Mzima Springs. Tsavo Gate is 48 km (30 miles) closer to Mombasa, and a main access point for visitors from the coast. If traveling by public transportation, get off at Mtito Andei and pray for a lift with another tourist vehicle.

Looking like a desert outpost, Salt Lick Lodge provides a viewing platform for Kenya's wildlife.

CHYULU HILLS

Now protected as a national park, the southern foothills of the Chyulus contain a couple of worthwhile establishments for the well-heeled, both run as Maasai community ranches. **Ol Donyo Wuas** ((02) 882521 FAX (02) 882728 E-MAIL Bonham.luke@swifkenya.com, Box 24133, Nairobi, is a small lodge run by Kenya legend Richard Bonham in partnership with the local Maasai (extremely expensive, all-inclusive). Stunning rooms make the most of views of Kilimanjaro, and even the toilets look directly out over the plains. Horse-riding is a specialty here, but access isn't: most guests fly in on private chartered planes, often Richard's own.

AMBOSELI

It's not just the animals that attract visitors to Amboseli National Park, but also magical Kilimanjaro, the largest mountain in Africa at 5,895 m (19,340 ft). Hemingway immortalized it in his *Snows of Kilimanjaro,* later filmed in Amboseli. When the border was being drawn between German Tanzania and British Kenya, Queen Victoria put a kink in the line to give the mountain, sight unseen, to her cousin, Emperor of Germany. As amusing as this story is, it reflects the callousness of the nineteenth-century partitioning of Africa, where all it took was the stroke of a pen to divide one country from another, and brother from brother.

Though Kilimanjaro seems so close from Amboseli's flat open plains, its peak is almost 50 km (31 miles) away, across the Tanzanian border, making it a major expedition for the Kenyan tourist. On your own, this means an extra visa for Tanzania, a re-entry visa for Kenya, road tax in Tanzania (approximately US$60), and US$20 (in United States currency only) per person for entry into the Kilimanjaro National Park. It may be wiser to return to Tanzania as a separate destination. If your aim is just to climb Kilimanjaro, bear in mind that Mount Kenya offers easier climbing to a higher altitude, without needing climbing gear, expertise and pre-planning, while taking the "Coca-Cola Route" up Kili is little more than a trudge. If you are dead set on visiting Mount Kilimanjaro, Let's Go Travel can arrange a tour and help you with the visas.

For many who visit Amboseli, the mountain can be as elusive as its wildlife, but the early riser is usually rewarded with an unobscured view of Uhuru Peak, the summit, and Mawenzi, 5,151 m (16,900 ft). During the day, clouds usually play hide and seek about one or both peaks. Sometimes they become so thick you are unaware of the mountain's presence. If you have arrived on a cloudy afternoon, look to the south early the next morning. The mountain is so huge it is incredible how it can completely disappear.

Even without Kilimanjaro, Amboseli, just a four-hour drive from Nairobi, has much to offer. It has a unique ecosystem and variety of game. There are five different wildlife habitats — the seasonal lake bed of Lake Amboseli, swamps and marshes with a few sulfur springs, open plains, yellow-barked acacia woodlands, and lava rock thornbush country. It's not huge, at 392 sq km (151 sq miles), and a couple of days are enough to cover most of the paths.

Amboseli is probably the best place to watch elephants in Kenya; if you'd like to learn more about them, *Elephant Memories* by Cynthia Moss, an American scientist who has studied them in Amboseli since 1972, is the best book available.

In recent years, poaching has driven many elephants into Amboseli, where Moss's research project has followed their lives and where, perhaps, the presence of many scientists and observers has provided a slight protection. Nonetheless, the poaching continues. *Elephant Memories* chronicles one example:

"Torn Ear was just reaching for a small succulent herb that was nestled in amongst the grass when a quick movement to her left caught her eye. She whirled toward the movement and there were two men only 30 yards away. Without hesitation she put her head down and charged toward them. She did not even hear the explosion before the bullet ripped through the light airy bone of her forehead and penetrated deep into her brain. She was dead by the time she fell forward onto her head and tusks and skidded along the ground for several feet from the momentum of her charge. Her son was hit next, first in the shoulder, which made him scream with pain and rage, and then through his side into his heart … The men turned and began to run but let off one volley of shots, missing most of the elephants but catching Tina in the chest with a shot that went into her right lung … it took seven shots in her head and neck and shoulders before Wendy fell and died.

"Teresia took them to the far side of Meshanani, a small hill up on the ridge above the lake. There was some protection here, and Tina could go no farther. The blood pouring from her mouth was bright red and her sides were heaving for breath. The other elephants

Every tourist who visits the game parks of Kenya is helping to protect the elephants by manifesting his or her interest in Africa's wildlife. In addition, we can all help by refusing ever to purchase any item made of ivory, even if it's sold as an "antique," by adding our support to the East African Wildlife Society, the World Wildlife Fund and other conservation groups, and by joining in international efforts to discourage ivory smuggling which is almost entirely organized by Japan, Taiwan, Hong Kong and China.

crowded around, reaching for her. Her knees started to buckle and she began to go down, but Teresia got on one side of her and Trista on the other and they both leaned in and held her up. Soon, however, she had no strength and she slipped beneath them and fell onto her side. More blood gushed from her mouth and with a shudder she died.

"Teresia and Trista became frantic and knelt down and tried to lift her up. They worked their tusks under her back and under her head. At one point they succeeded in lifting her into a sitting position but her body flopped back down. Her family tried everything to rouse her, kicking and tusking her, and Tallulah even went off and collected a trunkful of grass and tried to stuff it into her mouth …"

Despite the continuing threat of poachers, the elephants of Amboseli have become accustomed to tourist vehicles, and they generally will not flee if you wish to sit and watch them as they go about their daily routine — showers, dust baths, around 16 to 18 hours of grazing and playful bouts of rock or stick throwing.

You can also expect to see waterbucks, Maasai giraffes, buffaloes, Coke's hartebeests, common zebras, elands, gazelles and impalas. Cheetah and lion sightings are almost sure bets.

Entry to Amboseli is US$27, children US$10 and vehicles are charged at Ksh200.

Zebras, like domestic horses, are playful and generally unafraid to block the road.

WHERE TO STAY

Among the better lodges in the park are:
Amboseli Serena Lodge ((02) 710511 FAX (02)
718103, Box 48690, Nairobi (very expensive,
full board), and **Tortilis Camp** ((02) 748307/27
FAX (0154) 22553 or (02) 740721 E-MAIL cheli
peacock@africaonline.co.ke WEB SITE www
.chelipeacock.com, Box 39806, Nairobi (extremely expensive, all-inclusive). Less good
than they used to be are **Amboseli Lodge** and
Kilimanjaro Safari Lodge both ((02) 227136

At Namanga, a pretty town 75 km (47 miles)
west of Amboseli on the border with Tanzania, is the **River Hotel** ((02) 330775, Box 4,
Namanga, a very scenic array of cottages
under shady acacias with a good restaurant
serving Kenyan cuisine. The rate is Ksh1,500
bed and breakfast for doubles. Camping is
also available at Ksh150 per person. Also in
Namanga are a couple of cheaper *hotelis*. Since
Namanga lies on the direct route south from
Nairobi to Amboseli, it can make a nice stop
for lunch, or for the night if you're taking your
time or started late.

FAX (02) 219982, Box 30193, Nairobi (expen-
sive, full board). Near Lemito Gate is the
slightly dilapidated **Kilimanjaro Buffalo
Lodge** ((02) 227136 FAX (02) 219982, Box 72630,
Oloitokitok (expensive, full board). **Ol Tukai
Lodge** ((02) 540780 FAX (02) 543810 E-MAIL
blockreservations@net2000ke.com, Box 40075,
Nairobi (expensive, full board), near Cynthia
Moss's elephant research station, is better.

South of Serena Lodge is a **campground**
run by the Maasai (Ksh600 per person). Sites
are flat, dry and well-spaced, usually with
water but few amenities. The wildlife is so
tame that elephants and giraffes often pass
through. Most campers leave a large fire burn-
ing upon retiring. Because of the nearby
marshes, mosquito netting is a must.

HOW TO GET THERE

From Nairobi, join the lines of heavy traffic
heading southeast on the Mombasa Road.
Turn right 25 km (16 miles) out of town, onto
the A104 towards Arusha. At Namanga,
165 km (103 miles) south, turn left onto
the C103 for the final 75 km (47 miles) to
Amboseli on dirt road. By public transportation it is easy to get to Namanga but hard
thereafter. Hitching will be your only option.
The quickest way to get to Amboseli is with
Airkenya , which flies at 7:30 AM daily from
Wilson Airport (US$88).

LEFT: Mount Kilimanjaro's snow-capped peak.
ABOVE: Kilimanjaro Lodge in Amboseli.

The Coast

Throughout time, Kenya's coast has had a separate, but connected, history to the inland cultures. This remains somewhat true today. For tourists, there's a great difference between a coastal resort and a game park lodge.

Coastal development has primarily catered to those who wish to relax in the sun, dine well and be entertained at night. Most Kenyan coastal resorts are like those at Miami Beach or the Caribbean, with the major difference being that they generally cost less. However they also offer the opportunity to explore Kenya, whether the inland world of

The Indian Ocean offers some of the best snorkeling and diving in the world. The water is calm and crystal clear during the dry months, and the marine life is astounding. Because there are relatively few motorized coastal fishing boats (one deep-sea fisherman estimates that there are fewer than 300 for the entire 480-km/300-mile coast and fewer than 20 north of Kilifi), fish here can reach enormous sizes.

In the marine parks at Malindi, Watamu Bay and Shimoni, the coral reefs grow relatively undisturbed with resident populations

game and parks or the coastal life of weekend discos and local restaurants.

Typical coastal development is based on large hotels catering for sun 'n' sand visitors. Luckily, there are exceptions: notably the areas of Watamu Bay, Lamu, and Shimoni.

As the coastal resorts have been developed mainly for and by the European market, there is a preference for employees speaking Italian, German and English. Unlike the practice in other parts of Kenya, Swahili is the first, and often the only, language spoken at home. Beach-boys concentrate on the main resort strips north and south of Mombasa; travel further, or stay in any area for length of time, and you are rarely bothered.

of fish so numerous and colorful as to defy description. Outside the parks, however, the coastal coral reefs have been abused, and fishing keeps the shoal size down. At low tide, you can walk along the beaches and find pools that often contain small fish and a variety of crustaceans. You can also watch the fishermen setting nets from the shore or dhows. In recent years, the spear gun has been introduced. Many a young fisherman, weaned from his canoe carved from a mango tree by offers of nets from the West, has now progressed to goggles, snorkel and spear-gun to earn his livelihood.

OPPOSITE: Traditional Arab dhows still ply the coast of Kenya. ABOVE: The old and the new blend in Mombasa's skyline.

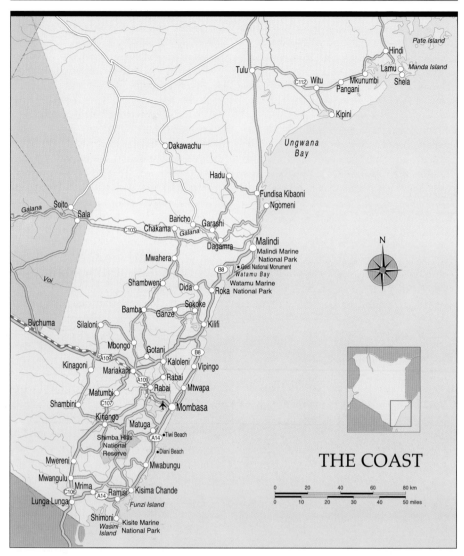

THE COAST

0	20	40	60	80 km
0	10	20	30	40	50 miles

Except at river inlets and bays, the ocean bottom slopes gently out to wide fringing and barrier reefs. There are three main reefs, starting with the sheltering onshore reef, often exposed at low tide and heading out to three kilometers (two miles) offshore, a fertile home to the ocean's big fish some 30 m (100 ft) below sea level. Occasional small atolls, such as at Shimoni, complete the wide variety of habitats that make Kenya's coast the marine treasure-trove of East Africa. The water near the shore is heated to surprisingly high temperatures. Average monthly temperatures for offshore surface waters vary from 25°C (77°F) in the fall to 29°C (84°F) in

the spring; at low tide, it's possible to find shallow pools over 35°C (95°F). Even at high tide, the coastal water is warm and it's possible to swim for hours without getting cold. As the sun sets and beaches become shaded, it's often warmer in the water than out, although the coastal breeze is more likely to cool than chill.

Kenya's coastal beaches are of the finest white sand. During and after the northeast trade winds, called the *kaskazi* (December to April), they are swept clean by an offshore current and virtually no debris is present. Unfortunately, a change of direction, precipitation and current during and after the southeast trade winds or *kusi* (May to November) brings seaweed to shore. This is the coast's low season and bargain hotel prices can be negotiated, especially in the north around Watamu, while further north still, in Lamu and Kiwayu, most hotels close completely. The seas run high and there is daily rain. Many of the deep-sea fishermen take their boats out of the water, but in any case they are unable to ride the reef out to the open sea. Further south, around Diani, Mombasa and Shimoni, the weather is less severe and beach surf breaks from July onwards are fine.

High season on the coast is December through mid-February. Rain is infrequent, the water is calm, snorkeling is excellent, the fish are numerous, and there is usually enough wind to make windsurfing exciting. Even if you are not interested in sailing, the breeze will be welcome, because without it, the heat and humidity can be exhausting.

The pace of life along the coast is slow. "Coasties" are famously more laid-back than their "upcountry" brothers. For these Islamic believers, life is tranquilly easy. Traditionally, there has been an abundance of fish for the taking, bananas, coconuts, mangoes and papayas grow wild, and small garden plots supply plentiful vitamins for a family's sustenance. No wonder it's hard to find labor to work in the tourist industry.

In dress and architecture, the Arab influence, dating from as early as the sixth century, is undeniable, particularly in the ancient towns of Lamu, Malindi and Old Mombasa. The elegance of the thirteenth through fifteenth centuries, the height of coastal Kenya's power and affluence, has disappeared, but in the ruins of Gedi and the island of Lamu, you can still capture a glimpse of the past.

Reminders of the period of Portuguese domination during the sixteenth and seventeenth centuries are Mombasa's Fort Jesus and a small chapel and monument in Malindi. This period created much disruption but left little mark on the daily life of the native Kenyans. Although Catholicism endured in the Portuguese colonies of the New World, it never really took hold in Muslim coastal Kenya, and once the Portuguese left, so did their influence.

As in earlier times, the coast today is separated into individual spheres of influence. There is Mombasa with its northern resort strips, linking into a nightlife center but with beaches that recede at low tide to the distant horizon. To the south are the self-sufficient resorts of Tiwi and Diani. For the independent traveler the best areas are further afield The first place of interest is quietly charming Kilifi, then Watamu Bay for deep-sea fishing and the offshore marine park, then the nightlife resort of Malindi with its Italian restaurants and casinos. A short air hop reaches Kenya's northern coast, the Swahili island of Lamu, and a mangrove coast leading up to the exclusive hideaways of Kiwayu.

Head south from Mombasa over the Likoni Ferry to Tiwi and Diani Beaches, and further south towards Tanzania to Shimoni, with the offshore Wasini Island and the marine park of Kisite.

The road between Malindi and Shimoni is paved and in relatively good condition — one roadside stop is proudly called the "New Surface" café. This link makes it easy to reach the different marine parks, ruins, coastal forests, wildlife areas and old towns that line Kenya's shore. The road to Malindi is also good, but from there north to Lamu and Pate becomes a bit of a challenge. Unpaved, and often impassable during the rains, even in good weather it is an endurance test and best circumvented by a short air hop.

MOMBASA

Mombasa is Kenya's second largest city and its only deepwater port. In many ways, it is the country's lifeline to the world. Once a scarcely developed island in a mangrove-lined bay with dhows in the harbor, today Mombasa is crowded and busy with container berths at Kilindini ("place of deep water") on the west side of the island. The surrounding mainland sprawls with industrial development and suburbs.

There are no bathing beaches on Mombasa Island, so you may choose not to stay here, but the Old Town and Fort Jesus will make one- or two-day trips worthwhile.

Mombasa appears on Ptolemy's map as Tonika, and was probably the most sophisticated and largest of the coastal city-states in Kenya in the early days. It resisted Portuguese domination in the fifteenth and sixteenth centuries and was looted and burned by them on four separate occasions. As a result, only a few archaeological remains of its early glory have been found. It is interesting to note that Mombasa's population in 1500 was estimated at 10,000, roughly the same as medieval London. Fort Jesus remains a reminder of the eventual Portuguese victory that cost the lives of every native of Mombasa who had not fled the island, and ultimately every Portuguese stationed there.

After the Portuguese came a period of Omani control that was scarcely more peaceful, as the governing Mazuri family and the Sultan were constantly at odds. These differences led directly to reluctant British involvement in Kenya when Mombasa became a protectorate.

From the end of the nineteenth century until 1906, Mombasa boomed. Government buildings were erected and affluent Indian merchants constructed large two- and three-story houses along the main roads. Most of the Old Town dates from this period. In 1906, the government headquarters moved to Nairobi, but Mombasa still remained Kenya's major commercial and industrial center until after World War I. Though still a major industrial center today, Mombasa has lost its former splendor.

GENERAL INFORMATION

Grandly surveyed by the much-photographed arch of twin tusks, Mombasa's business center is along Moi Avenue, which splits in the east into Nkrumah and Makarada Roads, and this is where you'll find the police station, most travel agents, banks, airlines and banks. To the east, nearest the coast, are the most interesting areas: the brooding bulk of Fort Jesus, and the Old Town. This is best explored on foot, with an early start to avoid the sultry heat of a tropical midday.

Unusually for Kenya, there is a **Tourist Information Office** ((011) 225428 FAX (011) 228208 E-MAIL mcta@africaonline.co.ke, Box 99596, in Moi Avenue near the tusks, which is open 8 AM to noon and 2 PM to

4:30 PM Monday to Friday, and 8 AM to noon Saturday. The staff are, however, more enthusiastic than effective as they suffer a characteristic shortage of printed material.

Taxis, generally can be found at all the sites of tourist interest, but **Kenatco** ((011) 227503 offers a fixed-price, 24-hour alternative. In case of medical problems **Panddya Memorial Hospital** ((011) 314140, Dedan Kimathi Avenue, has an ambulance service and full medical facilities. Out of hours, this is where you'll have to go to buy medicaments, though **Yudah Pharmaceuticals** ((011) 316028, Duruma

Road, is open from 9 AM to 10 PM Monday to Friday, and until 8 PM on Saturday. If you're heading out to the bush, temporary coverage can be arranged with **Africa Air Rescue** (AAR) ((011) 312405, Harbour House, Moi Avenue. If you need to check your e-mail there are a couple of cybercafés, with more opening daily. Try the **Online Café** ((011) 220008, Yusuf Ali Mansion, Moi Avenue, open 8 AM to 7 PM weekdays, or **Clicks Netcafe** ((011) 221579, Superior House, Makarada Road, open 8 AM to 6 PM.

WHAT TO SEE AND DO

Mombasa is built on an island. A causeway heads inland — and to the airport — while the relatively new Nyali Bridge heads off to link up the northern resorts of Nyali, Bamburi and beyond. Access to the south and Diani Beach is by the endlessly shuttling Likoni Ferry. Don't try to save money by swimming across as sharks are plentiful and have very urban appetites.

Old Town

The streets of Mombasa's Old Town are narrow and not designed for automobiles. They are just wide enough for a camel or a donkey with panniers to pass, or for the hand carts (*mkototnei* or *hamaili*) still used in the area today.

Although most of the buildings date no earlier than the early 1900s, they often stand on older foundations, and show strong Arab influence. The Fort Jesus gift shop sells an excellent historical guide, *The Old Town Mombasa*, which gives a history of the town and details for a self-guided walking tour. With it, you can trace the lines where the Portuguese built a wall to separate the "Cidade dos Portugusos" (Portuguese City) and the "Cidade dos Moros" (Moorish or Swahili City). But nothing remains of the wall that was said to be one and a half meters (five feet) wide with several towers and three gates.

The Old Town has numerous mosques, each built by different groups of Muslims arriving at various times in Kenya. There are many colorful buildings with intricate grillwork, a few with fretted balconies. The carved wooden doors described by Portuguese chroniclers have long ago disappeared, many lost when the Portuguese burned the city, but the stone *baraga* seats are still found flanking the doors of many Old Town houses. Examples of carved doors can be seen in Fort Jesus; the best surviving examples grace homes in Lamu, further north on the coast.

Mombasa also boasts Kenya's first public library, as well as an open-air pavilion, Jubilee Hall, built to commemorate Queen Victoria's diamond jubilee in 1897. There's also Government Square, a hub of colonial activity in the 1890s. Glen's Building was named for a dog called Glen owned by a government official, Sir Ali bin Salim. The dog appears in many photos of Sir bin Salim taken at state functions.

Fort Jesus

Fort Jesus, a national historical monument, is a testimony to the determination of the Portuguese to control the coast of Kenya, and to the tenacity of Mombasa's inhabitants in retaining their identity and culture. Once inside (entry fee is Ksh350 per person), you are isolated from everyday Mombasa, just as the Portuguese were. The fortress is not unlike medieval castles along the Mediterranean.

The fort is very well maintained. Several major buildings and the ramparts looking toward the sea are restored. In one barracks

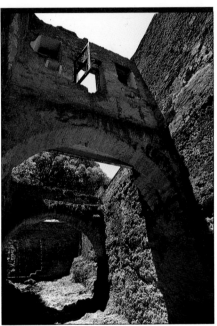

room, drawings of ships, churches, and figures in armor have been uncovered, revealing the longing of many Portuguese sailors for a more familiar home. There are the foundations of a chapel, a storeroom, and dwellings or shops against the inland wall. Fort Jesus is impressive, and although it might lack some of the charm and romance of European fortresses it catches the nervous isolation of Europe's first settlers, the Portuguese sailors charged with maintaining a precarious toehold on the East African shore, where threats came from both land and sea.

OPPOSITE: The strong influence of Islam on the coast results in many mosques. ABOVE: Fort Jesus in Mombasa: "Nothing remains but deathless fascination."

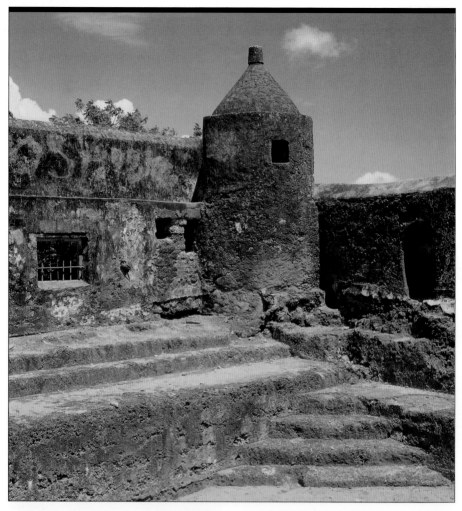

There are several carved doors in the fortress, not original, but hung for display. Also preserved are chambers with carved beams and inlaid inscriptions that were decorated by the Omani after they defeated the Portuguese in the eighteenth century. These rooms are reminiscent of the splendor of the Moorish castles of Spain, a few with traces of poetry similar to that which embellishes the Alhambra.

A museum in the main courtyard houses "treasures" from the wreck of the *Santo Antonio de Tanna*, which sank in Mombasa Harbor in 1697. The museum also has an extensive display of pottery recovered along the coast. Some of these are over 1,000 years old, from as far away as China. The pottery finds are keyed to the ancient settlements and ruins along the coast. This is a good place to begin if you plan to tour the coastal ruins. It also has a small collection of Swahili artifacts from Old Town Mombasa.

The fort has a gift shop selling reasonably priced craft items and an excellent selection of books on Mombasa and the coast. Proceeds from the shop help support restoration and maintenance of the site. You can tour the fort by yourself, as it is adequately marked, or you can hire a guide. The guides are very well-informed and can usually give their tour in Swahili, Italian, German or English.

SHOPPING

Mombasa is a rather more restful place to look for handicrafts and fabrics than Nairobi, with a relaxed, tropical heat calming the bargaining process and a provincial moderation muting some of the opening prices. Thanks to its long tradition of coastal trading it is also important for fabrics, all neatly contained in a single, specialized street, Biashara Road, where *kangas* are the specialty, brightly-colored textiles with proverbs (generally in Swahili) making the cloth more memorable. The main tourist shopping area is along Moi Avenue, from the Tusks to Digo Road, and gets more hassle as you go along. A good place to visit first is Haria's Gift Shop on Moi Avenue (near the tusks), which gives a good idea of the "correct" prices.

WHERE TO STAY

Most people staying here cross Nyali Bridge to the north and choose one of the many resort hotels that line the coast. These are listed later on under THE SOUTH COAST, page 267, and under NORTH OF MOMBASA, page 271.

There are those, however, who prefer to stay in the city itself, even though water supplies are erratic and, in the wet season (April to June, October to early December), what water there is needs to be purified. Perhaps because Mombasa Island lacks a beach, recent years have seen many of the city center hotels deteriorate if not close down completely. The remaining establishments are good value. The **Lotus Hotel** ((011) 313207 FAX (011) 220673, Box 90193, Mvita and Cathedral Road, is probably the best but is often full (inexpensive, B&B). The **Royal Court Hotel** ((011) 223379 FAX (011) 312398, Box 41247, Haile Selassie Road, is centrally located, but avoid the single rooms, which are oppressively small (mid-range, B&B).

For less expensive rooms, there's the decaying charm of the **New Palm Hotel** ((011) 311756, Nkruma Road (inexpensive, B&B). The **YWCA** is on the junction of Kaunda and Kiamba Avenues: good in that it takes both men and women, bad in that it caters mainly to stays of a month or longer.

If you want to stay at the ocean for a week or so, you might consider renting a house or cottage. Prices range from Ksh750 per day for one bedroom to Ksh10,000 per day for a villa. **Let's Go Travel** ((02) 447151 or (02)

441030 FAX (02) 447270 or (02) 441690 E-MAIL info@letsgosafari.com WEB SITE www.letsgosafari.com, Box 60342, Nairobi, can make advance reservations or help with immediate reservations. Reservations are rarely necessary except during December, January and August. Travel agents in Mombasa usually have listings of houses available up and down the coast. You can also ask residents when you find an area where you'd like to stay. The houses are generally sparsely furnished, but come with cook and housekeeper. Though the cook and housekeeper get a wage

from the owner or manager, it's customary to leave Ksh500 for each of them for each week you're there.

Both north and south of Mombasa are numerous coastal resorts. Each hotel at least tries to have its own appeal, and the quality and type of food varies. Most are relatively modern, have standard resort accommodations and quote prices in United States dollars or sterling. To head south along the coast from Mombasa Island means using the Likoni ferry, which makes the southern resorts feel pleasantly isolated from the bustle of city life, and the beaches are better than

OPPOSITE: Even in Fort Jesus the Portuguese were never safe. ABOVE: Mombasa's sun sets to the distant call of countless muezzins.

those an equivalent distance from town to the north. Accommodation options in these resorts are listed below.

WHERE TO EAT

Even if you don't stay in town, Old Town Mombasa is one of the best places in Kenya to experience the local cuisine. An excellent stop for lunch after visiting Fort Jesus is **Surya Restaurant** on Nyeri Street, Mombasa's best Ethiopian restaurant. The wood-paneled front room has plastic tablecloths and is aimed at the local market. Behind is a large, shaded courtyard with traditional furniture and rather smarter style. Whenever you eat at local restaurants wash your hands in the sink provided or in the jug and bowl brought to you as not to do so is considered very rude. And as in all Muslim societies, eat only with your right hand. Food is served on a base of *ngara*, a flat Ethiopian bread that also serves as knife and fork. Mounds of spiced meats and vegetables are designed to be picked at and shared, with costs in the range of Ksh200 per person. The Surya is open for lunch and dinner.

A few doors up is Mombasa's best Swahili restaurant, **Recoda**, but it opens only for dinner. If you're early enough you can sit outside at sidewalk tables and watch the inhabitants go about their evening routine. There is no menu: the waiters will explain what has been prepared for the day, usually mild curry-flavored stews, fish cooked in coconut milk and *pilau* (spiced rice with meat). Desserts include iced, pureed papaya with slices of orange, mango and banana, or chilled, pureed avocado with milk and spices. Prices, once again, in the region of Ksh200 per person. Don't expect a wine list — or even a beer — at these two restaurants, but they will provide cutlery if you ask. They're both worth visiting for the excellently prepared and quite unique food, and I'm still trying to work out which I prefer.

HOW TO GET THERE

The main road from Nairobi, the A109, links Mombasa with Nairobi, 485 km (303 miles) away. Several buses leave Nairobi every day for Mombasa, but although the road is being repaired, a journey that once took as little as six hours now can often take twice as long. Don't complain too much: not so long ago it could easily have taken 20 hours or more. The best service is with **The Connection** ((011) 221361, Vogue Travel, Jubilee Insurance Building, Moi Avenue, Ksh1,000. There are other bus companies charging half as much, such as **Akamba** ((011) 316770, Jomo Kenyatta Avenue, Mombasa.

An overnight train links the two cities and takes 12 hours. Reservations are essential for traveling first or second class; two or three days in advance are generally enough to secure a berth. Without a reservation you'll end up traveling on the benches in third. Reservations can be made in person at Nairobi Station, one and a half kilometers (one mile) from the city center on Station Road, or at Mombasa Station, on Haile Selassie Avenue. Rather less securely, reservations are apparently taken by telephone — Nairobi ((02) 221211, Mombasa ((011) 312221 — or perhaps are easiest through a travel agent such as **Let's Go Travel** ((02) 447151 or (02) 441030 FAX (02) 447270 or (02) 441690 E-MAIL info@letsgosafari.com WEB SITE www.letsgosafari.com, Box 60342, Nairobi.

Alternatively, many visitors arrive at Mombasa's Moi International Airport, which is on the mainland 10 km (six and a half miles) from the city. Although there are no scheduled flights from Europe into Mombasa there are plenty of direct charter arrivals. Domestically, **Kenya Airways** ((02) 210771 or (02) 229291 FAX (02) 336252, Box 41010, Nairobi, and ((011) 221251 FAX (011) 313815, Box 99302, Mombasa, flies five times every day from Nairobi International Airport for US$80. **Airkenya** ((011) 229777/229106 FAX (011) 224063, TSS Nkrumah Road, Mombasa, with an office at the airport ((011) 433982 FAX (011) 435235 E-MAIL info@airkenya .com, WEB SITE www.airkenya.com, Box 84700, Mombasa, also runs up to six flights a day from Nairobi's Wilson Airport, with one-way tickets costing Ksh5,385. The flights take an hour and a half. Airkenya also has flights up to Malindi, Lamu and Kiwayu. There's also a very useful daily flight provided from Mombasa to the Masai Mara operated by **Blue Bird Aviation** ((02) 602338 FAX (02) 602337, Box 62045, Nairobi.

Fixed-fare taxis head from the airport to the major resorts, while those going on safari will usually leave directly from the airport.

AROUND MOMBASA

Around Mombasa, there are several sites to lure you from the beach, or to occupy your time if you've overdone the sun. All these can be easily reached from Mombasa's satellite resorts in Diani to the south, or the northern resort areas.

could worship. Near the north-facing wall of the mosque are several tombs, one of which has an interesting inscription, which translated reads: "Every soul shall taste death. You will simply be paid your wages in full on the Day of Resurrection. He who is removed from the fire and made to enter heaven, it is he who has won the victory. The earthly life is only delusion."

Entrance fee to Jumba is Ksh200; you can buy a guidebook to the site at the entrance. The ruins are smaller and less intricately planned than Gedi to the north, but after a

JUMBA LA MTWANA NATIONAL MONUMENT

A short drive north along the coastal highway, just past Mtwapa Bridge, is **Jumba la Mtwana National Monument**, ruins of a fourteenth-century town. Situated right on the beach, the town, whose Swahili name means "Mansion of the Slaves," gives one the impression that at its peak Jumba was much more in the mainstream of coastal commerce, with nearby Mtwapa Creek as a safe anchorage. The site is dotted with the giant-trunked baobabs, some of which could have existed when Jumba was inhabited.

The most interesting of the ruins is the mosque by the sea. According to archaeologists, it has a separate room in which women

wander around you can stroll onto the beach, which has a stand of aerial rooted pines, the mangroves of the pine family.

BAMBURI NATURE TRAIL

Closer to town is Bamburi Nature Trail (open daily, Ksh500 per person), the most zoo-like park you'll find in Kenya. There are somewhat tame hippos called Sally, Potti and Cleopatra, aldabra tortoises, crocodiles, a tilapia aquaculture project that produces over 30 tons of fish per year, pelicans, crowned cranes, antelopes, and a family of serval cats. An attached restaurant called

The coastal mangrove swamps are a dense haven for bird life.

Whispering Pines is good for lunch. Set amongst the casuarina trees it provides a welcome breath of the bush experience at a cost of about Ksh400 per person. Thursdays to Saturday the restaurant stays open for evening meals.

The nature trail is a rehabilitated quarry owned by the Bamburi Cement Factory, which moves its operation north and west as its mining techniques dictate. The quarry revegetation began in 1971 with the planting of hardy casuarina trees from Australia. Now a dense forest of whistling pines has taken

To get the most of a trip to the reserve, consider staying a night. If you're equipped (food, cooking equipment and mosquito nets), there are the superb **Shimba Hills Self-Service Bandas** (US$10 per person) overlooking a steep, thickly-vegetated ravine where the air is cool and refreshingly dry. The view east is magnificent and the sunrise across the Indian Ocean is beyond description.

Alternatively, **Shimba Hills Lodge (** (02) 540780 FAX (02) 543810 E-MAIL blockreservations @net2000ke.com, Box 40075, Nairobi (expensive, half board), is a night-viewing lodge built

hold and the ground below is starting to recover its fertility.

SHIMBA HILLS NATIONAL RESERVE

Even if your primary interest is the beach and the sun, you shouldn't pass up an opportunity to explore at least one of Kenya's game parks and see the animals. Easily accessible from the coastal highway is Shimba Hills National Reserve. Wildlife here is not as abundant as in Amboseli or the Masai Mara, but you can often see the rare sable antelope. With luck, you can find genets, elephants and civet cats and, occasionally, leopards. Entry fees are US$20 per person per day, US$5 per child, and Ksh500 per vehicle.

along the same lines as Treetops (see THE ABERDARE MOUNTAINS, page 208) but with infinitely more style and charm. Children under seven are not permitted. Shimba Hills is a good coastal version, a sturdy and comfortable tree-house in the heart of dense jungle. If Shimba is the only wildlife reserve you will visit, by all means stay at the lodge for a night. Elephants occasionally visit the waterhole and bushbabies are attracted to the activities. Shimba Hills National Reserve is the only place where you'll find the rare sable antelope, which can be seen along with other game on the morning or the evening game drives.

The lodge overlooks an emerald glade of dense coastal rainforest with giant cycads. In the early morning and late afternoon, you can sometimes see a leopard; giant monitor lizards are numerous. Animals are now well used to whispering visitors in their domain. There have been sightings of elephants at night, but these are rare at present.

Nearby — but just outside Shimba Hills National Park — is the **Mwalugange Elephant Sanctuary** (US$10 entry), a community-based project to protect a large population of elephants marooned by encroaching human development and preserve their migratory routes. Accommodation here is at **Travelers Mwalugange Elephant Camp** ((0127) 51202 E-MAIL travellershtl@swift mombasa.com, Box 87649, Mombasa (very expensive). Reservations can also be made through **Traveler's Beach Hotel** ((011) 485121 FAX 485678, Box 87649, Mombasa.

How to Get There

Shimba Hills is 30 km (19 miles) southwest of Mombasa, and even nearer Diani Beach Resort, while the access road to Mwalugange, just to the northwest of the reserve, is slightly more demanding. Although it is an easy drive in your own vehicle, it is easier and usually cheaper to buy a package to Shimba from one of Mombasa's travel agents.

RABAI

A 45-minute drive west of Mombasa (towards Nairobi, turning north at Mazeras on C-107) is Rabai, site of Krapf and Rebmann's mission. It was from here that they left on their separate expeditions, which led to the mapping of Mounts Kenya and Kilimanjaro. The ruins of Krapf's house can be seen; Rebmann's is still occupied. The people of Rabai will be glad to show you around.

Krapf departed on several expeditions from this mission at Rabai. He became the first white man to cross the Tsavo River, to explore the Yatta Plateau in what is now Tsavo East National Park, and to locate Mount Kenya. Local tribesmen had described the mountain as taller than Mount Kilimanjaro, which no one had climbed because of "the intense cold and the white matter which rolled down with great noise" — a reference to the snow avalanches that now, with world climate change, no longer occur on Mount Kenya.

THE SOUTH COAST

Heading south from Mombasa means using the Likoni Ferry, which shuttles cars and flooding pedestrians across 400 m (a quarter of a mile) of water to the mainland and the southern strip of the B8 coast road. This tends to give the southern resort areas a more timeless, relaxing atmosphere even though, as the crow flies, they are quite close to the city. The beaches tend to be better than those an equivalent distance north of Mombasa, with the ocean — and the fringing coral reef — nearer to land.

Thread straight through the suburb of Likoni, scene of some of the worst disturbances in the 1997 elections and still with an uneasy atmosphere. This quickly fades. Although some hotels have been built on the shore here as Likoni Beach merges into Shelley Beach — it's not especially recommended: the sea goes a long way out at low tide and it's prone to seaweed. If you do want to stay here, try the **Anglican Church of Kenya Guest House (ACK)** ((011) 451619, Box 96170, Mombasa, which is good value, and convenient for public transportation although a bit of a walk from the beach (inexpensive, B&B).

TIWI BEACH

It's better to carry on south: after 20 km (12.5 miles) two turns to the left head off into the small, cottagey atmosphere of Tiwi Beach, four kilometers (two and a half miles) from the B8 coastal road. Traditionally this area is popular with Kenya residents and backpackers who shudder alike every time they see the enormous Traveler's Beach Hotel that has been built on the coast and stay instead in a range of smaller chalet-type developments. Few *matatus* mean that visitors without a car will find most of Tiwi's beach lodges feel quite isolated; access is by taxi or rental car and the pleasures quiet, beach-based ones. One of the best is **Tiwi Sea Castles** ((0127) 51220 FAX (0127) 51222, Box 96599, Likoni (inexpensive, B&B), while another is **Sand Island Beach Cottages**

Craftsman sculpts attractive tropical hardwoods for tourists.

((0127) 51233 FAX (0127) 51201 E-MAIL hat field@form-net.com, Box 5516, Diani, which is closed May and June (mid-range, B&B). Both conform to the general pattern of lodges here, which is to have self-contained cottages, ideal for families, where guests stay for weeks — or months. The liveliest bar is at **Twiga Lodge** ((0127) 51267, Box 96005, Mombasa, which also has rooms (but not very good ones).

DIANI BEACH

Ten kilometers (six miles) further south at the small town of Ukunda a left turn leads down to the resort of Diani, the most developed stretch of Kenya's coast. There's even a **Tourist Office** (0127) 2227 FAX (0127) 2156, Box 702, Ukunda, behind the Agip Gas Station, 8 AM to 1 PM, 2 PM to 5 PM Monday to Friday. There's a taxi rank here as well.

Treating where the road from Ukunda meets the coast road as point zero, the resort spreads out to north and south. Generally, the southern direction is better, passing most of the major hotels, a couple of small shopping centers and most of the best restaurants and nightclubs before becoming, once more, unspoiled. There's more forest squeezing between the vacation-style resorts, and colobus monkeys swing around. One kilometer (less than a mile) north of point zero is the small **Diani Beach Hospital** ((0127) 2435/6, beside the Diani Complex shopping center.

What to See and Do

The classic Diani activities are scuba diving on the fringing reef or game fishing out in deeper waters. For game fishing, **Grand Slam Charters** are endlessly helpful and accommodating, while the best dive operator is **Dive the Crab**. Both are bookable through Safari Beach Hotel ((0127) 2726 FAX (0127) 2357, Box 90690, Mombasa. Day-trips from Diani head down to Kenya's deep south for the very best diving: Shimoni, the offshore island of Wasini, and the Marine National Park of Kisite. At a cost of US$80 (US$85 if you're being picked up from the northern resorts) these excursions include a sail by dhow out to the best snorkeling area and an after-swim feast of crab and seafood

that renders most people comatose. Fortunately wicker beds are laid out under trees. Reserve through **Kisite Dhow Tours** ((0127) 2331 FAX (0127) 3154, Box 281, Ukunda. There are plenty of other dhow operators offering day-trips. Amongst the best are **Kimazini Funzi Dhow Safaris** ((0127) 3182, Diani Beach Shopping Centre, who tour Funzi Creek, visit local schools and have lunch on a desert island; and **Funzi Island Lazy Lagoon** ((011) 225546 FAX (011) 316458, Box 90246, Bodo Village, with a range of tours, including bird- and croc-watching. All pick up guests from their lodges. Away from the water, Leisure Lodge, north of the junction, has an 18-hole golf course. Jadini Forest breaks out between developments to the south, providing a refuge for countless colobus monkeys.

Where to Stay

Most of the hotels here depend on European tour operators for their business: walk-in rates, for room only unless otherwise stated, are steep and trade discounts are huge. Generally, therefore, it is cheaper to buy a package vacation from home. There are exceptions: most notably a small Seychellois restaurant called **Boko Boko** (/FAX (0127) 2344 (inexpensive) at the northern tip of the resort road, opposite Neptune Village Hotel; they have four en-suite guest rooms available. This represents exceptional value here. The German-run **Diani Beachalets** ((0127) 2180, Box 26 Ukunda, is a well-run place with a range of accommodation options to suit all budgets (very inexpensive to inexpensive), and is quietly set south of the main Warandale Cottages.

Otherwise it's back to international-standard luxury. Four kilometers (three miles) south of point zero is the sophisticated but welcoming **Safari Beach Hotel** ((0127) 2726 FAX (0127) 2357, Box 90690, Mombasa (very expensive), possibly the best, closely followed by its two neighboring sister hotels, **Jadini Beach Hotel** (expensive) and **Africana Sea Lodge** (expensive). Three kilometers (two miles) north of point zero is the good-value **Southern Palms Beach Resort** ((0127) 3721 FAX (0127) 3381, Box 365, Ukunda (expensive). For families, especially, the all-inclusive option can be attractive. There are a few all-inclusives here but the best — and the best value — is **Papillon Hotel** ((0127) 2627 FAX (0127) 2216 E-MAIL onearth@africa online.co.ke, Box 83058, Ukunda (expensive, full board), formerly known as Lagoon Reef, five and a half kilometers (three and a half miles) south of point zero. Traditionally the cheapest beachfront hotel is **Nomad** ((0127) 2155 FAX (0127) 2391, Box 1, Ukunda (mid-range but negotiable), four and a half kilometers (three miles) south. Perhaps it's too cheap, as Nomad totters along, seemingly on the verge of bankruptcy, holding out

clubs, but it is worth getting out occasionally, and the best nightlife clusters about three kilometers (two miles) south of point zero: it's here you'll find **Ali Baba's Restaurant**, perhaps the most atmospheric eatery on the East African coast, set deep underground in limestone caverns. For evening drinking, the Kenyan watering-hole next door is the **Forty Thieves Bar** where "YMCA" echoes from disco speakers over the sea. For a more Kenyan experience cross the road to the open-air **Bushbaby** night club, or the rather more hardcore **Shakatak** next door. Alter-

against any attempt by its snooty neighbors to drag it upmarket.

To the south of Diani is the luxurious, but ecologically very unsound, **Chale Paradise Island** ((011) 222502 E-MAIL islands@africa online.co.ke, Box 12396, Mombasa (expensive). Well, it was a nice island until they built this resort all over it. Further south again, just short of Shimoni, is Funzi Island, connected to the mainland at low tide, where **Funzi Island Club** ((0127) 2044, Box 1108, Ukunda (expensive), is a really exclusive tented camp set amongst the mangrove. Total paradise.

Where to Eat

Generally, guests look to their own resort hotels for a choice of restaurants and night

natively, take a *matatu* or drive to the town of Ukunda on the main coast road: for instance, at the (unlicensed) **Happy Moment** café, it's a struggle to spend more than US$2 on a meal.

How to Get There

Take the Likoni Ferry from Digo Road, Mombasa and follow the A14 coast road, which stays near, but not in sight of, the ocean, and the beaches are clearly-marked turnings to the left. Tiwi comes first, 20 km (12.5 miles) and two turnings south of Likoni. The Diani turning is another 10 km (six miles) further

Tiwi Beach is a favorite with backpackers and ideal for a longer stay.

south, at the town of Ukunda. Turn left and drive three kilometers (two miles) to a strip of tarmac that runs along the back of the beach developments. Turn right for most of the hotels and restaurants. Drive carefully here: there are ladders to let the colobus monkeys cross the road but they still sometimes use the road, and have very little traffic sense.

Diani is easy to get to by public transportation. Buses and *matatus* leave from the Likoni Ferry throughout the day and take about 30 minutes. Many buses and *matatus* go directly to the beach, although it might be necessary to disembark at Ukunda if your bus is heading to Tanzania. If heading for Tiwi Beach, taxis lurk around the turning and offer the only alternative to a long hot walk to the coast.

SHIMONI

Shimoni is a low-key coastal resort catering primarily to deep-sea fishermen, but it offers excellent snorkeling in Kisite Marine National Park, subterranean caves, and Wasini Island to explore.

Kisite Marine National Park is one of Kenya's three offshore reserves where fishing and collecting shells and coral are strictly forbidden. Because of this, the underwater spectacle is unrivaled. You can snorkel anywhere off Shimoni or Wasini Island, as the sea is calm and clear. The best viewing, however, is around Kisite Island. There are organized trips from the hotels along Diani Beach or reserve directly with **Kisite Dhow Tours (** (0127) 2331 FAX (0127) 3154 Box 281, Ukunda.

The cost — US$80 per person including transfers — includes a sailing-dhow crossing to the island, snorkeling equipment rental, and a lavish banquet lunch after which most people collapse on rattan beds spread around under shady trees. Alternatively, walk to the small and friendly Wasini Village. The Kisite National Park has probably the best snorkeling in Kenya and qualified divers can also rent scuba equipment.

The town of Shimoni takes its name from the Swahili *shimo,* meaning caves, which refers to a series of underground coral grottoes. A path from the Shimoni jetty leads to

a ladder entrance. Bats now inhabit the caves, but legends claim that they were once used for storing slaves or were the secret refuge of the locals against Maasai raids. They evoke thoughts of pirate ships and hidden treasures among the nooks and crannies that some claim extend for 20 km (12 miles). The adventurous should bring a flashlight although the area around the entrance is well-lit by sunlight filtering through holes like the one through which you descend.

WASINI ISLAND

A short boat ride offshore from Shimoni is Wasini Island, a small scrub-covered atoll. It measures five kilometers by one kilometer (about three and a half miles by two-thirds of a mile) and is home for a few fishermen. There are no cars; it is a bit like living adrift on the sea. You can wander around the island, explore a raised dead coral garden alive with birds and butterflies instead of fish, swim and snorkel off the beach in front of the village, and discover the ruins of an Arab-African town around which the present village is built. The **Wasini Island Restaurant** caters to snorkeling groups during the day although it closes for the months of May and June.

WHERE TO STAY

Shimoni Reef Lodge ((011) 471771 FAX (011) 473249 WEB SITE www.africa-direct. com, c/o Reef Hotel, Box 82234, Mombasa, caters mainly to keen scuba divers (mid-range), while the **Pemba Channel Fishing Club (** (011) 3132749 FAX (011) 316875, Box 86952, Mombasa, is a club (in the British sense) for serious deep-sea fishermen (very expensive, half board). They do, however, open their doors to nonmembers who share their fishing interests.

If you'd prefer to stay on Wasini Island itself it is always possible to stay at **Mpunguti Guest House**, where rooms cost Ksh1,000 per double, bed and breakfast, or it is possible to camp for Ksh200 per person. Negotiate hard with a boatman for a dhow ride across to the island: how much they charge depends on how much money they think you have; Ksh800 would be a reasonable price.

HOW TO GET THERE

To get to the south coast from Mombasa, drive to the end of the Digo Road and down the ramp to the Likoni Ferry. Two boats shuttle across the water and it's rare to wait more than 20 minutes. Pay at the office before driving on board if in a vehicle; the charge is Ksh25. Pedestrians travel free. *Matatus* and buses wait on the other side. Kenya Bus Service buses leave every 20 minutes or so. For Shimoni, a couple of buses and *matatus* each day go directly; otherwise take anything heading for Lunga Lunga on the Tanzanian border and get off 32 km (20 miles) early at the Shimoni turning. You'll then have to hitchhike the last stretch.

If driving your own vehicle, the A14 coast road stays near, but not in sight of, the ocean, and the beaches are clearly marked turnoffs to the left. The Shimoni turn is 70 km (44 miles) south of Likoni. Then a *murram* road takes you the final 14 km (nine miles) to the tip of the peninsula.

NORTH OF MOMBASA

To the north of Mombasa the new Nyali Bridge has brought the northern beaches within easy reach of the city and given the hotels a rather busier feel. The beaches aren't great, but it has settled into the liveliest place on Kenya's coast, as a chain or bars and clubs break up the chain of resort hotels, whose entertainment tends to the cheesy, along the beach. Easy access to Mombasa keep it lively, while foreign exchange means the resorts of Bamburi, Nyali and Shanzu suck all the best bands and entertainers out of the city. There are water sports here, of course, generally run by the resort hotels and aimed at their packaged clientele, but plenty of people get away without bothering themselves with too much daylight.

There is no real center to the three beach suburbs, spreading out along the Indian Ocean coast: rather there's a line of hotels along the waterfront catering to foreign tourists, while the indigenous population has largely moved to the inland side of the main road.

There's no resentment, though. Kenyans are not likely to spend much time tanning on the beach and are generally happy to let

visiting *mzungus* (white people) pay huge prices for being near a sea which, for bathing purposes, is outclassed by their hotel swimming pools. The beach itself shelves gently, and for much of low tide the water is well out of range.

WHAT TO SEE AND DO

The leading attraction here is Bamburi Nature Trail, see page 205, and Rabai, see page 267. There is also **Mamba Village** ((011) 472709 FAX (011) 472281 E-MAIL mamba@africa

online.co.ke, Box 857223, Mombasa, Links Road, 8 AM to 6 PM daily, Ksh500 adults, Ksh250 children, which is the largest crocodile farm in Kenya. It has camel and horse riding, a tropical garden and a disco, as well as the chance to try a croc-burger. The **Marine Aquarium**, 9 AM to 6:30 PM daily, Ksh250 adults, Ksh150 children, is right next door and includes a snake farm and horses that can be rented for rides.

WHERE TO STAY

Prices here are seasonal, and there are bargains to be had after the peak months of

The coast has been built over millions of years by coral growth.

December to February. There are more than 30 large hotels along this stretch of coast, and so there's little point trying to be exhaustive here, especially as the package-orientated establishments offer such big discounts to tour operators that walk-in travelers are actively discriminated against.

The first place you reach leaving Mombasa Island, and which rather breaks this rule, offers probably the best value on the entire coast: the newly-built but strangely empty **Orchid Bay Hotel** ((011) 473238 FAX (011) 471365, Nyali Road (inexpensive, B&B). Perhaps prices will go up when it gets better established but it is rather a beach resort without a beach. The most comfortable place here, staying well clear of the package market, is perhaps **Tamarind Village** ((011) 474600 FAX (011) 473073 E-MAIL tvlmsa@africaonline .co.ke WEB SITE www.tamarind.co.ke, Box 95805, Mombasa (very expensive), with one- to three-bedded apartments overlooking the harbor. Attached to the city's best restaurant, at least you can be sure of a good breakfast.

The longest-established, and perhaps the best hotel for holidaymakers is **Nyali Beach Hotel** ((011) 471567 FAX (011) 471987, Box 1874, Mombasa (expensive, half board), which is a family-friendly place with a good range of water sports. Rather cheaper is the **Traveler's Beach Hotel** ((011) 485121 FAX (011) 485678, Box 87649, Mombasa (expensive, half board). Somewhat more expensive, but with a notable "Adventurer's Club" for children, is **Voyager Beach Resort** ((02) 446651 or (02) 447929 FAX (02) 446533 E-MAIL info@heritage hotels.co.ke WEB SITE www.heritagehotels .co.ke, Box 74888 Nairobi (very expensive, half board), which is large but cheerful. One of the largest hotels in this area, and certainly with the longest beach frontage, is the very smart **Whitesands** ((02) 713333 FAX (02) 715566, E-MAIL reservations@sarova.co.ke WEB SITE www.sarovahotels.com, Box 72493, Kenyatta Avenue, Nairobi (very expensive, half board).

Step away from the package market and there are some places for travelers who prefer non-packaged, self-contained accommodation, even if they can sometimes be overshadowed by the nearby resorts. Top of the league is **Bamburi Chalets** ((011) 485706 FAX (011)

Rainbow reef shelters a myriad of tropical fish.

485594, Box 84114, Mombasa (expensive, per cottage), sleeping six self-catering, with the less expensive **Baharini Chalets** ((011) 487382 FAX (011) 486302, Bamburi Beach, Box 90371, Mombasa (inexpensive), which has a popular (and in Kenya this isn't always such a good thing) bar. For basic, inexpensive rooms, try **Mombasa Safari Inn** ((011) 485094, opposite the Mombasa Continental Resort in Shanzu, Box 87452, Mombasa (very inexpensive). On a real budget, head away from the tempting ocean waters and go inland and go indigenous: **Monique Hotel** ((011) 474231, Box 97263, Mombasa (very inexpensive, B&B), won't break any budget and includes breakfast.

Most hotel rates in the Mombasa region are negotiable. If you're arriving in the high season and want to reserve in advance, try one of the hotels listed above directly, but you might find better value by asking your travel agent to help — tour operators have often negotiated the keenest rates. Even in December, January and August, you should, in the current climate, be able to pick and choose where you want to stay. Charter airlines from Europe and Canada often include several nights at coastal hotels for the price of a round-trip ticket (see TRAVELERS' TIPS, page 291). This option gives you the security of a place to stay on arrival and time to decide how and where you are spending the remainder of your vacation.

WHERE TO EAT

In the early evening, **Mtwapa Marina Pub** at the northern limits of Mombasa's northern resort sprawl is a good place to watch the sun go down over a beer or three. Meals are available, but for food there are other places to go. Most of the resort hotels have their own specialty restaurants, of which the better ones are **Sher-e-Punjab** at the Travelers Beach Hotel, and the grills at the **Mombasa Safari Inn**, opposite Mombasa Continental Resort. One of Mombasa's best restaurants, with international prices, is the **Tamarind Restaurant** ((011) 471747, overlooking Mombasa's Old Port. It's expensive — but well worth it — and there's a top-floor casino to try to recoup the service charge. Reservations are usually needed. **Splendid**

View Café ((011) 314763, near the Planet shopping center, doesn't actually have any such thing, but the Indian cuisine is very good for less than Ksh1,000 per person.

NIGHTLIFE

For nightlife, there are a number of options along the waterfront, and in many ways it is easiest just to walk up the beach and see which bands are playing, where. To make a start **Beach Corner** at the Baharina Chalets, Shanzu Beach, is a bit of a pick-up joint, with the **Cha Cha Bar** rather calmer. Later on, **Tembo Disco**, just north from the Bamburi Nature Trail, and the **Bora Bora Club** at Ocean View shopping Plaza, offer some of the best music and lighting on the coast.

HOW TO GET THERE

From Mombasa, any number of *matatus* head along the main coast road. Taxis also ply the route, and it doesn't take long to get used to the pricing structure: it's rather less than the fixed fares quoted by Kenatco. Driving yourself, the route, across the Nyali Bridge and following the main road, is umistakable.

THE NORTH COAST

North of Mombasa and the Nyali, Bamburi, and Shanzu hotel strip, there is little development. Most of the coastal land up to Kilifi is the privately owned Vipingo Sisal Estate, one of the largest sisal estates and Kenya's most impressive. The sharp-pointed sisal plants in neatly lined rows cover the landscape in an endless sea of dark sage-green.

Sisal's succulent leaves, which can grow up to one and a half meters (five feet) have sharp spikes at the tips, and when not "in bloom" sisal is easily mistaken for pineapple. (Pineapples are grown at the coast and they are the best I have eaten anywhere, even better than the famed Hawaiian ones.) The bloom of the sisal plant is a three- to six-meter-tall (10- to 18-ft) rigid stalk that bears yellow flowers. A coarse, yellow-white fiber is obtained from a process of crushing and beating the succulent leaves. These dry one- to two-meter-long (three- to six-foot) fibers are then used to make twine and rope for nets, hammocks and carpets. Sisal was one of Kenya's major exports until lighter synthetic fibers elbowed it out of the world market. Nonetheless, Vipingo is still in operation and a major employer on Kenya's north coast.

The monotony of the sisal rows is broken frequently by huge, light-gray, almost silvery, baobabs. These trees are without leaves for most of the year, bearing leaves only after periods of heavy rain. Most Africans consider the baobab a sacred tree. They can live up to 2,000 years, and at Vipingo, when one eventually dies, it is removed.

The baobab looks like a normal tree until it is about four and a half meters (15 ft) tall. Then its trunk begins to swell and continues to swell throughout its life. Some trees reach a diameter of six meters (20 ft) and the trees look somewhat absurd with trunks almost as broad as they are tall.

There are several local legends as to why the baobab looks the way it does. One suggests that the baobab was once the most beautiful tree in Africa, but it was also very proud and boasted too much. As punishment, God turned it upside down, making its beautiful foliage its roots. Another claims that the first baobab refused to stay planted in one place. It wandered the countryside causing trouble. When God caught it, he planted it upside down as punishment.

The baobab's green nuts can be used to make flour and the leaves and fruit-pulp are a Kenyan cure for fever. Inside its thin bark, the trunk is soft and pithy, storing a great amount of moisture. During periods of drought, elephants rip the baobabs apart and extract the water.

KILIFI

Kilifi is the first town north of Mombasa with any tourist amenities. Originally dependent on trading with traffic waiting for the ferry, a 1991 bridge has left it rather without purpose. But as the locals say, it's "a bit cool." It has several *hotelis* in town, a motel, and two coastal resorts. When the Portuguese arrived on the Kenyan coast, Kilifi was known as Mnarani and was centered on the south bank of Kilifi Creek. Ruins of the town are situated on a high cliff above the creek and include a pillar tomb and mosques. There is little

mention of this establishment in Portuguese or Arab writings of the times, and one theory is that the settlement was solely a slave trading center, not mercantile and agricultural like Mombasa, Malindi, Lamu and Pate.

The best hotel around here is **Kilifi Beach Resort (** (0125) 22264 FAX (0125) 22258 WEB SITE www.clubsinternational.com, Box 537, Kilifi, six and a half kilometers (four miles) north (expensive, half board). The **Mnarani Club (** (0125) 22320 FAX (0125) 22200, Box 1008, Kilifi, used to be run by Clubs International (expensive, all-inclusive), but at time

of going to press might have been changing to a good-value, room-only hotel. On a budget, behind the Agip station on the highway going north is the **Mkwajoni Motel and Restaurant (** (0125) 22474, Box 171, Kilifi (very inexpensive, B&B). It has clean rooms with mosquito nets, but be warned: the rooms surround a disco that operates Wednesdays, Fridays and Saturdays. On these nights the similarly priced **Dhows Inn (** (0125) 22028, south of the bridge, is a quieter bet. North of the cashew plantation are grazing lands, a coconut grove or two, and the start of the Arabuko-Sokoke Forest, a designated UNESCO Biosphere Reserve.

Lantern-sailed outriggers along the coast.

WATAMU BAY AND WATAMU MARINE NATIONAL PARK

Watamu Bay is the prime destination for this part of the coast, a quiet community sandwiched between two UNESCO Biosphere Reserves: the forest (Arabuko-Sokoke) inland and the marine park offshore. Watamu Marine National Park has superb snorkeling, or "goggling" as it is locally called. As at Shimoni in the south, fishing of any kind is forbidden in the park and the variety of fish, coral and anemones is phenomenal.

Sometimes, a thousand or more gregarious and colorful fish may surround a swimmer. Among the common species are butterfly fish, angelfish, golden trevally, cardinal fish, hawkfish, white-breasted sturgeons, blue-lined snappers, rock cod (groupers) and jewelfish. The rock cod can grow to several hundred kilograms in weight, and hide under coral outcrops; most of the others are very small, from one to ten centimeters (one-half to four inches) in length.

Low tide is the best time for snorkeling because the sea water filters the sunlight, and the red end of the spectrum disappears after the first one to two meters (three to six feet) of depth, depending on water clarity. Thus the reef will appear much more colorful at low tide as there is less water covering it.

The local hotels all have boats to take you to the reef and along the coast for Ksh300 to Ksh450 per person, although the park entrance fee is also US$5 per person per day. The park extends the length of the ocean in front of the hotels, and you won't be charged an entrance to swim as long as you're not using a mask and snorkel. If you want fins, ask at the dive centers at **Hemingways** or **Ocean Sports** (see WHERE TO STAY, below). To protect the reef none of the standard snorkeling operators include fins: they argue you'll see more without them. Some of the largest fish are near shore, hiding under the moored boats in an area known to the early settlers as "The Larder." For scuba diving, the best operator is **Aqua Ventures (** (0122) 32008 FAX (0122) 32266, next to Ocean Sports.

At the south end of Watamu Bay is another drowned river valley, **Mida Creek**. It is lined with low-lying mangrove swamps and mud flats. A boat tour of Mida Creek is a pleasant way to spend a morning or afternoon and it can be combined with snorkeling stops in the marine park.

Late April, just before migration, is the best time to watch the birds in Mida Creek. The more expensive hotels in Watamu run boats daily to the marine park and Mida Creek, and have boats that can take you deep-sea fishing. Their catch includes blue and black marlin, sailfish, shark, bonito and tuna. Kenya is at the forefront of East Africa's tag-and-release program though it has to be said that many fish caught die of shock and exhaustion. If you're tempted to give game fishing a try, see GAME FISHING, page 22 in TOP SPOTS, and SPORTING SPREE, page 40 in YOUR CHOICE.

ARABUKO–SOKOKE FOREST

To fill your time away from the beach in the Watamu Bay area, you will find the Arabuko-Sokoke Forest, the largest surviving lowland jungle in Kenya. It has stands of hardwoods and rubber trees and the borders of the forest, thanks to its Biosphere listing, seem relatively secure. You can hike along the many dirt tracks and logging roads and will see birds, butterflies and, if you are lucky, the Zanzibar or Aders' duiker, a 35-cm (14-inch) antelope, or the forest's two unique species, the Scopps owl and the elephant shrew (which rattles, occasionally, across your path like a very large rat).

GEDI NATIONAL MONUMENT

Gedi National Monument is the most extensive of the ruins on the Kenyan coast. It comprises the remains of a city constructed in the late thirteenth- or fourteenth-century that was at its peak in the middle of the fifteenth century and was abandoned in the early seventeenth century. Its history is somewhat a mystery. No one is certain exactly when it was founded and by whom. Unlike most of the Arab-African towns, it did not have a harbor and was possibly not a major commercial or political power. Nonetheless, the quantity and quality of porcelain discovered here indicate that its inhabitants were prosperous. The city had a palace that covered about a tenth of a hectare (a quarter of an acre), houses with sunken courtyards, numerous mosques, ornate pilaster tombs, and inner and outer protective walls.

Archaeologists suspect that only a few of the buildings were still occupied in the sixteenth century. By the end of the seventeenth century, Gedi was empty. The writings of the Portuguese from this period shed no light on the history of this mysterious city.

In the seventeenth century, the invading Galla from Somalia either massacred or chased away the inhabitants of all the Arab-

take a dislike to visitors and toss fruits and nuts on the unsuspecting. Recently a new visitors center has been built to formalize what has been learned of this lost coastal culture, replacing the small museum that used to display some of the artifacts uncovered during the excavations between 1939 and 1958. You can purchase a booklet at the entrance that guides you through the town and along the walls, though Abdallah, the manager of the visitors center, is the best local guide, and really brings the site to life. The **Gedi Museum** ((0123) 32065 is open daily.

African cities between Juba River in present-day Somalia and Mtwapa, 24 km (15 miles) north of Mombasa. Gedi was probably no exception. In the second half of the nineteenth century, the Galla were in turn attacked by Somalis and Maasai and lost control over the northern coastal area. The site of Gedi was never reoccupied or rebuilt, but a nearby town, also named Gedi, has been built. There is a school, a few shops, and numerous homes and small farms.

A national historic site, Gedi has been partially excavated and the grounds are well maintained. A tall coastal forest that has grown up around and in the site all but dwarfs this 18-ha (45-acre) town. It is now home for vervet monkeys who frequently

The Ksh200 admission also gets you into the neighboring butterfly project (see below).

KIPEPEO BUTTERFLY PROJECT

One of the few good things to result from the Rio Conference on climate change, the Kipepeo Butterfly Project has started to reap benefits for local farmers living on the border of the Arabuko-Sokoke Forest. At least eight farmers, working from makeshift frames on the edge of the forest, are breeding butterflies for export to Europe. At the heart of this project is a butterfly center by the Gedi Ruins, where the pupae, often more

Watamu Bay Marine Park protects some of the best coral on the coast.

beautiful than any jewel, are packed in cotton-wool for the journey to the West. This has brought US$50,000 to the local economy, in an area that already contains at least 260 butterfly species, fluttering through the dense trees of the forest in vivid bursts of color.

WHERE TO STAY

There are three main resorts in Watamu. **Turtle Bay (** (0122) 32003 FAX (0122) 32268, Box 10, Watamu, is an all-inclusive hotel popular with tourists from Europe (very expensive, all-inclusive). **Hemingways (** (0122) 32624 FAX (0122) 32256 WEB SITE www.hemingways.com, Box 267, Watamu, is a luxury hotel catering mainly — but not exclusively — to big-game fishermen (very expensive, half board). Local Kenyans tend to walk a few meters up the beach for the family-owned **Ocean Sports (** (0122) 32008 FAX (0122) 32266 E-MAIL oceansps@africa online.co.ke, Box 100, Watamu (mid-range, half board), with lunch as a supplement. However, in the heat of the coast, half-board is adequate, with afternoon tea with fresh homemade scones instead of lunch. During May and June, admittedly when seaweed cloaks the beach and the boats are unable to cross the offshore reef, Ocean Sports reduces its rates dramatically. As it should. It's called "Open Shorts" locally, but for the ageing Kenya Cowboys who droop on the bar at this time of year this seems little more than wishful thinking. More sensibly Hemingways closes completely through May.

Unless you've very keen on a hotel atmosphere, by far the best place to stay is **Baraka House (** (0122) 32250 E-MAIL tara@baraka house.co.uk WEB SITE www.barakahouse .co.uk, Box 402, Plot 24B, Mida Creek Road, Watamu (very expensive), a superbly comfortable beach property that can be rented as a whole. With three luxury en-suite rooms this can be very good value for groups, though it can be a bit expensive for singies or couples.

On a budget, look to Watamu village, a 30-minute walk up the beach and across a headland from Watamu Bay but a world apart, culturally. The (very inexpensive) **Dante Hotel (** (0122) 32083, next to **Happy Nights Disco**, doesn't offer breakfast, while opposite, **Veronica (** (0122) 32243 (very inexpensive), does. Whichever, Happy Nights Disco is a blast on weekends.

HOW TO GET THERE

It takes just over an hour to get to Watamu from Mombasa. Leave Mombasa on the B8 coast road and after 90 km (56 miles) turn right at Gedi Village. Pass Gedi National Monument and drive four kilometers (three miles) to the beach. By public transportation, take a bus or *matatu* heading for Malindi, and get off 24 km (15 miles) early at Gedi village. Further *matatus* will reach Watamu village. Alternatively it is possible to fly to Malindi with Airkanya's daily service and take a taxi back to Watamu; the cost to cover the 24 km (15 miles) should not be much more than Ksh1,000.

MALINDI

Malindi was the city-state that in the fourteenth century sent a Kenyan giraffe to China, gift of the Sultan of Malindi to the Chinese emperor, which was transported by one of China's most renowned navigators, the Ming Dynasty's Admiral Zheng He. The gift probably served a twofold mission. First, it attempted to prove to the isolationist emperor that the lands beyond China did have something to offer. Secondly, the Sultan wished to establish direct trade with the Chinese fleets that had, since the sixth century, sailed only as far as India or Arabia to purchase slaves and other East African goods. Malindi also welcomed and entertained Vasco da Gama on his visits to the Kenyan coast, but has since lost some of its previous charm to tourism: a rapid boom in Italian development ended in a bust from which it will take years to recover and silt has affected both its marine park and beaches. The old town is a mishmash of Arab-style buildings, few of which are older than 1900, and boom buildings from the 1930s, while to the north are the rather grander reminders of the 1990s boom.

Most of Malindi's old buildings went to ruin after its ruling family moved to Mombasa in the sixteenth century. When the Portuguese captured Mombasa, they installed Malindi's royal family as titular head of the coastal communities.

Without a ruling family, Malindi's power and prosperity declined. The port no longer attracted merchant vessels and Malindi became a ghost town. Gone are the inlaid doors described by the early Portuguese visitors. Tourism in the past 25 years revitalized the town, and left it hanging. During the peak of the high season (December and January, and, later on, in August), the town is flushed with tourists, mostly German and Italian, while at other times bars and hotels stand empty. The high tide of this seasonal invasion still leaves a **Tourist Information Office** ((0123) 20747

WHERE TO STAY

The smartest option here is the newest: the **Woburn Residence Club** ((0123) 30073 FAX (0123) 31183 WEB SITE www.woburnrc .com, Box 33, Malindi (expensive), seven minutes' walk from town by the Galana Hospital, with as many comforts as you could happily throw a stick at and accommodation mainly in apartments and suites. It's owner-run and small enough to remain intimate and friendly.

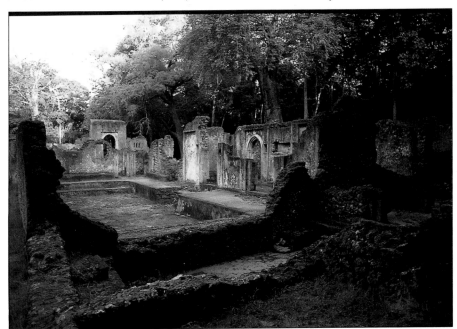

FAX (0123) 30429, Utali Parade, Harambee Road, Box 421, Malindi, 8 AM to 4:30 PM Monday to Friday. There are taxis everywhere, but you can also call **Baobab Taxis** ((0123) 30499. If you need medical treatment urgently, **Galana Hospital** ((0123) 2083, Lamu Road, is the best. For e-mail try **Bit House** in the Malindi Complex shopping center.

Located at the mouth of the Sabaki River, Malindi's bay often turns red due to seasonal runoff from upstream overgrazed land. This makes Watamu Bay a better choice for divers keen to spot the coral, though most dive schools are prepared to travel for good reefs. The coral in the **Malindi Marine National Park** suffered lasting damage from the El Nino floods in the 1990s and has not yet recovered.

The main resort hotels, all rather less expensive booked overseas as a package, are set well back from the beach. The **Driftwood Beach Club** ((0123) 20155 FAX 214120, Box 63, Malindi (mid-range), is the nearest refuge, for Kenya Cowboys who fail to get into Ocean Sports in nearby Watamu, or for the all-inclusive beach experience there is **Lawfords** ((0127) 3081 FAX (0127) 3439, Box 37, Ukunda. But the best of these big international package places is the most southerly: the **Eden Roc** ((0123) 20480 FAX (0123) 203333, Box 350, Malindi (expensive), also with some fan-cooled rooms (mid-range), is great for families and not too smart — perfect for the rather

Ruins of the thirteenth- to fifteenth-century Arab city of Gedi.

scruffy charms of the town. Though a recent change of management has dragged it nearer the twenty-first century, it's still two and a half kilometers (one and a half miles) south on the "British" side of the city center. For something a little different, the **Kobokoni Riding Centre** ((0123) 21273 FAX (0123) 21030, Box 857, Malindi (expensive), north of town, offers an beachfront atmosphere for horsey romantics.

On a budget, in Malindi town there are several small hotels, the best of which, though sandwiched between a bus station and a mosque, is **Ozi's Bed and Breakfast** ((0123)

fly from Nairobi's International Airport to Malindi. They have a Malindi office at ((0123) 20237, Box 634, Malindi. **Airkenya** ((02) 501421/3 FAX (02) 500845 E-MAIL info @airkenya.com WEB SITE www.airkenya.com, Box 30357, Nairobi; ((011) 229777 FAX (011) 224063, Nkrumah Road, Mombasa; or ((0123) 30808 FAX (0123) 21229, Box 548, Malindi, fly here too — and on up the coast — from Mombasa and also link Malindi with Nairobi. The fare between Malindi and Mombasa with Airkenya is a very reasonable Ksh2,000, and from Nairobi (via Mombasa), Ksh5,385. If

20218, Seafront Road, Box 60, Malindi (very inexpensive, B&B), although its position between mosque and bus station might make for a restless night. If driving, the **Starlight Hotel** ((0123) 30424 FAX (0123) 21225, Box 194, Mama Ngina Street, near the market, has secure parking (very inexpensive).

you're depending on this flight to catch an international connection, reconfirm often as overbooking does happen. Frequent buses and *matatus* link Mombasa with Malindi but traveling north to Lamu overland is not currently recommended, even though convoys of *matatus* occasionally make the trip.

How to Get There

Malindi is two hours by car from Mombasa along the coast road. It can also be reached by air from Nairobi or Mombasa: the flight from Mombasa offers a spectacular half-hour overview of the fringing coral reef of the shore. **Kenya Airways** ((02) 210771 or (02) 229291 FAX (02) 336252, Box 41010, Nairobi,

THE LAMU ARCHIPELAGO

North of Malindi, when the paved road ends, you enter a no-man's-land that Somali bandits (*shiftas*) rule. The landscape is flat with marshy green and arid brown stretches. During the rainy season, the route north is impassable in any vehicle; bus service is often interrupted for weeks. Even in the dry season, *shiftas* make the route unsafe. Visitors wanting to go further north to Lamu usually fly from Malindi, Mombasa or Nairobi.

There are daily flights from Malindi and Mombasa, and if you are in a hurry you can tour Lamu in a day, flying up in the morning and returning the same night. But that's not really long enough. Lamu is the most exotic site on the Kenyan coast, a mini-Katmandu-by-the-sea, that appeals particularly to long-staying backpackers, lone travelers and the occasional honeymoon couple.

religious refugees from the Arabian or Persians regions of the Caliphate.

These refugees, like those who migrated to Malindi and Mombasa, became the religious, political and economic force in the area. They assimilated parts of the native population and culture. Lamu and the nearby islands of Manda and Pate were part of the Portuguese Indian Ocean empire. The Portuguese constructed a fort on Pate, but apparently never had a large force on Lamu or Manda. From the number of old buildings still standing, it seems reasonable to

From the airport a dhow takes new arrivals from the mainland to Lamu; the slow approach to the toytown buildings of the old city center transports you back to the nineteenth century. There is one automobile, belonging to the District Commissioner, but it's a rarely used status symbol. Electricity has only just arrived. Donkeys and dhows are the only transportation, and mostly both are wind-powered. The pace of life is accordingly slow.

Archaeologists and historians have established that the island has been inhabited since about AD 1200, though the towns of Lamu and Shela on Lamu Island did not exist until the fourteenth to fifteenth century. The founders of Lamu and Shela were most likely

assume that the inhabitants did not openly oppose the Portuguese, but maintained their cultural and religious identities without aggravating their rulers. There are reports of the Portuguese executing one of Lamu's sheiks for collaboration with the Turks in the late sixteenth century — a minor punishment when you consider the massive slaughter and pillage the Portuguese inflicted on Mombasa.

Lamu became prosperous in the seventeenth century when Pate's harbor began to silt in. It reached its peak of affluence in the eighteenth century. From the ancient poetry of the region and a few western accounts,

A luxury restaurant in Malindi. Malindi and Lamu are the most interesting places to stay on the coast.

historian J. de V. Allen has reconstructed life on the island then:

"Rich men clad in fine silks and turbans moved about surrounded by crowds of retainers, young men who competed, both individually and collectively in personal display, in witty exchanges, in composing poetry and epigrams and also in ceremonial sword-dances. There was a constant buzz of activity, with business being transacted in the streets and coffeehouses, workmen and slaves building or refurbishing houses, heavily-laden sailing boats entering or leaving

"Warfare, when it occurred, was an occasion for impassioned speeches, the wholesale distribution of invulnerability charms, and menacing processions accompanied by the beating of many gongs." (J. de V. Allen, *Lamu Town*.)

Lamu, Pate and Manda aligned themselves with Oman and later Zanzibar, when Seyyid Said moved his court there, and thus traded regularly with European and American merchants. There was a period of German occupation in the late nineteenth century, but by then, the islands' prosperity

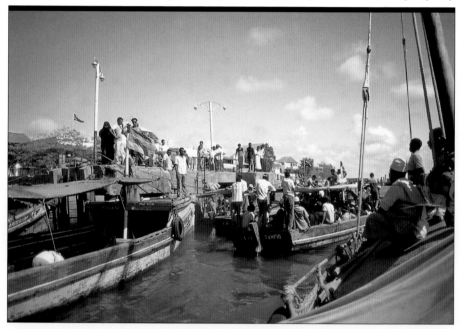

the harbor, and great men coming and going on the eternal safaris which are still so much an integral part of Swahili life.

"Music was provided for the master of the house when he returned home, also massage and baths (both hot and cold) and couches strewn with jasmine. While the women, probably already in seclusion for much of their lives, lived for the weddings and other occasions when they could congregate to dance their own dances and compete with each other in poetry and song, and concentrated meanwhile on enjoying life as much as they could without exciting their husband's suspicions. The art of enjoying harem life is one in which Lamu women have become, over the centuries, very skilled.

was already in decline. Pate's harbor was completely silted in, Manda never had a good deepwater harbor, and Lamu's could not accommodate the new steamships.

LAMU

Lamu is an amalgam of twelfth- through eighteenth-century buildings in Arab style, with its traditional town plan still intact. Streets are narrow and have the dual purpose of providing shade and producing a slight wind tunnel effect. There are over 20 mosques, the oldest, Pwami, dating from 1370.

ABOVE: Dhows are still used for daily transport on this island without cars. OPPOSITE: A few coastal artisans still construct dhows by hand, as on Lamu.

Lamu's ornately carved wooden doors, wall niches and plaster detailing generate the greatest interest, being close to hypnotic in their intricacy. Most of them are distinctly Arabic, but some include universal motifs often found in Celtic, Phoenician and Roman designs.

Daily life takes place out of doors; artisans work on their doorsteps, businessmen meet on verandas, children play anywhere and everywhere. Although the absence of cars is certainly a factor in this style of life, this has been the rhythm here for centuries.

The **museum** at Lamu is one of the best in Africa. Housed in a classic open-centered building, the museum has a room depicting a Swahili wedding. It also features excellent displays on coastal maritime culture, a collection of ivory and brass *siwas* (ceremonial horns), and exhibits of daily life of the Swahili and the non-Swahili peoples of the nearby mainland. Here, you can buy J. de V. Allen's guide, *Lamu Town*, which gives a detailed history of the area and an excellent description of the historic buildings in the town and the island.

Women still live in relative seclusion, though this is beginning to change. The people of Lamu are social and convivial, most of them sharing common ancestors and history.

Processions occur frequently. The most common are the *ziara*, or visits to the graves of holy men. There are festivals for weddings, betrothals, and funerals.

Annually, on the last Thursday in Rabai al-Awal, the week-long festival of **Maulidi** begins (currently in the summer and moving back through the year, according to the lunar calendar). Lamu is then overcrowded as pilgrims come from all over Kenya, Tanzania, Uganda and Arab countries as well. The island is alive with traditional dance, song and open-air religious ceremonies.

Lamu is the most populous island in the archipelago. The long white beaches are a 40-minute walk from Lamu town (or a 50Ksh dhow ride), near Shela village. Walk far enough and many will be deserted; but don't sunbathe nude or topless as someone will appear and take offense.

The reefs offshore offer good snorkeling, but only from November through February; at other times visibility is a problem. Windsurfing and deep-sea fishing are always available. When the wind is up, you can also body surf — the only place apart from a few dangerous locations further south where this is possible in Kenya.

If you have an extra day (or two) to spend in the area, it is worth visiting **Pate**. There are plenty of dhows providing ferry service; departure times depend on the time and weather. There are no hotels or restaurants on the island, but residents meet the ferry boats offering rooms and meals. You can spend only a day, but make sure your dhow or another is going back in the evening. In any case, it is best to bring your own food and water. Around the island (on foot), there are the modern villages of Kizingitini, Bajumwali, and Nyabogi, which have a few carved doors, and the ancient towns of Pate, Siyu and Faza.

runs the best bar in town (there are only about five) on its rooftop terrace. For both, contact **Romantic Hotels** (/FAX (0121) 33107, Box 4, Lamu. The small hotels in town are more in keeping with the mood of the city: **Casuarina Guest Lodge** ((0121) 33123, Box 12, Lamu (very inexpensive, B&B, with bargaining), is one good example that rejects commission-paid touts. Hoteliers — and their friends — make finding a hotel on your own a significant challenge. Usually there is too much help, and bargaining is expected.

WHERE TO STAY

The best tourist-class hotel on Lamu is located a 40-minute walk — rather quicker by dhow — from town, but it is right on the edge of the town's nearest beach. The very comfortable **Peponi Hotel** ((0121) 33154 FAX (0121) 33029 Box 24, Lamu (very expensive, full board), is closed annually from April 15 to July 1 but is still the best place to eat and sleep on the island.

In the town of Lamu itself, the two smartest places are owned by the same organization. On paper the best is their **Lamu Palace** (mid-range), though **Petleys** (inexpensive, room only), despite recent refurbishments, is more atmospheric and still

HOW TO GET THERE

Part of the reason Lamu has retained its special character is that access to it has always been far from easy. Not only is the road north of Malindi in extremely poor condition, and generally becomes impassable at the onset of the rains, but the entire route is plagued by *shiftas* (bandits).

Occasionally, convoys of buses and trucks make it through this hazarous route, but for most visitors access to Lamu is by air, with reasonably regular flights from

OPPOSITE: Lamu's population LEFT reflects the influence and immigration of northern Arab traders and RIGHT most women go modestly veiled. ABOVE: Sunset falls over a timeless sailing dhow.

Nairobi and Mombasa, and less regular flights from Malindi, on **Airkenya** ((02) 501421/3 FAX (02) 500845 E-MAIL info@air kenya.com WEB SITE www.airkenya.com, Box 30357, Nairobi; or ((011) 229777 FAX (011) 224063, Nkrumah Road, Mombasa; or ((0123) 30808 FAX (0123) 21229, Box 548, Malindi; or ((0121) 33445 FAX (0121) 33063, Box 376, Lamu. The fare to fly from Malindi to Lamu is US$7 one way. It is possible to charter a dhow from Malindi to Kiwayu, but allow a few days for the journey, at least. Take plenty of water.

extremely expensive, all-inclusive **Kiwayu Safari Village** ((02) 503030 FAX (02) 503149 WEB SITE www.kiwayu.com — Kiwayu Safari Village can also be booked in Nairobi through Cheli and Peacock ((02) 604053/4 or (02) 603090/1 FAX (02) 604050 or (02) 603066 E-MAIL chelipeacock@africaonline.co.ke WEB SITE www.chelipeacock.com, Box 39806, Nairobi.

Just offshore on Kiwayu Island, the generally very busy **Munira Camp** ((02) 512543 FAX (02) 512213 E-MAIL bigblue@africaonline .co.le, Box 40088, Nairobi, is the rather less

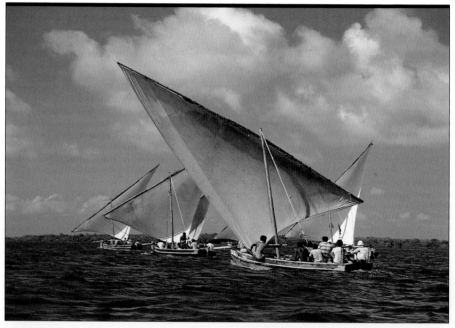

KIWAYU

Isolated in the far northeast of Kenya are two final outposts of luxury, accessible only by air and offering the sort of comforts only huge amounts of money can buy. By all accounts, it's worth it.

The emphasis here is on leisure, with most guests relaxing thoroughly and fast. Even so, Kiwayu is surrounded by one of the country's least-visited nature reserves and within a few kilometers are the "hanging gardens" growing from the great baobab trees of Kitangani.

Kiwayu is primarily a beach destination though, with the smartest of its small handful of tourist resorts being the luxurious, if

sophisticated alternative favored by Kenyan nationals (very expensive, all-inclusive).

Finally, there's an Italian-run luxury lodge called the **Blue Safari Club** ((02) 890184 FAX (02) 890096 WEB SITE www.blue safariclub.com (extremely expensive, all-inclusive). Access is generally by air, using **Airkenya** from Mombasa via Malindi and Lamu (US$150 one-way), although it might be possible to arrange (long) transfers by speedboat from Peponi's in Lamu, or a very long (think overnight) trip in a local dhow.

ABOVE: Dhows are a major means of transportation among the islands of the Lamu archipelago. OPPOSITE: Lamu's shady, colorful open market.

Travelers' Tips

GETTING THERE

Finding a reasonably priced ticket to Kenya takes time and a fair amount of persistence.

FROM THE UNITED STATES AND CANADA

No flights fly direct, non-stop to Kenya from North America, and a change of plane and airline will be needed, usually in Europe. Depending on departure point, length of stay and season, the APEX fare will be around US$2,500 to US$3,500. KLM's code-share link with Northwest Airlines and Kenya Airways make them amongst the most frequent fliers, with a comprehensive range of departures across the United States. Routing through the United Kingdom can give the best rates: operators in London have access to consolidated fares and special rates with safari companies and beach resorts. Student travel companies such as STA or Council Travel offer low fares. Refer to advertisements in the travel sections of major newspapers for more specialists — book by credit card for added security.

FROM EUROPE

Your options are greatest from Europe. Prices and restrictions vary. There are direct flights from London, Paris, Amsterdam, Brussels, Copenhagen, Frankfurt, Madrid, Moscow, Athens, Rome and Zurich on regularly scheduled airlines: British Airways, Air France, Sabena, SAS, Lufthansa, Iberia, Aeroflot, Olympic Airways, Alitalia and Swissair, respectively. Some fly daily, but most once or twice weekly. Kenya Airways, now a code-share partner with KLM, flies from Paris, London, Amsterdam, Zurich, Athens, Frankfurt, Rome and Cairo on a daily basis. APEX fares are the most reasonable you can get with these airlines, and from the United Kingdom these can cost as little as US$600 round trip, even with scheduled airlines. Some companies will restrict your length of stay and flexibility to change travel dates at this price so check conditions before you part with your money.

For cheaper fares, often on the regularly scheduled flights, you should contact a travel agent who is familiar with the charter and consolidator scene. In the United Kingdom, one of the best is **Flightbookers** ((0171) 7572444 FAX (0171) 7572200 WEB SITE www .flightbookers.net, 177-178 Tottenham Court Road, London W1P OLX, with further branches around the United Kingdom.

FROM AUSTRALASIA

There are no direct flights or to Kenya. A stopover is inevitable. Most direct is via Mauritius using Air Mauritius' weekly flights from Perth: a code-share arrangement with Ansett opens this route up to New Zealand and Australian cities. Perth is lucky again with flights to Nairobi and Harare. Kenya's substantial Asian population ensures plenty of flights from India, so good linkages exist from from Australia via various cities in Asia, especially Bombay. Good services are also supplied by Middle Eastern Airlines, including Gulf Air and Emirates. Flying via the United States is not only much longer but also raises the problems already faced by Americans trying to get to Africa, but Kenya can be fitted into round-the-world itineraries. Specialist operators include **Africa Travel Centre** ((02) 9267 3048, Level 12, 456 Kent Street, Sydney NSW 2000, and in New Zealand ((09) 520 2000, 21 Remuera Road, Box 9365, Newmarket, Auckland.

ARRIVING (AND LEAVING)

VISAS

To the despair of tour operators and hoteliers, visa requirements do change regularly. When things are going well the government will try to introduce substantial visa charges, to be waived when things are going badly. Visas are required for all visitors except citizens of some British Commonwealth countries and several other countries with which Kenya has reciprocal agreements, namely Denmark, Ethiopia, Germany, Finland, San Marino, Spain, Sweden, Turkey and Uruguay. However at time of going to press all United Kingdom and United States citizens

The first view of Nairobi is from the air as your plane comes in to land.

needed visas, at a cost of £35 sterling or US$57 per person. Citizens of Australia, Nigeria and Sri Lanka also need visas. Although any currency will be accepted, credit cards are not.

These requirements are subject to change and should be checked with Kenya government offices abroad or a travel agency before departure. If visas are required, best get them before leaving home: airport lines can be long and the requirement that the visas must be bought with a hard currency mean that lines move slowly. Standard tourist visas

or a valid certificate of loss, leaving Kenya can suddenly get bumpy.

The import of fruit, plants, seeds, or animals is prohibited. Your dog or cat may accompany you, for which you must submit a health certificate to the same office as for your visa to obtain an entry permit. However, dogs are not allowed in national parks and reserves.

If you have any ivory articles (jewelry), make sure you can prove in which country the ivory was purchased by means of a receipt, or else it will probably be confiscated.

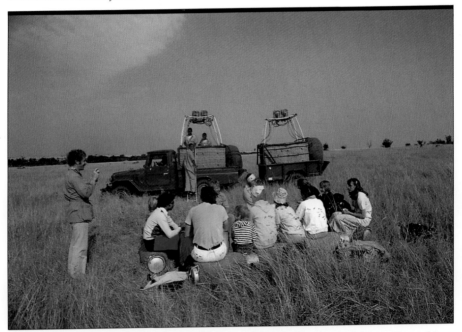

are valid for 30 days and for one entry. Passports must be current for six months from your date of entry into Kenya.

CUSTOMS ALLOWANCES

Travelers over 16 years of age may import duty-free up to 200 cigarettes or 50 cigars of 250 grams (eight and three quarter ounces) of tobacco, one liter of alcoholic beverage and a quarter-liter of perfume. Personal effects, including unexposed film, cameras and accessories, may be temporarily imported duty-free, but laptop computers and other valuables may well be listed in your passport so they can be checked off when you depart. Without the same laptops or cameras,

Avoid any hassles and leave ivory objects at home.

Firearms and ammunition require a permit issued by the Central Firearms Bureau, Box 30263, Nairobi. In view of the recent crackdown on poachers, these permits are difficult to acquire.

Export of ivory, rhinoceros horns, game skins, game trophies and all other anatomical relics of wildlife is strictly forbidden, as is export of live animals, birds and reptiles, except by licensed dealers.

AIRPORT TAX

To leave Kenya, it is necessary to pay an airport exit tax of US$20 (in United States

Travelers' Tips

currency *only*). Officially, this should be integrated into the cost of the ticket, but this hasn't always worked. If you didn't pay this with your ticket make sure you have US$20 spare when you get to the departure gate: changing money at the airport can be time-consuming and it's not unknown for harassed tourists to be tricked into changing more than they wanted to at a very poor rate. The need for all currency transactions to be noted in your currency declaration is no longer generally required.

EMBASSIES AND CONSULATES

As a rule of thumb, allow six weeks to get your visa from one of the Kenya diplomatic missions listed below, or from the British consulate if Kenya has no diplomatic representation in your country. When time is tight, advise the appropriate mission so it can speed your application. Kenyan embassies and consulates abroad include the following:

Australia ((02) 6247 4788, 33 Ainslie Avenue, Box 1990, Canberra.

Austria ((01) 633242, Rotenturmstrasse 22, 1010 Vienna.

Belgium ((02) 230 3065, Avenue Joyeuse Entrée 1-5, Brussels.

Canada ((613) 563 1773, Gillia Building, Suite 600, 415 Laurier Avenue East, West Ottawa, Ontario.

Egypt ((02) 704 455, 20 Boulos Hanna Street, Box 362, Dokki, Cairo.

France ((01) 4553 3500, 3 Rue Cimarosa, 75116 Paris.

Germany ((0228) 356041, Villichgasse 17, 5300 Bonn 2.

Italy ((06) 578 1192/808 2718, CP 10755, 0014 Rome.

Japan ((03) 479 4006, No. 20-24 Nishi-Azobu 3-Chome, Minato-Ku, Tokyo.

Netherlands ((70) 350 4215, Konninginnegracht 102, The Hague.

New Zealand — No representation: apply to the Australian consulate.

Sweden ((08) 218 300, Birger Jarlsgatan 37, 2tr 11145, Stockholm.

Uganda ((041) 231 861, 60 Kira Road, Box 5220, Kampala.

United Arab Emirates ((02) 366300, Box 3854, Abu Dhabi.

United Kingdom ((020) 7636 2371, 45 Portland Place, London W1N 4AS.

United States — Embassy **(** (202) 387 6101, 2249 R Street NW, Washington, DC 20008; Consulate **(** (212) 421 4740, 866 United Nations Plaza, Room 486, New York, NY 10017; **(** (310) 274 6635, 9150 Wilshire Boulevard, Suite 160, Beverley Hills, CA 90212.

Foreign embassies and consulates in Kenya iclude the following:

United States Embassy ((02) 537800 FAX (02) 537810 E-MAIL usis@usis.africaonline.co.ke, WEB SITE usembassy.state.gov/nairobi, Barclays Plaza, Loita Street, Box 30143, Nairobi.

Australian High Commission ((02) 445034/9 FAX (02) 444718, Riverside Drive, Box 39351, Nairobi.

British High Commission ((02) 714699 FAX (02) 719082, E-MAIL bhcinfo@iconnect.co.ke, Box 30465, Nairobi.

Canadian High Commission ((02) 214804 FAX (02) 226987, Comcraft House, Haile Selassie Avenue, Box 30481, Nairobi.

French Embassy ((02) 339978 FAX (02) 339421, Ninth Floor, Barclays Plaza, Loita Street, Box 41784, Nairobi.

German Embassy ((02) 712527/8 FAX (02) 714886, Eighth Floor, Williamson House, 4 Ngong Avenue, Box 30180, Nairobi.

South African Embassy ((02) 215616/8 FAX (02) 223687, 17th Floor, Lonrho House, Standard Street, Box 42441, Nairobi.

New Zealand Consulate ((02) 722467 FAX (02) 722566, Minet ICDC Insurance, Third Floor, Minet House, Nyere Road, Box 47383, Nairobi.

TOURIST INFORMATION

This is where Kenya really hasn't got its act together. Even the Kenyan tourist office in Britain has been closed recently, and in Kenya itself you'll be relying, apart from a few under-funded bureaux on the coast, on the impartiality of those who work within the tourist industry and, often, on the kindness of strangers.

Fortunately, in Kenya strangers can be very kind indeed.

A balloon flight can be relaxing way to visit Kenya's national parks Here balloonists appreciate an alfresco champagne breakfast after an early-morning trip.

TRAVEL AGENTS

If you're going on your own, you may want to make reservations ahead of time. **Let's Go Travel** ((02) 447151 or (02) 441030 FAX (02) 447270 or (02) 441690 E-MAIL info@letsgo safari.com WEB SITE www.letsgosafari.com, Box 60342, Nairobi, will do this for you and answer most questions you may have about road and travel condition. In all our wanderings through Kenya, Let's Go Travel has consistently received good reports from its clientele. Efficient and informative without being pushy, they provide useful help to all classes of traveler, although it has to be said that there are other agencies in Kenya that are just as helpful.

GETTING AROUND

BY BUS

Buses of all sizes and shapes, and communal taxis or *matatus* go virtually everywhere in Kenya, except through most national parks and reserves. Prices are minimal, depending on owner and operator, but are usually below Ksh5 per kilometer (half-mile). They are famously crowded but somehow, there's always enough room — just barely. This hasn't changed the fact that drivers are more concerned with speed than safety. Schedules are often erratic; drivers will rarely leave without an overfull load. Nonetheless, they will get you to your destination, and can run into some exciting adventures along the way. *Matatus* and buses are cheap. Hitchhiking is not generally recommended, and is most unwise near cities — the only exception might be in very rural areas where it is the only way to get around.

BY TAXI

In Nairobi and Mombasa, there are taxi services at reasonable prices. The cabs have no meters so always agree the price to your destination before getting in. Bargain or ask a different driver if you think the price too steep.

The minimum rate is generally Ksh200: don't accept higher minimums. Even in

Nairobi Ksh300 should get you a long way, and even the international airport shouldn't be more than Ksh1,000. In general, taxis are usually around when needed, but they rarely cruise, and only in Nairobi and Mombasa are there dial-up taxis. If you're unsure about your return ride, book a taxi ahead.

BY TRAIN

The Mombasa–Uganda Railway, now Kenya Railways, provides nightly service between Mombasa and Nairobi, and Nairobi and Kisumu. The night trip to or from Mombasa to Nairobi is particularly recommended. With a private compartment and an excellent railroad meal, it feels a bit like the old Orient Express, or the still-marvelous trip on the Trans-Siberian Railway from Moscow to Vladivostok.

To reserve a seat on the train, you generally must make arrangements at the train station in Nairobi, Mombasa, or Kisumu, where you may be told no first-class tickets are available. If so, buy a second-class one and visit a nearby travel agency, where they may be able to upgrade your ticket to first class for a nominal fee. If this arrangement strikes you as peculiar, try going to a travel agency first. A word of caution: the travel agency may send you to the train station ...

BY CAR

Car Rental

It's possible to rent both two- and four-wheel-drive vehicles in Nairobi and Mombasa; occasionally it's possible also to rent four-wheel drives (with or without drivers) at some hotels and lodges.

If you plan to drive only during the dry season (July to September, January to March) and avoid the Northern Frontier District, Mount Elgon, Tsavo East, Lamu and all the other areas off the main tourist circuit, you may be able to get by with a two-wheel-drive car. However heavy-duty tires are almost essential for occasional potholes that afflict even the best roads, let alone the collapsing surfaces of the worst.

Buses and *matatus* are Kenya's major form of transportation.

To ensure full freedom of travel, and to get into the backcountry (or to get practically *anywhere* during or after the rains), choose a four-wheel drive. Many of the roads in Kenya are so bad in the rainy season even a helicopter could get stuck in them. By sub-Saharan African standard they're not bad, but by any other they're dreadful.

There are special problems with renting cars in Kenya. First is cost. Bad roads are part of the reason why car rental is expensive, and this factor also means checking over the car for mechanical soundness is very important before driving off on an ambitious safari. There are also traps in the small print for the unwary. First is that cheap rates hide expensive charges per kilometer, often starting to click up your bill from the moment you edge out of the parking space. Rates rarely include CDW (Collision Damage Waiver), TP (Theft Protection) or tax at 17 percent. Even experienced travelers can be caught by insurance excess: some companies charge clients up to US$10,000 in the case of any accident, and that is when they've paid the CDW excess. Our best recommendation, in terms of vehicle reliability, price, and overall helpfulness, is **Central Rent-a-Car** ((02) 222888 FAX (02) 339666, Standard Street, Box 4939, Nairobi, while other reputable operators — with offices in Nairobi and Mombasa — include **Avis** ((02) 334317 FAX (02) 215421, Box 49795, Nairobi, and **Hertz** ((02) 214456 FAX (02) 216871, Box 42196, Nairobi. Central has more than competitive rates on both two- and four-wheel-drive vehicles, and their cars are clean, well-maintained, and reliable.

The second question is: what type of vehicle? The best four-wheel drive is probably a Landrover, followed closely by Mitsubishi Pajero and Toyota Landcruiser. Slightly cheaper — to buy or rent — is the Isuzu Trooper. I chose it after test-driving a number of similar vehicles and found I liked it most: it was comfortable yet rugged, roomy and solid but economical on gas. Due to its longer wheelbase, its ride is much smoother than the shorter Suzuki Sierra, which seemed also potentially hazardous and top-heavy. As experienced four-wheel drivers, we know the importance of freewheeling hubs that can be disengaged when two-wheel traction is insufficient.

If there are only two of you, it might be worth considering the four-seat model of the Suzuki Sierra (the two-seat version with a back bench being unstable on the road). The ride in the Sierra is a lot bouncier than the Trooper's, which becomes more and more important as you log more kilometers. If you're not going far, the Sierra may be fine. A compromise would be the Diahatzu Feroza, rather bigger and heavier than the Suzuki but still economical to rent: try Avis.

In any case, no matter what vehicle you choose, be sure it has sufficient seatbelts for each person traveling. Accidents are common in Kenya, and acceptable hospital facilities invariably distant.

Driving in Kenya

By Western standards, the roads in Kenya are poor. Even the best-surfaced ones have sudden jarring potholes, and the worst tarmac often entails a laborious, snaking slalom which leads some drivers to take to new tracks on either side. Many roads are still *murram*, or surfaced with local clay. If not regularly maintained these turn into rutted and unforgiving channels and however well prepared, any rain will transform the surface into mud more slippery than ice. This is even more of a problem if the surface is deeply rutted: the effect on the car is to make it, as the locals say, "dance." At any point roads can be blocked by trucks or cars that break down or simply get bogged.

Traffic is heavy, with slow trucks crawling up the steeper hills. Constant passing in the face of oncoming traffic can be wearing. Driving at night is not recommended, as other vehicles often drive without lights, and if they have them, rarely turn down the high beams. Blind corners are littered with unlit broken-down trucks, and a growing incidence of banditry and car-jacking make daylight hours the safest option. At any given time, some of the roads in the country will be unsafe due to cattle rustling or tribal disputes. The only way of finding out where it is safe to travel is to ask locally and place your trust in the answer.

Each Easter the East African Safari Rally takes place on public roads, and for much of March it seems that half the population is practicing speed-driving, often in heavy rain. Long distances irresistibly increase speed: watch out for speed bumps, often unmarked, which are frequent hazards near every school and settlement. Sometimes they are mere rumble strips, but often very serious mounds of tarmac that can bump the unwary driver hard against the roof and cause loss of control. Off the beaten track, road bumps are less of a problem than finding gasoline; sometimes it's necessary to phone ahead and ensure supplies are available at key lodges on your route. In any event, keep the tank well topped up, as it is easy to run dry in Kenya. Street signs are limited, and even major junctions are frequently unmarked. It's not even easy to get an accurate map, as the authorities regard these as classified information and seem to believe the average visitor is planning an invasion rather than a vacation.

Put off? Good. Because only the brave should head out behind the wheel of their own car. That said, the freedom of having your own vehicle can transform your experience, and a self-driver in Kenya is also rewarded with a considerable sense of achievement. All Kenya's roads have aspects of beauty. However, for the driver, appreciation of this is often glimpsed only in snatched glances from upcoming hazards on the way ahead. Roads subject to heavy traffic are usually the worst. The main road artery between Nairobi and Mombasa, for instance, is a bore: bad surface and slow trucks mean the view palls even for passengers. Many of the same trucks continue through towards Uganda and Africa's interior, taking their toll on routes across the Rift Valley, but better views compensate. Main roads not used by heavy traffic, dead-ending up towards Lake Baringo, Eldoret and Kitale are usually far better, and are considerably helped if their local MP is well-connected. At their best these roads can have light traffic and the only hazards are occasional potholes and stray animals.

Minor roads can deteriorate quickly over the wet season (April to June, October to early December), and their condition depends whether they have been graded. The little-used western route down from Kericho into the Masai Mara is one of the country's most scenic, but the dreadful *murram* surface

means that pleasure is tinged with concern: will you make it? In the wet season the answer is often no, although a little maintenance would make a great difference. The only way of finding out if this has taken place is to ask locally. The situation can change from mile to mile as well as year to year, but improvement is rare.

The condition of the vehicle is all-important. It is not always easy to find competent mechanics up-country, and there are plenty of situations where your life depends on the car's correct mechanical function. In general,

the driver is responsible for minor repairs that become necessary along the way, and just to complicate matters there are unscrupulous mechanics — especially around Kenya's third city, Nakuru — who specialize in tricking motorists into shelling out substantial amounts of money on unnecessary repairs. The favorite trick is to pour oil under your car when it's parked and then persuade you to visit their local garage. Don't let anyone take a wrench to your rented car without checking first with your rental agency. Travelers visiting Nakuru with a car and driver are faced with the same problem: often the driver will disappear for half an hour and come back with a mechanical fault. Nine times out of ten, your vehicle has been sabotaged. Understand that this will have happened often to most rental cars, and a quick glance underneath the hood will often make any competent mechanic blanche. Parts that should have been bolted will have been welded and mechanical parts thought

Checking the "Lunatic Line" in Tsavo.

essential in other countries will, inexplicably, be missing. When repairs are needed they are unlikely to be straightforward.

A further special hazard is the risk of carjacking. This is when armed thieves ambush your car while you wait for the gate to be opened in a private residence, or foolishly stray into the wrong part of town and then stop at a traffic light. The problem gets worse after dark. Asian drivers are often beaten up, while whites are generally treated with a weird civility, though as with all situations where there's a scared man—or some-

Courtesy on the road takes a slightly different form in Kenya. Whereas elsewhere flashing brights means "Go ahead," in Kenya it is more likely to mean "I am going ahead —keep clear" and often it just means "hello." Although in principle cattle, bicycles, ox-carts and pedestrians should get out of the way of trucks and cars, in practice frequent use of the horn serves as a useful reminder to people who might have forgotten that they are sharing the road with faster vehicles, and constant beeping that would seem rude and assertive in the West is perfectly acceptable

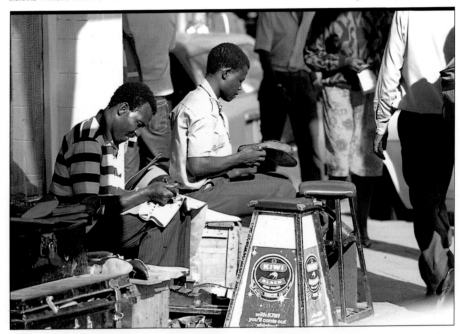

times woman—pointing a gun at your head there is a big element of risk.

There is no way to reliably avoid this risk, though knowing your way around clearly helps. Some vehicles are fitted with Cartrack, a vehicle-tracing transmitter that allows the local organizers, who employ their own policemen, to chase down and track stolen vehicles and, effectively, steal them back. This is a good safety aid, if fitted. Check perhaps with Cartrack ((02) 712780 FAX (02) 713010 directly.

The best map of the country for motorists is Freytag and Berndt's 1:1,500,000, which also includes reasonable city-maps of Mombasa and Nairobi as well as a useful 1:700,000 inset of the Kenyan coast.

in Kenya. Although it might seem harsh, it is no longer recommended to stop for broken-down vehicles or hitchhikers waving desperately by the side of the road: there have been too many cases of ambush or hijack.

In case of breakdown, pile branches or trees 50 m (50 yards) downstream on the road. It's a local equivalent to a warning triangle and will alert oncoming traffic, which might or might not have functioning lights. Get flat tires repaired as soon as possible: there are plenty of cheap puncture repair places (agree on the price first) in every village and, perhaps for this very reason, punctures seem to be far more common here than in any developed country. You never know when your next puncture might happen. Keep the doors locked when driving through cities, and be ready to step on the gas if approached. In the event of an accident involving a pedestrian or casualty, it is recommended to drive to the nearest police station rather than stopping to assist. Emotions can run high and the situation can spiral out of control to no one's benefit. It is wise to sacrifice common humanity and play things safe.

It is usual, when parking in towns or cities, to pay a small parking fee to private security guards or official parking boys: they will also, to a considerable extent, look after your car and its contents. A 20-Ksh note is useful here: motorists should make sure they keep a reasonable supply of these small blue notes, worth about 30 cents, as the alternative might be to part with a larger note, encouraging inflation as well as increasing the cost of traveling.

Finally, vehicles drive on the left side of the road.

Rules of the Road

1. DON'T DRIVE ALONE. Be sure to travel with at least one other person in your car. Several tourists who've rented cars recently for solitary wandering in Kenya have turned up dead.

2. DON'T DRIVE AT NIGHT. Kenyan roads are narrow, often in poor condition and can be singularly lacking in guard rails, center lines and other safeguards. Some of the vehicles coming the other way may be without lights or in dreadful mechanical shape ("Brakes? What brakes?"); large trucks often break down (particularly on hills) and are not infrequently left on the road in the dark with no hazard lights or other indication (the normal breakdown alert is to spread branches along the roadside).

3. DON'T GET OUT OF YOUR VEHICLE IN THE PARKS AND RESERVES unless it's allowed at the specific place where you are. Lions have attacked tourists, but buffaloes, hippos, crocodiles and even elephants are more dangerous. Alternatively, take advantage of the many wonderful places where it's safe to walk around. If you have any doubt, check with rangers, lodge personnel or local folk.

4. DON'T CAMP JUST ANYWHERE. Many of the parks and reserves have reliable campsites at minimal cost, and the rangers can keep

you up-to-date on the best places. But camping at non-designated areas can lead to trouble, from both people and animals. Particularly in the Northern Frontier District, be careful where you camp.

5. NEVER LEAVE THINGS IN YOUR TENT, particularly food. Lock them in your car. Baboons will tear a tent apart for a box of cookies; elephants will crush it for a cabbage; as friendly and honest as the Kenyans are, there are still a few who'll rip you off (particularly on the coast or in the cities). Crime in rural areas is minimal but in the cities stay alert: crime rates are approaching American levels.

6. IF YOU'RE A WOMAN, you can expect few male hassles, but keep alert. I've met single women hitching the Northern Frontier who've had nothing but fun, and lots of women driving (two to a car). But, especially in Nairobi and on the coast, take no chances.

7. IF YOU BREAK DOWN in the middle of nowhere, or run into any other kind of trouble, you'll probably be overwhelmed with help. Kenyans are unusually kind and sympathetic, and have a national ethic of peace and assisting others. Their tribal philosophies, often summarized as "African socialism," in most cases require treating a stranger almost as family. But follow your instincts — if somebody makes you uptight, act accordingly. Breaking down at night in any major city represents real danger. Try to avoid any such situation.

ACCOMMODATION

While the rates at some of the upcountry resorts and game lodges might look horrendous, bear in mind that they usually include all meals (there is, in any case, rarely anywhere else you can eat), all game activities and the services of a skilled and knowledgeable guide.

Trying to arrange your own safari and book lodges on arrival might be more satisfying but is unlikely to save you money. The "milk run" safaris that link a few game parks together in a quick package are particularly competitive and the major operators will have negotiated better deals than you will be able to privately.

Shoe-shine boys in Nairobi.

Moderately priced "Kenyan" hotels used mainly by locals but also used by expatriates and, occasionally, tourists, can usually be relied upon to provide perfectly adequate accommodation; although most bars in these hotels will probably tend to double as informal brothels, the pressure is rarely severe. Every major town will have one or more hotels that used to be grand in colonial times and are still open for business, charmingly starting to become rundown. Rates priced in Kenya shillings are almost always lower than those rated in dollars and often you'll find a great atmosphere: such places are almost always family-run. A double, with a good dinner and breakfast, at a "Kenyan" hotel, can run as low as US$30 for a comfortable, clean room with a private toilet and bath. Places quoted in Kenya shillings are invariably looking more to a resident market and are invariably cheaper. The service is more offhand, the food more African. Prices take a quantum leap in those establishments aimed at the overseas visitor, which will generally quote their rates in dollars.

For the purposes of this book accommodation costs have been calculated on two sharing, per night, and are B&B (bed and breakfast) unless otherwise stated. Half-board comes with breakfast and dinner included. Full-board indicates all meals are provided. All-inclusive means that extra services, such as game drives, alcoholic drinks, or water sports, are included in the rate. At the top end of the Kenyan travel market some serious charges are imposed, and the "Extremely Expensive" is a new category all of my own of which I am very proud. Perhaps, however, I just suffer from the poverty characteristic of the guide-book writer.

The price bands used in this book, in United States dollars, are, for a double room:

Very Inexpensive	under $10
Inexpensive	$11 to $50
Mid-range	$51 to $100
Expensive	$101 to $200
Very Expensive	$201 to $400
Extremely Expensive	over $400

Young elephants usually stay with their mothers for seven to ten years or more, females often forming a two- or three-generational matriarchal clan.

Tented Accommodation

In general, tented camps in Kenya are just as comfortable — and expensive — as stone-built lodges. If taking your own tent, it should be roomy enough to move about in and close securely at the bottom and doors, with reliable mosquito screens.

You can rent tents and some camping equipment from **Atul's (** (02) 228064 FAX (02) 225935, Biashara Street, Box 43202, Nairobi.

Those who are willing to rough it can find board and lodging at very inexpensive rates in campsites in most national parks, charging from US$1 a night upwards. More usefully still, often having a tent will open up rarely-visited regions where the lack of accommodation means you'll have the place to yourself.

Don't, however, fly-camp. The remote area sare just those where the forces of law and order are spread most thinly, populated areas are always much less safe at night, and wild enclaves might harbor animals to whom a human in a tent is just a well-wrapped tasty morsel.

EATING OUT

Regular readers of the *Traveler's Companion* series might notice the comprehensive WHERE TO EAT sections in many of the smaller towns and settlements featured in these pages are strangely missing. There is a good reason for this. While there is a choice of restaurants in the larger cities and in tourist areas, in most Kenyan towns you will be most likely to find your hotel is the only place that can be relied on to provide food. There is little tradition of eating out amongst rural Kenyans, and if you do find a restaurant its quality will probably depend on what has died and how recently. The WHERE TO EAT section has been included where justified.

BASICS

ELECTRICITY

Electricity is 220–240 volt, 50 cycles and most of the smarter establishments use three-prong plugs as found in the United Kingdom. Less ambitious establishments also use two-pin plugs with round connectors. It is useful to carry adapters for many kinds of outlets, which can be purchased at most hardware stores in Nairobi. The larger hotels will have adapters, as well as separate outlets, for 110–120 volt razors, but often these will not provide full power. In remote areas electricity is generally provided by generators, which operate only during specific hours each day. Even in urban areas, however, electrical power cannot be guaranteed. Don't rely on electrical appliances like curling irons, hairdryers, etc. This will also have the effect of keeping your luggage light.

TIME

Local time is three hours ahead of Greenwich Mean Time; Kenya does not have daylight savings time. During winter, it is two hours ahead of continental Europe (only one hour during summer) and eight hours ahead of New York (seven hours in summer).

WEIGHTS AND MEASURES

Weights and measures in Kenya are metric. Distances are measured in meters (just more

OPPOSITE: The world's fastest land animal, the cheetah, runs down his prey in short sprints. ABOVE: Two of the black rhinos to be seen in Kenya's game reserves.

than a yard) and kilometers, as are speed signs. Multiply by 1.6 to convert kilometers to (approximate) miles: one kilometer is five-eighths of a mile. Fuel is sold in liters, (4.5 liters = 1 Imperial gallon, while 3.8 litres = 1 US gallon), and beer is usually sold in 500-ml bottles, which are just more than a pint. Vegetables are sold in kilograms, with one pound equal to 4.5 kg. Temperatures, generally, are expressed in Celsius.

PUBLIC HOLIDAYS

Public holidays follow the Christian calendar, with New Year's Day, Good Friday and Easter Monday, Christmas Day and Boxing Day. June 1 is Madaraka Day, celebrating the granting of self-government; October 10 is Moi Day (with crowds paid to celebrate this one at the moment); October 20 is Kenyatta Day and December 12 is Independence Day.

CURRENCY

The unit of currency is the Kenya shilling (Ksh), divided into 100 cents. Notes are in denominations of 500, 200, 100, 50, 20, and Ksh10. The blue Ksh20 note is sometimes called a "Kenya pound" and is a useful tip for services both small and large. Coins are 5, 10, and 50 cents and 1 Ksh. At the time of publication, **exchange rates** were US$1 for Ksh78.75 and 1 euro for Ksh66.52.

Any amount of foreign cash or travelers' checks may be brought into the country, and the old currency declaration forms, made ridiculous by the ATM's all around the country, are no longer important. The black market in currency has also ceased to exist, and you should not be tempted to change on the streets. Changing money in banks can be interminably slow, but will give you better rates than you'll get in your hotel.

Banks are open from 9 AM to 3 PM, Monday to Friday and most from 9 AM to 11 AM on Saturdays. All transactions, whether the bank is empty or full, seem to take 20 minutes and involve plenty of forms. Licensed exchange bureaux and hotel cashiers generally stay open longer, give a marginally worse exchange rate, but do the transaction quickly. ATM machines give the best rate of all with cash advances on Visa and Master

Card if you have a PIN number. They are found in all major towns but sometimes run out of money or break down: look for branches of Barclays. There are machines throughout Nairobi as well as Nyeri, Meru, Kitale, Nakuru, Diani, Kisumu, Kisii, Embu, Thika, Nyahururu, Kakamega, Naivasha, Limuru, Mombasa, Bungoma, Nanyuki, Eldoret, Kericho and Malindi. Travelers' checks are useful for carrying substantial amounts in relative safety.

Banks at the Mombasa and Nairobi airports are supposedly open 24 hours.

Your Visa, Mastercard, American Express and Diners Club cards will be accepted by many hotels and shops.

Many national parks, hotels and services catering to the tourist market quote their prices in United States dollars. Those that quote in Kenya shillings are looking more to a resident market and are invariably cheaper. The service is more offhand and the feel more African. Those quoting in dollars are slicker and sometimes lack the Kenyan feeling. I have kept this distinction by quoting prices as the service providers quote them.

ETIQUETTE

Etiquette, in Kenya, is usually relaxed. On the generally Muslim coast, topless bathing on public beaches is needlessly provocative and should be avoided. It is easy too to run foul of political sensibilities. Never tear up a Kenyan banknote (though some may, literally, fall apart on you) as this is seen as a deep insult to the country. Don't take photographs of the president, his palace, or the national flag, and you can get into trouble if you pull your camera out at airports and near police stations. If you suddenly find your car pushed off a Nairobi street by a flood of motorcycle outriders, pull off completely, get out of your car, and stand respectfully. In due course President Moi will pass.

HEALTH

It's strongly recommended that you talk with your own physician when planning a Kenyan vacation. At present, the only certificate required is for yellow fever for travelers from endemic areas. However, it is recommended that visitors take anti-malaria medication; beginning 10 days before they leave and continuing until three weeks after their return. Ask your doctor for advice.

It is generally stated that tap-water in Nairobi and other cities is potable, although our experience does not always bear this out. If you're susceptible to stomach upsets, it's wise to treat all water supplies, and to ask before drinking the water in lodges and hotels. Peel your fresh fruits and vegetables, or wash them with potable water. Avoid uncooked foods from sidewalk stands. Even with these precautions, you may get a mild attack of dysentery or the "runs." If you are struck with a serious case of dysentery, the best medication is available in pharmacies under the name of Gabboral, which has replaced Flagyl, but many doctors think that wiping out the stomach's natural gut flora with high doses of antibiotic is the worst thing to do with an upset stomach. Personally, I find the old Caribbean favorite of a teaspoonful of Angostura Bitters mixed with five times as much Coca-Cola invariably settles things down. There are numerous pharmacies with well-qualified staffs to help in the event you do become ill, but they may not have familiar brand names. If you use medication regularly, bring it with you.

Nairobi and Mombasa have modern, well-equipped hospitals, capable of dealing with any emergency, but even smaller towns usually have reliable clinics. Health insurance is strongly recommended: get it before you leave home and make sure it covers you for travel in Africa. If you are planning to spend a lot of time in the bush, it would be wise to make sure evacuation by Flying Doctor is covered.

AIDS is in Kenya, is heterosexual and widespread. If you need an injection, make sure it's a new needle, or bring your own, and in the event of needing a blood transfusion (which is to be avoided if possible) try to contact your embassy: often they have lists of healthy donors.

Make sure your tetanus vaccination is up to date to avoid this inoculation in the event of a bad cut. In general, avoid any inoculation. Do not swim in fresh water. As in most

of Africa, still fresh water is infested with bilharzia, a parasite that enters the body and causes a general deterioration in health. Treatment is usually effective and straightforward, but there can be complications. Note that flowing water is generally clear of bilharzia, so whitewater rafting is fine, but still water is dangerous, ruling out swimming in Lake Victoria. Take local advice before taking any quick dip.

Remember that Kenya straddles the equator and the sun is directly overhead for longer periods of time than most of us are used to.

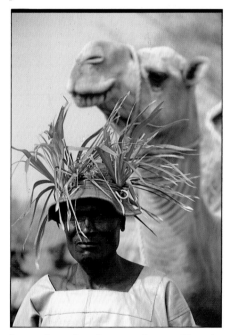

Sunstroke and sunburn are dangers. If you're sensitive to the sun, consult your doctor or pharmacist about the best sunscreen to use. Even if you have never burned, use sunscreen during your first days of exposure and avoid prolonged exposure during the middle of the day. For children, a T-shirt while swimming is always a good precaution. This is highly recommended also when snorkeling, because time passes quickly and reflection from the ocean surface magnifies the effect of the sun. Children should always use sunscreen, which should be reapplied regularly.

A member of Kenya's northern desert anti-poaching unit. The government has adopted a shoot-to-kill policy in a last-ditch attempt to save its remaining elephants.

Bring a sun hat or invest in one on arrival, and use it. Sunstroke's nausea and dizziness can ruin several days of your visit.

The altitude at Nairobi and the highlands can also cause discomfort to some travelers in the form of drowsiness and passing dizziness. Such mild symptoms usually pass in a couple of days once you've become acclimated to the thinner air, but travelers attempting to climb Kenya's mountains should take the risk seriously and take time to acclimatize. Altitude sickness can kill. Headaches or trouble breathing mean it is time

Make use of these services rather than leaving money, passports, or travelers' checks in your room. In Nairobi, Mombasa and other cities, don't wear jewelry on the streets or walk after dark — especially past bush areas where muggers can lurk. Strangely, street crime is worst on weekends, when you're dealing with students: they're much brighter than the down-and-outs (known as "Parking Boys") whose ambitions usually extend only as far as snatching necklaces and watches. In taxis, don't rest your arm on the window if you're wearing an expensive watch, as it

to lose altitude fast, even if someone has to carry you, until the symptoms disappear. Then spend a day acclimatizing before continuing your climb.

SECURITY

Opportunistic crime is increasingly common, especially in the cities. In rural areas the temptation can overwhelm — and penalties are harsh if they are caught. It is unfair to tempt — often very poor — locals by leaving out goods they could not possibly buy. Never leave cameras, handbags and other valuables unattended or visible in your locked vehicle, even in the bush. Most hotels and lodges have safes where you can leave your valuables.

may well be torn free. Car-jacking is an increasing problem in Nairobi and Mombasa, but seems confined to certain suburbs. Stick to the main roads and try to avoid driving at night and you should be safe.

ANIMAL WATCHING

For the wildlife observer, a pair of binoculars and the Collins *A Field Guide to the Natural Parks of East Africa*, *A Field Guide to the Birds of East Africa*, and *A Field Guide to the Butterflies of Africa*, all by J. A. Williams, are essential. At all the parks and reserves, wardens are more than happy to explain what species you can expect to see, where and when to find them, and the "rules of the game."

In general, the "rules of the game" are speed limits of 30 km/h (19 mph), confinement to vehicles except in specifically designated areas, and, of course, no shooting except with a camera. Travel after dark and before dawn (6:30 PM to 6 AM) is strictly forbidden and enforced. There may be variations from one park or reserve to another, so it's best to check the regulations each time you pay an entrance fee. No matter how cute, friendly, docile, cuddly or harmless animals may seem, they are all wild and are potentially dangerous. Young animals invariably

the arid regions a little more green than usual, the dangers of sunstroke and sunburn somewhat reduced, and the ocean as refreshing as ever. Particularly now the climate in Kenya is less predictable, there is a lot to be said for off-season travel. Accommodation is easier to find and the staff have more time to spend with you individually explaining the countryside and its attractions. May is probably the exception: many hotels and lodges close for refurbishment and roads during rainy seasons are even more dreadful than usual.

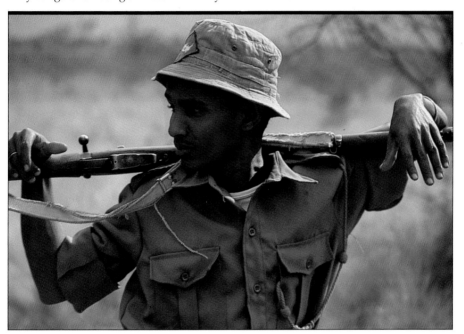

have parents who might kill you for disturbing their offspring.

WHEN TO GO

Being on the equator, the Kenyan "season" is anytime, with the winter months (December through February) and the school holidays (July and August) the busiest. During these times, it's advisable to make arrangements ahead of time for safaris and coastal accommodations.

During the rainy seasons (April to June, October to early December), you can frequently get reduced rates on hotels, but many safari outfitters do not operate then due to impassable roads. The animals are still there,

WHAT TO BRING

Year-round, you will need to bring lightweight comfortable clothing, which is preferable wash-and-wear. Away from the coast, most of Kenya is well above sea level, which makes the climate perfect: warm in the day and pleasant at night. Dress is casual throughout the country. For footwear, again the key is comfort. Canvas or running shoes are ideal, and only the more adventurous travelers — those attempting the peaks of Mounts Kenya or Elgon, or those taking a camel safari or a

OPPOSITE: Twenty-seven tons of ivory, confiscated from poachers, go up in smoke. ABOVE: Until recently Kenya's anti-poaching unit was equipped with ancient Enfield rifles.

walking tour of the parks or reserves — will need hiking boots. Locally made boots and shoes are good and inexpensive, but it's better to come with broken-in, supple shoes. Sandals are only suitable for wearing in town and on the beach, and not suitable for walking in the bush.

Whether your plans include an overnight in the mountain lodges or not, bring a warm sweater and light waterproof jacket as the high altitude means that evenings can be cool and, beyond the occasional open fire, heating is unlikely. A good combination is a polar fleece pullover and a windbreaker or K-way. In the bush, long pants are preferable to shorts, and shirts with long sleeves that can be rolled down to protect you against the sun and insects are recommended. Your clothes will get covered with the ever-present red dust of Kenya, so make sure they are all washable. Laundry is done almost every night in safari camps and lodges, or you can wash it out yourself and it's usually dry by morning. Of course, don't forget a swimsuit.

If you have made arrangements for a safari, your outfitter will provide you with a list of things to bring. Follow their advice, as they are professionals with years of experience in making Kenya vacations as comfortable as possible for visitors.

Don't forget to pack a flashlight, spare batteries and binoculars. Sunscreen and a hat are necessities for everyone. You may want to wait and buy your hat in Nairobi, where there is a wide choice, and if time permits you can get an entire safari outfit made-to-measure.

PHOTOGRAPHY

Since the game-hunting ban in 1977, most legal "shooting" of wildlife has been done with cameras. Print film is readily available throughout the country, especially in Nairobi, but slide film isn't. Processing can be quick but the quality variable.

A 35-mm camera, with a telephoto lens of at least 300 mm is ideal, and films of varying speeds are recommended: 400 ISO for dusk, sunrise, and dense vegetation; 64 and 200 ISO for midday on the savanna, and 1,000 ISO or higher for night shooting in

lodges like The Ark and Treetops (see THE ABERDARE MOUNTAINS, page 208). If you are using a APS (advanced photo system) camera, be warned that film supply and film processing may not be readily available in some places.

But don't weigh yourself down with a lot of bulky and new equipment. If photography will be a major part of your Kenyan vacation, ask the advice of a professional at your local camera store. Then decide which combination of camera, lenses and film fits your style of shooting best. It might be better to use familiar equipment even if it's a fixed lens or compact camera than to waste precious time trying to operate an unfamiliar camera. The animals won't wait for you to change lenses and focus. You will miss not only the shot, but also the enjoyment of observing the animals.

On the other hand, a lion or giraffe who seems close at hand will end up shrunken and distant in a normal 50-mm SLR or compact camera slide or print — so if you have the means and a bit of experience, a telephoto lens (at least 200 mm) is a real advantage. The most important thing, however, is to have fun: if you're too hung up on getting a picture of whatever strange beast stands before you, you'll miss the opportunity of seeing it in a relaxed, enjoyable fashion.

Be sure to keep your film as cool and dry as possible; never expose film canisters or camera to prolonged heat or direct sunlight, as on the dashboard or rear ledge of your car. The best time to take pictures is early morning or late afternoon — the light's best and the animals more abundant. Always pay attention to your light meter reading. If your subject's in the shade, get your reading from him, not from a sunlit area.

Always ask permission before you take pictures of anyone. Many Kenyans are afraid of cameras; there is a widespread feeling in Kenya that being photographed robs the subject of his or her soul or of a future life — and perhaps they're right. Others are willing to take the chance for a posing fee. Always agree on the fee before you shoot. Usually, a few shillings will do, but occasionally you'll encounter someone, typically a Maasai, who'll demand outrageous fees. Negotiate or walk away.

COMMUNICATIONS

POST

Mail service from Kenya is good, taking three to six days to reach Europe or the United States. And the stamps are beautiful! Main post offices in Nairobi are open from 8 AM to 6 PM, others from 8:30 AM to noon, and 2 PM to 4 PM; some up-country post offices are open only in the morning. More expensive hotels and lodges sell stamps for postcards and letters.

TELEPHONES

With the Kenya telephone service, you can direct-dial domestic and international numbers, but in general the telephone system is expensive and inefficient. Telephones are provided in some hotel rooms, but be aware that hotels can and do add hefty surcharges to an already large bill. Often charges are made — and high ones — for calls even if they don't go through, so even unsuccessful attempts to send faxes can result in an expensive bill. It is more practical to make your international calls from the post office. Even from a post office or private phone, long-distance calls in Kenya are very expensive as well as being unreliable. Don't chat too long.

TELEGRAMS, TELEX AND INTERNET

Telegrams can be sent by phone through the operator. Telex and fax facilities are available at many post offices or private businesses, providing direct dialing to most major international cities on a 24-hour basis. Internet bureaus are just starting to become available in the business centers of the larger hotels and small offices in Nairobi, but they are invariably expensive: they usually charge in dollars for the time you're on the machine, as well as to send or receive e-mails. Increasing numbers of Internet cafés now grace the streets of Nairobi and Mombasa, often with very low costs — as little as Ksh3 per minute.

At the moment, Internet cafés haven't spread beyond the towns of Mombasa and Nairobi. In a country where the telephone system is so bad, however, commercial establishments are increasingly switching to e-mail for their business communications. In upcountry areas your hotel might let you borrow their computer, or let you use your own through the telephone system, but the connection speeds are just too slow to make even e-mail effective and recreational surfing is impractical. Just to make it worse, long-distance calls (to the hubs in Nairobi or Mombasa) are very expensive.

SWAHILI

Swahili is the *lingua franca* of Kenya, and English the language of business and commerce. English is taught in schools all over the country, so you can usually make yourself understood everywhere.

Nonetheless, whenever you travel, it is always appreciated when you attempt the native language. Swahili is one of the easiest languages to learn. The pronunciation is entirely phonetic, and the grammar need not worry a beginner. For the vowels, A is pronounced as in *father*, E as the *a* in *day*, I as the *e* in *see*, O as in *go*, and U as the *o* in *do*. The consonants are generally pronounced as in English. If people ask — and they will — if you speak Swahili, *"kidogo sana"* — meaning "very little" — is less abrupt than "no."

SOME BASIC EXPRESSIONS AND VOCABULARY

Politeness and Introductions
hello *jambo*
good-bye *kwaheri*
good morning *habari ya asubuhi*
good afternoon *habari ya mehana*
good evening *habari ya jioni*
how are you? *habari?*
I am well (I am very well) *mzui (mzui sana)*
please *tafadhali*
thank you (very much) *asante (sana)*
what is your name? *jina lako mani*
my name is … *jina langu ni …*
excuse me *samahani*
I am sorry *pole*
yes *ndiyo*
no *hapana*

Places and People

hotel (or occasionally just foodhut)   *hoteli*
room   *chumba*
bed   *kitanda*
police   *polici*
hospital   *hospitali*
street   *barabara*
airport   *uwanja wa ndege*
river   *mto*
mountain   *mulima*
where?   *wapi?*
where is the hotel?   *hoteli iko wapi?*
what?   *nini?*
Mrs.   *bibi*
Mr.   *bwana*
Miss   *bi*
who?   *nani?*
I, me   *mimi*
you (singular)   *wewe*
he, she   *yeye*
we   *sisi*
you (plural)   *ninyi*
they   *wao*
woman   *mwanamke*
man   *mwamamume*
child   *mtoto*
mother   *mama*
father   *baba*
daughter   *binti*
son   *mwana*
wife   *mke*
husband   *mume*
friend   *rafiki*

Food

food   *chakula*
coffee   *kahawa*
tea   *chai*
beer   *tembo* or *pombe*; *Tusker*, the name of the leading brand, is usually good enough.
ice   *barafu*
meat   *nyama*
chicken   *kuku*
fish   *samaki*
bread   *mkate*
rice   *wali*
butter   *siagi*
sugar   *sukari*
vegetables   *mbogo*
fruit   *matunda*
water   *maji*
milk   *mazima*
salt   *chumvi*

pepper   *pilipili*
dessert   *tamutamu*

Common Kenyan Dishes

githeri   beans and maize
irio   peas and other vegetables with maize
matoke   steamed bananas
mkate mayui   a flour and egg mixture
mrere   cooked green vegetables
muhogo ya kuchoma   roasted cassava with chilies and lemon
nyama ya kuchoma   roasted meat
samosa   Kenyan sandwich
sukuma wiki   boiled spinach (or kale)
ugali   maize meal

Numbers

half   *nusu*
one   *moja*
two   *mbili*
three   *tatu*
four   *ine*
five   *tano*
six   *sita*
seven   *saba*
eight   *nane*
nine   *tisa*
ten   *kumi*
eleven   *kumi na moja*
twelve   *kumi na mbili*
twenty   *ishirini*
twenty-one   *ishirini na moja*
thirty   *thelathini*
forty   *arobaini*
fifty   *hamsini*
sixty   *sitini*
seventy   *sabani*
eighty   *themanini*
ninety   *tisini*
hundred   *mia*
one hundred   *mia moja*
two hundred   *mia mbili*
thousand   *elfu*

Adjectives and Adverbs

good   *mzuri*
bad   *mbaya*
cold   *baridi*
hot   *moto*
now   *sasa*
quickly   *haraka*
slowly   *pole-pole*
big   *kubwa*

small *kidogo*
more, another *ingine*
much, more *mwingi*
that *yule*
this *huyu*
sweet *tamu*
cheap *rahisi*
expensive *ghali*

Directions

right *kulia*
left *kushoto*
turn (right) *geuka (kulia)*
go straight *enda moja kwa moja*
where are you going? *una kwenda wapi?*

Time

now *sasa*
today *leo*
tomorrow *kesho*
yesterday *yana*
morning *asubuhi*
afternoon *alarsiri*
evening *jioni*
nighttime *usiku*
daytime *mehana*
day *siku*
week *wiki*
month *mwezi*
year *mwaka*
Sunday *Jumapili*
Monday *Jamatatu*
Tuesday *Jumanne*
Wednesday *Jumatano*
Thursday *Alhamisi*
Friday *I jumaa*
Saturday *Jumamosi*

Shopping

money *fedha*
cent *senti*
how much? *ngapi?*
how much does this cost? *inagharimu pesa ngapi?*
that's expensive *wawezakupunguz*
shop *duka*
cigarettes *sigareti*
newspaper *gazeti*
clothes *nguo*
shoes *viatu*

Recommended Web Sites

Kenya has been slow to get online, though the dreadful general state of its telecommunications have helped a late surge. The most relevant newsgroups for Kenya are rec. travel.africa and soc.culture.kenya. The following sites might be of interest.

Kenya News www.kenyanews.com, updated every weekday, is a worthy source of up-to-date information about events and news stories in Kenya. It's a great introduction to the issues in the country and a good way to stay in touch after your visit. Kenya's leading national paper online, *The East African Standard* www.eastandard.net, carries all the stories, and is searchable too.

Africaonline's Kenya Site www.africa online.co.ke has a good range of general information about Kenya, and **Kenyaweb** www.kenyaweb.com is especially comprehensive, with a virtual Nairobi tour of what's on. **Kenyalogy** www.kenyalogy.com offers interesting information about the country and its national parks, with pictures; also in Spanish.

The Kamusi project's **Swahili Online Dictionary** www.yale.edu/swahili/concerns itself with Kenya's widest-used language. Don't waste your visit shopping for souvenirs: you can buy them all at **Curios200** www.curios2000.com and contribute to the homeless by doing so.

Friends of Arabuko-Sokoke Forest www .watamu.net tells you all you need to know about the forest and the village of Watamu, online. **Kenya Birds** www.kenyabirds.co.uk is a wonderful and very detailed site showing what birds are found, where. A must for birders.

Trying to link conservation initiatives nationwide is **African Websites** www.african conservation.com/kenya.html, while the **East Africa Wildlife Society** www.eawild life.org is the official site of this worthy conservation movement, who also publish the influential *Swara* Magazine.

Three Routes Scuba Diving Guide www.3routes.com/scuba/africa/keny/ index.html provides up-to-date links to Kenya's main diving operators, not necessarily those whose contact details are in the text of this book.

The Kenya Embassy in Washington DC has a cosular services site, **The Kenya Embassy** www.kenyaembassy.com, which is good place to find out the current situation regarding frequently changeable visa requirements.

To keep abreast of new cybercafés across Kenya, try **Net Café Guide** www.netcafe guide.com/africa.htm

Recommended Reading

Literature relevant to Kenya tends to concentrate on three main aspects of the country. The drama and glamor of exploration and the colonial years inspired some of the most famous books, often made into films, while the spectacular and intriguing natural history of the country has provided the base material for many glossy coffee-table books, a number of autobiographies where the animals play leading roles and a few more scientific tomes, and the African experience, with all its tribal complexity, has left relatively few literary traces. In all these categories, market forces have done little to ensure the immortality of the written word, and many of the best titles are now out of print. Kenya is one place where time spent in second-hand bookshops or searching web sites such as www.abe.com are likely to be especially rewarding.

For literature from the colonial era, some titles have been kept in the public eye by the later attentions of the movie industry. Thus *Out of Africa* by Karen Blixen (first published 1937 under the penname of Isak Dinesen), a tale of a Dutch settler's relationship with a colonial settler, is still the best-known tale of a Nairobi where hunting was a way of life. The material for the film of the same name, however, drew more on the biography of the author, *Isak Dinesen: the Life of a Storyteller*, by Judith Thurman (Picador, first published 1984) which is rather more revealing and honest. Perhaps the books — and later films — that did most to put wildlife conservation on the world's agenda were written by Joy Adamson, including *Born Free, Living Free*, and *Forever Free* (first published 1960, 1961, 1962 respectively; now published as a trilogy by Pan), which relate to the author's time living amongst lions. Ernest Hemingway did his bit to immortalize Kenya, with books such

as *The Green Hills of Africa* (1935) and *The Snows of Kilimanjaro* (1948). Elspeth Huxley's books *The Flame Trees of Thika* (1959) and *Nine Faces of Kenya* (1991) provide a more autobiographical background. For a more informed overview of Kenya's early years there's still not much that can match Alan Moorhead's seminal tale of Burton, Speke and the race to find the source of the Nile, *The White Nile* (1901), which will have most readers booking their air ticket the next day for an exploration of their own.

When it comes to wildlife the keen reader is spoiled for choice. *Elephant Memories* by Cynthia Moss (1988) is a fascinating account of her observations — still continuing — of the elephants of Amboseli, while the same elephants also provide the material for Joyce Poole's *Coming of Age with Elephants* (1996). *Gorillas in the Mist* by Diane Fossey (1983) shifts the action just over the border into Uganda, but is still an insight into one of the world's most important conservationists.

For those with any interest in the natural world a good field-guide to Kenya's wildlife will be a great investment, both to aid identification in the field and as a souvenir of your visit. Some of the best are published by Collins, and written by John Williams, whose three titles cover the birds, butterflies, and national parks of East Africa. *The Field Guide to the Larger Mammals of Africa* by Chris and Tilde Stuart (1998) is a useful guide to have aboard your safari vehicle, as is the comprehensive *Field Guide to the Birds of Kenya and Northern Tanzania* by Zimmerman, Turner and Pearson (1999).

For an African perspective on Kenya, a good place to start is Jomo Kenyatta's *Facing Mount Kenya: the Tribal Life of Kenya* (1962), whose important reflections on the country he helped guide through independence are interesting from a political and anthropological point of view. One important but deceptively cheerful contemporary Kenyan writer is Meja Mwangi, whose titles include *The Cockroach Dance*, (1979) *Going Down River Road* (1976, now unfortunately out of print) and *The Return of Shaka* (1989 — generally available). Rather luckier with his publishers (Heinemann) is the altogether more serious Wa Thiong'o Ngugi, whose titles *I will Marry When I Want* (1982), *A Grain of Wheat*,

(1967) and *Devil on the Cross* (1982) are still in print, alongside *Decolonising the Mind: the Politics of Language in African Literature* (1986).

When it comes to conventional travel books, some of the best include Dervla Murphy's *The Ukwimi Road* (1994), an account of her cycle ride from Nairobi to Zimbabwe, while Shiva Naipaul's *North of South* (1980) is a readable and often very funny account of the country. *No Picnic on Mount Kenya* (1999) by Felice Benuzzi is essential reading for anyone intending to climb Kenya's highest mountain.

Photo Credits

Quick Reference A–Z Guide
to Places and Topics of Interest